Third Edition

Reading Problems: Assessment and Teaching Strategies

Margaret Ann Richek
Northeastern Illinois University

JoAnne Schudt Caldwell
Cardinal Stritch College

Joyce Holt Jennings
Northeastern Illinois University

Janet W. Lerner
Northeastern Illinois University

ALLYN AND BACON
Boston • London • Toronto • Sydney • Tokyo • Singapore

Series Editor: Virginia Lanigan
Series Editorial Assistant: Nihad Farooq
Cover Administrator: Suzanne Harbison
Marketing Manager: Kathy Hunter
Manufacturing Buyer: Aloka Rathnam
Editorial-Production Service: Electronic Publishing Services Inc.

Copyright © 1996, 1989, 1983 by Allyn & Bacon
A Simon & Schuster Company
Needham Heights, Massachusetts 02194

Library of Congress Cataloging-in-Publication Data

Reading problems : assessment and teaching strategies / Margaret Ann
   Richek ... [et al.]. — 3rd ed.
     p. cm.
   Includes bibliographical references and indexes.
   ISBN 0-205-16388-2
   1. Reading disability. 2. Reading—Remedial teaching.
I. Richek, Margaret Ann.
LB1050.5.R53 1996
372.4´3—dc20   95-23367
                                                    CIP

Printed in the United States of America

10 9 8 7 6 5 4 3   99 98 97

*This book is dedicated to
the many students who have touched our lives
and inspired us.*

Contents

LIST OF TABLES

Preface

This book is concerned with helping the many children, adolescents, and adults who encounter difficulty with reading. Designed as a text for undergraduate and graduate students, it guides prospective and present teachers in assessing and teaching students with reading problems.

Reading Problems: Assessment and Teaching Strategies is a comprehensive survey of teaching strategies, formal and informal assessment, theory, and research. The reader will find information both from the field of reading and from allied fields, such as special education, bilingual education, medical science, and policy studies. Together, this forms a coherent framework for helping students with reading problems.

The book includes both newer strategies and more traditional approaches to helping students with reading problems. It is important for teachers to be familiar with all approaches, so that they have a wide variety of strategies from which to choose. Recent research has clarified the reading process and provided important strategies, many focusing on using meaningful literature to help pupils with reading problems. These new insights provide a rich source of innovative diagnostic and teaching methods. At the same time, more traditional techniques remain useful. This text integrates time-tested methods with newer perspectives to provide effective programs for helping students with reading difficulties.

The text is also a valuable resource for teachers. Hundreds of instructional strategies are presented in an immediately usable form. Many are illustrated by "strategy snapshots," examples of actual use in a classroom. These are drawn from our own experiences in working with pupils in Reading Centers at our universities and with at-risk students in schools. In Chapters 5 through 11, we present informal assessment tools (immediately before each set of strategies) which can be used by teachers without any special materials. In addition, there are extensive lists of formal assessment instruments and good literature (including informational material and poetry). This practical information is combined with readable, understandable summaries of the research and theory that form the basis of the methods and materials suggested.

We have tried to retain both the readable style and the combination of theory and practice that characterized previous editions. In addition, however, this third edition has been thoroughly updated and reworked. A valuable addition to this text is a new, extensively field-tested informal reading inventory, completely ready for use. Developed by Joyce Jennings, one of our authors, it is unparalleled in its child-centered passages. This informal reading inventory may be freely copied and used by students.

Three more changes to the third edition of this book are noteworthy. First is the inclusion of a chapter on "Emergent Literacy" (Chapter 5), which provides information on helping children (and adults) who lack fundamentals necessary for beginning to read. Second, "Literacy in a Diverse Society" (Chapter 12) deals with teaching reading to a population that is increasingly diverse in background, language, and age, and includes strategies for working with community memebers.

Finally, in this edition, we have split the presentation of assessment strategies into three parts, enabling it to be more easily assimilated and integrated with instruction. The first (in Chapters 2 and 3) presents information about pupil background (accompanied by parent, pupil, and school interview forms) and an overview of informal assessment (dealing with informal reading inventories). This information is presented first, since it is often used first when working with a pupil. Next, in Chapters 5 through 11, assessment strategies in each area of reading are coupled with teaching strategies in that area. Finally, technical, in-depth information, such as a theoretical and research-oriented discussion of factors relating to reading disability, issues related to severe reading difficulties, and extensive discussion of standardized tests is presented in Chapters 13, 14, and 15.

Our book is presented in fifteen chapters. The first, "Reading Ability and Disability" provides a framework for instruction by presenting an overview of reading problems coupled with a discussion of the reading process. Chapters 2 and 3 deal with assessment, providing an overview of background information on pupils and a detailed discussion of the informal reading inventory. Chapter 4 presents an "Overview of Instruction," and is particularly rich in suggestions for leading students to reading and providing a motivating environment. The use of computers in instruction is also included.

Chapters 5 through 11 deal with various aspects of reading including Emergent Literacy, Word Recognition Accuracy, Word Recognition Fluency, Comprehension of Narrative Text, Comprehension of Expository Text, Listening Comprehension and Meaning Vocabulary, and Writing. Each chapter presents a general discussion of an aspect of reading, informal assessment strategies, an extensive array of instructional strategies, and useful materials.

Chapter 12 deals with Literacy in a Diverse Society, focusing on issues, strategies, and materials for dealing with students from different backgrounds and age groups (including adolescents and adults) who speak different languages. Sections are also presented on working wih parents.

Since Chapters 13 through 15 present information of a more technical nature, they have been placed at the end of the text. However, these chapters can be used in any order. Chapter 13 presents an in-depth discussion of factors relating to reading disability, as well as technical tools for assessing these factors. Chapter 14 contains information and strategies for dealing with severe reading disabilities. This chapter is especially noteworthy in its detailed treatment of Attention Deficit Disorders, special education laws, and new insights from medical research into the brain. Finally, Chapter 15 presents technical information on standardized tests.

The appendices provide many resources. Appendix A is an extensive list of published tests. Appendix B includes many materials that can be used with pupils who have reading problems. Appendix C contains a newly developed informal reading inventory, which has been extensively field tested and can be freely reproduced and photocopied by students.

The third edition of this text retains the comprehensiveness and clarity of the first two editions while adding new insights into the reading process and new developments in the field. These include emergent literacy, more informal assessment, more emphasis on literacy in a diverse society, many new startegies, and a completely new informal reading inventory. Updated sections on changes in special education, Title I legislation, and developments in medical research also reflect new trends.

Many people have contributed to this book. We wish to thank the reading professionals who deepened and extended our understanding of issues and strategies by taking the time to answer personal inquiries. We thank the graduate students, undergraduate students, and pupils we worked with for giving us detailed feedback on instructional strategies. The indispensible reference librarians of Northeastern Illinois University worked tirelessly to ensure accuracy for references and publishers. The staff at Allyn & Bacon, including Virginia Lanigan, Nihad Farooq, and Mary Beth Finch, provided invaluable assistance in developing this manuscript. Finally, reviewers Dr. Patricia H. Duncan, Virginia Commonwealth University; Donald McFeely, Indiana University of Pennsylvania; and Barr W. Taylor, East Carolina University provided many helpful suggestions in shaping this text.

Margaret Ann Richek
JoAnne Schudt Caldwell
Joyce Holt Jennings
Janet W. Lerner

Reading Ability and Disability

Introduction

- Soon after Jason was born, his mother realized he was not developing normally. As time went on, he sat, crawled, and walked later than other children. His speech was slow and difficult to understand. Jason's dedicated parents provided him with several years of speech therapy and motor training. They insisted that he receive an extra year of preschool education, but even this intensive education did not elim-inate Jason's problems. He entered our Reading Center at the age of eleven, a fifth grader reading at a second-grade level. Small for his age and clumsy, he was falling behind his classmates, both socially and academically. As the rest of his class read from a literature series, Jason struggled with the easy-to-read *Curious George.*

- Born to a substance-addicted mother, eight-year-old Diane was brought to our Reading Center by her grandmother. She was a special education student who had extreme difficulty when reading even the simplest material. Diane's poor achieve-ment and lack of discipline confounded her teachers, who had given up even attempting to teach her to read.

- Part of a struggling Russian immigrant family, Ilya's parents were not able to make arrangements to take him to kindergarten. Although apparently intelligent and able, Ilya had imperfect mastery of oral English. By the end of the first grade, when he entered our Reading Center, he was half a year behind his peers.

- Gail's mother became concerned when her daughter's once-excellent grades began to fall in fourth grade, as schoolwork concentrated increasingly on science and social studies. Gail seemed confused by difficult words, sentences, and concepts in her textbooks.

- Because of many learning problems, Roy had been classified as a special educa-tion student. Despite his teachers' best efforts, he had entered high school with a second-grade reading level. Finally, unable to pass the written examination for a driver's license, he came to our Reading Center in a desperate cry for help before graduation.

Our book is dedicated to these five youngsters and to the many other students who have attended our Reading Center. Although reading problems are a national concern, each child (or adult) faces the failure to read individually. For many, the results are heartbreaking. Reading problems can devastate students and their families. In school, these children are forced to face their inadequacies day after day, often to be met with rejection by teachers and peers. Students with reading problems may be fed a daily diet of textbooks they can-not read and homework they cannot do. In response, they may turn to misbehavior or sim-ply give up, displaying "learned helplessness." Not surprisingly, poor readers often suffer from low self-esteem. As these children mature, they find that the doors to personal enrich-ment and career opportunities are closed.

Educators, parents, physicians, and psychologists, as well as society in general, share a concern about individuals who do not learn to read. However, the primary responsibility for teaching reading belongs to teaching professionals. The teacher is the coordinator and deliverer of instructional services, the person most able to help youngsters with reading problems. Throughout our nation, hundreds of thousands of classroom teachers, reading teachers, and special education teachers help these students to read better and to enjoy read-ing.

This book will help teachers to instruct children like Jason, Diane, Ilya, Gail, and Roy. It contains many instructional strategies and diagnostic tools that you may use to understand and aid students in their struggles to read. To do something well, people must enjoy doing it. Hence, it is important to inspire a love of reading. For this reason, our book also refers to many books of children's literature and materials that will help students to realize the wealth of information and enjoyment that reading can provide. The strategies and materials we present in this book have helped these five youngsters, and countless others. We hope that the students you teach will also benefit from them.

Reading Problems: A National Dilemma

Although teaching is a personal activity, professionals need to understand the overall situation of reading problems. For this reason, having focused on students as individuals, it is also worthwhile to consider reading problems from a national perspective.

Society suffers when citizens cannot read adequately. People with low reading levels comprise many of the unemployed, high school dropouts, the poor, and those convicted of crimes. The problems of our schools, the growth of poverty, and the loss of family values all show some association with poor reading.

In response to national concerns about education, the U.S. Congress passed The Goals 2000: Educate America Act in 1994. The goals, which are scheduled to be met by the year 2000, include literacy for all adults in the United States. To accomplish this, according to the United States Office of the Secretary of Education (1994), schools need higher standards, new approaches to teaching, accountability, and partnerships with the community.

How serious is the problem of illiteracy in the United States? About 23 million adults are classified as functionally illiterate, with basic skills of fourth grade or below. Another 35 million semiliterate adults have skills below the eighth-grade level. Illiterate and semiliterate adults account for 75 percent of the unemployed, 33 percent of mothers receiving Aid to Families with Dependent Children (AFDC), 85 percent of the juveniles who appear in court, and 60 percent of prison inmates (Orton Dyslexia Society, 1986). *The National Adult Literacy Survey* (United States Department of Education, 1994) shows that adults on the lowest level on the literacy scale (44 percent) are more likely than those on the highest level (4 percent) to live in poverty.

Increasingly, illiteracy has been seen as an important factor in the U.S. economy. Fifteen percent of people in our work force are functionally illiterate. A lack of reading ability often hinders those seeking employment. The New York Telephone Company (NYNEX) reported that it gave a simple 50-minute exam on basic reading and reasoning skills to 21,000 applicants for entry-level jobs. Only 15 percent passed (Simpson, 1987)!

Increasing technology in today's world demands that workers constantly retrain. Due to automation, jobs based on manual labor are disappearing, to be replaced by occupations that demand a high level of technical skills, such as the ability to operate a computer. Unskilled and semiskilled workers find fewer jobs; they are likely to end up chronically unemployed. Furthermore, the lack of reading skills among large numbers of young adults threatens to divide society deeply between the highly literate and a low-income, low-achieving underclass unequipped for educational and professional advancement. One study of the literacy skills of young adults has warned that, unless improvements are made, a large part of the U.S. labor force will become progressively less capable of doing highly skilled work. Low literacy levels among the U.S. population may not allow leadership to be maintained in a changing, technological world (Venezsky, Kaestle, & Sum, 1987).

These societal problems are reflected in our schools. The U.S. Department of Education estimates that almost one-third of the school population has significant learning problems (Will, 1986), and most of these are reading related. Students with reading problems are found throughout our schools.

- Some students are found in regular classes and receive no special help.
- Some students are served by school or state-sponsored programs.
- California and Pennsylvania are among the many states that provide programs for reading assistance.
- Other students are served through Title I provisions. Title I/Chapter I* is a federal program that funds basic skills education for students in low-income areas. Seven million children, most of whom have reading problems, are served through this funding source (Long, personal communication, 1995).
- Approximately 5 million children receive special education services through the Individuals with Disabilities Education Act (IDEA) (1995). Sixty-three percent of these children need help in reading and other language-related areas.

Special reading assistance, if available, may be given in many different instructional situations. Some students who receive special education services are placed in *self-contained classes* and do not receive any instruction with nondisabled students of their own age. For other students, special education and reading instructional help is given in *resource rooms* for a small portion of the day; at other times students with reading problems are in *regular classrooms*.

A recent trend is a growth in *inclusion*, in which all students are served in regular classrooms. For special education students, this may be called the *Regular Education Initiative* (REI). In inclusion settings, reading specialists and special education teachers go into the regular classroom to assist students who have problems.

Despite all of these sources of help, many students with reading problems still receive no additional assistance. They, and their often overburdened classroom teachers, must face these difficulties without the aid of special teachers or programs.

Factors Associated with Reading Problems

Reading problems are rooted in (1) factors within the individual, (2) factors within the home, social, and cultural environment, and (3) factors in the school environment. At times, all of these factors may play a role in any one student's reading problem.

Factors within the Individual

Without a doubt, many reading problems stem from factors within the individual. Every teacher has known students such as Jason, the first child described in this chapter. Despite a dedicated family, a nurturing school environment, and many economic advantages, Jason continued to struggle with reading.

Problems within the individual have been a focus of research for over 100 years. In 1896, the physician P. Morgan described "word blindness" in an otherwise normal individual who could not learn to read (Hinshelwood, 1917). Other physicians, particularly neurologists, followed with reports of similar cases (Critchley, 1970; Cruickshank,1986; Orton, 1937; Rabinovitch, 1989). Many of these researchers speculated that reading disabilities were associated with neurological factors.

As psychologists and educators joined this research tradition, they found that many children who had apparently normal neurological development nevertheless had reading prob-

---

*"Title I" programs were called "Chapter I" for several years. We use both names to refer to this federal program.

lems. Nonmedical professionals found that many factors other than neurological ones were associated with poor reading. These included visual–motor problems, delayed speech, a history of reading disability in one's family, and the inability to process information (Perfetti, 1985; Robinson, 1946; Stanovich, 1982a,b).

After much research, the combined fields of medicine, psychology, and education have not identified any one definitive cause of reading disabilities. Some of the most complete studies (e.g., Robinson, 1946) have shown that, even within one individual, reading problems have many causes. However, several types of factors that *contribute* to reading problems within the individual have been identified. These include physical factors (such as neurological ones), emotional factors, and language factors.

Reading problems may vary considerably in severity. Within the population of reading-disabled students there appears to be a core of extremely disabled individuals, who acquire each word with extreme difficulty (Kavale & Forness, 1987; Rabinovitch, 1969). These students are sometimes called *dyslexic* (Vellutino, 1987); their needs are addressed in Chapter 14 of this book. Fortunately, such individuals comprise only a small fraction of individuals with reading problems.

Factors in the Home, Social, and Cultural Environments

The home, social, and cultural environments in which children grow can also influence their ability to read. One child whose story we have told—Diane—grew up in an environment that could not nurture school achievement. Homes that are plagued with poverty and family instability and neighborhoods where violence is commonplace produce children who are "at risk" for school failure. Sadly, many social and economic indicators show that the number of such children is rising.

- The child poverty rate rose by more than 11 percent during the 1980s and was almost 18 percent in 1989 (Kameenui, 1993). Since 1987, 25 percent of all preschool children in the United States have been born into poverty (Hodgkinson, 1991).
- Every year, about 350,000 children are born to cocaine-addicted mothers. Those who survive have many learning and behavioral problems. The cost of preschool therapy for these children, and for those suffering from fetal alcohol syndrome, is estimated at $40,000 per child (Hodgkinson, 1991).
- On any given night, it is estimated that at least 50,000 children are homeless (Hodgkinson, 1991).
- Violence in society continues to increase. In 1994, 32 percent of adults listed violence as a primary concern of their lives (*Chicago Tribune,* 1994).

At times, even a well meaning, stable family may not be able to prepare a child for the school situation. Such was the case with Ilya, whose family was not able to enroll him in kindergarten, or to prepare him for reading instruction in English.

Problems within the individual (such as health and emotional problems) tend to increase when students live in difficult environments. Poorer mothers are less likely than more affluent ones to seek prenatal care. Alcohol addiction in parents may affect a child in two ways simultaneously: the child may be born with fetal alcohol syndrome and the parent may not have the energy to nurture the child's education. Thus, individual causes and environmental causes combine to produce an increased risk for reading problems.

Children who are hungry or homeless have little energy to focus on school. Their over-burdened, often undereducated parents and guardians may lack the time and skills to nurture literacy by sharing books with them, encouraging them to do homework, or communicating with their teachers. Some families are able to rise above their problems and provide warm, nurturing places that support education, but the sad fact remains that children born into poor or unstable families are at risk for educational failure.

The home environment has increasingly become a factor in the reading problems of children. Even in affluent neighborhoods, teachers notice an increase in family breakup. School problems are multiplied in less fortunate settings. As family instability becomes commonplace, teachers in *all* schools are instructing "at risk" children.

Factors in the School Environment

Surprisingly, research indicates that some school practices can contribute to reading problems. Is it possible that teachers, whose job is to help, can actually be doing some things that are harmful? Think back to Diane, whom we introduced at the beginning of this chapter. Diane's teachers had entirely given up teaching her to read; instead they simply read everything to her. When other children had reading time, Diane was expected to sit quietly and do nothing.

Although such dramatic lack of reading instruction is rare, school instruction often does little to help children with reading problems. In an intensive study of one school, Juel (1994) found that a child who is a poor reader in grade one has an 88 percent of being a poor reader in grade four.

Why is school instruction often ineffective in helping to solve reading problems? One important reason is that students with reading problems do not read much in school. In an extensive line of research, Allington (1977, 1983, 1984, 1986) and Stanovich (1986, 1993–4) compared the reading of low-achieving and average students. They found that unskilled readers spend less time reading than do average students, and that low-achieving students read only a third as many words as average students. This means that students with reading problems are not practicing enough to improve their reading abilities. With little reading, they make little progress.

Students with reading problems are a challenge to teach, but it is important to provide them with the best instruction possible. This book is filled with suggestions that aid youngsters in breaking the cycle of reading failure and help them to love reading. Since students with reading problems are already lagging behind, we do not have a moment to waste!

What Is Reading?

A physician trying to heal a sick patient must have an understanding of the healthy human body. In the same way, in order to help a student who has reading problems, a teacher must understand what good readers do. Many studies have been done that examine the reading process. The findings of these studies have enabled us to improve our understanding of reading, and thus to improve our ability to teach it.

When people read, they actually construct their own meaning of a text (Rosenblatt, 1983; Anderson & Pearson, 1984). In other words, people create their own mental version of what they read. The reader, the material, and the reading situation all contribute to the meaning that is constructed (Rumelhart, 1985; Wixson et al., 1987).

Constructing Meaning

Imagine that you are reading a novel. Rather than simply acquiring information, you are actively creating, in your mind, your own personal version of the material you are reading. The version you make is not exactly like what you read on paper. Instead, you, the reader, contribute to the construction of meaning. You visualize the characters and the scenery in a story. In fact, your mind probably even supplies details that aren't in the book.

You can prove this by comparing your mental "image" of a character in the novel with that made by a friend. You will find that no two people's images are ever exactly alike. Most people have had the rude shock of seeing a movie made from a favorite book and realizing that the actors look nothing like the image they created when they read!

To prove to yourself that reading is actually constructing meaning in your own mind, read this short selection:

> The minute she saw the weight register on the scale, she realized she was the winner. She knew exactly how she would spend the prize money.

What meaning do you construct from this passage? Perhaps you "see" a dieter involved in a contest to lose weight, looking forward to buying new clothes. Or, you might imagine a farmer getting an award for the largest livestock or pumpkin and planning to spend it on a new tractor or a family vacation. You might imagine a person who caught a large fish, and the money might be reinvested in expensive fishing equipment. Perhaps you thought of even another interpretation. Isn't it true that the meaning you constructed reflected your background and life experiences?

Sadly, students with reading problems are often reluctant to construct their own meaning and interpretation of the text. Instead, the terror that they might get something "wrong" prevents them from interpreting the text in an imaginative way. This fear is reinforced when teachers ask large numbers of factual questions, giving a perception that reading is a "right" and "wrong" act. Chapter 8 of this book provides several suggestions to foster personal responses in students when they read. This enables them to create their own meaning in the text, and results in better and deeper comprehension.

The Contribution of the Reader

As we have mentioned, the meaning that is constructed during reading depends upon three key contributions: the *reader;* the *material* that is being read; and the *reading situation.* Let's explore how each of these influences the process of meaning construction, or reading.

The *reader* forms the cornerstone of reading, for meaning is actually constructed in the reader's mind. The reader activates and controls the reading process. The reader's *background, interest, attitude, purpose,* and *ability* dramatically influence the reading process.

Reading builds on the reader's background knowledge, and the richer or more detailed this background is, the richer the reading experience will be (Hirsch, 1987; Daneman, 1991). All of us have an easier time reading about familiar topics. A child who has ridden horses is able to understand the terms about horseback riding in the children's book *Black Beauty* (by Sewell). This child will have pleasant associations with the book and will find it relatively easy to identify with the problems of the characters. In contrast, a child who brings little background knowledge to *Black Beauty* is likely to have a less rewarding reading experience.

The background information a reader has is often called *schema.* Researchers have learned much about reading using schema theory, the study of how people store knowledge in their minds and use it to assimilate new information (Spiro, Bruce, & Brewer, 1980; R. C. Anderson, 1984).

There are two reasons why it is important that teachers help low-achieving students to build up their background information. First, research has shown that these students have less background information than their average-achieving peers. Second, since students with reading problems often have difficulty recognizing words, they need clues to help them. A good grasp of background information enables the student to use the clue of meaning (or context) when a word cannot be immediately recognized.

The effects of improving background knowledge can be shown through the third-grade reading instruction that we planned for a school with many at-risk children. One reading, "Through Grandpa's Eyes," dealt with the concept of blindness, and how blind people can cope through their other senses. Before children worked with the story, teachers read to them an encyclopedia article about blindness. Next, teachers listed story words that could be identified through other senses, such as "marigold" and "cello," and the children determined how each could be identified, whether by taste, touch, hearing, or smell. Prepared with these background knowledge activities, when the children read the story, their understanding of blindness and of the five senses helped them to comprehend subtle ideas and to recognize words.

Interest is another important way that the reader influences the reading process. Have you ever noticed that many people don't read the sports section of a newspaper until a hometown champion sparks their interest? Interests seem to be particularly important during childhood, as children pursue dozens of series books, such as *Baby-Sitter's Club* (by Martin), or read intensively about a favorite topic, such as dinosaurs.

Interest can be a critical factor in helping students with reading problems. Engagement in a subject can keep a struggling reader both absorbed in a book and wanting to read other books. Ten-year-old Georg, a child in our Reading Center, refused to read until his tutor discovered his passion for snakes. Suddenly he was devouring fact books on snakes, snake stories, and snake poems. Throughout this instruction, Georg was gaining critical practice in reading. He was delighted when his father bought him *Snakes* (by Wexo) and *Amazing Poisonous Animals* (by Parsons) for Christmas.

Of course, interest and background are related. People who are interested in a topic will read about it and, as they read, increase their background information. Therefore, when teachers build their students' interests in what they are reading, they also deepen their students' reading processes.

The attitude of the reader is also an important factor in constructing meaning (Beach & Hynds, 1991). Because of an unfriendly teacher, long ago, in a high school physics class, one adult finds any article about physics almost impossible to understand. On the other hand, warm memories of a chemistry teacher make this subject more readable. Many students with reading problems are literally afraid of books. Nine-year-old Kenisha experienced a magical feeling of achievement after she read and enjoyed her first hard-cover book. This feeling was made even stronger by her former fear of books. For those who teach students with problems, developing positive attitudes toward reading is an extremely important and sometimes very challenging task. Many suggestions are given in Chapter 4.

A reader's purpose also affects the reading process. Good readers use strategies that fulfill their purposes for reading. Most people use a phone book, for example, simply to locate the number they want. They turn as quickly as possible to the right page, locate the number, and close the book. Unfortunately, many students with reading problems are not this efficient. We still remember, with horror, a reading-disabled teenager who was trying to locate the name "Weiss," starting from page one of a telephone book! When we read to fulfill our purposes, we are doing *strategic* reading (Paris, Wasik, & Turner, 1991). Strategic reading is difficult for students with reading problems.

Finally, the reader's ability plays a part in meaning construction. Students with reading problems must often struggle to recognize words and comprehend text. Therefore, they have less energy to pay attention to the meaning of what they are reading.

As teachers, we owe our best efforts, our warmest smiles, and our most effective techniques to the students who experience reading problems. Providing these is what this book is all about!

The Contribution of the Material

The *material* (or *text*) read is a second contribution to the construction of meaning. Without the text, there would be no reading, for the reader uses the material as the input from which to construct meaning. The material sets limits on the construction of meaning that the reader may make. A person reading a manual about health care may decide that some of the author's points are more important than others, or may even disagree with some things. However, the reader would probably not think the manual was about using a computer!

Finding the right materials is particularly important for a student who experiences reading difficulties. As we showed in the case of Georg, interesting materials (in his case, about snakes) can be a key factor in the success of instruction. Finding books that are interesting, yet not too difficult, may be a particular challenge. This point is addressed in several chapters of this book, and a list of easy, but interesting, reading is given in Appendix B.

Students must also learn how to handle many different types of materials. Good readers can often teach themselves to read their science texts, computer manuals, and novels strategically. In contrast, readers with problems need direct instruction in the strategies appropriate for different types of reading.

The Contribution of the Reading Situation

The *reading situation* forms a third contribution to meaning construction. One element of the reading situation is the task the reader must accomplish. Imagine that you are leisurely reading—and enjoying—Ernest Hemingway's novel *The Old Man and the Sea*. In fact, you are enjoying this novel *despite* the fact that it was assigned for an English class. Suddenly, you realize that you have a test on the book tomorrow. The reading situation changes dramatically. You read hurriedly, focusing on getting through the book, and (since this is an English class) trying to understand what it "means." In later years, your memory of this

What is the reading process like for students with problems? In one study (Liebert, 1970–1) professors asked university students to read text written in a mirror (or backwards) form.

The text looked like this.

Instantly, the backwards text transformed excellent readers into individuals with reading problems. Here is how they reacted:

- I resorted to finger pointing to keep my place in a maze of unfamiliar print. . . . I guessed words, repeated words and phrases continually.
- I guessed, repeated, reversed, inverted, and giggled. To be specific, I became entirely frustrated.
- What was most frustrating to me after correctly identifying . . . the word, was the awkward inability to recognize the identical symbol in other locations. . . . Such words as *and*, *the*, *as*, or *but* were particularly troublesome.

Although the print was normal in size, the readers felt it was too small.

- . . . all of the words were so close to each other that they were hard to recognize. . . . *O*'s looked like *a*'s, *f*'s like *t*'s, *b*'s like *h*'s, etc.
- It would have been a help to have the print considerably enlarged.

As readers struggled, their fluency disappeared and comprehension was lost. In less than 10 minutes, they developed negative attitudes, lowered self-esteem, and undesirable behaviors.

- I laughed, looked around to see the reaction of other people, became fidgety.
- I gave up quite easily. After the test I was quite weary and felt headachey.
- This nervousness, insecurity or frustration was shown by pointing with my pen and glancing up to see if I were being closely observed by the teacher.

If these are the reactions of skilled adults after ten minutes, what must be the feelings of schoolchildren who face reading problems year after year? Is it any wonder that they lose their places, complain about small print, fidget, and suffer from lack of self-esteem? As one adult in the experiment stated:

- I now can really feel strong sympathy toward children who are faced with a similar situation 180 days a year.

novel (or put another way, your construction of meaning) will probably include unpleasant associations of rapid reading and tension.

Students with reading problems often find themselves studying difficult material at a rapid pace to meet classroom demands. They rarely have time to enjoy true leisure reading. It is important that teachers structure their activities so that they *can* read for enjoyment.

The environment in which we read is another factor in the reading situation. We relax by reading magazines or novels on a couch or in a bed. (These situations often result in an even more relaxing nap!) Teachers should do all they can to make the environment inviting for students with reading problems. A well-organized, colorful room with bean-bag chairs and pillows with which to curl up and read helps them to experience reading as pleasurable. Chapter 4 gives many suggestions for creating a pleasant reading situation and environment.

The Components of the Reading Process

Accomplished readers are able to construct meaning from reading without conscious effort and to combine many abilities into the single act of reading. However, teachers who deal with low-achieving students need to be aware of the different components involved in learning to read, so that we may know when students need assistance in using them.

In this book we have addressed these topics separately, providing distinct chapters to help you teach each one. However, remember that our ultimate goal is for the student to experience the act of reading as a pleasurable and informative whole.

Some of the components of good reading are:

- knowing what reading is and how to deal with books (emergent literacy, Chapter 5)
- recognizing words accurately (word recognition–accuracy, Chapter 6)
- recognizing words with ease and fluency (word recognition–fluency, Chapter 7)
- understanding and being able to study and learn what is read (comprehension and studying, Chapters 8 and 9)
- understanding language structures and word meanings (language and meaning vocabulary, Chapter 10)
- responding actively to reading (the reading/writing connection, Chapter 11)
- enjoying and appreciating reading (motivation and reading environment, Chapter 4)

To illustrate the components of reading, an excerpt from the *Miami Herald* newspaper (Phillips, 1990) has been reproduced. Read it, and, after the excerpt, let's consider each component of the reading process:

Ephemeral Ixia Plant Kept Off Federal Endangered List

In 1791, writing of his travels through the wilds of Florida, naturalist William Bartram admired the "azure fields of cerulian ixia" gracing what is now greater Jacksonville.

What Bartram witnessed was one of the most ephemeral delights in Nature's bouquet: a violet-blue wildflower that blooms for as little as a few hours every two decades.

The plant, now called Bartram's ixia, is so reclusive that the U.S. Fish and Wildlife Service proposed listing the species as endangered. But the agency reversed that decision last month after timber companies produced evidence that *** plant is hiding out on thousands of privately owned pine lands in several northeastern Florida counties.

"Ephemeral Ixia Plant Kept Off Federal Endangered List," by Michael Phillips. Reprinted with permission of the Miami Herald.

The companies, through the Florida Forestry Association, argued that timber harvesting actually helps the plant. Ixia bulbs are drawn into bloom by fires, bulldozers, and other soil disturbances.

Emergent Literacy

As an adult, you realize that newspapers supply information about the world. You also know how to identify the title of an article, and that reading, in English, is done from left to right. Such knowledge is usually learned in the preschool and kindergarten years, but students with reading problems may still be mastering emergent literacy skills long after these ages. Emergent literacy is discussed in detail in Chapter 5.

Word Recognition: Accuracy and Fluency

It seems almost silly to state that we need to recognize the words *accurately* in order to read this text. Of course we do! But word recognition is partly a product of our comprehension. In the text above, one word has been replaced by asterisks. You probably guessed that the missing word is "the." In fact, fluent readers don't even bother to fix their eyes on some of the small words in text such as "the" and "is," since this type of word can often be predicted from our general comprehension of the material. In this way, our comprehension of material actually contributes to the words we recognize.

However, we can only use our comprehension abilities to guess a small proportion of the words in our reading; we must learn to read most of them accurately. Accurate word recognition is often difficult for disabled readers. One study found that 77 percent of students with reading problems felt that the difficulties they experienced were due to difficulty in recognizing words (Miller & Yochum, 1991). More about word recognition accuracy is found in Chapter 5 of this book.

In addition to recognizing words accurately, we need to read them quickly and *fluently*. Otherwise our reading will be labored and unenjoyable, and we will lose meaning. Reading fluently has recently been recognized as "the missing ingredient" (Anderson, 1981) in instruction for problem readers. It is addressed in Chapter 7 of this book.

Comprehension and Studying

Comprehension is the essence of the reading act. The many levels of comprehending include drawing on background experiences (or schema), literal comprehension, higher-level comprehension, and being able to study and learn from text. These different levels of comprehension are strongly related.

In order to comprehend material effectively, readers require some background knowledge. In fact, in these days of environmental concerns, most readers are aware of the efforts to save rare plant and animal species that are addressed in the ixia article. You may also be conscious of the growing concerns of businesses that use natural resources (such as lumber, water), as they find their activities affected by efforts to save wildlife. You probably know that Jacksonville is a city within the state of Florida, located in the southeastern United States. The organized background that you have enables you to build the bridges to your experiences and connect what you read to what you know.

Literal comprehension, or understanding the information stated directly in the text, is another part of comprehension. Yet, even here, the good reader picks and chooses, remembering the most important facts. You may remember that the plant mentioned in the article was named after a man who lived a long time ago. You are less likely to remember that his name was William Bartram or that he described the plant in 1791.

Perhaps the thing you are most likely to remember is your construction of the central thought of the article. Formulating this thought is part of higher-level comprehension. The main thought we construct is a little different for each of us. In our case, it was: "A pretty, but rarely blooming Florida plant was taken off a federal endangered species list." In this way, we actively participate in the reading process by constructing meaning.

Another form of higher-level thinking consists of the inferences, or implied information, we draw from the text. The experienced reader will draw many. For example, in the first paragraph, the reader will infer that two hundred years ago the metropolitan area of Jacksonville was not developed. In the second paragraph, it seems that the plant was put on the endangered species list because it is hard to find. In the fourth paragraph, we might infer (although it is not stated) that the forestry industry does *not* want the plant on the endangered list. We might further draw the conclusion that the forestry industry wants to harvest timber on lands that they were forbidden to lumber because of this plant.

Critical or evaluative thinking is also a part of higher-level comprehension. As you read, you are probably developing a point of view about whether the ixia plant should be kept on this list. You are evaluating the information given in the light of your thinking and experiences. What might motivate lumber companies to ask that the ixia be taken off the list of endangered species? Perhaps you feel that the lands will not be maintained as lumber sites, thus helping the flowers, but will eventually be developed as housing or commercial sites. In this case, you would probably oppose taking the ixia off of the endangered list.

Although your task was not to study this article, the accomplished reader can easily understand how to gain information from it. In school, students are often called upon to study (gain information) from their textbooks. This continues throughout adult life, using books, manuals, directions, and many other materials. The ability to study is important in school and daily life.

Students with reading problems need work in many areas of comprehension and studying. As mentioned earlier, they do not construct meaning effectively in their minds, the way we did when we constructed a central thought for this article.

In addition, low-level readers are particularly at risk in content-area subjects, such as science, social studies, and health. These are areas in which the reading is "expository," or focuses on giving information (rather than telling a story).

In this book we deal with the comprehension of *narratives* (or stories and novels) in Chapter 8, and the comprehension and study of *expository* text (informational materials, such as textbooks) in Chapter 9.

Language and Meaning Vocabulary

To read a text effectively, you must understand its sentence structures and word meanings. Yet it is certainly possible to read something without understanding every word in it. In fact, using your comprehension processes, you are able to increase your vocabulary as you read. When you started, the word *ephemeral* may have been unfamiliar to you. From the clue in the text "blooms for as little as a few hours every two decades," you probably figured out that it means "lasting for a short time." If you did know the word before you read the passage, your knowledge has been reinforced with another example. In a similar way, *azure* and *cerulean*, which also may have been unknown to you, are now somewhat more familiar. You may realize that both are adjectives (in fact, they describe shades of blue.)

In addition to knowing vocabulary, you need a knowledge of difficult language structures to read this article. It contains a quote from 1791 that was rather formal by today's standards. It also contains many long and complicated sentences. For example, the second sentence ("What Bartram witnessed . . .") has 30 words and many complex structures.

To summarize, you needed a knowledge of word meanings and language to read this text. Yet, at the same time, you also acquired new word meanings and gained experience with language as you read it. The more students read, the more word meanings and language they will acquire (Stanovich & Cunningham, 1993; West, Stanovich, & Mitchell, 1993). This is one important reason that teachers need to encourage students with reading problems to read as much as possible.

The language we understand is the natural limit of our reading ability. Meaning vocabulary is an extremely important factor in reading, particularly in the intermediate and upper grades (Davis, 1968; Stanovich, 1986). Students with reading problems lag behind their average-achieving peers in both language development and meaning vocabulary. Chapter 10 contains many motivating ideas to help build the language and vocabulary of low-achieving readers.

The Reading–Writing Connection

Perhaps it seems strange to include writing as a part of reading. Yet we have already pointed out that, as we read the article, we mentally constructed its central thought. In other words, we composed (or "wrote") in our minds. As we are constructing our own meaning, we are always composing, so reading actually involves "writing."

Reading the ixia article involves composing in our minds. However, when students actually take pencil in hand and write down their thoughts, they learn even more about reading. Trying to spell gives them insights into sound–symbol relationships (or phonics). Creating their own writing shows them that somebody actually *writes* what is read, and that they can write too! Thus, students acquire a sense of control over reading. In this book, the reading–writing connection is addressed in Chapter 11.

Enjoyment and Appreciation

The article cited above is on a controversial topic of current importance. The editors of the *Miami Herald* decided that it would interest you; that is why they printed it. In addition, the writer (Michael Phillips) tried to write it in an engaging way. He reminded you of a time long past; he conjured up images of wild blue flowers in a forgotten wilderness. People do what they enjoy and appreciate. In order for the reading act to be complete, the reader's interest must be engaged.

Suggestions for helping students with reading problems to enjoy reading are found throughout this book, but are particularly concentrated in Chapter 4. We give many different strategies and materials that you can use to motivate your students.

As you can see, the reader is an active participant in the many parts of reading. Although these parts can be analyzed separately, fluent readers are not aware of most of them. For, in accomplished reading, these processes interact with each other and take place simultaneously. Our goal as teachers is to foster such accomplishment; yet, when instructing students with reading problems, we must be aware of the component parts of reading so that we know how to develop each one.

An Overview of This Book

This book provides teachers and prospective teachers with techniques for assessing and helping students who are experiencing reading problems.

In Chapter 1, we have discussed the widespread nature of reading problems and some of the factors that contribute to them. We have defined the many components of the skilled reading process.

In Chapter 2, Obtaining Background Information, we discuss background factors, both within the individual and in the environment, that may contribute to a reading problem. We also provide interviews and related tools to help you assess these factors.

Chapter 3, Assessing Reading Achievement: Overview and Informal Measures, provides a framework for diagnosis and assessment. This is followed by a thorough discussion of informal measures you can use to identify a student's reading level and determine patterns of strengths and weaknesses. One important instrument, the Informal Reading Inventory, is discussed in detail.

Chapter 4, An Overview of Instruction, deals with overall principles of providing motivating and effective instruction for students who experience reading difficulties.

Chapters 5 through 11 deal with component parts of reading. In each chapter, we give (1) the abilities involved in the particular area of reading, (2) specific strategies for assessment, and (3) instructional strategies. The chapters include:

Chapter 5 – Emergent Literacy

Chapter 6 – Improving Word Recognition Accuracy

Chapter 7 – Improving Word Recognition Fluency

Chapter 8 – Improving Comprehension of Narrative Text

Chapter 9 – Improving Comprehension of Expository Text

Chapter 10 – Improving Language Abilities: Listening Comprehension and Meaning Vocabulary

Chapter 11 – Reading and Writing

Chapter 12, Literacy in a Diverse Society, presents special considerations needed when teaching students who speak English as a second language and strategies for teaching in today's multicultural society. In addition, resources are given for working with parents. Finally, the special needs of adolescents and adults are presented.

Chapter 13, Factors Related to Reading Disabilities, gives a detailed, theoretical description of the factors associated with reading problems. We discuss factors both within the individual and in the environment, presenting relevant research and in-depth assessment tools.

Chapter 14, Severe Reading Disabilities, addresses the concerns of severely disabled readers. We address the characteristics of these students and of programs designed to serve them. We give new research insights into severe reading disabilities and we present several instructional options for addressing the needs of these students.

Chapter 15, Assessing Reading Achievement: Formal Measures, presents a discussion of formal tests, including a presentation of types of tests, considerations in using tests, how standardized tests may be interpreted, and an overview of many specific, widely used instruments.

Appendix A gives a description of tests that are widely used in the reading diagnosis. Appendix B gives resources of materials for students with reading problems.

In Appendix C, we present an informal reading inventory, which you may administer to your students. Our book concludes with a list of references.

Summary

Teachers bear the primary responsibility for instructing students who have reading problems. Reading problems are associated with difficulties in life, including poverty, unemployment, and problems with the law. Since they lack skills, individuals with reading problems are often unable to train for jobs in an increasingly technological society.

It is estimated that one-third of our school population has learning problems, and most of these are related to reading. Such students may receive help through Title I programs, the special education Individuals with Disabilities Act (IDEA), or through state or locally funded programs; however many students with reading problems receive no special help. If help is given, students may be placed in a self-contained setting, a resource (or "pull out") setting, or in an inclusion (regular classroom) setting.

Factors associated with reading problems include those within the individual and those in the environment. Factors within the individual include physical factors (including neurological ones), language factors, and emotional factors. Although neurological problems first received intense focus, the causes of reading problems are quite complex.

Environmental factors include the home, social setting, culture, and school. In today's society, increasing numbers of students come from homes that cannot support literacy. The school environment has not proven entirely effective in eliminating reading problems. A key problem is that students with reading problems do not do enough reading to develop the ability to read effectively.

Reading is the construction of meaning from text. The reader constructs meaning in his or her own mind; and each reader constructs this meaning a bit differently. The reader contributes to meaning construction through background, interest, attitude, purpose, and ability. The text that is read also contributes to the meaning that is constructed. Finally, the reading situation contributes to reading through the task and the environment.

We are often not conscious of the components of the reading process as we read, for, in good readers, these components are used unconsciously and automatically. However, in order to help students with reading problems, teachers must be able to identify these components. They include emergent literacy, word recognition accuracy and fluency, comprehension and studying, the understanding of language structures and word meanings, an active response to reading (the reading–writing connection), and the enjoyment and appreciation of reading.

Obtaining Background Information

Introduction

Accurate assessment helps teachers to plan the best possible instruction for students. Chapters 2 and 3 provide information on gathering and analyzing data about students and their reading. In Chapter 2, we discuss background information. In Chapter 3, we concentrate on the assessment of reading abilities. Both kinds of information are essential to good teaching.

In this chapter, we examine ways to obtain a broad understanding of a student's background. We divide background information into two parts: (1) the student's environments, including home, school, social, and cultural, and (2) background factors within the individual, including emotional, physical, and language development. We then provide specific methods of gathering information.

Background factors can profoundly affect a student's reading. In Chapter 1, we gave several examples of this. Some were of students whose *environmental* background did not foster reading development—Diane's family could not provide a stable home life; Ilya missed a year of important preparation when he did not attend kindergarten. For other students, problems in reading seem to come from *within the individual*—Jason's reading problems were related to his physical development.

At times, identified problems can be corrected. For example, a student with visual difficulties may be referred to an eye doctor, receive corrective lenses, and show immediate reading gains.

Often students face problems that cannot be resolved easily. For example, a teacher has little ability to affect a difficult home situation. But even in that instance a teacher can make a difference. During a time of family turmoil, a student may need a compassionate, understanding adult. Knowing background information enables the teacher to deal sympathetically with a fragile human being and to adjust instruction to special needs.

Our discussion of background factors in this chapter is oriented to the immediate, practical needs of teachers. More theoretical, research-oriented information is presented in Chapter 13, "Factors Related to Reading Disability," and in Chapter 14, "Severe Reading Disabilities."

When dealing with background factors, it is important to remember that these have a complex relationship to reading problems. A factor may coexist with a reading problem, but not actually cause that reading problem. For example, some students manage to achieve well in school despite difficult home lives. For other students, however, problems at home may impede learning. Thus it is important to interpret background information judiciously.

Information About the Environment

Students live in several environments: the home, the school, the social, and the cultural environment. Each one of these influences how a youngster thinks about reading, the desire to learn, and the access to reading materials. In addition, these environments interact. For example, a difficult situation at home may contribute to difficulty making friends in the social realm and to trouble in cooperating with teachers at school.

The Home Environment

The home exerts a powerful influence on the development of reading and writing. Parents play an important role in modeling the value of literacy and bringing children to books, and the general home situation can influence a student's academic achievement. Events such as divorce or a move to a new neighborhood can affect a student's ability to profit from school reading instruction.

Parents as Models for Literacy.
Parents are a child's earliest and most important literacy role models. If parents read for both recreation and information and provide many reading materials at home, the child learns to value literacy. Parents also stimulate a love of books by reading to their children, taking them

to the library, and buying books as gifts. A home environment that is rich in books and in literacy activities fosters success in reading.

A reading teacher can determine whether the home supports and values literacy by interviewing the parents or by asking them to fill out a questionnaire. What information is helpful? Some of the questions to ask parents about their own reading habits are: Do they read regularly? Do they subscribe to newspapers and magazines? Do they buy books? Next, parents should be asked about literacy interactions with their child. Do they regularly read to their child? Do they encourage their child to read? Do they take their child to the library or buy books for the child? Do they subscribe to any children's magazines? Do they limit television viewing? Responses to such questions indicate how parents and other family members, including grandparents and older siblings, foster literacy at home.

Information obtained directly from a student can also give insights into how literacy is modeled at home. As you gather information from interviewing and working with your students, you learn whether there are books at home and if reading is done regularly.

What can a reading teacher do if the home does not nurture literacy? We have found that many parents are grateful for teacher suggestions about improving literacy in their homes. Often, the parents of students with reading problems are worried about their child's future and have misgivings about their own parenting skills. A few suggestions often help both to foster a sense of family security and to enhance literacy. For some families, these suggestions will reinforce the good things they are doing already.

1. Provide a good reading/studying environment. Advise parents to provide a quiet, stable, well-lighted place in which their child will study. Supplies (paper and pencils) and reference materials (dictionaries, maps) should be located near this area. Make sure that the television is off during homework or reading time.

2. Share literacy with the child. When parents read to young children, they promote an interest in reading, foster language development, and share close family experiences. If the child is older, parent and child can share reading time as they each read silently. Students of all ages enjoy reading material that they have mastered to a parent who listens enthusiastically. Encourage parents to take children to a local library and to look for a helpful children's librarian, who will aid them in locating suitable books.

3. Accept the child as he or she is. It is often difficult to admit that one's own child has a problem. Some parents deny that difficulties exist or hold unrealistic expectations for their child. Children are sensitive to their parents' disappointments. To prevent a reading problem from becoming a family problem, it is important for children to know that parents accept and love them as they are.

4. Help the child to feel secure and confident. Encourage activities that a child does successfully. Playing baseball or basketball, taking cooking lessons, or just being dad's special helper may acquire a very special meaning for a child with reading problems.

When parents are unable to provide literacy experiences at home, teachers must nurture a love of literacy during instruction. Classrooms filled with different types of books and magazines, invitingly displayed, show students that literacy is important. Give students time to browse through and share these materials. Teachers can also read to students on a regular basis, asking them to share their own thoughts and feelings about the selections. More suggestions for teachers are given in Chapter 4.

General Home Situation.

Children are profoundly affected by what happens to their families. They are often dramatically touched by a move to a new location, divorce or separation of parents, the death of relatives, or leave-taking of older siblings. It may be impossible for a child to pay attention to reading instruction when the father has just moved out or the mother has taken a new job and will no longer be at home after school.

Through a parent interview, we often collect helpful information about a family. This includes the names, ages, and occupations of the parents; the number and ages of siblings; names of other family members that are living in the home; and the members of the nuclear family (parents, siblings) who are not living at home. During this interview, we ask parents to share any other information that might help to explain their child's difficulties. Often parental insights give valuable ideas for cooperation between a reading teacher and the family.

Occasionally, the parent interview reveals that a family situation is causing stress for the student and contributing to difficulty in school. Although teachers cannot intervene in a divorce or prevent an impending move to a new neighborhood, they can be sensitive to a student's feelings and emotional needs. At such critical times, the reactions and guidance of an understanding teacher may be more important for the child than direct instruction in reading. Our work with Shannon at our Reading Center illustrates this point. When Shannon's parents separated, she reacted with fits of crying and withdrawal from other children. We realized that there were certain topics that would upset her, so we allowed her to select her own materials for instruction. Shannon avoided books about families, choosing instead nonsense books such as *Chicken Soup with Rice* (by Sendak) and books featuring brave young children, such as *Hatupatu and the Birdwoman* (by Cowley) and *Where the Wild Things Are* (by Sendak). These selections proved to be key elements in improving her reading.

Teachers can help students cope with difficult home situations by:

1. Being sensitive. Sensitivity in talking to students and allowing them to express their feelings is very important.
2. Reducing demands. Teachers may want to "go easy" on students for a while by reducing both academic and behavioral demands.
3. Being aware of the student's living situation. Teachers should be knowledgeable and understanding about the student's living and legal custody arrangements. If parents do not live together, make sure the appropriate parent receives communications. With permission from the custodial parent, both parents may be informed.

The School Environment

Many factors in the school environment can influence reading achievement. Information about educational history, school attendance, and instructional methods helps us to understand the student's problem and forms a basis for cooperation between *all* the professionals who are helping a student.

Educational History.

By gathering information about a student's educational history, teachers learn what the youngster has already experienced and are able to select new options for instruction. Students differ widely in their educational histories. For some, first grade is the initial instructional experience; others enter first grade with a rich history of preschool and kindergarten. Some students are barely six years old when they first encounter formal reading instruction; others are almost seven. Some students have repeated a grade or have received an extra year of kindergarten instruction. Some children have received private tutoring; some have been placed in special school programs.

Educational history may offer some hints about the seriousness of a student's problem. For example, a student who has had many enriching experiences, such as preschool education and previous tutoring, and still has difficulty in reading, probably has a serious problem. In contrast, a student who comes with no preschool education or history of special reading help may simply have lacked the opportunities needed for learning to read.

Educational history is gathered from many sources: interviews with parents and/or students, teacher interviews and questionnaires, cumulative school records (which follow the student from year to year), portfolios, and report cards. If you are not a staff member at the student's school, you must obtain written permission from parents before contacting school personnel.

A complete history of schooling covers several areas.

1. Ask about preschool experiences, including the length of nursery/preschool education and kindergarten attendance.
2. Ask about the student's age (in months and years) when the student entered first grade; children exposed too early to reading instruction often have problems (Olson, 1989).
3. Ask if the student has ever repeated a grade; if so, try to determine the cause of retention.
4. Ask if the student is currently in, or has ever been in, a special school program. Placement in such programs as special education, special reading, or Chapter I/Title I can influence the type of instruction and attention a student receives. If the student is in a special program, is the placement full-time or part-time? Does the student receive supportive help in a "resource room" setting or in the regular classroom?
5. If previous diagnostic work has been done for the student through the school or a private agency, ask the parents to bring in a copy of the findings. It is necessary to have written consent from parents or guardians to contact these professionals.

School Attendance.

Absence from school and frequent transfers can be harmful to a student's progress. Some children are absent from school for weeks at a time, missing critical instruction. Other students change schools several times during the year, resulting in abrupt changes in the teaching they receive.

Information about school attendance can be obtained from parents, teachers, and cumulative school records. Try to determine how many times the student has been absent in the current school year and in earlier years. Instruction missed in first and second grade seems to have a particularly damaging effect on reading progress. Extended absences are also harmful. It is important to determine how long the student has been in a particular school, and how many different schools the student has attended. Ask about the reasons for frequent absences or transfers.

School Instruction.

The type of reading instruction that students receive dramatically affects their ability to read. Often students with reading problems have received instruction that does not match their unique needs. Some have not received enough direct instruction in critical concepts. Although the typical student often learns word recognition and comprehension strategies from extensive reading, low-achieving students may need direct, sequenced lessons. Biemiller (1994) found that direct and prescribed practice in reading was more beneficial to some students than a less controlled literature approach to reading.

At other times, low-achieving students are given books that are too hard for them. The basal reading series of the 1990s contain more difficult words, complex concepts, and longer selections than earlier series (Hoffman et al., 1994). If the whole class is using one text-book series or novel, poorer readers may not be able to read it successfully. Even teachers who group their students for reading are likely to have one or two very low readers who cannot handle the easy books that are comfortable for the rest of the reading group. As a consequence, these poor readers have no material at their level, and little opportunity to read.

Information about a student's first experiences with reading instruction may provide insights into how a problem developed. Was the student ready for reading instruction? Was the initial method suited to the student's needs? Did the reading problem start in first grade, or were the student's early experiences successful? Reading problems that begin in first and second grade often involve word recognition abilities; problems that develop in the inter-mediate grades (or later) tend to focus on comprehension and language abilities.

Information about school instruction can be obtained from school personnel, parents, and students. The school is a particularly valuable source. Teacher interviews and questionnaires, school records, and information about schoolbooks and assignments all provide insight into instruction. In gathering information from the school, the reading teacher should try to gather a full picture of instruction and progress. Is the student receiving specific reading instruction, or is reading addressed only as a part of other subjects (such as social studies and science)? If reading is taught as a subject, is a reading textbook series used? If so, which one, and at what level is the student placed? If novels and trade books are used, which ones has the student read? Is the class organized into reading groups, or is the whole class instructed together? Are word recognition and comprehension strategies taught directly? Are students given strategies for reading in social studies, health, and science books? Does the class have time to do recreational reading? If so, are books provided at the student's level? Is writing encouraged? How is the student performing in such areas as math, science, social studies, art, and physical education?

The student's own perceptions about reading instruction can also offer valuable insights. Interviews and informal conversations provide information about whether a student likes reading class (or instruction) and whether the books and stories are easy and interesting to read. Ask the student what activities take place during reading instruction? Are stories and novels read orally or silently? We have found that students with reading problems often would like to change something about their instruction. For this reason, we often ask them, "If you could change one thing about reading class, what would it be?" A student's perceptions of reading can also be very revealing. You might ask the student what reading is or what makes a good reader.

Parents' perceptions of the school environment come from their child's comments, homework examples, report cards, and teacher conferences. During an interview, ask the parents to describe the type and amount of homework. Ask parents if the student brings books home from school to read. Parents often have strong feelings about instructional factors that may have contributed to their child's reading problems. Obtaining this information from parents is important in fostering a cooperative spirit between the school and home.

Sometimes, the information suggests that school factors may have, indeed, contributed to the reading problem. What can you, as a reading teacher, do? It is, of course, impossible to change the past. Furthermore, assigning blame to a particular school or teacher is not really helpful. It is very difficult for a classroom teacher to be responsive to the special needs of one individual while dealing with a group of 25 to 35 students. A reading teacher *can* make helpful suggestions to the school and can foster cooperation among all of the professionals who are trying to help the student. For example, one reading teacher suggested the titles of easy books for a low-achieving student to read during recreational reading time in his class. Another reading teacher worked with the classroom teacher to adjust difficult homework assignments for a special-needs student.

In some cases, information about past instruction is helpful in planning an effective current reading program. Ten-year-old Gregg loudly stated that he hated school reading class and "all those hard worksheets." Gregg defined reading as "saying the words right," which explained his lack of interest and enthusiasm for it. To help him overcome negative past experiences, his reading teacher avoided any tasks that resembled school instruction and emphasized comprehension rather than accurate word pronunciation. Gregg selected the stories that he and his teacher read together. They paused periodically to discuss and predict what might happen next. Since Gregg enjoyed art, the tutor encouraged him to illustrate parts of the story and vocabulary words. At the end of the semester, Gregg proclaimed that these lessons "weren't real reading classes but I learned to read better."

The Social and Cultural Environments

Reading is a social process, since, during reading, an author communicates his (or her) ideas to the reader. Because of the social nature of reading, a student's relationships with parents, teachers, and peers can affect reading achievement. Social interactions occur through specific personal relationships and through the student's general cultural environment.

Successful social interactions can provide the student with feelings of high self-esteem and confidence that encourage reading achievement. Unfortunately, for many poor readers, the social sphere is yet another area of personal failure. Students with reading problems are often rejected by their classmates and viewed with disfavor by their teachers. They may be a source of concern to their parents. As a result, poor readers often have difficulty relating to others.

In today's schools, reading instruction tends to be a social experience. Students often read orally in pairs or groups, sharing thoughts and feelings about a novel or working in cooperative groups. These activities can be burdensome to a student who lacks ability in social interaction. Students who are poor readers may withdraw in shame when they have to share their reading.

The student's general cultural environment may also affect reading progress. Some students are surrounded by peers who do not value literacy. In addition, the student's cultural background may make asking a teacher for help a difficult and uncomfortable experience.

Reading teachers should gather background about both the student's social and the more general cultural environment. Often the parents' description of their child's social interactions is informative. Ask the parents to describe their child's relationships with them and with siblings. Does the student have many friends? Do these friends value education? What is the student's relationship with the teacher and classmates? Does the student willingly join in group activities or prefer to work alone. Is the student shy and withdrawn, or outgoing?

Interviewing the student about friends and interests can also be useful. Does the student see reading as something that friends and family value? Does the student spend time with friends? What are the student's interests? Such information provides hints about how to make reading a motivating experience.

At times the investigation of a student's social relationships indicates that there is some cause for concern. However, we often find that these relationships improve when academic problems are alleviated. When the student reads better, feelings of success provide more confidence in social interactions. Thus, by offering good instruction, reading teachers can often affect both a student's achievement and her or his social relationships.

At other times, a teacher's use of a student's interests may draw him or her more comfortably into social interactions. Eamon, the poorest reader in his third grade class, seldom interacted with his peers. During recess, he stood in the corner of the playground; at lunch, he usually sat and ate alone. To help him, the reading teacher made a point of talking to Eamon alone whenever possible. Discovering that Eamon was passionately interested in snakes and had two pet reptiles at home, she gave him several books about snakes and asked him to bring his pets to school. The eager fascination of the other children motivated Eamon to talk about the care of his pets and how they should be handled. The teacher also read several books about snakes to the class, and encouraged Eamon to critique them. Were the facts accurate? Had Eamon ever see a snake do that? As Eamon became the class "snake expert," he gradually increased his willingness to participate in class activities and to seek out the company of his peers.

Carefully planned reading with peers can promote social and reading competence. Jennifer, a sixth-grade student in our Reading Center, was reading at the third-grade level and had a history of negative social interactions. To improve reading and social skills, Jennifer was paired with Samantha, a fifth-grade student. The two girls read *Charlotte's Web* (by White) at home, and returned to the Reading Center to discuss difficult words, the characters in the book, and the plot. Sharing the reading experience helped Jennifer to overcome her shyness. Jennifer and Samantha became good friends as they enjoyed the positive social experience of reacting to good children's literature.

At times when a student's culture does not value academic achievement, instruction can be made relevant by reading and writing about interesting topics, such as popular TV programs and movies, video games, and "hot" musicians or comedians.

Information About the Individual

Many of the factors that contribute to reading problems are found within the individual student. In this section, we discuss information about emotional status, physical health, and language development.

Emotional Information

Poor readers often display emotional problems that impede learning. Not surprisingly, many students who have problems in their social environments (discussed in the previous section) also display emotional problems.

For some students, problems with learning to read may result in emotional problems. For example, some children withdraw and refuse even to attempt to read or write. Seven-year-old Carlos eagerly participated in classroom activities that did not involve reading or writing. However, when the teacher asked students to take out their books, Carlos would either put his head down on the desk or turn his chair away from the teacher. To avoid meeting repeated failure, Carlos had decided not to read anymore.

If learning has been a painful experience, some students develop a block against all school activities. Others react by becoming hostile or aggressive. Still others develop self-images of poor readers; since these students believe that they are "dumb," they give up trying to learn. Other students become overcome with anxiety, and may start to shake or stutter when asked to read.

For another group of students, the reading problem may be a result of an underlying emotional problem. For example, some of the students in our Reading Center first developed problems with literacy just as their parents were separating or going through a divorce.

Teachers, parents, and students themselves can all offer insights about emotional factors that may affect reading achievement. The teacher, who sees the child in class, can note reactions to instructional activities. The parents can describe the child at home and with peers. Finally, the perceptions of the student are perhaps the most revealing.

What types of school information is useful in determining a student's emotional state? It is helpful to know whether the student works independently in class. Does the student cooperate well with others? Does the student pay attention and follow directions? Is there evidence of emotional outbursts, inappropriate behavior, or depression? Does the student willingly participate in reading activities? How does the student interact with others?

From interviewing a parent, the reading teacher can also gain insight into a student's interactions, behavior, and attitudes within the family and with friends. For example, can the child take enough responsibility to do chores and complete work? Does the youngster often withdraw from peer groups? Does the child seem unhappy?

Of course, simply observing and interacting with a student also gives much information. Observation of a student's behaviors and attitudes during reading class can make you aware of that student's emotional state. It may also be possible to observe a student during regular reading instruction in school. Finally, as you interact with a student, you will be able to judge the appropriateness of responses.

At times, you may suspect that emotional factors may be affecting reading. However, since a reading teacher is not a psychologist or psychiatrist, directly addressing emotional problems is not an appropriate role. Rather, a reading teacher may best address these problems by planning sensitive instruction.

Donny, one student in a group of five, was very hostile during reading instruction. He accused the teacher of liking the other children better and of thinking that he was "dumb." He deliberately dropped books and pencils, loudly complained of a stomach ache, and refused to answer questions or to read orally. In fact, his behavior totally disrupted group activities. To help Donny, his reading teacher made a special effort to spend some time with him alone. She read orally with Donny, praising him when he was successful and gently helping him when he met difficulties. Donny enjoyed this private attention, away from the possibly negative reactions of others. Slowly Donny's trust in his teacher developed into an improved self-concept, and his behavior during group reading activities became more cooperative.

Physical Information

Many physical factors affect a student's ability to read, including hearing problems, vision problems, general health problems, and neurological dysfunction. In this section, we provide a brief overview of these factors.

Hearing Problems.

A hearing loss, even if it is moderate or temporary, can greatly impede reading instruction. A student who cannot hear the teacher, or who cannot differentiate the sounds needed for phonics instruction, will often develop reading problems. However, the most serious effect of hearing loss is that it impedes normal language development, which is the basis of reading.

When students cannot hear adequately, all of their communication skills are impaired. This can result in problems with vocabulary, grammar, and verbal thinking skills. Hearing loss is most devastating if it occurs during the language acquisition years (between the ages of two and four).

Because of the importance of adequate hearing, students need to be screened for possible hearing impairment. Often schools do this, or preliminary screening may be done by a reading teacher (see Chapter 13).

Additional information can also help to pinpoint a problem in hearing. The reading teacher can ask the parents if there are any speech problems, such as slurred speech or difficulty in making sounds. Has the student suffered frequent ear infections? Does the student turn her or his ear to one side while listening? Does the student seem inattentive or ask for information to be repeated? Does the student fail to respond immediately when called? Of course, if you observe such behaviors during your own work with a student, you should immediately request a screening for hearing loss.

What should be done if a teacher suspects a hearing problem? As we have mentioned, many schools and reading clinics have devices for screening students. However, since the testing of hearing is complex, and the results may vary from time to time in children, a reading teacher cannot make a definitive diagnosis. Rather, if screening devices or symptoms suggest a hearing loss, the parents or school should be referred to a professional in the field, such as an audiologist.

Reading teachers can also adjust their instruction to meet the needs of a student with a hearing loss, or a suspected hearing loss. Remember to sit close to and face the student directly when speaking. If the student does not respond directly to questions or comments, try to repeat them in a cheerful fashion, letting the student watch you pronounce the words.

Vision Problems.

The ability to see clearly is critical to the reading process. Vision problems may be quite complex, involving difficulties in seeing close up or far away, or in focusing both eyes together. In addition, certain students may have difficulties with glare, fluorescent lights, and different colors. Since vision changes rapidly for children, it should be tested often.

As with possible hearing loss, a reading teacher should try to determine whether the student has a vision problem. School records or parents can provide the results of recent vision screenings. Reading teachers can also administer vision-screening tests (see Chapter 13).

Visual behaviors that indicate problems include:

avoidance of reading and writing

holding a page very close or at an unusual angle

losing one's place while reading

frowning, squinting, or scowling during reading

headaches, rubbing the eyes, or covering one eye

What can a teacher do to help a student with a suspected vision problem? First, if a screening test or student behaviors indicate a vision problem, the youngster should be referred to a vision professional (optometrist or ophthalmologist) for further testing.

If a reading teacher is dealing with an uncorrected vision problem, certain accommodations will make the student more comfortable. Use books with larger type if they are available. Some computer software allows the teacher to adjust the size of the print. In addition, it may be possible to record some of the student's books on audiotape.

General Health Problems.

Since learning is an active process, it requires that a student be alert, energetic, and concentrated for long periods of time. Poor physical health can impair the ability to do this. Through parent interviews and questionnaires, reading teachers can determine whether there are any medical conditions that may affect learning or if students suffer from conditions or take medications that affect the ability to concentrate.

What can a teacher do when a student suffers from health problems? Sensitivity to the needs of the student is often crucial. Meghan suffered from severe allergies and the strong medication that she took during certain times of the year tended to make her somewhat lethargic. Knowing this, her reading teacher praised Meghan for the work she completed and never suggested that Meghan was not trying her best.

Neurological Problems.

All learning, including the ability to learn to read, is neurologically based. The reading process demands an intact and well-functioning nervous system; a neurological dysfunction can destroy reading ability.

Children with damaged neurological systems are often "hard core" disabled readers who have extreme difficulty learning to read (Vellutino, 1987), or are labeled *dyslexic* (see Chapter 14). Thus, if assessment of a student's reading (as we describe in the next chapter) suggests a very serious reading problem, a teacher might consider the possibility of a neurological examination.

To probe further, ask the parents if any other member of the family has experienced a very serious reading problem. A history of a difficult pregnancy and delivery may also point to neurological damage. Certain studies suggest that some reading problems may be hereditary (Lyons et al., 1991). Other signs of possible neurological dysfunction are: a history of clumsiness, slow physical development, and accidents that have involved damage to the brain.

There is evidence that Attention Deficit Disorder (ADD), a problem that affects the ability to concentrate, is caused by neurological problems (Lerner, Lowenthal, & Lerner, 1995). Students who suffer from ADD are often prescribed medications, such as Ritilan, to help control their behavior.

Finally, many practitioners believe that children with learning disabilities may also have subtle problems in their neurological functioning. Students with learning disabilities are entitled to special services under the provision of the Individuals with Disabilities Education Act (IDEA)(1995).

Information on possible neurological problems can be gathered from the parents, from school records, and from specialists (such as physicians) who have been consulted by the child's parents. If students with suspected neurological problems have been diagnosed as having ADD or a learning disability, the school will have already gathered much information about these students. For example, thorough testing is required for every special education student in order to comply with the regulations of the Individuals with Disabilities Education Act (see Chapter 14). With parental consent, these records can be released to a reading teacher.

What can be done if a teacher suspects that a student may have a neurological dysfunction? If students need further testing, they should be referred to physicians specializing in pediatrics and neurology, or to appropriate professionals in their schools.

However, it remains the responsibility of the teacher to teach these students to read. Can we help them? The answer is a resounding *yes*. At one time, it was thought that very specialized methods were required to teach students with neurological difficulties to read. More recent studies suggest that the same methods that are effective with all students who have reading problems will also work with those who have a neurological dysfunction (Vellutino, 1987). A reading teacher who concentrates on effective and motivating methods will often help these students to make substantial gains. Be aware, however, that students with neurological problems (or suspected neurological problems) may improve at a slower rate and may need longer and more intense instruction than most reading-disabled students.

Information about Language Development

Since reading is language expressed in written form, a student's language development forms the basis for all reading. The ability to express and receive thoughts through language is fundamental to being able to read. A student who is confused about oral language sounds will have difficulty pronouncing written words. A student who does not know many word meanings will gain little information from reading, even if he or she can pronounce all of the words.

In other instances, a student's language patterns may be mature, but may differ from the language used in school. Many at-risk students come to school speaking languages other than English. They need rich experiences in learning English, plus experiences reading in their native languages, to develop high-level comprehension. Other students, who speak nonstandard dialects, may lack both exposure to more standard English language patterns and a feeling of pride and proficiency in their own dialect.

A reading teacher can easily obtain background information about the student's language. Simply listening to or conversing with a student gives many valuable insights. A student who speaks in long sentences, provides full answers to questions, and is able to use many words probably has an excellent language base for reading. Unfortunately, many students with reading problems speak haltingly in short sentences, using just a few words.

Joey, for example, was in kindergarten, yet his language patterns resembled those of a three- or four-year-old. He often used his name instead of a pronoun or used pronouns incorrectly. "Joey needs crayons" or "Me need crayons" were typical utterances. Similarly, eight-year-old Paul had difficulty dictating even a single sentence to his reading teacher.

In addition to observation, interview questions can reveal much about a student's language. Ask the parents whether their child's language development was slower than that of other children or was within a normal range. Did their child experience any speech difficulties? Has there been any language or speech therapy? To obtain information about language differences, ask parents what languages are spoken in the home, and whether or not the child knew English when entering school. A history of class placements, including bilingual services or ESL (English as a Second Language), often gives much information about a student's proficiency in English.

What can be done if a teacher suspects that language problems affect a student's reading? At times, evaluation by a language professional (speech therapist or language specialist) may be needed to pinpoint the precise source of difficulty. However, in many other instances, a reading teacher can foster the development of rich language by employing enjoyable instructional strategies, such as reading language-rich storybooks to the student, encouraging conversation, and developing knowledge of abstract concepts (see Chapter 10).

Twelve-year-old José, a student in our Reading Center, could speak and understand basic English, but he lacked the English skills to read more sophisticated material. His tutor began by reading selections from the daily newspaper that focused on news about Mexico, his homeland. José enjoyed helping his tutor with the pronunciation of Spanish names. They then discussed what was happening in Mexico, reading portions of the articles together several times. Finally José attempted to read articles alone. At one point, he joyfully exclaimed, "That's what "NAFTA" looks like!" José and his tutor continued this process, moving gradually into other familiar topics such as television and sports. As he did this, he began to locate cognates—words that are the same in Spanish and English—to help his tutor learn Spanish.

Methods of Collecting Information

As we have shown, there is a wealth of important background information that may be collected about a student with reading difficulties. This information helps us to understand the factors that contribute to a reading problem. It also aids us in planning effective and motivating instruction.

Generally, background information is collected at the beginning of our work with a student. The assessment tools most frequently used are (1) interviews and questionnaires, (2) informal talks with the student, parents, and professionals, (3) records of previous testing, school achievement, or report cards, and (4) observation.

The Interview and Questionnaire

Interviews and questionnaires with informed and concerned people yield information about the student that cannot be obtained in any other way. In these two formats, those concerned with a student's reading problem are able frankly and fully to state important information.

The Interview.

In an interview, a reading teacher follows a prescribed set of questions, asking them orally of the person who is being interviewed. A teacher can interview parents, the student, or the classroom teacher. The personal and informal atmosphere of an interview encourages the sharing of valuable information in a sympathetic setting. We generally interview the parents separately from the student, using different interview forms. A reading teacher who works outside the student's school may get valuable information from interviewing the classroom teachers and other professionals in the school. However, *written permission* must be obtained from the parents before a student's school may be contacted. Some important procedures will ensure a successful interview.

1. Begin by telling the parents, student, or classroom teacher that this information will be kept confidential.
2. Strive for an amiable, open atmosphere. Briefly discussing a neutral topic, such as the weather or sports, can reduce initial fears or discomfort about the interview process.
3. Avoid indicating disapproval of responses.
4. Follow a directed plan. You should know what questions to ask before the interview begins. These questions should be in front you so they will not be forgotten.
5. Take notes, since it will be difficult to remember everything that was said. Explain why this is being done. If the person being interviewed asks about what he or she said, cheerfully read the notes back aloud.
6. Since there are important legal and moral considerations involved in the interview, it must be kept confidential. If you wish to tape-record the interview, you must obtain written consent from parents, guardians, or the professionals involved. The presence of another individual during the interview also requires consent. Finally, information shared at an interview or any other part of the assessment procedure cannot be released to another agency without parental permission.

The Questionnaire.

Like an interview, a questionnaire consists of a group of questions that is responded to by parents, a student, or another professional. However, the list of questions is responded to in writing. A questionnaire may simply be mailed to the respondent, filled out, and mailed back. Alternatively, it may be filled out in the presence of the reading teacher.

Questionnaires are valuable when a face-to-face interview is not feasible. In our Reading Center, we often mail questionnaires to the classroom teachers of the students we serve, since they have difficulties coming in for interviews. In addition, because questions are responded to independently, the use of a questionnaire enables parents, students, and classroom teachers to formulate thoughtful responses and to take the time to gather valuable information about developmental history, school attendance, and grades. However, questionnaires may be unproductive with parents and children who find writing difficult.

The Parent Background Information Form.

Table 2.1 (located at the end of this chapter) presents a sample form for gathering background information from parents. We suggest that, if possible, this form be used as an interview, rather than as a questionnaire.

The Student Background Information Form.
Table 2.2 presents a student information form, which can be used either in an interview or as a questionnaire. Questions about student interests help to establish rapport with a student and give the teacher information to motivate and personalize reading instruction. Questions may be modified to suit your locality (for example, adding skiing or surfing).

A final section, based on the work of Burke (1976), gives information on how the student thinks about reading. We often find that low-achieving students think that reading is just saying words, and, not surprisingly, they do not focus on meaning. These questions also explore the student's reading strategies. Many students with reading problems will just "sound it out" as the only strategy they use to cope with an unknown word; they do not realize that meaning can also be used. Other low-achieving students have unrealistic pictures of good readers and believe that such readers know all the words and never make mistakes.

The School Information Form.
Table 2.3 presents a form useful for collecting information from the student's school. Remember that written permission from parents or guardians is needed whenever you contact a student's school.

Informal Talks

In addition to interviews and questionnaires, informal conversations throughout the semester can keep providing valuable insights. Twelve-year-old Adam continued to share his frustrations with homework assignments through the school year, enabling us to help his classroom teacher modify them.

The parents of another child revealed, over an informal cup of coffee, that he had had extensive difficulties immediately after birth. This information, not given on an initial interview, was shared only as the parents became more comfortable with us. The reading teacher should be alert to opportunities to gather information through these continuing, informal means.

We have found it important to keep in touch with parents as instruction continues. Continued contact with parents provides teachers with valuable information about how students are reacting to instruction, whether they are improving, and if their attitudes toward reading are becoming more positive. Finally, contact helps families to encourage children to read at home.

School Records and Materials

School records, previous diagnostic reports, report cards, and student portfolios (organized collections of student's work) kept in school are all valuable sources of information. In addition, cumulative records, which detail a student's progress over a number of years, help us to gain information about the history of a reading problem. Reports, such as an Individual Educational Program (IEP), done for special education students under the provisions of the Individuals with Disabilities Education Act (IDEA), are also valuable sources of information. Encourage parents to allow you access to school information, for it enables you to gain a more thorough and balanced view of a child's reading problem.

Observation during Reading Lessons

In our discussion of background information, we presented many types of information that could be gathered through direct observation of your student. Factors such as social interactions and language information are perhaps best illustrated through direct observation. As a reading teacher, you can make observations as you work with a student. However, if possible, it is useful to observe a student in many different settings. Student reactions and behaviors often vary according to the environment in which we observe that student. A student who is quiet and cooperative in individual instruction may be noisy and defiant in a large class. In fact, sometimes a description of one student in these two settings is so different that we wonder if the same individual is being observed! To gain a realistic picture of students, it is helpful to observe them in natural settings (at parties, on the playground, in their classes) as well as in special reading classes.

As you make observations, be sure to note them in writing for future reference. Further information about observations is given in Chapter 13.

Summary

This chapter deals with collecting background information on students with reading problems, including information about the environment and information about the individual. Background factors interact with reading problems in complex ways; it is possible for a background factor to coexist with a reading problem, and yet not cause that problem.

Environmental factors include the home environment, school environment, social environment, and cultural environment. The home influences a child, as parents serve as role models for literacy and provide a general environment that nurtures the child. The child's school history, attendance, and school instruction also affect a reading problem. Often, students who have reading problems are not receiving instruction that meets their needs. Students with reading problems also tend to have social difficulties. They may also come from a culture that does not support literacy.

Background information about the individual may be collected about emotional status, physical status, and language development. Students with reading problems may have emotional difficulties. Sometimes these emotional problems are alleviated as reading improves. Physical information includes hearing problems, visual problems, general health problems, and neurological problems. Students with ADD and Learning Disabilities may have subtle neurological problems. Students with reading problems may also have difficulties with language development.

Information may be collected through interviews, the filling out of a written questionnaire, informal talks, school records and materials, and observation.

Table 2.1 **Parent Information Form**

| Student's Name | Grade | Age | Birthdate |

| Person Being Interviewed | Relationship to Student | Interview Date |

List three positive things about your child.

1. _____

2. _____

3. _____

Environmental Information

Home Environment

Members of family present in home

| Name | Relationship to Student | Age | Birthplace | Occupation |

_____

_____

_____

Family members not living in home

_____

_____

Describe any reading or learning problems experienced by family members.

_____

What reading materials are available in your home? _____

_____

What reading activities, including reading to or with your child, are done at home? _____

_____

_____

_____

Table 2.1   **continued**

Describe your child's TV viewing. _____

_____

What are your child's responsibilities at home? _____

_____

What are the attitudes of family members toward reading? _____

_____

School Environment

Describe your child's preschool and kindergarten experiences. _____

_____

At what age did your child enter first grade? _____

Describe your child's reading experiences in first grade. _____

_____

Has your child repeated any grade? If so, why? _____

Describe your child's current school and classes, including any special placements (special education, bilingual instruction). _____

_____

Describe the homework your child gets. _____

_____

How does your child do in areas other than reading (e.g., math, spelling, handwriting, social studies, science, gym)?_____

_____

Has your child's school attendance been regular? _____

Describe any extended absences from school. _____

continued

Table 2.1 **continued**

Describe your child's reading instruction, including grouping within the class, if any. _____

_____

Does your child receive any special help in school? If so, describe. _____

_____

Describe any testing your child has experienced. _____

Describe help outside school your child has received (summer school, outside tutoring). _____

_____

When did a reading problem develop? _____

What may have contributed to this problem? _____

Social and Cultural Environment

Describe your child's relationship with family members. _____

_____

Describe your child's friends and social group. _____

_____

What are your child's interests and leisure activities? _____

_____

Information About the Individual

Emotional Information

Describe any evidence of emotional tension, or lack of confidence in your child. _____

_____

Does your child seem to be happy? _____

What is your child's attitude toward reading? _____

_____

Table 2.1   **continued**

Physical Information

How would you compare your child's physical development with that of other children of the same age?

_____

_____

Describe pregnancy, delivery, and child's early history. _____

_____

Describe your child's general health. _____

Describe any specific illnesses, allergies, or accidents. _____

_____

Describe any medications your child is taking. _____

Has your child ever been unconscious? _____

Does your child seem to have difficulty maintaining attention? _____

Give the date, tester, and recommendations from last hearing test. _____

Has your child ever experienced a hearing loss? _____

Give the date, tester, and recommendations from last vision test. _____

Describe any "glasses" your child has been asked to wear. _____

Language Development

What languages are spoken in your home? _____

What languages does your child speak? _____

Has your child received any bilingual or ESL services? _____

Has your child received any speech or language therapy? _____

How did your child's early language development compare to that of other children? _____

_____

Table 2.2   **Student Information Form**

Your Name	Age	Grade	Today's Date

Who lives at home with you? _____

_____

What are some things that you and your family do together? _____

_____

What are some of your favorite books? _____

Do you read at home? _____

Do you get books from the library or store? _____

What are some of your favorite TV shows? _____

What are some of your favorite movies and videos? _____

What kind of music do you like? _____

Who are your favorite actors, singers, and stars? _____

What are your favorite sports and teams? _____

What sports do you play? _____

What kinds of pets do you have? _____

Do you have any chores to do at home? _____

What is your favorite subject at school? _____

What are some subjects you don't like? _____

Do you have reading groups, or does the whole class read together? _____

_____

Do you have a separate reading class? _____

_____

Table 2.2   continued

What are the names of some books you are reading in school? _____

_____

What happens in your class during reading time? _____

_____

Do you like learning to read? _____

If you could change one thing about your reading class, what would it be? _____

_____

What kind of homework do you get? _____

_____

Who are your best friends at home? _____

Who are your best friends in school? _____

What do you like to do with your friends? _____

_____

Do you ever have trouble hearing things? _____

Do your eyes ever hurt? _____

Do you ever have trouble seeing the board in school? _____

Do you ever have trouble seeing the print in books? _____

What clubs do you belong to? _____

What lessons do you take? _____

What are you interested in? _____

What do you want to do when you grow up and finish school? _____

continued

***Table 2.2* continued**

Why do people read? _____

What do you do when you come to something you don't know while you are reading? _____

_____

Who is the best reader you know? _____

What makes this person such a good reader? _____

_____

Table 2.3   **School Information Form**

Student's Name   Grade   Date Form Completed

Person Completing Form   Position (teacher, principal, special teacher)

School Attendance

How long has this student attended this school? _____

Describe regularity of attendance. _____

Reading Performance

Is this student having problems in reading? _____

Describe these problems. _____

_____

When did the problems begin? _____

Describe the areas of strength and weakness in reading. _____

_____

Please describe reading instruction, including whether it is taught as a separate subject, whether students are grouped (if so, what is student's group), whether classes are changed, whether a reading series or separate books are used for instruction, and what supplementary materials are used.

_____

_____

_____

_____

_____

Please name some books this student is reading. _____

_____

Table 2.3 **continued**

Describe student's progress in other areas, including spelling, writing, math, science, social studies, and gym. _____

_____

Describe help the student receives in addition to regular classroom instruction. _____

_____

Describe student's independence, task completion, ability to follow directions, and ability to pay attention. _____

_____

Describe homework. Is it completed? _____

_____

Does this student read for pleasure? _____

Does this student seem tired at school? _____

Does the student appear to have any vision or hearing problems? _____

What language(s) does this student speak at school? _____

How does this student's physical development compare to that of others? _____

_____

Has any testing been done at school? If so, please provide a summary below, or attach information.

_____

_____

How does this student's oral language compare to that of other students? _____

_____

CHAPTER 3

Assessing Reading Achievement: Overview and Informal Measures

Introduction

In this chapter we describe the process of assessing a student's reading performance. We begin by presenting two general questions that form an overview of diagnosis. Next, we discuss both formal and informal assessment. We then devote a major portion of the chapter to informal measures, and in particular the informal reading inventory, a fundamental tool that gives many insights into a student's reading.

Other tools for informal assessment are given in Chapters 5 through 11. In addition, an in-depth discussion of formal tests is presented in Chapter 15.

General Diagnostic Questions: An Overview

The process of assessing reading involves more than giving tests. In fact, a good reading teacher uses tests, background information, and observation to formulate answers to diagnostic questions. A reading diagnosis is thus a thoughtful synthesis and interpretation of all the information that is collected about a student.

What questions need to be answered about the student? Assessing a student's reading achievement involves answering two general questions: (1) How severe is the reading problem? and (2) What is the general area of the reading problem?

How Severe Is the Reading Problem?

Since resources for special reading help are scarce, it is important that we allocate them to the students who need them most. In fact, some of the students who are referred for help actually do not need it. Sometimes it is very easy to recognize that a student has a reading problem. For example, a child who has finished second grade and still cannot read a first grade text is clearly having difficulty. On the other hand, at times students have been referred to our Reading Center simply because they were not selected for a gifted program.

To determine the severity of a reading problem, we need to determine at what level a student is reading and to compare this to the level at which that student should be reading. We compare

1. The student's current reading level to
2. The student's appropriate reading level.

By appropriate level, we mean the books and stories that are used in the student's classroom, both for reading and for content area instruction (math, social studies, science). Usually, appropriate materials mean those at a student's grade level. However, if the student's class is reading at a higher level, then appropriate materials are at that higher level.

Note that the opposite of this is not true. Children who are experiencing problems in school are often placed in special classes where they read materials well below their grade level. For example, a fourth grader might be in a special class that is reading second-grade material. In this case, second-grade text is *not* an appropriate level; the appropriate level for this student would be the fourth grade level, the actual grade placement.

A student who can read at an appropriate level with acceptable word recognition and comprehension does not have a reading problem. However, if a student cannot read appropriate materials, there is a reading problem, and our next step is to determine the severity of that problem. The difference between the student's grade placement and the grade placement of the text he or she can read shows us how severe a reading problem is.

How do we know whether a student's problem can be classified as severe? Guidelines provided by Spache (1981), presented in Table 3.1, compare a student's current grade placement with the student's reading level. As you can see, the younger the student, the less difference is needed to define a reading problem as severe.

Table 3.1   Criteria for Determining a Severe Reading Problem

Student's grade placement	*Difference between grade placement and reading level*
Grades 1, 2, 3	One year or more
Grades 4, 5, 6	Two years or more
Grades 7 and above	Three years or more

Source: Spaehe (1981).

Using these criteria, a student who is placed in fourth grade but is reading at the second grade level would have a reading problem that is severe. A fourth-grade student reading at the third-grade level would have a reading problem, but not a severe one. A fourth-grade student reading at the fourth-grade level would not have a reading problem.

The severity of the student's reading problem helps us to determine what type of special instruction is most effective. Students with severe reading problems may require long and intensive intervention, in daily classes with individual instruction. In contrast, students with less severe problems may blossom in small group settings that meet once or twice a week.

What Is the General Area of the Reading Problem?

As we discussed in Chapter 1, reading consists of many different components, or areas. Problems with reading fall into several general areas:

1. problems with emergent literacy;
2. problems with word recognition accuracy;
3. problems with word recognition fluency;
4. problems with comprehension;
5. problems with language and meaning vocabulary.

Some students may have problems in only one of these general areas. Other students may have problems in a combination of areas. Deciding the general area of a student's reading problem is important, for this information helps you, as a reading teacher, to deliver the most effective instruction.

Problems with Emergent Literacy.
Emergent literacy refers to the understandings and skills that underlie reading. These include the knowledge that print stands for meaning, the recognition of alphabet letters, and the ability to recognize letter sounds. Although most students have acquired emergent literacy skills by the time they enter first grade, some students with reading problems continue to lack them long after formal reading instruction has begun.

Problems with Word Recognition Accuracy.
Many students with reading problems cannot recognize words accurately. They lack strategies, including phonics and the ability to use meaning or context, for word identification. For example, trying to read a passage about farms, nine-year-old Carlos pronounced the word "farm" as *from, form,* and *for.*

Without accurate word identification, a student cannot comprehend a passage. For example, Carlos's summary of the farm passage was "They—the kids—were going someplace."

Problems with Word Recognition Fluency.
In addition to recognizing words accurately, readers identify them quickly. Words that we recognize instantly, without any need for analysis, are often called sight vocabulary. When we read fluently, we read text without stopping to analyze words. Fluency is important because human beings have limited memories. If we direct all our attention to figuring out the words, we will have difficulties understanding what the author is saying because we will have no resources to devote to comprehension (LaBerge & Samuels, 1974). Only if we rec-

ognize words quickly can we devote attention to comprehension. One of our students, Sofia, did a flawless oral reading of a story about Johnny Appleseed. However, since she labored over many words, she read slowly and without fluency. As a result, she could answer only three of ten comprehension questions.

Problems with Comprehension.

Many students have problems comprehending what they read. At times, youngsters do not actively construct meaning, but simply read in order to pronounce words or answer questions. Thus they are not reading to comprehend. There are several different levels of comprehension: applying background knowledge to what is being read, gaining important facts (literal comprehension), organizing what is read, drawing inferences, and thinking critically (all parts of higher-level comprehension).

However, at times, poor understanding of text may be rooted in causes other than comprehension. For example, a student who lacks adequate word recognition may not be able to comprehend material. Sofia, whom we mentioned above, could not comprehend material because she lacked word recognition fluency. Similarly, apparent problems in comprehension may actually be caused by underlying problems in understanding language and word meanings.

Students need comprehension strategies when they read storylike or narrative text. Learning from expository text, or studying, is also part of comprehension; many students with reading problems do not know how to summarize, take notes, or prepare for multiple choice and essay examinations.

Problems with Language and Meaning Vocabulary.

Since reading is a language process, our ability to read cannot exceed the language we can understand and the word meanings we already know. Students who can pronounce words as they read but cannot understand them are not really reading. Aushabell, a second-grade student in our Reading Center, had recently arrived from Turkey. She could read orally with amazing accuracy. However, she had little idea of what she was reading, for she lacked understanding of such common English words as *mother, school, run,* and *night.* Many other students in our Reading Center do speak English fluently, but lack the rich language patterns and meaning vocabulary needed to read more sophisticated stories, novels, and textbooks. In fact, problems with underlying language and word meaning have been recognized as an extremely important factor in reading disabilities for intermediate and upper-grade students beyond grade three (Stanovich, 1986).

In summary, effective overall reading assessment involves answering two questions: (1) What is the severity of the student's reading problem? and (2) What is the general area of the student's reading problem? We can answer these questions by observing and working with a student and by administering assessment tools. Often a single assessment tool, such as an informal reading inventory, can answer both questions, as well as provide much specific information about a student.

An Overview of Formal Assessment Measures

In reading diagnosis, we use both formal and informal tests. By formal tests, we mean commercially and formally prepared instruments. Many formal tests are norm-referenced or "standardized." Using norm-referenced tests, we can compare a student's score with the sample of students who were used to standardize the test (the "norm sample"). To assure that we can compare student scores with the norm sample, we must strictly follow the procedures for test administration, scoring, and interpretation. Unlike informal assessment measures, the teacher cannot adapt or change formal testing procedures.

Other formal instruments are called "criterion-referenced" tests, and these are constructed from a different theoretical view. Instead of comparing a student's score to the norm group, a criterion-referenced test determines whether a student has mastered certain competencies, such as specific reading skills. The student's score is compared to a cut-off score (or criterion) set by the authors of the test.

There are several types of formal reading tests, each offering a different type of information. Formal tests that assess general reading abilities usually give a student's reading level and suggest general areas of reading strengths and weaknesses. Other formal tests are used for more specific or diagnostic reading assessment and assess strengths or weaknesses within a certain area (such as word recognition). We present a thorough discussion of formal measures in Chapter 15.

An Overview of Informal Assessment Measures

Informal measures refer to tools, other than published instruments with prescribed procedures, that can be used to collect information about a student's reading. We can modify informal measures to suit the needs of our students and the information we want to gather. In this chapter we describe the informal reading inventory. In Chapters 5 through 11 we describe various informal measures for evaluating various components of the reading process.

There are three key differences between formal and informal measures.

(1) Informal measures have not been normed, or standardized, on large populations of students, as have many formal tests. Therefore, we cannot use informal measures to compare one student's performance with that of others. To make such comparisons, we must use formal tests that have been normed.

(2) Informal measures are flexible. Since informal measures have not been standardized, teachers can feel free to make modifications in test procedures, adapting them to serve the specific needs of the diagnostic situation. In contrast formal measures must be administered in the same way to all students. Because of their flexibility, many reading teachers consider informal measures to be the cornerstone of reading assessment.

Informal tests allow us to personalize assessment to the needs of the student and tailor our testing to account for the different backgrounds, interests, and attitudes that students have. For example, fifth-grade Jon was very interested and active in sports. Jon insisted that although he wasn't doing well in school work, he could read sports material "like a champ." When we carefully chose different selections, we found that, indeed, he comprehended a fifth-grade narrative about the soccer star, Pele, very well, but could read at only a third-grade level when the subject was plants or frontier life. This informal assessment told the reading teacher that Jon's background and interest had a marked effect on his reading.

(3) Informal measures often give a more authentic assessment than formal ones. By authentic assessment, we mean assessment measures that are similar to the actual reading tasks

a student does in school. In such measures, students read longer selections, summarize them, and answer questions, just as they would do in a typical classroom or when reading for their own information or enjoyment.

For example, to get a picture of why eleven-year-old Duane was failing in social studies, his reading teacher asked him to read a selection from a textbook and take notes as if he were preparing for a test. His difficulties with this task enabled his teacher to precisely pinpoint his instructional needs.

In contrast to this use of authentic materials, many formal tests measure the ability to read short passages and answer multiple choice questions. These tasks do not represent what real readers do on a daily basis.

To summarize, informal measures allow teachers the flexibility to adapt assessment so that it gives maximum information about how students, materials, and classroom situations interact to affect a reading problem. In this way, teachers can best determine how students can meet the demands of school reading.

The Informal Reading Inventory

The informal reading inventory (IRI) is one informal assessment instrument that is widely used in reading diagnosis. IRIs provide one of the best tools for observing and analyzing reading performance and for gathering information about how a student uses a wide range of reading strategies.

The IRI is an individual test that is administered to a single student. In an IRI, a student reads graded passages orally and silently and answers questions about them. As a student does this, the teacher records performance in word recognition and comprehension. Generally, passages are given at the preprimer, primer, first grade, and all other grade levels through the eighth grade. However, inventories vary in the levels they present. In addition, many inventories contain graded lists of words, which are used to help place students into the appropriate passage level.

Passages in IRIs are representative of or are taken from textbooks at different grade levels. Thus, a teacher can see how a student functions with classroom-like materials (Johnson, Kress, & Pikulski, 1987). Because it is classroom-based, the information gained from an IRI is often more useful and realistic than the results of a standardized test.

There are many different types of IRIs. Some are published as separate tests (see Appendix A) and others are available with reading textbook series. Teachers may also construct their own IRIs. We include an IRI at the back of this book (see Appendix C). Whatever IRI you choose, remember it is an informal measure that you can adapt for different purposes and needs.

Obtaining Answers to General Diagnostic Questions

The IRI helps us to obtain information on the two general assessment questions we presented in the beginning of our chapter: (1) What is the severity of the student's reading problem? and (2) What is the general area of the student's reading problem?

To answer the first question, the reading teacher determines an instructional reading level for the student. This is the level of material that the student can read with instructional support (such as that found in school). The teacher then compares the instructional level on the IRI to the level of reading appropriate for the student. This comparison shows the severity of the reading problem. For example, a student who has an instructional level of fifth grade on the IRI and is in fifth grade does not have a reading problem. On the other hand, a fifth-grade student who has an instructional level of first grade has a severe reading problem.

The IRI can also help to reveal the general area of the reading problem. Through listening to a student read orally, the teacher can determine whether word recognition accuracy or fluency are problems for the student. Through asking questions and having students retell passages that have been read, the teacher can assess comprehension. Through presenting passages in a listening mode to the student, the teacher can determine whether the areas of language and meaning vocabulary are problems.

Finally, because the IRI is an individual test, during its administration, a teacher has opportunities to make diagnostic observations that answer many different questions. Does the student read better orally or silently? Become easily frustrated? Point to each word or regularly lose the place in reading? Does the student have particular difficulty with drawing conclusions in material? The IRI is a rich source of these and many other insights.

However, IRIs, like all other assessment tools, have some limitations. For example, examiners, especially untrained ones, can miss some problems with oral reading (Pikulski & Shanahan, 1982). In addition, a student's performance on a passage may be affected by the amount of personal interest in the subject, background knowledge, and text organization (Caldwell, 1985; Leslie & Caldwell, 1995; Lipson et al., 1984). Finally, the shortness of IRI selections (often a few hundred words) may not allow teachers to determine how well a student reads a multipage selection.

To obtain the greatest assessment value, teachers need to prepare carefully for administration of the IRI. They need to use professional observation and judgment in effectively translating IRI results into instructional decisions. In short, the IRI is only a tool for your use in gathering diagnostic information.

Administering and Scoring the Informal Reading Inventory

Each published IRI comes with directions for administration that may vary in detail from other IRIs. All IRIs have some common features, however, and the directions that we give are based upon these.

The informal reading inventory consists of a series of graded reading selections followed by questions. Some IRIs, like the one we provide in Appendix C, also contain graded word lists. The teacher can use these lists to decide which passage to administer first. The student reads passages (orally or silently) at different grade levels and stops when the material becomes too difficult. After the student reads each passage, the teacher asks comprehension questions. For passages read orally, the teacher records reading errors (or miscues) and student responses to the questions. For passages read silently, the teacher records the time needed for reading and the responses to questions. (In addition, you may wish to record the time it took students to read oral passages and to ask the student to retell a selection in his or her own words.)

The percentage of reading miscues determines word recognition accuracy. (The time needed for reading, which determines word recognition fluency, may also be used to judge passages, if you wish.) The responses to questions determine the comprehension score. In turn, word recognition and comprehension scores determine three reading levels for the student: the independent level, the instructional level, and the frustration level.

Each level is expressed as a grade level (from preprimer through eighth grade). Teachers can use these three levels to determine the severity of a reading problem as well as to select reading materials for various purposes. Thus, a unique and valuable assessment feature of the IRI is that it gives guidelines for selecting classroom materials.

The three reading levels are:

- An independent level, at which a student can read without teacher guidance. Use this level for recreational reading.
- An instructional level, at which a student can read with teacher support. This is the level to use for reading instruction.
- A frustration level that is too hard for the student. The frustration level should be avoided.

Materials and General Preparation.

To give an IRI, select a period of about an hour to work with an individual student. For younger students and students who are extremely nervous, you may want to divide the testing into two periods.

Materials you will need usually include:

1. A student copy of the IRI for word lists and passages
2. A protocol (or teacher copy) for word lists and passages
3. A stopwatch
4. A tape recorder
5. A clipboard

Seat the student across from you and hand him or her the student copy of the passage to read. The student copy contains only the passage, without the questions. You will record oral reading miscues (errors) and responses to questions on a teacher copy, referred to as a protocol. The protocol also contains questions to ask the student. We suggest placing your copy on a clipboard for ease in handling.

Even experienced examiners find it helpful to tape the entire session so that they can refer to it later. Explain to the student that you are taping because you can't remember everything. Then place the tape recorder off to one side to reduce its intrusion into your testing situation. Since using the tape recorder often makes students nervous, you might ask your student to state his or her name and the date, and to play these back to test the tape recorder.

If you wish to record the speed of your student's reading, you will need a stopwatch. Again, explain what you are doing, allow your student to handle the stopwatch for a short time, and then place it off to one side.

To help prepare a student for the IRI, explain that he or she will read passages both orally and silently and answer questions after each passage. Finally, tell the student that the material will become progressively more difficult.

Administering Word Lists.

Many IRIs provide a set of graded word lists. A student's performance on reading these lists of words provides a quick way to determine which passage in the IRI the student should read first. Word lists generally start at the preprimer level, and continue up through the sixth-grade level. At each level, there are 20 to 25 words.

Students usually begin by reading the easiest list. As your youngster reads from the student's copy, record responses on your teacher's copy. If the student recognizes a word instantly, mark a "C" in the untimed column. If the student must analyze the word, mark "C" in the untimed column. We suggest that you administer the graded word lists until the student scores below 70% on any list (for example, six errors out of twenty words). The highest word list level at which the student scores 70% (or better) is an acceptable level for timed and untimed presentations added together. To select the first reading passage for the IRI, subtract two levels from this isolated word recognition level. Here, for example, are fourth-grade Reyna's scores on the IRI word lists:

Preprimer 90%	Grade 2 80%
Primer 100%	Grade 3 55%
Grade 1 80%	

Grade two is the highest level at which Reyna scored 70% or above. The teacher subtracted two levels from this and began testing Reyna at the primer level.

If students score very low on the word lists, begin by testing at the preprimer level or eliminate the IRI and use emergent literacy assessments (see Chapter 5).

In addition to determining which passage to administer first, a student's performance on word lists can provide important diagnostic information about word recognition abilities. By looking at incorrect responses on a word list, the reading teacher can gain insights about how a student analyzes words. We can see, for example, whether students are matching letters and sounds (phonics). We can also determine if they use structural analysis, such as examining prefixes and suffixes. Table 3.2 shows Reyna's responses to the second-grade word list.

If we look at Reyna's incorrect responses, we can see that she is able to use sounds (such as *t, dr, wh*) at the beginnings of words, but does not always use correct vowels and ending sounds. This information provides the reading teacher with suggestions of phonics strategies that need to be taught.

Administering Reading Passages.

If you have given a word list, you will know the passage level to administer first. If not, start at a level that you think will be easy for the student. Sometimes information from other testing or classroom performance can suggest a beginning passage level. Remember that it is better to begin too low rather than too high, for students who have difficulty on the first IRI passage they read often become very nervous. If you find that the first passage you have chosen is too challenging, stop the reading of the passage and immediately move down to an easier level.

Most IRIs provide passages for both oral and silent reading. In our experience, it is most efficient to administer all of the oral passages first, obtaining independent, instructional, and frustration levels for oral reading. We suggest that you then administer the silent levels, obtaining reading levels for this mode. (For an alternate plan, see the section on Special Issues in Using IRIs.)

There are several steps in administering IRI passages. These steps are appropriate for the IRI in Appendix C of this book, as well as for many other published IRIs.

Table 3.2 **Reyna's Scored IRI Word List, Level 2**

Target Word	Student's Attempts	
	Timed Presentation	*Untimed Presentation*
camp	c	
year	c	
spend	c	
whole	what	when
week	will	c
packed	pick	c
clothes	clap	c
dressed	dr...	drossed
brushed	c	
teeth	test	tooth
kitchen	c	
eggs	c	
toast	test	c
seemed	s...	c
forever	c	
shorts	c	
shirts	shark	shirk
tent	c	
year	k...	know
teacher	c	
world	work	c
playground	c	
classroom	c	
card	c	

1. Before reading, orally give the student a brief introduction to the topic (e.g., "This is a story about a girl who wanted to become a champion skater").
2. Ask a background question to determine how familiar the student is with the topic: "What do you know about championship skating?" This allows you later to determine whether problems with reading might be due to lack of background knowledge. (The IRI in Appendix C provides instructions and background questions.)

3. Hand the student copy to the student to read. State that, after reading is completed, you will ask questions. Have the student read orally (for oral passages) or silently (for silent passages). If the passage is to be read orally, tell your student that you will not be able to help with words, and that he or she can say "pass" if a word cannot be figured out. (See Special Issues in Using IRIs for a discussion of teacher aid.) If the passage is to be read silently, ask your student look up immediately when finished (so that you can record the time correctly).

4. For oral reading, record any differences between the text and the student's reading on your protocol. If you want to record reading speed, time the student on a stopwatch.

5. After the student finishes, take away the passage and ask the comprehension questions. If you want additional information, you may also ask the student to retell the passage in his or her own words.

6. Continue testing until you have determined independent, instructional, and frustration levels for your student. For example, if a student scores at an independent level for third grade, have the student read fourth grade passages. Continue moving up until you reach the student's frustration level. If a student scores at a frustration level on the first passage read, move down until you reach the independent level. The next section explains how to determine these levels.

Reading Levels Obtained from the IRI.

Using an IRI, a reading teacher can determine the student's independent, instructional, and frustration reading levels. The instructional level is particularly critical, since the severity of a student's reading problem is determined by *comparing the instructional level with the level at which the student should be reading* (usually the student's grade placement). For example, if a student's IRI instructional level is third grade, but he is in a sixth-grade class, he would have a severe reading problem.

How do we calculate reading levels? As we stated earlier, reading levels on an IRI are determined by performance on the passages (not scores on the word lists).

The level of an orally read passage is based upon (1) the word recognition accuracy score for the passage (2) the comprehension score. The level of a silently read passage is based upon the comprehension score.

The word recognition score comes from the number of miscues (or errors) that the student makes while orally reading a passage. The comprehension score comes from the number of correct responses on the comprehension questions. Table 3.3 lists the criteria we suggest for the different IRI levels.

Table 3.3   IRI Passage Criteria for Three Reading Levels

Reading Level	Word Recognition (%)		Comprehension (%)
Independent	98–100	and	90–100
Instructional	95–98	and	70–89
Frustration	Less than 95	or	Less than 70

Grading Word Recognition Accuracy.

We obtain a word recognition score from the student's oral reading of passages. To do this, we must (1) code this oral reading and (2) score this oral reading.

Your first step is to code oral reading. As the student reads, you will need to mark all miscues, using a standard system, so that you can later determine exactly what the student said. Commercial IRIs generally provide their own coding systems. For teachers who construct their own IRIs or use the one in Appendix C, we suggest the coding system presented in Table 3.4.

Omissions, additions, substitutions, and reversals usually count as word recognition errors. You might, in addition, want to *record* repetitions, hesitations, omissions of punctuation, and spontaneous corrections of errors. These four things do not alter text, so we do not recommend counting them as errors (McKenna, 1983). However, they can provide additional information on a student's word recognition strategies.

Table 3.4 **Coding System for Scoring IRI Passage Miscues**

1. *Omissions:* Circle.

   ☐ on ⟨the⟩ table

2. *Insertions:* Insert the added word above a caret.

   big
   ☐ on the ∧ table

3. *Substitutions, mispronunciations:* Write the word that the student said above the word in text.

   tablet
   ☐ on the table

4. *Reversals:* Same as substitutions.

5. *Repetitions:* Draw a wavy line below the words.

   ☐ on the table
   ~~~~~~~~~

6. *Words pronounced correctly but with hesitations:* Write an **H** over the word.

   H
   ☐ on the table

7. *Lack of punctuation:* Circle ignored punctuation.

   ☐ I saw Mary⊙ She was happy.

8. *Student corrections:* Mark with <u>SC</u> and cross out any previous responses.

   SC
   ~~tablet~~
   ☐ on the table

After coding oral reading, you need to score it. The easiest and most reliable way to score oral reading is to assign one point to each omission, addition, substitution, and reversal (Leslie & Caldwell, 1995). Two sets of extensive field testing (Leslie & Caldwell, 1995; Jennings, 1995) indicate that this scoring system places students at appropriate instructional levels. There are, however, some alternatives for scoring miscues (see Special Issues in Administering IRIs).

There are certain scoring problems that may arise during an IRI. We propose solutions to some of these based upon our field testing (Leslie & Caldwell, 1995; Jennings, 1995).

If a student repeatedly mispronounces the same word, we recommend counting it as incorrect each time. This reflects the fact that, if a student were reading an assignment in school, each mispronunciation would affect comprehension.

If a student omits an entire line or phrase, we recommend that you count it as one miscue. In this situation, it is likely that the student simply lost the place.

Proper names are difficult for students because they often do not follow regular phonics patterns. We recommend you do not count a mispronunciation of a proper name as incorrect unless it changes the sex of the character. For example, do not count the substitution of "Mary" for "Maria." However, do count the substitution of "Mark" for "Maria." Sometimes students use a nonword to pronounce a proper name such as "Manee" for "Maria." If the student says this consistently throughout the passage, do not count it as an error. If, however, the student pronounces it differently on other occasions, count it as incorrect each time. Follow these guidelines for names of places.

Miscues that reflect a student's speech patterns should never count as errors. In other words, mispronunciations due to dialect differences, speaking English as a second language, immature speech patterns, or speech impediments do not count as errors. For example, a student who speaks a dialect other than Standard English might pronounce the word "tests" as "tes," both in speaking and in reading an IRI passage. In such miscues, readers are simply recoding the written word into their own pronunciation. Pupils should never be penalized for such recoding.

After you have counted all of the errors on an individual passage, total them. Then compute the percentage of words read correctly in the passage. In the coded and scored passage in Table 3.5, there are 96 words, 4 errors, and 92 correct words. The percentage correct is 96%, an instructional level.

$$\frac{92 \text{ Words correct}}{96 \text{ Total words}} \times 100 = 96\%$$

To make this process easier, use Table 3.6, p. 56. Simply find the intersection between the number of words in the passage and the error count. For example, if the passage contains 103 words and the error count is 9, then the percentage correct is 91.

After you have determined a percentage of words read correctly, translate this percentage score into a level (independent, instructional, or frustration). To do this, see Table 3.3.

Grading Comprehension.

After the student reads each passage, the teacher asks questions to check comprehension. If the student's answer is incorrect, the teacher writes the exact student response; if correct, simply mark "C". The teacher obtains a percentage-correct score. For example, if the student answers 3 of 4 comprehension questions correctly, the comprehension score would be 75 percent on that selection. For your convenience, Table 3.7, p. 57 gives the percentage of correct scores for different numbers of comprehension questions. Translate the percentage score on comprehension into a level (independent, instructional, or frustration).

Determining Passage Levels.

Once you have scored both word recognition accuracy and comprehension, you are ready to determine a total level for that passage. If a student has read a passage silently, there is only one score that determines passage level: the comprehension score. Leslie, for example, read a fourth-grade passage silently and achieved at an instructional level for comprehension. Therefore, her level for that passage was instructional.

However, if a student has read a passage orally, the teacher will have both a word recognition accuracy score and a comprehension score to determine whether the passage is at a student's independent, instructional, or frustration level. If a student achieves the same level

Table 3.5   A Student's Coded Oral Reading of a First-Grade Level IRI Passage

Background: What kinds of animals could you find near water? Read this story about Nick and his dad watching animals.

Nick's Trip to the Lake

Once
Nick and his dad like animals. One ⟨day,⟩Nick and his dad went to the lake. They went to see the animals. They sat next to the lake. They were very still.

                                    out   Then
Then Nick saw a big duck. He saw the duck swim to ⌃a big rock in the lake. ⌃Something made the duck fly away fast.

Nick asked his dad, "Why did the duck fly away?"

                                                                              H
Nick's dad said, "Look over there." He showed Nick something in the lake. Nick thought he would see something big.

                                              SC
What a surprise to see a little green ~~frog~~!

Scoring System

Omissions ⬭		Repetitions 〰	
Insertions ⌃		Hesitations H	
Substitutions **Write the word**		Student corrections SC	

Words in passage	96
Errors	4
Oral Reading Accuracy Score	96%

for both word recognition accuracy and comprehension, it is easy to determine this level. For example, on a grade-2 passage, one student, Leslie achieved at an independent level for both word recognition and comprehension. Therefore, the second-grade passage was at an independent level.

However, students sometimes have different levels for word recognition accuracy and comprehension. In this case, we use the lower level to determine passage level. For example, on a third-grade passage, Leslie achieved an instructional level for word recognition accuracy but an independent level for comprehension. Therefore, the third-grade passage was at an instructional level. Table 3.8, p. 58 will help you to assign levels to oral passages.

At times, a student may achieve two (or even more) independent or instructional levels. For example, a student reading oral passages might achieve an instructional score on the primer, first-grade, and second-grade passages. If this happens, record the *highest* instructional level. In this case, the instructional level would be second grade.

Table 3.6 Percentages for Oral Reading Accuracy Scores
(Each number indicates percentage correct)

Number of Errors

Number of Words in Passage	1	2	3	4	5	6	7	8	9	10	11	12	13	14	15	16	17	18	19	20	21	22	23	24	25	26
28– 32	97	93	90	87	83	80	77	73	70	67	63	60	57	53	50	47	43	40	37	33	30	27	23	20	17	13
33– 37	97	94	92	89	86	83	80	77	74	72	69	66	63	60	57	54	52	49	46	43	40	37	34	32	29	26
38– 42	98	95	93	90	88	85	82	80	78	75	72	70	68	65	62	60	58	55	52	50	48	45	42	40	38	35
43– 47	98	96	93	91	89	87	84	82	80	78	76	73	71	69	67	64	62	60	58	56	53	51	49	47	44	42
48– 52	98	96	94	92	90	88	86	84	82	80	78	76	74	72	70	68	66	64	62	60	58	56	54	52	50	48
53– 57	98	96	95	93	91	89	87	86	84	82	80	78	77	76	73	71	69	67	66	64	62	60	58	56	55	53
58– 62	98	97	95	93	92	90	88	87	85	83	82	80	78	77	75	73	72	70	68	67	65	63	62	60	58	57
63– 67	98	97	95	94	92	91	89	88	86	85	83	82	80	78	77	75	74	72	71	69	68	66	65	63	62	60
68– 72	99	97	95	94	93	92	90	89	87	86	84	83	82	80	79	77	76	74	73	72	70	69	67	66	64	63
73– 77	99	97	96	94	93	92	91	89	87	86	85	84	83	81	80	79	77	76	75	73	72	71	69	68	67	65
78– 82	99	98	96	95	94	92	91	90	89	88	86	85	84	82	81	80	79	78	76	75	74	72	71	70	69	68
83– 87	99	98	96	95	94	93	92	91	89	88	87	86	85	84	82	81	80	79	78	76	75	74	73	72	71	69
88– 92	99	98	97	96	94	93	92	91	90	89	88	87	86	84	83	82	81	80	79	78	77	76	74	73	72	71
93– 97	99	98	97	96	95	94	93	92	91	89	88	87	86	85	84	83	82	81	80	79	78	77	76	75	74	73
98–102	99	98	97	96	95	94	93	92	91	90	89	88	87	86	85	84	83	82	81	80	79	78	77	76	75	74
103–107	99	98	97	96	95	94	93	92	91	90	90	89	88	87	86	85	84	83	82	81	80	79	78	77	76	75
108–112	99	98	97	96	95	94	93	92	91	91	90	89	88	87	86	85	85	84	83	82	81	80	79	78	77	76
113–117	99	98	97	97	96	95	94	93	92	91	90	90	89	88	87	86	85	84	84	83	82	81	80	79	78	77
118–122	99	98	98	97	96	95	94	93	92	92	91	90	89	88	88	87	86	85	84	83	82	82	81	80	79	79
123–127	99	98	98	97	96	95	94	94	93	92	91	90	90	89	88	87	86	86	85	84	83	82	82	81	80	79
128–132	99	98	98	97	96	95	95	94	93	92	92	91	90	89	88	88	87	86	85	85	84	83	82	82	81	80
133–137	99	99	98	97	96	96	95	94	93	93	92	91	90	90	89	88	87	87	86	85	84	84	83	82	81	81
138–142	99	99	98	97	96	96	95	94	94	93	92	91	91	90	89	89	88	87	86	85	85	84	84	83	82	81
143–147	99	99	98	97	97	96	95	95	94	93	92	92	91	90	90	89	88	88	87	86	86	85	84	83	83	82
148–152	99	99	98	97	97	96	95	95	94	93	92	92	91	91	90	89	89	88	87	87	86	86	85	84	83	83
153–157	99	99	98	97	97	96	95	95	94	94	93	92	92	91	90	90	89	88	88	87	86	86	85	85	84	83
158–162	99	99	98	98	97	96	96	95	94	94	93	92	92	91	91	90	89	89	88	88	87	86	86	85	84	84
163–167	99	99	98	98	97	96	96	95	95	94	93	93	92	92	91	90	90	89	88	88	87	87	86	85	85	84
168–172	99	99	98	98	97	96	96	95	95	94	94	93	93	92	91	91	90	89	89	88	88	87	86	86	85	85
173–177	99	99	98	98	97	97	96	95	95	94	94	93	93	92	91	91	90	90	89	89	88	87	87	86	86	85
178–182	99	99	98	98	97	97	96	96	95	94	94	93	93	92	92	91	91	90	89	89	88	88	87	87	86	86
183–187	99	99	98	98	97	97	96	96	95	95	94	94	93	92	92	91	91	90	90	89	89	88	88	87	87	86
188–192	99	99	98	98	97	97	96	96	95	95	94	94	93	93	92	92	91	91	90	89	89	88	88	87	87	86
193–197	99	99	98	98	97	97	96	96	95	95	94	94	93	93	92	92	91	91	90	90	89	89	88	88	87	87
198–202	100	99	98	98	98	97	96	96	96	95	94	94	93	93	92	92	91	91	90	90	89	89	88	88	87	87
203–207	100	99	99	98	98	97	97	96	96	95	95	94	94	93	93	92	92	91	91	90	90	89	89	88	88	87
208–212	100	99	99	98	98	97	97	96	96	95	95	94	94	93	93	92	92	91	91	90	90	90	89	89	88	88
213–217	100	99	99	98	98	97	97	96	96	95	95	94	94	93	93	93	92	92	91	91	90	90	89	89	88	88
218–222	100	99	99	98	98	97	97	96	96	96	95	95	94	94	93	93	92	92	91	91	90	90	90	89	89	88
223–227	100	99	99	98	98	97	97	96	96	96	95	95	94	94	93	93	92	92	92	91	91	90	90	89	89	88
228–232	100	99	99	98	98	97	97	97	96	96	95	95	94	94	94	93	93	92	92	91	91	90	90	90	89	89
233–237	100	99	99	98	98	98	97	97	96	96	95	95	95	94	94	93	93	92	92	92	91	91	90	90	89	89
238–242	100	99	99	98	98	98	97	97	96	96	96	95	95	94	94	94	93	93	92	92	92	91	91	90	90	89

Table 3.7 Percentages for Comprehension Accuracy Scores
(each number indicates a percentage-correct score)

Number of Questions	Number of Correct Responses: 1	2	3	4	5	6	7	8	9	10	11	12
1	100											
2	50	100										
3	33	67	100									
4	25	50	75	100								
5	20	40	60	80	100							
6	17	33	50	67	83	100						
7	14	26	43	57	71	86	100					
8	12	25	38	50	62	75	88	100				
9	11	22	33	44	56	67	78	89	100			
10	10	20	30	40	50	60	70	80	90	100		
11	9	18	27	36	45	55	64	73	82	91	100	
12	8	17	25	33	42	50	58	67	75	83	92	100

Combining Oral and Silent Levels into One Overall Level.
We suggest that you determine levels for oral reading and then determine levels for silent reading. Students often perform differently on oral and silent reading, and may achieve different levels for each one. However, in order to make instructional decisions, it is sometimes useful to combine your results for both modes of reading.

To combine oral and silent levels, first put the level of each oral and silent passage side by side, according to grade level. Then, if there is a difference between the two levels, choose the *lower* level for the total reading level.

We will use fifth-grade Leslie's scores as examples of finding an oral reading level, a silent reading level, and then combining them into a single reading level.

Leslie achieved these levels on *orally* read passages:

2 – Independent

3 – Instructional

4 – Frustration

In this case, Leslie's *oral reading levels,* which are quite easy to determine, are:

Table 3.8 Criteria tor Assigning Levels to Oral Reading Passages

Comprehension	*Word Recognition*	*Passage Level*
Independent	Independent	Independent
Independent	Instructional	Instructional
Independent	Frustration	Frustration
Instructional	Instructional	Instructional
Instructional	Independent	Instructional
Instructional	Frustration	Frustration
Frustration	Frustration	Frustration
Frustration	Independent	Frustration
Frustration	Instructional	Frustration

2 – Oral Independent Reading Level

3 – Oral Instructional Reading Level

4 – Oral Frustration Reading Level

On *silently* read passages, Leslie received these levels:

2 – Independent

3 – Independent

4 – Instructional

5 – Frustration

Based upon these passages, Leslie's *silent reading* levels are:

3 – Silent Independent Level

4 – Silent Instructional Level

5 – Silent Frustration Level

To determine Leslie's *combined* reading levels, we place results from each silent and oral passage side by side, and then choose the lower level.

Oral Reading Passages	Silent Reading Passages	Total Level
2 Independent	2 Independent	Independent
3 Instructional	3 Instructional	Instructional
4 Frustration	4 Frustration	Frustration
5 (not given)	5 Frustration	

Based upon this information, Leslie's total reading levels are:

2 – Combined Independent Reading Level

3 – Combined Instructional Reading Level

4 – Combined Frustration Reading Level

Assigning a combined reading level is helpful in situations where you need a general level for assigning school materials. For example, because Leslie's combined reading is instructional at the third-grade level, she should be placed in a third-grade book. However, if you know that the text will be read orally, she can use a fourth-grade book.

Interpreting the Scores of the IRI

The IRI is rich source of information about a student's reading. We now show how it can provide detailed answers to the two diagnostic questions we asked earlier in this chapter: How severe is the reading problem? What is the general nature of the problem? In answering these two questions, we add some procedures to ones have already given. These provide options for enriching the information you can get from an IRI.

How Severe Is the Student's Reading Problem?

To estimate the severity of a reading problem, the teacher should examine the gap between a student's (highest) instructional level on the IRI and the level of text that would be appropriate for that student.

Let's consider the case of Subash, a sixth grader whose IRI summary is presented in Table 3.9. His teacher reported that Subash's class is reading sixth-grade material. On the IRI, Subash's independent level is 2; he scored at an instructional level on both grades 3 and 4, so his instructional level is 4; and his frustration level is 5. The gap between Subash's appropriate reading level (6) and his highest instructional level on the IRI (4) indicates that he has a severe reading problem, according to the criteria by Spache (1981) mentioned earlier in this chapter (Table 3.1).

Table 3.9 **IRI Summary for Subash**

Level	Oral Passages			Silent Passages	Combined Reading	Listening
	Word Rec Level	Comp Level	Passage Level	Comp & Passage Level	Passage Level	Passage Level
Pre-P						
Primer						
1						
2	Ind	Ind	Ind	Ind	Ind	
3	Ind	Ins	Ins	Ins	Ins	
4	Ind	Ins	Ins	Ins	Ins	
5	Ind	Frus	Frus	Frus	Frus	Ind
6						Ins
7						Frus
8						

We now move to the second diagnostic question, determining the general area(s) of the reading problem. To answer this question, we will consider the areas one by one.

What Is the Nature of Word Recognition Accuracy?

How accurate is word recognition? We base our assessment on the student's oral reading score in passages. (Word recognition level in passages provides a more authentic estimate of accuracy than scores derived from reading isolated lists of words.) If a student's word recognition accuracy is below the third-grade level on IRI passages, this is one sign that the primary nature of the reading difficulty is word recognition.

Judging a student's word recognition accuracy also involves determining the strategies the student uses to recognize words. Only by knowing the tools that students use to identify words can we help them to develop missing skills. Miscues, mismatches between the text and what the student says, provide opportunities to analyze these strategies.

Some miscues show that the student is using meaning or context clues. A student using context might substitute a word that makes sense in the context, for example, "Kleenex" for "handkerchief." As we know, readers bring a vast store of knowledge and competence to the reading act. When students use contextual clues, they are using this store of world information to bring meaning to reading. The use of context clues shows a positive effort to preserve comprehension (K. S. Goodman, 1965; Goodman & Gollasch, 1980-1; Y. M. Goodman, 1976).

Other miscues show that the student is using phonics clues to recognize words. A student who uses phonics clues makes miscues that contain many of the same sounds as the words that are in the passage. However, the miscues will often not make sense in context. In fact, sometimes they are not even real words.

An exact recording of oral reading can be analyzed to see which strategies a student tends to use. We call this miscue analysis (Goodman, 1969). Some forms of miscue analysis are very complex; others are simple. However, they all share a common purpose: to determine reader strategies for identifying words. Almost all try to determine whether the reader pays primary attention to letter–sound matching, to meaning, or, like skilled readers, to both.

To help you analyze a reader's strategies, we present a form of miscue analysis adapted from Leslie (1993) and Leslie and Caldwell (1995). Table 3.10 presents the miscue analysis worksheet.

We ask 3 sets of questions about each miscue.

(1) Is the miscue similar in sounds to the original word?
    a. Does it begin with the same sound?
    b. Does it end with the same sound?

If the answers are yes, the student is paying attention to phonics when reading. We find that beginning and ending similarity is sufficient to determine whether the student is paying attention to letter–sound matching. We do not ask about middle sounds, since these are often vowels, which have highly variable sounds.

(2) Does the miscue retain the author's meaning?

If the answer is yes, the reader is paying attention to meaning, and using it to help recognize words.

(3) Did the reader correct the miscue?

Self-correction can indicate two things. Self-correction of an acceptable miscue, one that does not change meaning, suggests that the reader is paying attention to letter–sound matching. Self-correction of a miscue that changes text meaning suggests that the reader is paying attention to meaning during the reading process.

To examine reading patterns, choose about 20 miscues from instructional level text. Analyze them and record them on the sheet provided by Table 3.10. Now you can look for patterns. Several patterns typical of students with reading problems are given below.

1. If the student has a large number of miscues that do not change the author's meaning, the student is using the meaning (or context) of a passage as a clue to recognizing words. Another clue to use of passage meaning is the self-correction of miscues that do not make sense.

2. If the student's miscues show a high number of miscues similar in sound and a small number of miscues that retain the author's meaning, the reader may be paying more attention to phonics clues than to meaning. Some readers show a large number of miscues that are similar in sound to the beginning of the text word and a small number that are similar at the end. Examples are pronouncing *when* for

Table 3.10   **Miscue Analysis Worksheet**

Word in Text	Miscue	Sounds Alike		Meaning Is Retained	Corrected
		Begin	End		
Column Total					

wanted; *dog* for *don't*; *live* for *liked*; and *truck* for *teach*. In this case, instruction should focus on guiding the reader to look at all the letters in a word.

3. If the worksheet shows a pattern of miscues that do not contain the same sounds as the text words, as well as a small number of acceptable miscues or self-corrections, the reader may be a wild guesser, one who is not utilizing either phonics or context effectively.

In the examples presented in Table 3.11, the first student is using meaning clues, while the second is using phonics.

Table 3.11 **Examples of Oral Reading Patterns**

Example 1. *Use of Context Clues*

                                 sea   lots of
Kim lives on an island far out in the ocean. You may think that it would be fun to live on an island.
          unhappy   ^
But Kim is miserable. Kim hasn't seen her friends in a year. There is no one to play with or talk to.

There isn't even a school!

Example 2. *Use of Phonics Clues*

   likes   open
Kim lives on an island far out in the ocean. You may think that it would be fun to live on an island.
          mysterious   family   Then
But Kim is miserable. Kim hasn't seen her friends in a year. There is no one to play with or talk to.
Then
There isn't even a school!

What Is the Nature of Word Recognition Fluency?

To assess word recognition fluency, you can calculate rate of reading for oral and silent passages. To determine the number of words read per minute, or reading rate, take the number of words in the passage, multiply by 60, and divide by the number of seconds it took the student to read the selection. This will yield a word-per-minute score.

$$\frac{\text{Number of words} \times 60}{\text{Number of seconds to read}} = \text{Words per minute}$$

For example, Tammie read a second-grade passage that contained 249 words in two minutes and fifteen seconds (or 135 seconds). Two hundred and forty-nine multiplied by 60 equals 14,940. Divide this by 135 seconds and Tammie's reading rate for that passage is 110 words per minute.

What is a normal rate for different levels of passages? Guidelines for reading rates, based upon normal students at their instructional level are given in Table 3.12 (Leslie & Caldwell, 1995). You will notice that the ranges for reading rate at each grade level are quite wide. This is because individuals tend to have very different rates of reading (Carver, 1990).

When you have determined a student's reading rate at a certain grade level of the IRI, use that same level on Table 3.12 as a comparison. For example, Arliss read a third-grade oral passage at 135 words per minute. This is within the normal range of the third-grade level, 85–139 words per minute.

Table 3.12   **Reading Rates at Instructional Levels**

Level	Oral Reading Words per Minute	Silent Reading Words per Minute
Preprimer	13–35	
Primer	28–68	
First	31–87	
Second	52–102	58–122
Third	85–139	96–168
Fourth/Fifth	78–124	107–175
Sixth/Seventh/Eighth	113–165	135–231

In using the guidelines in Table 3.12, remember that they are only advisory, and reading rate must always be interpreted in relation to comprehension.

A student who reads below the lowest reading rate given for a passage level probably needs work in word recognition fluency, especially if comprehension is poor. A slow reader who cannot comprehend adequately is probably concentrating all of his or her attention on recognizing the words. This strongly suggests a need for fluency instruction. However, fluency instruction may be less important for a student who reads slowly but comprehends well.

At times, the teacher may only need to listen to a student to determine that there is a need in word recognition fluency. Slow, hesitant, expressionless reading, filled with pauses, suggests that a student must work hard to identify words and lacks the fluency essential for making sense of the author's message (Wilson, 1988).

What Is the Nature of Comprehension?

If both word recognition and comprehension levels are at the frustration level on a passage, the comprehension problems are probably due to poor word recognition. Because of this relationship, the student needs to concentrate on improving word recognition accuracy or fluency.

On the other hand, if word recognition accuracy and fluency are good, but comprehension is poor, the student probably has a problem in the area of comprehension, and needs to focus on comprehension strategies. If the problem is comprehension, careful analysis of an IRI can provide some important instructional hints.

Some students have problems in comprehension because they believe that reading is "getting all the words right." These readers are often very accurate and tend to self-correct miscues that do not change meaning. As a result, they do not actively construct meaning as they read. For example, Susan was asked to read an IRI passage containing the following sentences, "Bill's mom saw the dog. Bill asked, 'May I keep it?'" She read, "Bill's mother saw the dog. Bill asked, 'Can I have it?'" Then she paused and went back, carefully correcting each miscue. Susan's comprehension of the total passage was poor, probably due to her concern with accuracy. For a reader like Susan, it is important to emphasize that reading is meaning, not saying words.

An analysis of IRI questions may also give insight into comprehension patterns. In the IRI presented in Appendix C of this book, for example, questions are divided into literal and inferential questions. Comparing the percentages correct on these two types of questions helps to determine whether the reader is focused on factual information or able to draw inferences. You might also note whether a student appears to get the central focus of the passage or is more observant of details.

If you ask a student to retell a passage after reading it, you can see exactly how he or she constructs meaning. In judging a retelling, use these questions as guidelines for a narrative or story:

- Does the retelling contain the central events of the passage?
- Does the student remember the most important facts?
- Is the student able to retell the events in sequence?

More detailed guidelines for judging retellings are given in Chapter 8.

The IRI can also give insights into the adequacy of the student's background information. If you have begun each selection by asking the student questions to assess background, you will have a good idea of the richness of a student's prior knowledge. If you find that the student has problems with the background for several passages, your comprehension instruction might concentrate on enriching background information and applying it to reading.

Finally, when students read both oral and silent passages, you can determine whether they comprehend better after oral or silent reading. We often find that young or very disabled students are usually able to comprehend better after they have read orally. These students need practice to increase their comfort in silent reading. Other, more mature, readers comprehend better after silent reading than after oral reading.

Most IRIs are based on narrative passages. While these allow us to assess comprehension, it is more appropriate to judge study strategies from expository passages. In a section that follows, we address the use of IRIs that contain expository passages.

What Is the Nature of Language and Meaning Vocabulary?

Since reading is a language process, we can read only as well as we can understand language and word meanings. An IRI enables a teacher to determine a student's language level through finding a student's listening level.

To do this, the teacher reads IRI passages aloud to the student, starting at the reading frustration level, and asks the comprehension questions about the passage. The highest level at which the student gets 70 percent or more of the answers correct is the listening level.

The listening level provides an estimate of the student's listening (or language) comprehension level. If a student's listening level is lower than his or her grade level, that student needs to develop better language skills. Instruction should then focus on developing rich language and learning more word meanings.

In contrast, the example of Subash, the sixth-grader whose IRI summary sheet is in Table 3.9, p. 59, shows a student who has a good language base. Subash's high listening level (6) but lower instructional reading level (4) indicate that there is a two-year gap between his current reading level and his language level. The fact that his listening level is equal to his grade level indicates that his language base is sufficient for reading on grade level. No language development is needed for him; instead, he needs to work on reading.

You can also use the IRI to directly assess knowledge of meaning vocabulary. After the student has read and answered the questions in a passage, ask the student to define (or use in a sentence) key vocabulary words in the passage. Remember that you may have to pronounce words that the student has not read correctly in the passage. A student who knows the meanings of difficult words in a passage is indicating a strong vocabulary base. A student who cannot define these words or use them in a sentence is indicating a need for more development of meaning vocabulary. If a student cannot define a word in isolation, you might ask him (or her) to reread the sentence in the passage to see if context helps the student with word meaning.

Extending the IRI to Examine the Nature of Studying Expository Text.

Students who have problems studying can often comprehend narrative (storylike) text, but have problems with expository (informational) text. Typically, IRIs focus on narrative passages. However some, like the Qualitative Reading Inventory II (Leslie & Caldwell, 1995), offer both narrative and expository passages at all levels, enabling comparisons.

If the IRI you are using does not have both types of passages, use the narrative passages (which all IRIs have) to determine an instructional level for your student. Then, have your student read expository material at the instructional level to see how he or she handles material commonly used for studying.

Modifying the typical IRI procedure can often answer important questions about a student's ability to study. One extension of the IRI procedure can determine whether students can locate information to questions. To do this, give the student an IRI passage that was previously read, so that he or she can look at it. Then ask questions that were missed during the original administration, and see whether the student can use the passage to locate the answers to these questions.

Other modifications allow a teacher to assess the student's ability to locate main ideas and to take notes. To evaluate the ability to determine main ideas, give the student an instructional level expository passage along with a pencil. Then ask him or her to underline the most important parts of the selection. To investigate study strategies, ask the student to take notes on the passage as if he or she were studying for a test. A teacher can use these procedures with any text, not just an IRI.

Special Issues in Using IRIs

The informal nature of an IRI allows many options for administration and adaptation to the special needs of students. At times, you may face some issues that are difficult to decide. In this section, we discuss some of these issues and, in addition, present some alternatives for administering and interpreting the IRI.

Should the Teacher Pronounce Words for Students?

When reading IRI selections orally, a student may sometimes become "stuck" on a word. The teacher may be tempted to supply this word, in order to make the student more comfortable and able to continue. However, pronouncing words for the student may inflate the student's comprehension score, for understanding the passage depends upon reading the words accurately. To obtain the most accurate assessment, we strongly discourage teachers from supplying words. We suggest that you tell students to say "pass" for unknown words, and score these passages as omission errors. On the other hand, some guidelines for IRI administration permit teachers to aid students.

Are There Alternate Ways to Administer Oral and Silent Passages?

We have suggested that you administer all oral passages first, finding oral reading levels, and then administer silent passages. Then, we suggest you may want to use a procedure to combine both reading levels into a total reading level. While we are most comfortable with this procedure, some clinicians prefer to alternate the administration of oral and silent passages at each level.

What if IRI Results Are Unclear?

When administering an IRI, it is sometimes difficult to determine a stable level. What are some of the things that can happen? A student may score just slightly below the criteria for a specific level, for example, scoring 94% on one passage, only slightly below the frustration cut-off of 95%. At other times, a student may not do well on a certain topic. Should the teacher count these passages as frustration and simply discontinue testing? If you are unsure of the correct decision, we suggest that you continue to gather information by testing at higher levels or administering another passage at the same level.

At times, however, you will be not be able to come to a perfectly clear-cut decision, and may have to make exceptions to some of the scoring criteria. Since the IRI is an informal instrument, you should feel free to modify criteria by using your own judgment. You should, however, note that you have made an exception to the scoring criteria, and explain the reason for this exception.

Are There Alternate Ways to Score Miscues?

As we stated earlier, we feel that scoring each miscue as one error is the best and most reliable way to reach an appropriate reading level for your student. We have verified this recommendation with extensive field testing.

However, those miscues that do not change the author's meaning suggest that the student is comprehending the passage. For example, consider the following sentence. "The teachers divided the children into four groups." A substitution of "put" for "divided" would not affect meaning. On the other hand, the substitution of "from" for "four" does distort meaning. Some reading teachers prefer to count miscues that retain meaning ("put" for "divided") less severely than miscues that change meaning ("from" for "for"). If you wish to do this, count a miscue that retains the original meaning as one-half error. If a miscue changes the meaning, however, count it as one full error.

Which option should you use? Since the IRI is an informal instrument, you are free to choose the scoring system that makes you most comfortable. However, once you choose the scoring system that best fits your needs, you should use it consistently.

Are There Alternate Norms?

As with many informal measures, alternate criteria for determining reading levels have been suggested by others. Based upon our own field testing, the criteria we have suggested for word recognition accuracy and comprehension place students at appropriate reading levels. Our criteria reflect our experiences in developing an informal inventory with students who have reading difficulties. More information on norms for informal reading inventories is summarized by Johns (1993).

Summary

Assessing reading achievement involves answering two questions: How severe is the student's reading problem? and What is the general area of the reading problem?

Reading assessment measures may be divided into formal and informal. Formal reading tests are commercially prepared instruments. Formal, norm-referenced tests compare students with a representative sample of other students. Formal criterion-referenced tests measure mastery of specific skills.

Informal measures have not been normed on large populations as have standardized formal measures. Therefore, they may be used more flexibly and may be adapted to the needs of the student and the demands of the diagnostic situation.

The informal reading inventory (IRI) consists of a series of graded reading selections. The student reads increasingly difficult material until a frustration level is reached. IRIs measure both oral and silent reading. Three levels of reading are obtained: the independent level, the instructional level, and the frustration level. These levels are based on the student's oral reading accuracy and ability to comprehend the passages. Generally, separate passages are provided for oral and silent reading.

The IRI provides information about both the severity of a reading problem and its general area(s). Careful analysis of the IRI can suggest whether a student is having problems with word recognition accuracy, word recognition fluency, comprehension, language base and meaning vocabulary, or studying. Miscue analysis, the analysis of a student's oral reading deviations, allows the reading teacher to examine the strategies that a student uses to recognize words.

Special issues in using IRIs involve pronouncing words for students, administration of oral and silent passages, unclear results, alternative miscue scoring procedures, and alternative scoring norms.

An Overview of Instruction

Introduction

How can we best help students with reading problems? In this chapter we present an overview of instruction. Our topics include the components of effective instruction, general principles of instruction, guidelines for building rapport, considerations in delivering instruction, creating a community of readers and writers, and using computers to help students read.

Components of Effective Reading Instruction

Since students with reading problems are already behind their peers, instructional time is precious. This section describes the components of reading instruction that enable students to make the most effective progress.

Essential Components of a Reading Lesson

Two components are essential for each reading lesson: *reading experiences* and *reading strategies.*

Reading Experiences.

In reading, we "learn by doing." In fact, many students who are reading on level have acquired good reading skills simply by doing lots of reading (Anderson, Wilson, & Fielding, 1988). Thus, *students with reading problems need to read at every lesson.* Typically, during lessons, students read material at their *instructional reading level* (see Chapter 3).

Reading experiences are particularly critical for low-achieving readers, for these students actually read *less* than their average-achieving peers. After an extensive review of the research on time spent in reading, Johnston and Allington (1991) concluded:

> Currently we find a major characteristic of remediation is that participation rarely involves the reading of stories, magazines, or books; in fact, that students served by remedial programs typically spend less time reading any text and read less text during instruction than do nonparticipating peers. (p.993)

The unfortunate fact of very limited reading has been documented in many different settings, some of them quite surprising. Low-achieving students who are served by supplementary classes (Title I/Chapter I, special education), in addition to reading instruction in regular classrooms, actually read *less* than classmates who receive no special services (Allington & McGill-Frazen, 1989; Allington & Walmsley, 1995; Birman et al., 1987). One study found that special education services for students with learning disabilities often *reduced* the time devoted to reading instruction (Zigmond, Vallecorsa, & Leinhardt, 1980). Allington (1977) found that reading-disabled students in grades two through eight read an average of only forty-three words per reading session!

What are students doing if they are not reading? Much instructional time is spent on "skills and drills" and worksheets. Students themselves seem to know this. When Johnston, Allington, and Afflerbach (1985) asked students in Chapter I classes (now Title I) to name their most frequent activity, they overwhelmingly cited filling out worksheets.

However, students must actually read if they are to learn to read well. Compare learning to read with learning to drive, skateboard, or swim. Some of us have taken swimming lessons that required us to sit at the side of a pool doing exercises for breathing, kicking, and arm strokes. Yet learning these isolated skills did not make us swimmers. We became swimmers only after we learned to apply these skills *as we were swimming.* In the same way, students can only learn to read by applying what they learn about reading as they are actually reading a story or book.

Leading students with problems to do extensive reading is a challenging task. Stanovich (1986) describes a negative cycle called the "Matthew effect." The cycle begins when students who are not skilled readers avoid reading. Then, because they have not practiced reading, they become less skilled. In turn, because they are less skilled, they tend to further avoid reading, and so on. This continues until, tragically, the students are doing almost no reading. Baker (1993) presents a familiar portrait of what low-achieving readers do when other class members are reading independently:

> In each class a few low-progress readers spent much of their reading time wandering; getting a Kleenex, picking another book, dropping something on the floor and retrieving it, gazing around or at a page for several minutes.

As teachers, we need to prevent the "Matthew effect." Our most important job is fostering the desire to read, so that students will, ultimately, make learning to read a self-sustaining process. There are many ways to encourage students with problems to read.

(1) *Give students books that are easy for them.* If students have to struggle, they are likely to abandon reading.

(2) *Have students share their reading experiences.* When students feel that others take an interest in their responses, they are more likely to read (Baker, 1993). Thus, students read more if they form small groups and read the same books. The groups meet to share responses to the book (Richek, 1994).

(3) *Explore many different types of reading materials.* Help students to find books that match their interests. They can read scary books (a favorite of many children we know), books about snakes, joke books, bubble gum jokes, stories about other children, series books, comics, sports pages, and "News for Kids" in a local adult paper.

(4) *Encourage students to read books several times.* Repeated readings of a story or chapter improve both word recognition and comprehension (Stahl & Heubach, 1993; Pearson & Fielding, 1991; Dowhower, 1987). Reading a favorite picture book again helps beginning readers feel comfortable (Sulzby & Teale, 1991). Students also enjoy rehearsing material for choral reading and performing plays.

Strategy Instruction.

In addition to student reading, each lesson should include *strategy instruction*. In guided reading, the teacher combines *reading* with *strategy instruction* that teaches students *how* to read. In a reading strategy, students learn *how* to read as they are actively reading. Acquiring strategies allows students to consciously monitor and control their own reading processes. There are two essential characteristics of reading strategies: (1) They occur within the context of a reading situation. (2) They teach students how to think about reading.

Low-achieving students do not approach reading strategically (Daneman, 1991; Brown, Armbruster & Baker, 1986; Paris, Wasik, & Turner, 1991). They often passively accept inaccurate word identification and poor understanding, "going through the motions" of reading just to get through the material. When reading a textbook, they remember a few isolated facts, rather than trying to organize or connect information. In short, they do not know how to think about what they are reading (Stein, Leinhart, & Bickel, 1989; Williams, 1993).

Sadly, instruction for low-achievers rarely includes teaching strategies. In a wide-reaching study of Chapter I programs, Birman et al. (1987) found little emphasis on high-level thinking, and almost no instances of teaching reading strategies. However, research shows that low-achieving readers are capable of mastering the demands of reading strategy instruction (Rowan & Guthrie, 1989). There needs to be emphasis on teaching reading strategies in every lesson.

Teaching a reading strategy is different from teaching a reading skill. When a student fills out worksheets to identify the main ideas of short paragraphs, this is skills instruction. Since this activity is not connected to other reading that the student does, the student probably will not apply this gained knowledge when reading other materials. In contrast, strategy instruction teaches a student to think in a certain way and to apply this thinking to a variety of reading materials.

Teaching a strategy involves four key steps:

1. *Tell students why the strategy is important.* Like most people, low-achieving readers will do only what they consider to be helpful. Students want to know how a strategy will make reading easier for them.
2. *The teacher should model the strategy.* When teachers demonstrate a strategy and explain why each component is helpful, they help students connect activities with goals.
3. *Students should demonstrate the strategy.* By verbalizing or writing about the strategy, students demonstrate their understanding.
4. *Students should practice using the strategy.* Students should practice, first under the direction of a teacher, gradually developing independence.

All phases of learning a strategy include talking about thinking. In a strategy, thinking is "made public" through discussion, teacher modeling, and practice (Paris, 1986).

There are many examples of reading strategies. Students can be taught to use background knowledge, to predict, to find main ideas, and to use known words to figure out unknown ones. Strategy instruction can also help students with simpler tasks, such as how to choose and read a book independently.

Trina, a second-grade student in our Reading Center, was unable to answer any questions about the books she took home. Through probing, we discovered that Trina did not know the appropriate conditions for reading, such as turning off the TV and finding a comfortable seat. Trina also did not know how to choose books she could read, or how to keep her place while reading. In fact, Trina was not even aware that the sequence of pages was important. On one occasion, she told us that she had started on pages 9 and 10 of her book, and then had gone back to the beginning!

To help Trina master the strategies of choosing and reading books, the teacher discussed why these things were important. Then she modeled finding a comfortable, quiet place. She showed Trina's class why it is important to read a storybook in correct sequence. Next, students were asked to demonstrate their understanding by preparing "think cards" (Caldwell, 1990). In this activity, students write their own understandings of a strategy on an index card, which they keep with them when they practice the strategy. The card enables students to record the features of a strategy that are most useful for them. Because a think card is the student's own creation, it is an important step in transferring control of strategic reading from the teacher to the student. In making a think card, students demonstrate how they use a strategy.

A sample of Trina's think card for independent reading is shown below:

> How to Read a Book
> Be quite.
> No T.V.
> Start pag 1
> Yous somthig to tell
>   wher you are
> Ask dus this make
>   sens

Think cards are useful in many types of strategy instruction. In Chapter 6, we will discuss using them for word recognition strategies.

After Trina prepared her think card, she referred to it whenever she chose a book or read one independently. At first, this practice took place under the direction of a teacher. Later, however, Trina was able to practice her strategies independently, using her think card to guide her.

Other Important Program Components

As we have mentioned, each reading lesson should include reading and strategy instruction. In addition, there are three components that are important parts of a total reading program: (1) independent reading; (2) review; and (3) writing. Although these components may not be part of *every* lesson, they should be included in the student's total reading program.

Independent Reading.

To establish permanent reading habits, students need to read when they are not under direct supervision. Many schools and classrooms reserve 15–20 minutes per day when everyone in the school reads: the principal, teachers, students, and lunchroom staff. These reading times are often called SSR (Sustained Silent Reading) or DEAR (Drop Everything and Read). The model of adults "practicing what they preach" about reading is a powerful one.

In addition to reading in school, it is important for students to form the habit of reading at home. Students may read a chapter in a book under teacher supervision, and then read a chapter at home. Or they can choose books specifically for home reading.

When helping students choose books for independent reading, guide them to select materials at their *independent level,* which is an easier level than the *instructional level* often used for lessons. Children, like adults, like to curl up with an easy, amusing book or magazine. They can also reread favorite books. Independent reading should be fun, not work! Research shows that students make important gains when they read material that is easy for them. Extensive easy reading provides the practice students need to maintain the gains they have made in lessons (Anderson, Wilson, & Fielding, 1988; Berliner, 1981; Guthrie & Greaney, 1991).

Students can also read material they bring from home. Valuable reading and study strategies can be learned from *TV Guide,* newspapers, baseball and football programs, record jackets, popular magazines, and manuals. Using these materials demonstrates to students that reading is directly connected to their lives. One teacher asked primary students to each bring in something their parents read. The resulting display of college texts, telephone books, memos, and the Bible was a highly motivating experience.

Students with reading problems often have difficulty choosing appropriate books. When choosing a book, have students look at the cover, the length, and the size of the print. They can read the summaries on the back cover and ask opinions of friends who have read the book. Teachers can give short "book talks," describing the book briefly. In a book talk, the teacher holds up a book, describing it in an enticing way. Next, the teacher chooses an exciting part and reads it to the students. The reading should take no more than five minutes, and the excerpt should be from the first third of the book. Try to choose a reading that will keep your students in suspense, so they will want to read the book. Make sure to have copies of the book available after the book talk so that students can read the book for themselves. After you have given several book talks, students may want to give their own.

Readers who have enjoyed one book in a series, such as *Curious George* (by Rey), are likely to enjoy a sequel, such as *Curious George Gets a Medal.* Finally, students can learn the "five finger rule." In this, students read one page of a book, counting each unfamiliar word with one finger. If they count past five before the end of the page, they should choose another book.

Review of Material Learned.

Students with a history of low achievement must work hard to learn new concepts, and they need extensive review to remember those concepts. Review is especially important for beginning learners, who are still becoming familiar with the act of reading.

What should your students review? Older students can profit from review of difficult vocabulary words or important facts. Some keep a personal collection of words they have learned on cards, and review these cards periodically. Beginning readers can benefit from reading a story again, reviewing words containing a certain phonics pattern, or reviewing word cards. Review can also emphasize *strategies.* Since strategies involve a change in thinking, they are mastered slowly and require much review before they can be thoroughly understood and used.

Writing.

By becoming authors themselves, low-achieving students gain dramatically in their sense of power over reading. Students who write regularly come to feel a sense of control over both reading and writing, and to approach literacy with more interest. Students also enjoy expressing their opinions and showing their creativity through writing. Finally, through frequent writing experiences, students practice phonics by trying to spell words.

Students write in a wide variety of forms at our Reading Center:

- Seven-year-old Luis, who was at the beginning stages of reading, wrote "love notes" to his teacher, usually reading something like U AR PTE ("You are pretty"). These elaborately folded notes were given with instructions "For your eyes only."
- A group of fourth graders made a bulletin board displaying balloons featuring their favorite books.
- Heather, a sixth-grader, wrote a variation on *How Much Is a Million?* (by Schwartz) entitled "How Much Is My Allowance?"
- Alfonso, a seventh grader, composed an elaborate, multipage biography of his best friend.

The student-authored books that fill the library in our Reading Center motivate new students to make their own contributions. Writing is further addressed in Chapter 11.

Principles of Teaching Students with Reading Problems

The most important principle of teaching low-achieving students is to *provide extensive opportunities to read,* as discussed earlier in this chapter. In this section, we discuss other principles to help you plan effective instruction.

Begin Instruction at an Appropriate Level

Choose materials at the student's instructional level for teaching lessons. Materials above this level will frustrate students; materials that are too easy will not provide sufficient challenge. One of our students, seventh-grade Robert, had a fourth-grade instructional level. Since all of the materials in his regular classroom were at the seventh-grade level, the work was frustrating for him. On the other hand, in his Title I/Chapter I class, Robert was reading a book written on the second-grade level, which was too easy and wasted valuable instructional time. In our Reading Center, we located materials on his fourth-grade instructional level, and Robert's reading level improved rapidly.

However, instructional level is not an absolute guide. Readers' backgrounds or interests can often motivate them to deal with very difficult material. Joshua, a star high-school athlete, was able to read only fifth-grade materials, except when the subject was basketball. On this topic, he could read advanced newspaper and magazine articles with greater understanding than his teacher!

Support Instruction in the Regular Classroom

An important goal of supplementary reading instruction is to help students function better in regular classes. To accomplish this goal, special reading teachers need to be familiar with the curriculum of the student's classroom. The classroom teacher and reading resource teacher must jointly decide how best to help the student through collaborative planning and teaching (Allington & Broikou, 1988). If teachers do not communicate with each other and coordinate their programs, the student will suffer greatly.

We remember, with horror, a first-grade student who was confused by three conflicting forms of reading instruction. In his regular classroom, he received instruction in a traditional reading textbook series. In his Title I/Chapter I class, he was taught using the DISTAR system (see Chapter 14), which uses a special alphabet. In his learning disabilities resource room, he used the Orton-Gillingham method (see Chapter 14). Each teacher was unaware of what the others were doing. The student, who could barely master one method of learning to read, was bombarded with three different methods every day!

Resource teachers should teach strategies that help students to succeed in the regular classroom. This is especially important for students who are performing near the level of their regular classroom (Rowan & Guthrie, 1989).

Richek and Glick (1991) developed a model for supporting students in their regular classroom work. Before students read a story in their regular reading book, the resource teacher read background information to them. For example, to prepare students to read a story, "Jack's Star," featuring fireflies, the teacher read a children's encyclopedia article on fireflies. Then the story in the textbook was processed three times: (1) the resource teacher read the story to the students, stopping to ask for predictions; (2) each student reread the story with a partner; (3) the students dramatized the story as they read it. When the students then read the story (again) in their regular classroom, they were highly proficient. Cooperative efforts between the two teachers resulted in dramatic improvement in coping with regular classroom tasks, reading scores, and interest in reading (L. Glick, personal communication, 1990; Richek & Glick, 1991).

In preparing students to function independently in their classrooms, be aware of opportunities to give students progressively more difficult tasks and materials. For example, move them from a second- to a third-grade book. In addition, try gradually to increase the length of materials that students read. Teachers must ensure that students with reading problems do not get caught in the "rut" of simply proceeding through a workbook until they finish it.

Use Time Effectively

Since students with reading problems are already behind their peers, time is precious and must be used wisely. Much time in a school day is spent "off task," on activities such as taking students to and from class and passing out papers (Fisher et al., 1978a,b). This is a particular problem for low-achieving readers. Because many have problems controlling their behavior, teachers must spend important instructional time on discipline and management (Gaskins, 1988). Even calling on students to read orally can become a complex negotiation when low-achieving readers are involved. McDermott (1978) found that students in a top reading group spent three times as much time on task as did students in the bottom group.

How can teachers use instructional time effectively?

1. Streamline noninstructional activities by establishing routines for coming to class and settling down to work.
2. Call on specific students to increase their attention. Often teachers avoid calling on low-achieving or inattentive students, yet these are precisely the students who tend to be "off task."
3. Do not allow supplemental reading instruction to replace reading in the regular classroom. Supplemental instruction should be given *in addition* to classroom reading. (In fact, this is specified in current federal Title I/Chapter I guidelines.)

Use Silent and Oral Reading Appropriately

Reading instruction should include both oral and silent reading. At different times, both of these modes are appropriate.

Silent Reading.

Through silent reading, students gain control of the reading process and can pace themselves, review material, and deepen personal reactions to literature. Unfortunately, research shows that students with reading problems do little silent reading. Allington (1984) found that good readers read three times as much material silently as poor readers. Low achieving first graders read only 5 words silently per day! In a study of compensatory classes, Quirk et al. (1975) found that only 2 percent of time was spent on reading silently. Chapter 7 contains many ideas for encouraging silent reading.

Oral Reading.

Although silent reading is the more desirable mode, some oral reading activities are useful for increasing fluency and comfort (Hoffman, 1987). Beginning readers in particular are most comfortable reading orally. Many strategies for encouraging appropriate oral reading are given in Chapter 7.

Teachers of low-achieving students need to monitor oral reading wisely. Studies show that teachers tend to overinterrupt low-achieving readers who make miscues when they read orally. Allington (1980) studied what happened when two groups of primary grade students, reading in comfortable materials, came across words they did not know. When students could not figure out words immediately, teachers interrupted the students in a high-reading group 31 percent of the time; but they interrupted students in a low group 74 percent of the time!

Further, when high-achieving students missed a word, they were encouraged to figure it out for themselves. In contrast, low-achieving readers were often immediately supplied with the word by the teacher (Allington, 1980). Unfortunately, supplying words to students (called "terminal clues") results in the least gain in reading performance (Hoffman et al., 1984).

Allington also found that low-achieving readers were often interrupted, even when their miscues made sense. Thus, when high-group students made a miscue such as substituting *a* for *the*, the teacher stopped them only 10 percent of the time. When low-group students made such a misreading, teachers stopped them 56 percent of the time! Thus, teachers were unintentionally conveying to less able students that reading is *word-perfect performance*.

To encourage independence, teachers should limit interruptions for all students. If mistakes do not affect meaning, try not to stop students. When you do interrupt, encourage students to monitor meaning and figure out words for themselves. In addition, insist that other group members not interrupt readers by calling out words. The student who is reading needs time to figure out words independently. If the student wants assistance, he or she may hold up a finger, indicating "help me."

Of course, these guidelines for oral reading must be used sensibly. The teacher should assist students when they can read no further or have lost the meaning of the material.

Building Rapport

The value of a successful teacher–pupil relationship cannot be overestimated; it is more important than the methods or materials used for instruction. Several suggestions for building rapport are discussed in this section.

Acceptance

Students with reading problems need to feel that teachers accept them as individuals. Too often, by the time students are identified for special attention, behavioral problems have developed which invite rejection by teachers. Low-achieving students often suffer from low self-esteem, nervousness, and defeatism (Johnston & Allington, 1991).

One simple way of fostering a positive self-image in students is to show a genuine enthusiasm for your students' interests, be they Power Rangers, motorcycles, baseball cards, cosmetics, or ballet. Teachers' verbal comments set the tone for instruction.

Another way is to foster intrinsic motivation, which makes students feel that learning is its own reward. Praise for work well done is an important component in fostering intrinsic motivation. When giving praise to a student, it should be specific, relating to what has actually been done well. For example, if a student has demonstrated understanding of a story, you might say "You really understood that story!" This *specific* praise is much more powerful than nondescriptive comments, such as "good." Praise should also be contingent, given only when students do something well. Giving praise for things that have been done badly confuses students. An "I know you can do it if you try" attitude on the part of the teacher is also motivational for students. Finally, teachers should avoid making negative comments, for these are powerful disincentives to learning.

Security

Students with reading problems also need to feel secure in the instructional setting. One way to instill this is to start each instructional session in the same way, giving students a sense of routine.

Security may also involve a sense of personal space. Eleven-year-old Janet resisted coming to her special reading lesson. However, when the teacher made a "place" for her, covering the top of her desk with specially patterned paper, she felt she had a "home" and started to come willingly to class. If desks are shared with students who come at other times, movable name cards can be used.

Emotional security is crucial for allowing students to take such risks as reading difficult material. They need to feel confident skimming material for information without having to read every word. If teachers assure students that it is all right to make some mistakes, and that nobody is perfect, learners will take the kinds of instructional risks that are needed to become good readers.

Success

Students with reading problems are in desperate need of experiencing success. Too often, their lives have been filled with unrelenting failure. If you plan lessons so that tasks can be accomplished successfully, you will have taken an important step in building a solid relationship with your student.

Your own belief in the capabilities of your students is also important. In classic studies, Rosenthal and Jacobson (1968) and Cooper (1979) demonstrated that if teachers expect a student to succeed, that student's performance will improve.

Finally, your students need to believe in the power of their own efforts. Low achievers often suffer from feelings of "learned helplessness," believing that their efforts cannot affect success and that success (or failure) is due to "luck" (Abramson, Garber, & Seligman, 1980; Diener & Dweck, 1978). It is important that your students know that *their own efforts* will lead to improvement in reading and writing.

Charting progress (discussed later in this chapter) is one effective way to demonstrate student success. In another strategy, we keep tape recordings of students orally reading the same passage at intervals of a few months. When students listen to their own improved reading, they gain a substantial sense of accomplishment.

Delivering Instruction

How should instruction be implemented? In this section, we examine the setting for instruction, materials for instruction, and the use of individual, group, or cooperative instruction.

The Setting for Instruction

At one time, most supplementary instruction, both in special education and reading, was given to small groups of students in resource rooms, "pulling out" students from their regular classrooms. Although resource instruction continues in many schools, there are some problems associated with it. There is often a lack of coordination between the instruction of regular classes and resource rooms (Allington & Johnston, 1989). In addition, students who attend resource rooms may miss instruction in the regular classroom. Researchers have also found that the labels that students receive (e.g., reading disabled, learning disabled, dyslexic) often are somewhat arbitrary, and that, in reality, there are few differences in students bearing different labels (Garcia, Pearson, & Jiménez, 1994; Jenkins, Pious, & Peterson, 1988; Kamhi, 1992).

For these reasons, recent trends have provided more instruction in regular classrooms. In special education, *inclusion* or the *regular education initiative* provides that all students, regardless of the type or extent of disability, be taught in the regular classroom in the students' neighborhood schools. Title I regulations have also been changed to enable instruction for school populations as a whole, rather than being limited to specifically designated students who are taken out of their classrooms for instruction.

Today, many alternative models are being used. In some schools, the resource room arrangement, or "pull out" continues. In other schools, the resource teacher goes into the regular classroom to assist students. This arrangement is referred to as an inclusion, in-class, or "push in" model.

Is one model of instructional placement more effective than another? Although professionals have debated this issue hotly, some studies indicate that the placement of the student for delivery of services may make little difference in student achievement. Rowan and Guthrie (1989) found that, for Chapter I programs (now called Title I), pull-out and in-class models made no difference in achievement. What *did* affect achievement was how much active, teacher-directed instruction a student received, and how much content was covered in the lessons. While students in resource rooms lost more transition time than students in in-class models, the difference was only a minute or two per day. Thus, at the present time, it is not clear that one model is better than another.

For the *teacher,* the instructional placement *does* make a difference. In a resource room, teachers can arrange their own classrooms and allow students to make noise. However, these teachers may feel isolated and find it burdensome to assume the responsibility for getting students from place to place.

In an in-class model, supplementary teachers find it easier to communicate with the classroom teacher and to support the students' regular curriculum. However, some supplementary teachers report that they lose autonomy and are hesitant to plan instruction that is too exciting or different. In fact, classroom teachers may assign them tasks, such as helping students to complete worksheets, that do not allow them to make instructional decisions.

Materials Used for Instruction

A wealth of materials can be used to entice students to read and improve their achievement. Major types of materials are listed in this section. Materials designated specifically for reading instruction are found in Appendix B.

Trade Books.

These are books published for students' reading pleasure. Because they are geared for enjoyment and often provide extended reading, trade books are invaluable for low-achieving students.

Fiction books and novels get children "into" reading. Some favorite children's titles for easy books include *The Napping House* (by Wood), *Brown Bear, Brown Bear, What Do You See?* (by Martin), and *In a Dark, Dark Room* (by Schwartz). Intermediate choices include *Charlotte's Web* (by White), *Superfudge* (by Bloom), *James and the Giant Peach* (by Dahl), and *Scary Stories to Tell in the Dark* (by Schwartz). More advanced favorites include *The Indian in the Cupboard* (Banks) and *Where the Red Fern Grows* (by Rawls).

Series books, which repeat the same characters and story lines, help students with reading problems feel secure and accomplished. Favorite easy book series include *The Berenstain Bears* (by Berenstain), *Clifford the Big Red Dog* (by Bridwell), and *Curious George* (by Rey). Students take an important step when they begin to read "chapter books." Table 4.1 on page 80 gives favorite series of books that are divided into chapters. These books encourage students with reading problems to experience more extended reading.

Nonfiction books with factual information open up worlds of experience. Students enjoy such books as *Mummies Made in Egypt* (by Aliki) and *The Popcorn Book* (by de Paola).

Children's favorite fairy tales include *Cinderella, Goldilocks,* and *Snow White.* Children list Dr. Seuss, Judy Blume, Roald Dahl, Maurice Sendak, and the poet Shel Silverstein among their favorite authors.

Many popular easy trade books have been enlarged into big books (about 21 inches by 24 inches), enabling them to be shared easily with large groups. Other popular books have been recorded into audiocassette and video formats. Children enjoy hearing and seeing these stories presented in different ways.

An increasing number of trade books are written in a language other than English, or in English and a second language. These provide motivating reading experiences for students who do not speak English as a native language (see Chapter 12).

Remedial Reading Series Books.

These series of graded books are designed to be used as instructional materials for students achieving below grade level. They contain stories or articles, sometimes accompanied by comprehension questions and practice exercises. Examples of popular series are *High Action Reading Series* and *Reading for Concepts.* Generally, these books contain selections of only one or two pages.

Table 4.1 **Series of Easy Chapter Books**

RL indicates approximate reading level

Primary Level

Adventures of the Bailey School Kids, Dadley and M. T. Jones, Scholastic, **RL 2**
    Children find adults are gremlins, witches, aliens, etc.

Einstein Anderson, S. Simon, Puffin, **RL 3**
    Sixth-grader uses science to solve mysteries.

The Kids of Polk Street School, P. R. Giff, Dell Press, **RL 2–3**
    Second-grade class experiences humorous events.

Nate the Great, M. Sharmat, Dell Yearling, **RL 1–2**
    In very easy text, Nate solves many mysteries.

New Kids of Polk Street School, P. R. Giff, Dell Press, **RL 1–2**
    Very easy chapter books deal with kindergarten class.

Pee Wee Scouts, J. Delton, Dell, **RL 1–2**
    First- and second-grade boys and girls share scouting experiences.

Something Queer, L. Levy, Dell Yearling, **RL 2**
    Girl detectives solve mysteries in illustrated text.

Sweet Valley Kids, F. Pascal, Bantam, **RL 2**
    Second-grade girls have humorous everyday adventures.

Intermediate/Advanced Level

American Girls, J. Shaw, V. Tripp, S. Adler, Pleasant Company, **RL 4**
    Books about five American girls set at different times in history.

Angel Park All-Stars, D. Hughes, Random House, **RL 4**
    Little league baseball team combines humor with sports.

Encyclopedia Brown, D. Sobol, Bantam, **RL 4**
    Ten-year-old Leroy Brown uses encyclopedic mind to store facts.

Fear Street, R. L. Stine, Scholastic, **RL 5–6**
    More advanced versions of the Goosebumps series.

Goosebumps, R. L. Stine, Scholastic, **RL 4–5**
    Tales of the supernatural to give you goosebumps.

Matt Christopher Sports Stories, M. Christopher, publishers vary, **RL 4**
    Features heroic and human stories of many sports.

My Teacher Is an Alien, B. Colville, Pocket Books, **RL 5–6**
    Strange teachers inhabit a middle school.

Sweet Valley Junior High, F. Pascal, Bantam, **RL 4–5**
    Adventures of girls in a junior high.

Easy Reading Books.

Often called "high-interest/low-vocabulary books," these books are designed to provide enjoyable reading experiences. They contain longer stories and do not concentrate on skill development. (1) Some, such as the *Dolch First Reading Books,* provide reading practice throughout 75 to 100 pages with a total vocabulary of 200 to 500 words. Such books enable very disabled students to practice sight words several times. (2) Others, such as *Fantastic Mystery Stories* and *In Fact Series* are controlled for reading level but do not contain specific word lists, nor do they repeat a limited number of words. These books may be used with more advanced students, and they often incorporate such topics as sports, rock stars, and teenage problems. (3) Still others contain classic stories rewritten in easier language. Examples of these are *Jamestown Classics.*

Basal Readers, Literature Anthologies, Literature Textbook Series.
These are series of books often used in schools for reading instruction, and many low-achieving readers use them in regular classrooms. In this case, supplementary reading instruction should be aimed at providing success in reading the classroom series.

Sometimes reading series intended for younger students are useful with older, disabled students. Careful pacing and consistent practice make these materials easy; however, older students may react negatively to the childlike style and content.

Some reading series have been specially designed for use with low-achieving students. These books look like on-level readers, but are written at lower levels. For example, a book designed to be used with sixth graders might contain selections with a fourth-grade readability. Examples of such series are *Focus* (Scott Foresman) and *New Directions in Reading* (Houghton Mifflin), and *The Reading Connection* (Open Court).

Content Area Texts.
These are the books used in students' social studies, health, and science classes. Reading teachers may help students cope better in school by teaching them to use effective comprehension and study strategies with these expository texts.

Real-life Materials.
The abundant reading material that surrounds us includes newspaper articles, captions of pictures, magazines, manuals, advertisements, and travel brochures. The interest of such real-life material makes vocabulary control a matter of secondary interest.

Children's Magazines.
Children's magazines make excellent reading material. Currently, our Reading Center subscribes to many, including *News for You* (a 4-page weekly newspaper for limited-reading adults), *Sports Illustrated for Kids, World* (published by National Geographic), *Ranger Rick* (published by the National Wildlife Federation), and *Cobblestone* (a history magazine for intermediate students).

Plays.
Plays written for students help them to foster their sense of drama and engage them in motivated, expressive, oral reading. Some plays, called "Reader's Theater" have been developed specifically to be read. The *Sunshine Plays* and the *Perform Theater Workshop Playbooks* are examples of excellent series.

Individual, Group, and Cooperative Instruction

Students with reading problems may be instructed individually or in groups. For students with very severe difficulties in reading, individual instruction is often preferable, since it allows the teacher to monitor and respond to instructional needs. In addition, at times highly distractable students need an environment that protects them from irrelevant stimuli. Finally, in individual instruction students can avoid the embarrassment of peer pressure. According to McCormick (1995) students who received individual instruction have consistently outperformed those receiving group instruction.

However, since individual instruction is not always possible, teaching is often done in groups. We find that group instruction often has benefits for students past the very beginning stages of reading. Group instruction enables students to learn from each other. As students listen to the reactions others have to a story, their own comprehension deepens. Sometimes students can explain concepts to peers that the teacher has difficulties transmitting. Students can also share background knowledge.

Group instruction also helps students to become more active. They may ask each other questions about material, share and discuss predictions about what will happen in their reading, and study with each other. They have opportunities to interact and to share literacy experiences by taking parts in plays and writing to each other. Finally, group instruction enables students to develop close personal ties to someone who is like themselves. We have often seen friendships develop between students in groups.

Peer tutoring is a special type of group work in which students teach each other directly. Generally, one student is assigned to another as a tutor. Older students are often used to teach younger ones (cross-age tutoring), or the tutor and learner may be the same age. A noteworthy finding is that students who act as tutors often gain more in reading skills than do the students they are teaching (Sheenan, Feldman, & Allen, 1976). With careful teacher supervision, peer tutoring has proven to be worthwhile for both tutor and learner.

There are many other creative ways to group students. We have had lower-achieving readers in sixth and third grades go into kindergarten rooms to read to children. This fostered practice and a sense of accomplishment in the older students and delighted the kindergarteners!

In another grouping method, low-achieving students are put into pairs and asked to reread a story. Students take turns, alternating the reading by paragraphs or pages, or taking parts. Richek and Glick (1991) and Stahl and Heubach (1993) have reported excellent results for this strategy with primary children. Stahl and Heubach (1993) reported that it worked best when students chose their own partners.

However, working in pairs often challenges the social skills of low-progress students. To ensure that they will have a successful experience, it is best first to concentrate on something that is purely social. We have often asked students to form pairs and, making a shared response, complete these statements:

A food we both like is _____.

A TV program we both like is _____.

A color we both like is _____.

An animal we both like is _____.

A book we both like is _____.

A type of pizza we both like is _____.

It is important to remind students that they should formulate *group* answers, and not answer as individuals.

More advanced students, who are comfortable sharing, may read books independently, and then share their responses in a reading conference (Hornsby, Sukarna, & Parry, 1986; E. Costa, personal communication, 1990). Some questions that students might ask each other include:

- Does the author make you want to read on? How?
- What was the most exciting thing that happened?
- Was the book (or story) easy to read? Why?
- Would you recommend this book (or story) to a friend?

Working with groups of students is, of course, not limited to pairs.

In *cooperative learning,* students form small groups, and each group is responsible for the joint learning of its members. Cooperative learning fosters a sense of solidarity among students and often increases the enthusiasm as well as the mastery of all students. It is effective with low-achieving students, even if they are grouped with higher achievers (Johnson & Johnson, 1975; Slavin, 1984).

Creating a Community of Readers and Writers

Since reading and writing are used to communicate to other people, the more we talk, write, and communicate about our reading, the deeper and more motivating our literacy will be. In this section, we describe methods to build a self-sustaining community of readers and writers. Using these strategies, we find that our students come to look forward to their reading lessons and read willingly at home (Jennings et al., 1993).

Filling the Environment with Literacy Materials

When your room, school, and home are filled with motivating, colorful literacy materials, it is hard *not* to read and write. Classes should contain many books, displayed at students' eye level, with covers facing forward. This arrangement is far more inviting than seeing rows of book spines. We separate books by genre, putting adventure books, scary books, joke books, and sports books in their own separate, labeled baskets. We also give popular series their own baskets.

Reading materials should be varied in levels and interests. Big books, audiocasette and book sets, and videos of favorite books are also motivating. Picture books motivate all types of students with reading problems, including those in secondary school.

Students' own work can be included in displays. Books written by students, favorite jokes, and book jackets should be placed around the room. Teachers can also display student comments about books or illustrations of stories they have read.

Special corners can develop interests. In poetry corners, poems, including those written by students, are displayed on the wall, and poetry books are put on slanted shelves. A writing corner can include space to compose, different types of paper (notes, scented paper, neon paper), crayons, magic markers, pens, pencils, scissors, a word processor, and other materials that encourage written responses.

An area with a tape recorder and head phones can house audiotape and book sets. In working with three middle-school students on American history, we constructed an American history corner in our Reading Center. This corner featured books about the topic, a map of America, flags of the original colonies, and student writing.

Color and good design are important in creating an attractive environment. We have painted secondhand bookshelves red, yellow, and blue. The slanted shelf cardboard book displays used by bookstores to feature new books are quite useful. Since the displays are often thrown out after use, bookstores have been happy to donate them to us.

Physical arrangement should provide a space for students to read. Bean bag chairs, pillows, and carpets or carpet squares provide an environment that welcomes students to sit or lie down and look at books. You may provide a class library, or distribute books and reading places throughout the room. Fractor et al. (1993) suggest that an effective library is attractive, with well-defined boundaries, and a name. There are duplicate books to encourage student sharing, and space is also provided for this purpose. Props may include flannel boards, stuffed animals, book jackets, bulletin boards, and posters.

An effective learning community also features pictures of the students, parents, and teachers. In our Reading Center, we take "candids" of participants. We cut them into different shapes, back them with bright neon-colored paper, and change them weekly. Excited students, parents, and teachers enjoy seeing themselves in action!

Sharing Literacy

Sharing and reacting to books fosters literacy at all levels. Providing lots of books and sharing them can result in marked increases in reading and achievement (Elley & Mangubahi, 1983; Ingham 1982; Morrow & Weinstein, 1986).

Teachers who read books to students encourage them to later read these books for themselves. Reading to students is important at all grade levels; in one successful program, community readers came in to read to at-risk senior high students. Favorite authors included Erma Bombeck and Harry Caray (J. Monahan, personal communication, 1990).

Students may be encouraged to continue a book for themselves if a teacher orally reads the first few pages to them. Make sure to break off your reading at a suspenseful point, so that students will want to know what happens.

A book chain encourages several classrooms to share literacy. Small shopping bags, each containing one book to read to students, are distributed among classroom teachers (S. Ali, personal communication, 1994). The shopping bags are rotated every two days until each class has listened to every book. Doing this with seven third-grade rooms enabled at-risk students to share themed reading experiences. In one book chain, seven third-grade teachers shared the picture books *Two Bad Ants* (by Van Allsberg), *Horton Hears a Who* (by Dr. Seuss), *Amos and Boris* (by Steig), *The True Story of the Three Little Pigs* (by Sczieka), *Streganona* (by de Paola), *The Three Little Wolves and the Big Bad Pig* (by Trivizas), and *Bartholomew and the Ooblek* (by Dr. Seuss). After listening to each book, students voted for their favorite and justified their choice. The winner was *The Three Little Wolves and the Big Bad Pig*. Student comments (including those from a bilingual room, in Spanish) were displayed in the hall. The students were thrilled to read their words as they passed to gym and lunch! In another chain, children shared selected 7 poetry books. As a final project, students illustrated the poem "If You Were Only One Inch Tall" (by Silverstein) and displayed their artwork in the hall (Richek, 1994).

Several classrooms have used a *Great Books* book to encourage sharing. This is actually a large, blank artist's sketch pad, with each page reserved for one book that students have enjoyed. After they read a book, they write their comments about it. When looking for a good book, other students peruse the pages of the Great Book.

Visual displays also invite sharing. For example, after reading *The Ballad of Belle Dorcas* (by Hooks), 30 third-grade students each recorded their responses as a leaf on a tree, a central concept of a story (Y. Brown, personal communication, 1994). Students can record responses to different books. A class of fourth graders each read a fairy tale of their choice, and then rated it with one, two, three, or four stars (E. Costa, personal communication, 1990).

Author studies provide another effective way to encourage student sharing. Many students with reading problems fail to realize that books are written by real people. When teachers share the story of an author's life, and relate books to one another, students are able to personalize the connection to reading. When students read many books by the same author, they are encouraged to compare them. For example, Sam, a fifth grader in our Reading Center, became very interested in the work of Daniel Pinkwater (including *Fat Men from Outer Space* and *I Was a Second-Grade Werewolf*). Responding to this interest, we gathered all of Pinkwater's books and found information about him. (*Something About the Author,* 1986, is an excellent source for biographical information.) Eventually, Sam read all of Pinkwater's books, which provided some unexpectedly difficult, but highly motivating, reading. Other students have studied Henry Allard (*Miss Nelson Is Missing*), Tommie De Paola (*Streganona* and *Mummies Made in Egypt*), and Norman Bridwell (author of the *Clifford* books).

Displaying Literacy and Using Themes

How can students show their accomplishments? In our Reading Center, we choose a different theme for each semester and display books read by planning visuals based on this theme (Jennings et al., 1993). In the fall of 1993, we walked an orange neon bear around the room, recording each book (or book chapter) a student read on a paw print. Finally, our bear came out the door and into the hall. In the winter of 1994, we launched a space ship and brought it back to earth, leaving a cloud of "jet stream" stars, each recording a book read by an individual student. In the summer of 1995, students recorded their readings on dinosaurs, which were made into individual mobiles. Other themes have included the sea, folktales, and "around the world."

Displays may also record words and concepts learned, as well as books. Words that students have learned can be placed on charts. Eight-year-old Samantha enjoyed her personal "word worm" that the teacher displayed on the wall. Each segment of the worm represented a word she had mastered. A group of teenagers who were working to improve reading rate charted progress every day so that they could see how their rates were climbing. When charting progress, however, it is important to remember that publicly displayed charts may embarrass the student who makes few or no gains. For some students, records of progress should be kept private.

Using Computers to Help Students Read

Computers offer many instructional advantages for students with reading problems. They can dramatically expand the motivation and time spent practicing reading. Computers can-

"Our reading bear came out of the door and into the hall."

not (and should not) take the place of books for teaching reading, or supplant the teacher. The technology of the computer can, however, expand instructional possibilities.

The use of computers offers four advantages in helping students improve their reading.

1. *Computer instruction offers the poor reader more time for learning on a one-to-one basis.* Students are given the valuable time they need to practice and strengthen newly acquired reading abilities. Computers have been shown to hold the attention of students with reading problems, dramatically increasing the amount of "engaged time" spent in learning (Cosden et al., 1987).
2. *Computers can help develop automaticity (or fluency) in word recognition.* Students with reading problems often need extended practice before they can recognize words quickly. Practice with the computer helps the poor reader recognize words rapidly and accurately. Research has verified automaticity training on the computer for students with reading problems (Holt-Ochsner, 1992).
3. *The computer offers the student private instruction.* Because students usually work at a computer privately, potential problems with peer criticism, poor self-concept, and embarrassment are avoided.

4. *The computer offers the opportunity and time to think about the reading passage.* Computer programs that provide interactive feedback actually guide the student in problem solving and metacognitive skills. Further, since the computer provides immediate feedback, the pupil does not practice an incorrect answer for a long period of time.

Using CD ROMS the student can work interactively, making decisions on the direction of a story, its animation, talking capabilities, and color. One CD Rom early literacy program is called *Fly Ball* (Don Johnson Developmental Equipment).

There are an extensive number of high-quality software programs designed to captivate students as they help reading (Lewis, 1993; Male, 1994; Mead, 1995). Most are available for all major computer platforms: Apple II series, Macintosh, and IBM compatible computers.

Programs for emergent literacy reinforce recognition of pictures, letters, and words. In the simplest, the student touches a key and the screen shows a letter, graphics, and often some animation. Popular programs include *Muppet Learning Keys* and *Muppet Word Book* (Sunburst-Wings for Learning), *Early Learning Series* (Marblesoft), *Reading and Me* (Davidson & Associates), *The Playroom* (Broderbund), *Talking Classroom* (Orange Cherry Software), and *Bailey's Book House* (Edmark).

The computer provides a motivating, gamelike way to develop fluency of word recognition. Among software programs are *Edmark Reading Program* (Edmark Corporation), *Stickybear's Reading Room* (Weekly Reader Software), and *Paint with Words* (MECC).

Many programs developing word recognition accuracy concentrate on teaching phonics. Widely used ones include *First Letter Fun, Phonics Prime Time* and *Word Munchers* (MECC), *Tim and the Cat* and *Big Red Hat* (Harley), *Reader Rabbit* and *Talking Reader Rabbit* (The Learning Company), and *Word Attack 3* (Davidson & Associates).

Story experiences that develop comprehension for beginning readers include *Living Book Series* (Broderbund), *Reading Magic Library Series* (Tom Snyder Productions), *Peter Pan* (EA Kids), and *K. C. Clyde in Fly Ball* (Don Johnson).

Vocabulary development software often builds meaning vocabulary using standard presentation and a cloze (fill-in-the-blank) format. Programs include *Words and Concepts, I, II, III* (Laureate) and *Young People's Literature* (Sunburst-Wings for Learning).

Some reading comprehension programs that present passages followed by comprehension questions designed to elicit literal, inferential, and critical responses include *Readable Stories* (Laureate Learning Systems), *Those Amazing Reading Machines* (MECC), *Comprehension Reading Series* (Harley Courseware), *Twistaplot Reading Adventures* (Scholastic, Inc.), *Read 'n Roll* and *Speed Reader* (Davidson and Associates), *Stories and More* (IBM), *Super Solvers: Midnight Rescue* (The Learning Company), and *Reading Realities* (for inferences, Teacher Support Software).

Comprehension-based programs that use children's literature as a basis for developing reading and writing responses include *Explore-a-Story Series* (William K. Bradford), *The Ugly Duckling* (Byte Works), *Discis Books* (Discis Knowledge Research), *Fly Ball* (Don Johnson), *Living Book Series* (Broderbund), *Reading Magic: Moonlight Madness* (Hartley Courseware), and *Reading Magic Library Plus* (Tom Snyder).

In addition to these instructional programs, computers can be used in writing. This word processing application is discussed in Chapter 11.

Summary

Essential components of an effective reading lesson include reading experiences and strategy instruction. Students with reading problems usually read less than their peers, and need to read more. Strategy instruction occurs in the context of a reading situation and teaches students to think about reading. Teachers should explain why a strategy is important, model it, have students demonstrate it, and have students practice it.

Other important instructional components include independent reading, review of material learned, and writing.

The most important principle of teaching low-achieving students is to *provide extensive opportunities to read.* There are four other principles for teaching students with reading problems: (1) Begin instruction at the student's instructional level; (2) support instruction in the regular classrooms; (3) use time effectively so that students are applying the strategies they learn while they read in real text; (4) most reading should be silent, but oral reading can be used for specific purposes.

No matter which strategies you use, the relationship between the student and teacher is crucial. Building rapport includes accepting the student, providing a secure environment, and helping the student to feel successful.

Special reading instruction may be provided in a resource room or in student's classroom. Materials used for instruction may include trade books, remedial reading series books, easy reading books, basal readers, content area texts, real-life materials, children's magazines, and plays. Instruction may be individual, group, or cooperative. Although individual instruction may be superior, especially for very disabled students, group and cooperative instruction helps students to learn from each other.

Creating a literate community is important. Teachers can fill the environment with literacy materials, share literacy, and display literacy accomplishments using organizational themes.

Computers help students to gain the reading skills they need through independent, motivational practice.

Emergent Literacy

Introduction

In this chapter, we discuss the underlying concepts that students must develop in order to read. We use the term "emergent literacy" to refer to the gradual process children go through as they develop an understanding of written language.

At one time, the field of reading focused on "reading readiness" as a set of skills students needed before they could begin reading instruction. However, research has shown that children best develop the foundation for reading as they engage in activities with print. Rather than children being "ready for reading" at one point in their lives, the basis for reading is laid gradually, and involves speaking, listening, reading, and writing (Galda, Cullinan, & Strickland, 1993).

Unfortunately, many students with reading problems have not mastered these crucial concepts. If you have students who cannot comfortably read beginning level books, it is important to see whether they have developed the foundation needed for reading. Many such students, even those in intermediate grades, lack basic concepts about print. When we develop these concepts using books, stories, letters, and words, we see dramatic improvement.

In this chapter, we identify critical concepts that form the basis for beginning reading, discussing how to assess them and offering some instructional strategies to teach them. Although most disabled students progress using these techniques, there are some students with more severe disabilities who need even more intensive measures (see Chapter 14).

Emergent Literacy Concepts

There are six areas that form the foundation of literacy:

Oral language development

Concepts about print

Alphabet knowledge

Phonological awareness

Letter–sound correspondence

Beginning reading vocabulary

In this section, we discuss each of these concepts and provide informal methods by which to assess them.

Oral Language Development

As described in Chapter 4, reading, writing, listening, and speaking are all aspects of language. Students whose oral language is not well developed have difficulty with literacy.

Aspects of Oral Language Important for Literacy.
To read effectively, students need to be able to express and understand ideas fully. They also need to develop language skills specifically related to stories. For example, they must understand and be able to express the structure of stories. This includes realizing that stories have characters and events that occur in sequence.

Questioning is also a crucial language skill. To participate fully in lessons, students must respond to teachers' questions. They also need to ask questions to clarify their own understandings or seek information. Many students with language development problems have difficulty constructing or responding to questions.

We realized that Sean, a third grader in our Reading Center, had language problems during our "get acquainted" activity with him. When Sean's teacher asked him for a word describing himself, he could not answer. After many probes, he finally said "boy" and "brother." When he retold "Little Red Riding Hood" in his own words, he referred to the

Grandmother as "Mom" and to Little Red Riding Hood as "she." Finally, despite the many problems Sean encountered, he never asked for help in reading or writing.

Assessing Oral Language Development.

One way to assess students' oral language development is through teacher observations. In informal conversations, do students talk about interests or activities? When you ask students about important events in their lives, are the responses full accounts or one-word answers? Can students tell a story in sequential order and complete sentences? When students misunderstand directions or encounter a problem, do they ask for help?

Another method for assessing oral language development is to read a short story to students and ask them to retell it in their own words. A good retelling includes important characters and events in the story given in sequential order. (See Chapters 3 and 8 for further guidelines.)

Concepts about Print

An understanding of how print works is critical to emergent literacy. Students must realize that print on the page is read in a certain order and that it contains words.

Concepts Crucial to Reading.

Students need three understandings about print.

1. Print (not pictures) carries meaning.
2. Reading is "tracked," or followed, from top to bottom and left to right.
3. In print, words are separated by spaces.

Although these concepts are typically developed in the kindergarten years, some students with reading problems have not fully mastered them in the primary grades. Kelly, a first grader in our Reading Center, traced lines backwards, from right to left, as her teacher read them. Derrick, a second-grade child, thought that every spoken syllable he heard was a printed word. These children lacked fundamental concepts about print needed to identify and learn it.

Assessing Concepts about Print.

Clay (1993a) has devised an excellent test, *Concepts about Print,* to measure such understandings. Two books specifically designed for this purpose, *Sand* and *Stones* (see Appendix A), determine awareness of print as meaning, "tracking" of lines in text, and knowledge of what a word is. The test also measures awareness of inverted pages, transposed words, reversed letters, and sentences printed out of sequence.

In addition, many concepts about print can be measured without formal tests just by sharing a simple book with a student. Choose an 8- to 12-page book with one or two lines of text per page. The book should contain at least one multisyllabic word. To determine awareness of print as meaning, open the book and ask the student to point to "what we read." The student should identify print, not pictures. Next, to determine tracking, point to the print and ask the student to show you "where we begin to read," and "where we go next." Notice whether the student starts at the left for each line. Finally, for word awareness, ask the student to point to and repeat words after *you* have read each page. From this repetition, you can see whether the student can correctly identify a multisyllabic word as one word.

Alphabet Knowledge

Research shows that the ability to name letters is an excellent predictor of early reading achievement (Walsh, Price, & Gillingham, 1988).

Knowledge Needed for Reading.
Alphabet knowledge consists of two parts: recognizing letters and writing letters. Students must identify letters automatically and must be able to name them when they are presented in random order. In addition, students must know both upper and lower case letters.

Some reading disabled students, even in the third grade, still have problems with letter recognition. Allen, a third grader in our Reading Center, frequently asked the teacher how to make a *u* or a *j*.

Assessing Alphabet Knowledge.
A sample of an alphabet test is given in Table 5.1. To administer the task, ask your student to say each letter, reading across the lines. Next, ask the student to write these same letters as you say them. First, ask that the letters be written in lower case ("small") letters, then in upper case letters.

Phonological Awareness

Phonological (or phonemic) awareness is the knowledge that speech is built from sounds. For example, the word *bed* consists of three speech sounds, or phonemes: *b*, *short e*, and *d*. The word *sleep* consists of four phonemes: *s*, *l*, *long e*, and *p*, even though it has five letters; the *ee* combination makes only one sound. Consonants can also combine to make one sound; the word *sheep*, which is five letters, consists of three phonemes: *sh*, *long e*, and *p*.

Knowledge Needed for Reading.
Phonological awareness refers to students' knowledge of individual sounds in words and their ability to manipulate those segments (Stahl & Murray, 1994). Research shows that students' abilities to identify and manipulate these sound elements are highly related to reading achievement and spelling (Ball & Blachman, 1991; Byrne & Fielding-Barnsley, 1991; Dreher & Zenge, 1990; Stanovich, 1988a; van Ijzendoorn & Bus, 1994).

Phonological awareness includes a variety of abilities. Students must be able to identify and separate beginning sounds of words, identify and separate ending sounds, and substitute sounds within a basic pattern. They must also be able to rhyme. Finally, students need to be able to manipulate sounds by putting them together (or blending them), taking them apart (or segmenting them), and deleting them. All these abilities help students to master phonics in reading.

Assessing Phonological Awareness.
We assess phonological awareness by asking students to blend and segment sounds, as shown in Table 5.2. Other tasks (Stahl & Murray, 1994) include asking students to identify the first sound in a spoken word (e.g., "What is the first sound in 'table'?") or to say a word without a sound (e.g., "Say 'table' without the /t/.").

Table 5.1   **Alphabet Recognition Test**

A	S	D	F	G	H	J
K	L	P	O	I	U	Y
T	R	E	W	Q	Z	X
	C	V	B	N	M	
a	s	d	f	g	h	j
k	l	p	o	i	u	y
t	r	e	w	q	z	x
c	v	b	n	m	a	y
g	q	t	a	g	t	q

Table 5.2 **Assessing Phonological Awareness: Blending and Segmenting**

Directions: I am going to say some words in a special code and I want you to figure out the real word. If I say s/-/a/-/t/, you say *sat.* If I say /p/-/i/-/g/, you say *pig.*

Teacher says:	Expected Response	Student's Response
/d/-/i/-/g/	dig	
/p/-/u/-/l/	pull	
/b/-/e/-/d/	bed	
/f/-/a/-/s/-/t/	fast	
/s/-/o/-/f/-/t/	soft	

Directions: Now we will change jobs. If I say *bat,* you say /b/-/a/-/t/. If I say *feet,* you say /f/-/ee/-/t/.

Teacher says:	Expected Response	Student's Response
can	/c/-/a/-/n/	
tell	/t/-/e/-/l/	
dust	/d/-/u/-/s/-/t/	
sit	/s/-/i/-/t/	
fog	/f/-/o/-/g/	

NOTE: When a letter is enclosed in brackets (//), this indicates that you should say the letter *sound.*

Letter–Sound Correspondences

To read successfully, the ability to identify and manipulate sounds must be combined with the ability to associate these sounds with their corresponding letters (Ball & Blachman, 1991).

Relationship to Reading Achievement.
Students' knowledge of letter–sound correspondence is highly related to later reading achievement (Dreher & Zenge, 1990). Most important to emergent literacy is knowledge about beginning consonants.

Assessing Knowledge of Letter–Sound Correspondence.
To assess students' knowledge of beginning consonants, we give them a word and ask them to identify (1) the beginning sound of the word and (2) the letter of this sound. The words in the sample task in Table 5.3 are frequently found in beginning reading materials and all begin with single-letter initial consonant sounds. The task also includes some two-syllable words.

Students' spelling of unfamiliar words also reveals important information about letter–sound correspondences (Gentry & Gillet, 1993).

Table 5.3 **Assessing Letter–Sound Correspondences: Beginning Letter Sounds**

Practice: What is the beginning sound of *mat*? (Student should say /m/.) What letter makes that sound? (Student should say "M." If not, model and practice another word.)

Word	Beginning Sound	Beginning Letter
fish		
little		
ride		
want		
happy		

Beginning Reading Vocabulary

The earliest words children learn to read are from their environment. Children who recognize *MacDonald's, Cheerio's,* and *Don't Walk* are reading environmental print. As books, paper, and markers become a part of children's worlds, they make a transition from recognizing logos and signs to recognizing their names or *MOM* and *DAD.*

A child's first sight words play a critical role in emergent literacy, for emergent readers gain confidence by using their beginning sight words in reading and writing. These words also form the foundation for word analysis strategies, enabling students to use known words as a basis for learning about new ones.

Assessing Beginning Reading Vocabulary.
One way to assess early reading vocabulary is to ask students to write any words they know. This provides students with the opportunity to show you what they know instead of what they do *not* know.

Clay (1993a) recommends that teachers assess beginning reading vocabulary by developing a word list using fifteen high-frequency words drawn from the students' early reading materials and asking students to read these words. This method allows you to discover both which early reading words students know and what are their strategies for coping with unknown words. Allow ten minutes for students to repeat this activity.

Strategies to Develop Early Literacy Concepts

In this section, we suggest activities for developing emergent literacy concepts. Although we have presented separate assessment tools for different areas, in instruction we try to integrate these areas into a total literacy environment. Thus, one activity may foster several areas of emergent literacy (Foorman et al., 1991). As we have also emphasized, emergent literacy understandings are best taught within the context of real reading and writing, in literacy-rich environments. Because emerging into reading is a gradual process, the instructional activities used to support development overlap with those used for beginning reading and writing.

Oral Language Development

As we stated earlier, oral language development forms the basis for reading and writing. Three aspects of oral language development crucial to literacy are understanding and using oral language, understanding the structure of stories, and responding to and constructing questions.

Reading Aloud to Students.

Reading books aloud to children is valuable for helping them to develop language skills. Many students with reading problems have not had wide experience in sharing print with an adult. Reading to students enables them to experience the rich language of books as an adult models how reading is done. Children learn to follow a story structure and to engage in conversation about books. In the sections that follow, we give additional strategies that may be used as you read books aloud to children.

Directed Listening–Thinking Activity.

Often referred to by its initials, DL-TA, this activity is a modification of the Directed Reading–Thinking Activity (DR-TA) developed by Stauffer (1975) and discussed in Chapter 8. In DL-TA, the teacher reads the text aloud, stopping at crucial points to allow students to predict what will happen next and to confirm or revise previous predictions. These predictions and confirmations (or revisions) guide the students' understanding of the story.

After students are familiar with this strategy, you can alter it by stopping before the last section of text and asking students what they think will happen in the end. Ask students to draw pictures showing what they think will happen; they may then write or dictate a sentence or two about their pictures. Next, read the author's actual ending to the story and compare it with the students' endings.

Story Structure.

The structure of stories (also presented in Chapter 8) can be used to guide discussion of books a teacher reads to children. Focusing on story elements helps students to learn that (1) stories are organized in a predictable fashion; (2) special terms, such as *characters, events,* and *setting,* are used for stories. These understandings will help children both to read and to write stories.

After you read a story to your students, ask them, "Who is this story about?" or "Who are the main characters in this story?" Then ask the students, "Where does this story take place?" and "When does this story take place?" Next, ask students, "What is the main characters' problem?" and, finally, ask, "How do they solve the problem?"

We often place these questions on a chart in our Reading Center. Students can answer the questions with pictures from the story or refer to the chart as they retell stories or construct their own. Learning about the "language of stories" provides an excellent foundation for the more complex story grammars and maps used in later comprehension instruction.

Shared Book Experience.

In this strategy (Holdaway 1979), teachers imitate the "bedtime story" experience of young children. You can use the shared book experience with whole classes, in small groups, or with individuals. Students are drawn into the shared book experience by the quality of the stories shared, by your enthusiasm, and by the "sharing" format. We generally use "predictable" (or patterned) books, which contain repeated words or phrases and plots simple enough for students to predict outcomes. Some favorite predictable books include *Have You Seen My Duckling?* (by Tafuri), *Bears in the Night* (by Berenstain & Berenstain), *Where's Spot?* (by Hill), *Have You Seen Crocodile?* (by West), *The Carrot Seed* (by Krauss), *Titch* (by Hutchins), *Ape in a Cape* (by Eichenberg), *Is Your Mama a Llama?* (by Guarino), *Green Eggs and Ham* (by Dr. Seuss), *Too Much Noise* (by McGovern), and *The Very Hungry Caterpillar* (by Carle). A list of additional suggested titles is presented in Table 7.1 (on page 131). Predictable books support students as they attempt to read on their own.

The steps in a shared book experience are:

1. *Introduce the book.* Ask students to predict what it will be about as you clarify any concepts that may be unknown. Show the pictures of the book.
2. *Read the book aloud to students.* Point to each word as you read. Read slowly, but with expression rather than word by word. Position the book so that the students can see it. Then reread the book, inviting children to join you. If students do not join you in the rereading, encourage them by leaving off significant words. For example, for "I Know an Old Lady Who Swallowed a Fly," you might read:

   She swallowed a spider
   That wiggled and jiggled and tickled inside her
   She swallowed the spider to catch the fly
   But I don't know why she swallowed the fly . . .

   Who can resist joining in with "I guess she'll die"?
3. *Follow the reading with language activities.* The language-related activities developed from shared book experiences can focus on letter–sound correspondences, dramatization, learning new vocabulary, or any other aspect of literacy that you choose to develop.

   For example, if you choose to focus on letter sounds, select significant words from the story and draw pictures of them on index cards. Have students group the pictures by their beginning sounds. Next, introduce the letters that correspond to those sounds. Then, you might present a picture card and ask students to write the beginning letter.

A shared book experience may be extended over several days, as children reread and engage in several different activities.

Language Experience Activity.

The shared book experience is an excellent springboard for the language experience activity (LEA) (Warner, 1963). In an LEA, teachers and students compose an original story or retell a story in their own words. Generally students dictate to a teacher, who writes down their words on a chalkboard or large piece of paper.

To try this strategy, follow these procedures:

1. *Brainstorm ideas for a story.* Topics may include shared experiences, such as field trips, science experiments, special events, or stories read aloud. Choose one topic for your story.
2. *Take dictation from students.* Ask students to tell you the words you should write. At early stages, stories should be limited to four or five sentences. Write the words in large print.

3. *Read each word as you write it.*
4. *Reread each sentence, pointing to each word as you say it.* Have students reread each sentence with you.
5. *Reread the entire story with students.*
6. *Follow up with language activities.* For example, students might select three words that they can recognize or draw pictures to go with their story. If they draw pictures, they might choose to write caption for them.

Often teachers combine the language experience activity with the shared book experience to create a cohesive lesson. One second-grade Title teacher used this format with poetry to provide her students with rich language experiences, as seen in Strategy Snapshot 5.1.

Using Wordless Books.

Wordless books, which tell stories through pictures only and contain no text, can help students develop the skill of telling a narrative in sequence. In using a wordless book, you may wish to have students dictate a sentence for each picture. An alternative approach is to discuss the book with students, record their dictation, writing each sentence on a separate page, and have students illustrate the book. You can then bind the pages to create your own big book. Children can be encouraged to identify words that they know and to read their creation to others. Popular wordless books include *A Boy, a Dog, and a Frog* (by Mayer), *What?* (by Lionni), and *Apt. 3* (by Keats). Each of these authors has written additional wordless books.

Strategy Snapshot 5.1
● ● ● ● ● ● ● ● ● ● ● ● ●
A Shared Book Experience with an LEA.

Ms. Burgess, a teacher in a second grade Title I class, began with a favorite poem, *Honey, I Love* (by Greenfield), printed on chart paper. She pointed to the words and the students read along in a sing-song fashion.

Next, Ms. Burgess reread a favorite story, *Being Here with You* (by Nicola-Lisa, 1992), as part of a unit on friendship. Ms. Burgess introduced the LEA saying, "Today we're going to write a story like Mr. Nicola-Lisa's, except ours is going to be about our class, and how nice it is that we are all so different, but alike."

The students brainstormed ways they were alike and different. As the students talked about what they liked to do together, they recalled a picnic at which they met their seventh-grade penpals. The students created their own story, "Penpals in the Park."

Next, the class divided into teams. One team played a sorting game with the letters *p* and *b*. Another group used magnetic letters to write words selected from their story. The third group sorted picture cards under the headings "Alike" and "Different." The fourth group met with Ms. Burgess to read sentences they wrote about a previous story.

After several minutes, the students reassembled for Ms. Burgess to introduce a new book, *Three Friends* (by Kraus). As she read, Ms. Burgess pointed to the words in the text, and stopped occasionally to ask the students how they thought the characters could solve their problems. When she came to a word that started with *b* or *p*, she asked the sorting group for help.

Concepts about Print

The activities we described in the previous sections of this chapter help to develop crucial concepts about print. In this section, we present some additional activities to develop these understandings.

Echo Reading/Pointing.

The echo reading procedure that we presented earlier to evaluate concepts about print may also be used to teach these concepts. This reflects the fact that good assessment should have much in common with instruction (Teale, 1988).

In echo reading, teachers help students match the spoken word with the printed word. To do this, select a predictable book with limited print. First, read the entire book to the students. Next, read one sentence, pointing to each word. To "echo read," students reread what you have read as they also point to words. As students become more familiar with the process, the length students repeat may be increased. It is important to monitor students' pointing carefully; make certain that they point to each *word* rather than to each *syllable* that is read.

Counting Words.

In this activity (Cunningham, 1995), students recognize words in speech, a skill that prepares them to recognize them later in print. To do the activity, give students objects (blocks, Popsicle sticks) to use as counters. The student listens as you say a sentence at a normal rate. Then say the sentence again, pausing after each word. Students should move a counter for each word you say. Next, have students make up their own sentences and count the words in them.

Jumbled Sentences.

In this strategy, students count words as they reorder them.

1. *Begin with a story you have read or written with your students.* Ask students to write a sentence about the story. Most students write summary sentences. For example, in a story about a hungry dog, Ramon wrote, "Duffy gobbled up all our food." Students often draw a picture about the story and write or dictate a sentence in a practice book.
2. *Write the sentence on a large sentence strip.* Have students read their sentence to you. Then write the sentence on a large sentence strip. Next, read the sentence together as you point to each word.
3. *Have students rewrite their sentence on a small sentence strip.* Use the large sentence strip as a model. Students then reread the sentence and point to each word as they read it.
4. *Cut the large sentence strip into individual words and "jumble" them.*
5. *Have the students reassemble the sentence, using the small sentence strip as a model.* Then students reread the sentence.

We have found that many students who develop early reading problems need this physical separation of words to develop a strong concept of word.

Being the Words.

In this activity (Cunningham, 1995), students actually "become" one word. To start, the teacher should write the sentences from a predictable book onto sentence strips. You may, of course, need to duplicate words that are used twice in a sentence, or write some words using both lower case and upper case first letters. However, you need not make copies of words that reappear in different sentences. Cut the words from two sentence strips into individual words and distribute each word to a student. Make a separate card for each punctuation mark.

Now tell the students they are going to *be* the word they are holding. Display the first two sentences of the book, and read them together. Point to the words as you read them and ask students to look at their words to see if they have any matches. Students who have the words from those sentences come forward and arrange themselves in left-to-right order. Have the other students in the class read the sentences as you point to each "student/word." Continue this activity until you have made all the sentences from the book.

For older students, write the sentences on smaller cards and deal a few (like a deck of playing cards) to each student. When you display the sentence, the students must cooperate to construct it.

Alphabet Knowledge

In teaching alphabet knowledge, we combine letter names with letter sounds to help students progress more efficiently.

Memory Game.
Sets of cards, which can be easily made or purchased, are used in this game. A set of cards is placed face down on the table. Half contain pictures (no words) of objects, and half contain the letters representing the initial consonant sounds of those objects. Students turn pairs of cards over, trying to match the beginning sound of a picture card with its letter. When a match is found, students must name the object and identify the corresponding letter name.

Using Alphabet Books.
There are a variety of beautiful alphabet books that help expand children's world knowledge and appreciation of literature as they learn letters. Some of our favorites include *Alligators All Around* (by Sendak), *ABC* (by Burningham), and *I Love My Anteater with an A* (by Dahlov). Research by Stahl (personal communication, 1995) indicates that children's alphabet books that provide words which start with a letter sound (such as *dog* for *d*) also help in developing phonological awareness. Letters in an alphabet book should be shown in both upper and lower case (e.g., *D* and *d*).

Phonological Awareness

The phonological awareness assessment procedures we presented earlier may also be used as activities to practice phonemic awareness. In addition, we present others in this section.

Using Nursery Rhymes and Rhyming Books.
Chanting nursery rhymes develops phonological awareness, including the ability to rhyme. Traditional poetry and songs are excellent resources to use with younger children.

Teachers can also use the many excellent books that focus on rhyming to help develop this ability. Begin by reading a rhyming book to students. Next, reread it, but this time, leave out the word that "completes the rhyme," and ask the students to provide it. For example, in the sentences "It is a nice day; I would like to play," you would omit "play" and ask the students to supply it. Students can also create their own "silly" rhymes.

Excellent books to model rhyming include *Sheep in a Jeep* and its sequels (by Shaw), *The Hungry Thing* and its sequels (by Slepian and Seidler), and books by Dr. Seuss, such as *One Fish, Two Fish* or *Green Eggs and Ham.* For older students, use collections of poetry, such as *The New Kid on the Block* (by Pretlutsky) or *A Light in the Attic* (by Silverstein).

Identifying Beginning Sounds.

Yopp (1992) uses well-known tunes to help reinforce the skill of identifying initial letter sounds. One song is set to the tune of "Old MacDonald Had a Farm."

What's the sound that starts these words:
Basket, bug, and *Bill*? (wait for response)
/b/ is the sound that starts these words,
Basket, bug, and *Bill,*
With a **/b/** - **/b/** here and a **/b/** - **/b/** there
Here a **/b/,** there a **/b/,** everywhere a **/b/-/b/**
/b/ is the sound that starts these words, *Basket, bug,* and *Bill.*

NOTE: When a letter is enclosed in brackets (//), this indicates you should say the letter *sound.*

Rhymes and Riddles.

In Rhymes and Riddles (Cunningham, 1995) teachers select two groups of words, one to rhyme with *head* and the other to rhyme with *feet.* Next, ask students a riddle so that the answer rhymes with either *head* or *feet.* The children point to the part of their body which rhymes with the answer to the riddle. For example, if you ask "When you are hungry, do you want to...?" students should point to their *feet,* because *eat* rhymes with *feet.* You can repeat this game with other parts of the body. For example, you can ask students to answer riddles with words that rhyme with *hand* and *knee* or *arm* and *leg.*

Counting Sounds.

In this activity, students break apart words and count their sounds. To do the activity, select ten words that contain two to four phonemes each. The words should be regular; that is, if there are two sounds, there should be two letters. In fact, we recommend that you use only words with short vowels, consonants, and consonant blends (in which each consonant says a sound). Example words would be *it, man, bent, stop.*

Students listen to you pronounce a spoken word, say it themselves, and then move one object for each sound they hear. You can use craft sticks, cubes, or counters. Try to use objects that are all the same, such as blocks of one color, or similarly sized paper clips.

Begin by modeling the activity. Pronounce a word. Then pronounce each sound element of the word, moving a counter for each sound that you say. Finally, move the counters back together and repeat the word as a whole.

Next, repeat the procedure with the same word, but this time ask students to try the game with you. Repeat this procedure with another word. Model the segmentation task. Then ask students to join you. Stop after the second phoneme and see if your students can complete the task. If practiced over a period of several weeks, we have found substantial gains for students.

Deleting Phonemes.

In this relatively advanced activity, students take a word apart, remove one sound, and pronounce the word without that sound. You might introduce this activity by removing parts of compound words. For example, pronounce a word, such as *playground*, and ask students to say it without *play*. Students should say *ground*. Next, tell students to say *applesauce* without the *sauce*.

Next, ask students to say words, omitting single sounds. Ask students to say *ball* without the /b/. (They should say *all*.) Try several of these, asking students to omit the beginning sounds; then ask students to omit ending sounds. When students successfully can omit beginning and ending sounds from words, ask them to say a word, omitting a medial sound. For example, you might say "Say *stack*, without the /t/." The student should say *sack*.

Blending.

Yopp (1992) uses the familiar tune, "If You're Happy and You Know It, Clap Your Hands," to provide practice in blending phonemes together to construct words:

> If you think you know this word, shout it out
> If you think you know this word, shout it out
> If you think you know this word,
> Then tell me what you've heard,
> If you think you know this word, shout it out
> /k/ - /a/ - /t/

(Students should respond by blending the phonemes into *cat*.)

Letter–Sound Correspondence

As students develop stronger concepts about print and the ability to identify individual sounds in spoken words, they need to connect these spoken words with printed letters and words. We recommend that you start with initial consonant sounds. These are the easiest sounds for students to hear and segment, and they are therefore the easiest to associate to letters.

Acting Beginning Sounds.

Many students have difficulty breaking words down into their individual sounds and identifying these sounds. To develop this skill, Cunningham (1995) suggests that teachers start by working with individual sounds in words. Begin by showing a specific letter, such as *b*, and have all the students engage in an activity that begins with that sound as they repeat the sound. For /b/ students *bounce*; /c/ is *catch*, /d/-*dance*, /f/-*fall*, /g/-*gallop*, /h/-*hop*, /j/-*jump*, /k/-*kick*, /l/-*laugh*, /m/-*march*, /n/-*nod*, /p/-*paint*, /r/-*run*, /s/-*sit*, /t/- *talk*, /v/-*vacuum*, /w/-*walk*, /y/-*yawn*, /z/-*zip*.

Letter–Sound Manipulation.

As we have mentioned, in the beginning stages of reading, students look for familiar patterns and substitute sounds. Students who have experienced problems in early reading need to be taught this strategy.

In the Letter-Sound Manipulation strategy (Iversen & Tunmer, 1993), students remove letter–sound elements from words and substitute other letter-sounds. For example, a student may change the word *bat* to *cat*. Although this seems simple, it is actually a complex task. Richek (1995) recommends using magnetic letters for this task. To try this strategy:

1. *Select familiar words with simple patterns and several possible rhyming words.* Choose words students can recognize automatically. Next, create a list of words that rhyme with each word you plan to teach. An example list might be *mat, fat, bat, rat*. If possible, start with words built from the *at, in,* or *it* word families.
2. *Give each student a magnetic board with one of the words on it.* Ask students to read the word. Then ask students to remove the beginning consonant and read the resulting word.
3. *Give students a letter to replace the beginning consonant you have removed.* Ask students to read the new word.
4. *Give students three more consonants to make new rhyming words.* Ask students to read their new words.
5. *After students have made the new words with magnetic letters, ask them to write these words on paper.* When students have learned this strategy and can apply it to new words in print, they are ready for the more advanced word analysis strategies presented in Chapter 6.

Spelling.
Allowing students to spell words they have worked with provides practice in manipulating letters and sounds in print. As students gain in their understanding of letter–sound relationships, their writing will become more conventional. Encourage students to write freely and explore their own spelling. As they do this, try not to correct them, but rather let them explore their own understandings, whether or not they are completely accurate.

Beginning Reading Vocabulary

There are many activities that encourage students to develop the first sight words on which reading is built. You may make a collection of logos and children's favorite words. Some teachers prepare flash cards with words that are common in the environment. They cut out pictures from newspaper and magazine advertisements and label them. Children often enjoy bringing in and identifying food labels and wrappers. In "print walks," children and adults walk through a building, identifying all the times they see a certain type of print, such as the word *exit*, words about weather, or ten-letter words.

Many of the activities we have presented earlier, such as shared book experiences and language experience stories, help children develop a fund of sight words. However, students may also want directly to learn a number of important words by sight. These words, at first, might include their names, addresses, and words that they frequently see in reading or use in writing. Students might want to keep personal cards for each word, and to form them into sentences using the "jumbled sentences" activity presented earlier.

Summary

In emergent literacy, students surrounded by reading and writing gradually develop the foundation for these activities. Students with reading problems may lack some emergent literacy understandings. Six needed areas of knowledge include oral language development, concepts about print, alphabet knowledge, phonological awareness, letter–sound correspondences, and beginning reading vocabulary.

In oral language development, students need to express and understand ideas fully, understand how stories are organized, and develop the ability to answer and formulate questions. Instruction in oral language development includes retelling stories, composing original stories, developing questions, reading to students, the Directed Reading–Listening Activity, discussing story structure, shared book activities, language experience activities, and using wordless books.

Three concepts about print are crucial to reading: understanding that print carries meaning, how print is organized, and what words are. Instruction includes echo reading, counting words, jumbled sentences, and "being" the word.

Alphabet knowledge is strongly related to reading. Sounds can be taught with letter names. Instruction includes the memory game and the use of alphabet books.

Phonological awareness refers to the abilities to manipulate sounds, including segmenting, blending, rhyming, sound deletion, sound addition, and sound substitution. Activities include using nursery rhymes and rhyming books, identifying beginning sounds, rhymes and riddles, identifying sounds, counting sounds, deleting phonemes, and blending.

Letter–sound correspondences, identifying a letter and its sound, can be taught by acting beginning sounds, letter–sound manipulation, and spelling practice, as well as several strategies mentioned above.

Students' early reading vocabulary words come from their environments. As they are exposed to more print, students start to connect environmental print with specific words. Teachers and parents help the process by reading extensively to students, labeling objects in their environments, and collecting functional words.

CHAPTER 6

Improving Word Recognition Accuracy

Introduction

In order to read, we must recognize the words that are written on the page. Poor readers have much difficulty with word recognition. They pronounce words inaccurately or must often laboriously attempt to match letters and sounds. They often stumble even over familiar words. These struggles leave students with little energy to concentrate on comprehending the author's message (Goldman & Pellegrino, 1987; LaBerge & Samuels, 1974).

This chapter is aimed at helping students to recognize words accurately. We first explain the entire process of accurate and fluent word recognition. Next, we discuss the clues that enable word recognition accuracy: context clues, sound or phonics clues, and basic structural analysis clues. For each of these clue systems, we present both assessment strategies and strategies for instruction.

The Process of Word Recognition

Word recognition is a very complex process. Readers use a variety of clues which interact in a complex and wonderful fashion. Some clues, such as sight words, enable us to recognize words fluently, or quickly. Other clues, such as context, phonics, and structural analysis, help us to recognize words accurately.

Clues that Enable Fluent Reading: Sight Word Clues

A good reader identifies words easily. Right now, you are probably reading the words in this book with little effort, recognizing them immediately. As a result, you are paying attention to meaning, rather than to recognizing words, although you are actually doing both. Words that you recognize immediately, without any analysis, are called sight words. A large store of sight words allows people to read fluently.

Readers who do not know many sight words must use other, more laborious, clues to recognize words. The time and effort put into analyzing words may take so much attention that even when they have gotten the words right, these readers may have little idea of what they have read!

Clues that Enable Accurate Reading: Context, Phonics, Structural Analysis

Readers who cannot recognize words immediately must stop to analyze them. They can match letters and sounds (phonics), break a word into prefixes and suffixes (structural analysis), or stop and think which word would fit best in the passage (context). At times, they use all of these clues together.

Context Clues.

When readers use context clues, they use the meaning of a passage to help them recognize words. They employ their background knowledge and their understanding of the text to focus on meaning. Context can be a powerful aid to word recognition (Anderson, Wilkinson, & Mason, 1991). In fact, context clues are so effective that we often can predict words that are left out of text. See if you can do this in the story that follows.

The Zoo Trip
We went to the zoo. We fed peanuts to the big, gray _____. We watched the striped
_____. The _____ was funny with its long neck. The _____ swung from tree to
tree.
Answers: elephant, zebra, giraffe, monkey

Because of your experiences with zoos, you probably had little difficulty supplying the
missing words. You also used your understanding of how our language works. Readers
know, for example, that articles such as *the* and adjectives such as *striped* tend to come
before nouns. Even beginning readers use such language cues to help them identify words
(Juel, 1983).

However, context clues do not always work well for poor readers. (1) In order to use
context to recognize some words, a reader needs to identify most of the other words accurately. Students with reading problems often cannot recognize enough words to use context effectively (Adams, 1990; Pflaum et al., 1980). (2) Poor readers often lack the background knowledge necessary for using context clues. A student who knows little about zoos
would not be as successful as you were in reading the zoo passage. (3) Students with reading problems often lack knowledge about how language works. There is a strong relationship between facility in oral language and reading (Vellutino & Denckla, 1991), and many
poor readers have delayed or limited language development. Since these students have difficulty manipulating language, they cannot use context clues effectively. (4) Many low-
achieving students ignore the sense of what they are reading and focus only on matching
letters and sounds. (5) Other poor readers overuse context (Perfetti, 1985; Stanovich, 1986),
often making up their own story, which has little in common with the author's.

Sound or Phonics Clues.
Much research (Chall, 1967, 1979, 1983a; Stahl, 1992) has found that students who learn
the sound–symbol correspondences of English read better than those who have not mastered these critical skills. These studies suggest that phonics clues are a vital part of good
reading.

Phonics clues are helpful in identifying printed words *that we have previously heard.*
However, if we have never heard a word before, we will not be sure we are pronouncing it
correctly. For example, if we had never been exposed to the word *podium*, we could not be
certain whether it should be pronounced *po dye um* or *po dee um*.

Poor readers often have difficulty learning to use phonics. Irregularities in the English
phonics system can cause problems. In addition, students with reading problems may lack
phonemic awareness, which forms the basis for phonics (see Chapter 5). These readers are
unable to identify and manipulate the different sounds in spoken and written words.

Structural Analysis Cues.
Using structural analysis, readers identify meaningful parts in words. For example, they recognize the unknown word *playground*, through its two component words, *play* and *ground*.

In this chapter, we discuss basic structural analysis clues, including compound words,
contractions, and word endings. Compound words, such as *cowboy* and *playground*, are
formed from two words. Contractions are two words that have been abbreviated into one
by the use of an apostrophe (e.g., *can't, I'm*). Common words endings, which are often called
inflections, include *s* (plural), *ed* past tense), *er* and *est* (comparative), *'s* (possessive), and

ing (gerunds and progressive tense). Prefixes, suffixes, and roots, which provide more advanced structural analysis clues, are discussed in Chapter 10.

Students with reading problems tend not to use structural analysis clues effectively. They are often unaware of how endings on words such as *talks*, *talking*, and *talked* signal time and tense, and they often simply omit them during reading.

Assessing Context Clues

Context clues, or meaning clues, may be assessed using miscue analysis through student interview, and through comparison of words in lists and passages.

Miscue Analysis

As we describe in Chapter 3, miscue analysis, or an analysis of the errors students make during oral reading, is an excellent method to assess use of context clues. A student who supplies a word that *makes sense in the passage* is probably paying attention to context. A student whose miscue is a word that *does not make sense in the passage* is not using context clues.

The Student Reading Interview

Another way of assessing use of context is to ask the student about word recognition strategies. When we ask "How do you figure out a word you don't know?" many poor readers' only response is "sound it out." On the other hand, students who say that they reread or think about the meaning of the text are aware of how context can help in word recognition.

Comparison of Words Recognized in Lists and Passages

A third way to assess use of context is to contrast a student's ability to recognize a set of words (1) in isolation (or list form) and (2) in a passage. Students who can pronounce more words in a passage than a list are showing that they use context clues.

To construct this assessment, choose a passage at a student's instructional level and identify twenty words. First, ask the student to read these words in list form. Then ask the student to read the passage orally. For both readings, keep track of the number of targeted words read correctly. Students who recognize significantly more words in the passage than on the list are making good use of context clues. Some IRIs, such as *The Qualitative Reading Inventory II* (Leslie & Caldwell, 1995) and the one in Appendix C of this book, construct their word lists from the words that appear in the passages.

Teaching Context Clues

As we emphasize throughout this book, learning to recognize words is best done in the context of actual reading. If students with reading problems consistently read stories and books, they often naturally learn to make use of context clues.

However, some students need further instruction with strategies that focus attention on using context. In this section we discuss suitable strategies. In the next section, when we discuss phonics clues, we present activities for combining phonics and context.

Encouraging Students to Monitor for Meaning

Low-achieving students do not always demand meaning from reading. Often they continue reading long after the material has ceased to make sense to them. In fact, most of us have, from time to time, become aware that our eyes have been moving over the words, but we have no idea of what they mean. What do we do? As good readers, we know that the purpose of reading is to gain meaning, so we stop and reread. Students with reading problems, on the other hand, may finish an entire selection, proud for having "got the words right," but with no understanding of what they have read.

Thus, activities that focus on use of context clues should reinforce the idea that reading should make sense. To encourage monitoring for meaning, have students stop periodically as they read and ask themselves four questions: Did what I just read make sense to me? Can I retell it in my own words? Are there any words that I do not understand? Are there any sentences that are confusing to me? Students can remind themselves to do this by making bookmarks that display these questions. The teacher can also place brightly colored, removable dots in the margin at regular intervals throughout a reading as reminders for students to stop and ask themselves these questions.

Using the Cloze Technique

Cloze refers to rewriting a passage with words deleted and asking students to fill in missing words. Students can write the missing words or supply them orally. The zoo passage we gave is an example of a cloze passage. In supplying words, students practice working with context clues.

In constructing a cloze exercise, simply delete words from a passage. You can retype the passage, or just "blacken" the words out with a magic marker. Which words should you delete? For general practice, try deleting every tenth word. Students will not be able to supply *all* the missing words, but they will get general practice in using meaning to read. Cloze can also be used to help students focus on certain types of words. For example, you might choose to delete only adjectives or connectives (*and, but, unless*). You might even choose to delete parts of words, such as word endings.

There are also several options for how students can respond. You may provide choices for the deleted words or ask the students to write in, or say, the word that they think fits. Students may work alone or cooperatively to supply the words. If students write words into the passages, accept their spellings, even if they are incorrect.

Remember that, as students fill in the blanks of a cloze exercise, they are not really *guessing.* Instead, they are *hypothesizing,* based upon their knowledge of the world around them, the content of the passage, and their knowledge of English. It is important to remind students that they are consciously using these clues to predict words.

After students are finished filling in a cloze, go over the exercise and have them explain the reasons for their choices. Often this discussion demonstrates how class members used context clues, making everyone more aware of this process.

Assessing Phonics Clues

Phonics refers to the relationship between letters and sounds in our language. When combined with context clues, phonics provides a powerful tool for word recognition.

Perhaps no area in reading instruction has caused as much controversy as phonics instruction. Some people see it as a cure-all for the ills of education (Flesch, 1979); others take a less extreme view, believing it is merely very important (Anderson et al., 1985; Chall, 1967, 1979, 1983a). Still others oppose direct phonics instruction, contending instead that wide reading will allow children to internalize key letter–sound matches (Goodman, 1979).

Unfortunately, past instruction has given phonics a bad reputation. Children with reading problems filled out numerous phonics worksheets and were often ceaselessly "skilled and drilled" at the expense of reading and enjoying meaningful text. Such overconcentration on isolated phonics drills robbed students of precious instructional time to do the actual reading that would teach them to apply their phonics. As a result, many children confused filling out skill sheets with real reading. We know many poor readers who have spent years with phonics workbooks still cannot use phonics to help them read.

Our view is that students who can use phonics abilities *while they are reading* have a valuable set of strategies. Direct instruction in letter–sound matching can be extremely helpful for low-achieving readers. In the following section, we provide suggestions for assessing a student's knowledge and use of phonics clues.

Miscue Analysis

As we discussed in Chapter 3, miscue analysis can provide insight into a student's use of phonics. Analyzing miscues can tell you (1) whether a student knows and applies phonics in reading and (2) which particular letter–sound patterns the student can use. If a student's miscue contains the same sounds as the correct word, that student is using some phonics clues to read. For example, Chrissy read "the children were going on a trip" as "the chicken were going on a top." This shows that she knows, and uses, the sounds of *ch, short e, n, t,* and *p,* but may need instruction in the sounds of *short i, l, d,* and *tr.* A teacher would need to confirm this knowledge, however, by listening to Chrissy read an entire passage.

Miscue analysis allows you to assess how students use phonics as they are actually reading. In this way, you can see how their use of phonics clues interacts with their use of context and structural analysis. However, in miscue analysis you are limited to an analysis of the words in the passage. To obtain a better overview, you can combine miscue analysis with a more systematic test of phonics principles.

Tests of Phonics Principles

Another way to assess knowledge of phonics principles is to construct a list of *nonsense words* (or *pseudowords*) that contain important sound–symbol relationships. Since these "words" cannot be known by sight, the student must use phonics to decode them. An informal phonics test using pseudowords is given in Table 6.5 (at the end of this chapter). Although this assessment provides a precise assessment of phonics knowledge, it is important to remember that nonsense words are not an *authentic* assessment of phonics, since such words do not appear in real-life reading. In addition, some young children may be reluctant to pronounce nonsense words and may simply make real words out of them. For these reasons, it is important to use a pseudoword assessment together with a miscue analysis. Finally, when analyzing phonics knowledge, remember that students with reading problems are somewhat inconsistent in their knowledge. For this reason, you may need to review patterns that you thought your students had already mastered.

Teaching Phonics Clues

Teachers have many important decisions to make about teaching phonics. In this section, we present instructional options and specific methods for helping students with reading problems to use phonics as a tool in recognizing words.

Presenting Patterns and Rules

Basic ways to organize phonics instruction for your students include (1) teaching phonograms, and (2) teaching important principles or generalizations.

Phonograms.
You may want to organize your instruction around the teaching of phonograms, or word families, such as *pin*, *win*, *tin* or *hop*, *stop*, *mop*. A phonogram pattern is made up of a vowel and following consonant (or consonants). Children seem to learn word families easily and naturally (Adams, 1990; Moustafa, 1993; Stahl, 1992). In addition, phonogram patterns are more regular than many phonics generalizations. Table 6.1 lists common phonograms.

To decide which phonograms to teach to your students, look at their pattern of miscues. Also examine the words in books for beginning readers. Many of these words illustrate common phonograms, and teaching a phonogram in combination with a book helps youngsters to realize that phonics helps us gain meaning from text.

Table 6.1   Common Phonograms

ad, ag, an, ap, at, aw, ay, ack, ail, ain, air, ake, ale, all, ame, and, ang, ank, are, ash, ast, ate, ave
ed, en, et, ear (bear and dear), each, eal, eep, eet, eck, end, ent, ess, est
id, in, ip, it, ick, ide, ike, ile, ill, ine, ink, ire, ish, ight
op, ot, ow (how and blow), oy, oat, ock, oin, oil, oke, old, ole, one, ong, ook, oom, ore, oast
ug, ue, un, uck, ull, ure, use

Phonics Principles.
A second option for phonics instruction is to teach important principles or generalizations. An example of a phonics principle is that a silent *e* at the end of a one-syllable word makes the preceding vowel long (as in *cane* and *stone*). Some important generalizations have been identified as extremely useful for children to learn (Clymer, 1963). Table 6.4, at the end of this chapter, lists these in approximate order of difficulty.

Choosing the Teaching Sequence

Good phonics instruction involves learning *both* by a *focus on words* and *application in reading*. Therefore, if you start with a phonogram or a phonics principle (focus on words), you next need to practice this in reading (application in reading). On the other hand, if you start by having students read (application in reading), you next need to focus attention on phonograms or principles (focus on words).

Starting with Phonograms.

If you are using phonograms (or word families) as the basis of instruction, you will want to choose a word family and several example words (see Table 6.1). If you choose the *at* family, for example, you might use *at*, *fat*, *rat*, and *sat*. We often start by having children arrange letters to make different words. To provide manipulatives, write each letter on a card or use magnetic letters. If you are using a full set of alphabet letters, arrange them in alphabetical order, so that students can find them easily.

Select your word family and then ask your students to pronounce (or make) different words containing the chosen phonogram. You might first ask the student to make *at*, then perhaps *rat*, and then *sat*. As children manipulate these patterns, they learn important vowel and consonant correspondences. Remember, however, that students will need to have the emergent literacy skill of rhyming to do this (see Chapter 5).

Taking a phonogram such as *ill* and building new words, such as *hill*, *pill*, *gill*, *silly*, *miller*, and *million*, helps students to extend phonics knowledge past the beginning stages and into more advanced words. Many different word families can be used in two and three syllable words.

To provide application in reading and writing, you might ask children to make up sentences with these words or to write the words in a word journal. Further application in reading can be provided by easy children's books that concentrate on phonograms (see Appendix B).

Starting with Phonics Principles.

If you are teaching a phonics principle, introduce the generalization, and then use several words to illustrate it. For example, to show how a final *e* changes the short *a* sound to a long *a*, use words such as *cap*, *cape*, *mad*, *made*, and *rat*, *rate*. After some work with single words, have your student read materials that contain these word patterns. A last and very important step in learning a phonics principle is applying it in general reading material, such as stories, novels, and textbooks (see Appendix B and chapter section "Reading Books with Regular Phonics Patterns").

Starting with Words from Reading.

It is also an excellent idea to start phonics instruction with *reading* by choosing words that students could not pronounce in their texts (Harp, 1989). Words that children have difficulty writing are also excellent choices. Choosing words from reading and writing helps low-achieving readers connect phonics to meaning.

If, during oral reading, students come to a word they do not know, tell them the word and mark it in your book. After the story has been read and enjoyed, you can return to the problem words and use them to teach phonics clues. If children are reading silently, you can ask them to identify words that gave them trouble.

Wilson (1988) suggests the "Brain Power Word" strategy for students working in groups. Either before or after reading a story, each student selects two to three words that he or she thinks are important for everyone to know. The students write these words on cards and give them to the teacher, who then pronounces and displays them. Finally, the teacher analyzes the phonics clues that could be used to pronounce these words. For example, if the word *display* were chosen, the teacher might point out the two syllables, including the short vowel used in *dis* and the *ay* pattern used in *play*. "Brain Power Words" are not threatening, since the student does not have to pronounce them and each student chooses words that are important for everyone in the group.

Using Analogies to Teach Phonics

Asking students to memorize phonics principles is not always effective. In fact, research indicates that most people (including students with reading problems) learn phonics, not by memorizing rules, but by recognizing patterns used in similar and known words (Gough & Hillinger, 1980). In other words, we pronounce new words by using known words. This is called decoding by analogy. Suppose you come across a word you have never seen before, such as "tergiversation." How do you manage to pronounce it correctly? You use word elements that you know: *ter* as in "term," the word "giver," and *versation* as in "conversation."

You can teach students with reading problems how to do this. When they meet an unknown word, ask them to think of an analogous one. For example, if the student is unable to decode the word *bay*, you might ask, "Can you think of a word that ends like this word?" If the child can't supply an analogy, you might say, "Think of the word *day*." The use of word families helps students to recognize and use these analogies. At the end of this section, we describe the Benchmark Program (Gaskins & Downer, 1986; Gaskins et al., 1989), which uses analogies to teach phonics.

Combining Phonics Clues and Context Clues

Perhaps because they have had so much difficulty recognizing words, poor readers often confuse phonics with reading. Since they think that reading is simply sounding out words, they need to learn that pronouncing words is only a step toward gaining the author's meaning. As they read, students need constantly to ask themselves "Does this make sense?" They must remember to check whether their pronunciation efforts result in meaning. Of course, this involves combining context clues and phonics. Two strategies to help students use these clue systems together are (1) cross-checking and (2) the four-step procedure.

Cross-Checking.
This variation on a cloze procedure is recommended by Cunningham (1995). The teacher writes a sentence that contains one covered word. To supply this word, students "cross-check" phonics clues with context clues. Teacher and students first read the sentence, saying "blank" for the covered word. Next, the students offer suggestions as to what the missing word might be. All reasonable suggestions are written down where the students can see them. (If a student offers a suggestion that does not fit, the teacher reads the sentence, inserts this word and demonstrates how the sentence does not sound right.) The teacher then uncovers the first letter/s. All words that do not begin with these letter/s are crossed out. Finally the teacher uncovers the entire word and points out that, although many words might fit in the blank, our pronunciation must match the letters chosen by the author.

The Four-Step Strategy.
At a more advanced level, the four-step strategy combines the use of several different clues to recognize words. In this sequence, students learn to use the steps that skilled readers employ when they figure out unknown words. They first use context clues, then phonics,

---

Strategy Snapshot 6.1
• • • • • • • • • • • • • •
Using Cross-Checking

Ms. Tate uses cross-checking with a small group of poor readers to stress that pronunciation should make sense. She presents them with the sentence. "Jane wanted to buy some _____" and asks what words would fit in the blank space. The children's suggestions, including *candy*, *clothes*, *cookies*, *books*, *raisins*, *flowers*, *toys*, *pets*, *shoes*, and *dolls*, are written on the board. When one child suggests *money* and another offers *friend*, Ms. Tate reads the sentence with those words inserted and asks if it makes sense. The children agree that it doesn't. Then Ms. Tate uncovers the first letter which is a *c*. The choices narrow to *candy*, *clothes*, and *cookies*. The children agree that all three make sense and when their teacher uncovers the entire word, they eagerly call out, "candy." Ms. Tate then gives them additional words which also start with *c* (*city*, *children*, *country*, *caps*, *cards*) and asks them if they make sense in the sentence. She reminds children that, when a word is pronounced, they have to check for meaning.

---

and then structural analysis clues. We have found that this sequence is successful in showing baffled readers how to integrate and apply their word recognition skills.

The first step is to explain the strategy and model how to use it for several words. After that, remind students to use it whenever they read. In one fifth-grade reading class, students made a list of all the words they had figured out using the four-step strategy, and how many steps were needed to figure out each word!

The steps are:

1. If you don't know a word in your reading, first reread the sentence and try to figure it out (context clues).
2. If that doesn't work, sound out the first part and reread the sentence (phonics clues).
3. If you still don't know it, look for word endings and try to figure out the base word (structural analysis clues).
4. If you still haven't figured it out, sound out the whole word. Remember you may have to change a few sounds to make the word make sense (phonics clues).

Making Students Aware of Their Strategies

We have presented several strategies to help your students figure out unknown words in print. However, to really master a strategy, your students need to become aware of what they are doing. How can you help them?

First, remember that students need to see strategies modeled many times before they can use them. You can do this by showing them, over and over again, how you use these strategies to figure out unknown words.

You can also display the strategies. To do this, put the strategies on a poster or have each student make a bookmark containing the steps in a strategy. One teacher created a bulletin board entitled "How to Read Words" and put the observations of children on the board. Another teacher placed a large tree branch in a bucket of sand and called it the "thinking tree." As students learned strategies for identifying words, they wrote them on cards and hung them on the thinking tree.

Finally, teachers can ask students to talk about how they use strategies. Helping students periodically to review steps stresses the "how" of phonics instruction. Students can write down their own strategies on "think cards" (see Chapter 4). When students create their own versions of strategies, they personalize what you have taught them. Table 6.2 presents examples of some student think cards.

Table 6.2 **Examples of Student Think Cards**

(These retain original spelling)

Tiffany, grade 3

"When I read a book I use a strategie that strategie is to look at the pictures the pictures help me figure out what I an reading abot. When I use a strategie when I don't know a word frist I sond out the word if I get the word then I use by mackground knowlede of what I know abot the word."

Mark, grade 3

"If I come to a word in a sentence I don't know I think of a word with the same sounds as the word I don't know and see if it make sense. 1. kitchen, kitten, mitten 2. book, cook, hook, look, shook." (dictated to his teacher)

LaTonya, grade 2

"You think of a word you all redy now then you should get the word. Or tack the word in parts. Sound the word out a cople times. Think of a word you now in it. Does the word fit? grump jump"

Dealing with Exceptions

Sooner or later, students will come across words that are exceptions to the phonics rules or patterns that you are teaching. Rather than treating this as a problem, you can use it as an opportunity to make students aware that phonics does not always work.

For example, when you ask for words that have a "silent e," students may suggest *have* and *love,* two words that are exceptions to the rule that the first vowel in the word takes a "long" sound. Write down such exceptions, and tell the students that these words "don't play fair." Low-achieving readers often enjoy making lists of exceptions to use for sight vocabulary instruction. Exceptions also make students aware of the need to combine phonics and context clues.

You can also remind youngsters that a particularly difficult word can be skipped, if they can make sense out of the rest of the reading. If all else fails, students can ask someone for help.

Ideas for Practicing Phonics

To effectively learn phonics, students need to consistently practice letter–sound patterns. Only through extended use can low-achieving students learn to apply phonics quickly and accurately. In this section, we give ideas for ways to practice phonics.

Making Words.

Making Words (Cunningham & Cunningham, 1992; Cunningham & Hall, 1994a,b) involves students in actively thinking about letter–sound patterns as they use letters to make different words. This activity focuses on many different phonics patterns, as children spell different words within a big word. By spelling, they practice creating phonics patterns. At the end of the activity, they can note similarities and differences among the words they have made.

To do the Making Words activity, you choose a word such as *thunder* and identify *all* the words that can be made from it. Make seven cards, each containing one letter in *thunder*. Make larger squares with the same letters for your use at a chalkboard ledge. Now ask the students to make the words that you say. Begin with the shortest words, move gradually to longer words, and finally to the seven letter word *thunder*. The sequence might look like this: *red, Ted, Ned, den, end, her, hut, herd, turn, hunt, hurt, under, hunted, turned,* and *thunder*.

Making Words can be used with an individual or with a group. If you are working in a group, have individual children or pairs form each word. Then, when they have finished, have one student come to the front of the room and arrange your large letter cards into words from memory.

As each word is made, write it on a card. When all the words have been made, you will have a list of words that you can use to sort according to phonics patterns. For example, you might have students sort all of the words (made from *thunder*) that contain *ur, er,* or *ed*. Or you might have students sort into piles the words that contain short vowels and long vowels. Remind students that when they meet a new word or when they need to spell an unknown word, they can use these patterns to help them (Stahl, 1992). We discuss another word sorting activity in Chapter 7.

Using Worksheets.

As you are probably aware, there are many different commercially produced worksheets and phonics books containing exercises for practicing phonics. However, many of the activities used in these materials involve youngsters in relatively passive activities, such as circling words and filling in letters.

Such practices do not lend themselves to the critical application of phonics during real reading, nor do they involve students in thoughtful problem solving activities. In truth, we have seen low-achieving readers complete worksheets by guesswork without even referring to the directions.

If used on an occasional basis, worksheets can provide examples of a phonics pattern and give some independent practice. However, worksheets *cannot* substitute for direct, teacher-led instruction, for having children supply their own examples, or for practicing the use of phonics as students are reading.

Reading Books with Regular Phonics Patterns.

Activities for practicing phonics in isolated words are enjoyable, but they will not allow students with reading problems to master phonics principles. *To master phonics, your students must read, read, read.* Only by getting practice figuring out unknown words while they are reading will students be able to *use* phonics. For this reason, this section and the next focus on materials to help students apply phonics in reading.

Students with problems can profit from using reading materials that are not only meaningful, but also present many phonetically regular words (Anderson et al., 1985). Of course, at times such books can sacrifice good text and an interesting story line in their efforts to include phonetically regular words. Reading "the fat cat sat on a mat" may not particularly excite children who have seen the Indiana Jones movies or Ghostbusters! Fortunately, there are some books using phonetically regular words that are enjoyable for children.

Trachtenberg (1990) has identified tradebooks that repeat different phonics elements. Examples of these follow.

> **Short a**: *The Fat Cat* (by Kent); *There's an Ant in Anthony* (by Most)
>
> **Long a**: *The Paper Crane* (by Bang); *Taste the Raindrops* (by Hines)
>
> **Short and long a:** *Jack and Jake* (by Aliki)
>
> **Short e**: *Elephant in a Well* (by Ets); *The Little Red Hen* (by Galdone)
>
> **Long e:** *Ten Sleepy Sheep* (by Keller); *Have You Seen Trees?* (by Oppenheim)
>
> **Short i:** *Willy the Wimp* (by Browne); *Small Pig* (Lobel)
>
> **Long i:** *The Bike Lesson* (by Berenstain); *If Mice Could Fly* (by Cameron)
>
> **Short o:** *Drummer Hoff* (by Emberely); *Flossie and the Fox* (by McKissack)
>
> **Long o:** *The Giant's Toe* (by Cole); *The Adventures of Mole and Troll* (by Johnston)
>
> **Short u:** *Big Gus and Little Gus* (by Lorenz); *Thump and Plunk* (by Udry)
>
> **Long u:** *The Troll Music* (by Lobel); *"Excuse Me—Certainly!"* (by Slobodkin)

Other series of very easy books built around phonics patterns are given in Appendix B.

Practicing Phonics in General Reading.

Phonics patterns are truly mastered only when students have had a large amount of practice using these patterns to figure out words in their general reading. By general reading, we mean stories, novels, poems, and textbooks that students read everyday, and that are not controlled for phonics patterns. As they use phonics to figure out unknown words in interesting stories and selections, students with reading problems learn that phonics helps them to construct meaning. Ask them to pick out words with phonics patterns they have studied.

Since poems contain many regular words, they can serve as a rich source for phonics practice. In Strategy Snapshot 6.2, we show how one poem acts as a basis for a complete phonics teaching sequence.

Teaching Multisyllabic Words

As children move beyond beginning reading levels, they face the challenge of recognizing increasing numbers of multisyllabic words (words of more than one syllable). Some are relatively easy to pronounce, such as a single-syllable word joined to a common ending (*jumping*, *teacher*) or a compound word (*cowboy*, *airplane*). However, other multisyllabic words (*lilac*, *assisted*, *autograph*) are more complex. Recognizing such words is important because they often carry much of the meaning of a text.

Students with reading problems seem to have particular difficulty with multisyllabic words for several reasons. (1) Many students are simply scared by lengthy words, and refuse even to try them. We have often seen students "freeze" in front of words that contain eight or nine letters. (2) Students forget to combine phonics and context clues when they meet a long word. Unfortunately, many poor readers who have learned to use context for recog-

Strategy Snapshot 6.2
• • • • • • • • • • • • • • •
Using Poetry to Teach Phonics

Mr. Lutz based a phonics lesson on the poem "Recipe for a Hippopotamus Sandwich" (by Silverstein). After he and his students read and discussed its silly story, he asked children for words that sounded alike. As they suggested *make, take, cake; ring, string,* he wrote each on the chalkboard under the headings *ake* and *ing.* Asked for more examples of these patterns, the children came up with and listed (in the proper place) *wake, sing,* and *rake.*

Mr. Lutz asked the children how knowing *ake* and *ing* would help them, getting them to verbalize the fact that they could use these sound patterns to figure out to new words. To demonstrate, Mr. Lutz wrote "I will bring popcorn to the party." He asked them to pretend that they did not know "bring." How could they use the *ing* in the word?

To apply this principles to other phonograms, Mr. Lutz picked out the words *slice* and *bread* from the poem, asking children for other words that contain the sounds of *ice* and *ead,* and creating two more lists of word families. When children offer *led* as a rhyme for *bread,* Mr. Lutz pointed out that words that sound alike can be spelled differently (or are exceptions).

Finally, Mr. Lutz copied the words from the board onto cards, handing some out to each child. As each child held up and read a word card (e.g., *nice*), another child supplied a word with the same phonogram (e.g., *twice*).

nizing single-syllable words revert to only matching letters and sounds when faced with long words. Using a combination of clues is very important for multisyllabic words, because they tend to contain irregular sound patterns; thus, students need to check what they have "sounded out" with the sense of the sentence. (3) Since students with reading problems often have limited meaning vocabularies, they may never have heard a particular long word before. If we have heard a word and know its meaning, being able to pronounce even a few parts may be enough to identify the entire word. However, if a word is not in our meaning vocabulary, we cannot check pronunciation against meaning.

There are several instructional strategies that help poor readers deal with long words.

Collecting Long Words.
In this strategy, we ask students to collect long words that they can read. In doing this they become aware that they can (1) pronounce many long words, and (2) use these long words to figure out words that they do not know (Cunningham, 1995). Having a collection of big words that students know also reduces the threat that such words often pose for low-achieving readers. As they become more comfortable with long words, they become eager to learn more.

To implement this strategy, as students read, ask students to note long words that they find interesting or important. Don't ask them to select unknown words, as this may be threatening. Very often, however, students with reading problems will choose words that they have found difficult. To remember the targeted word, students can check them lightly with a pencil, use page markers or Post-it notes, or write the words on a separate sheet of paper.

Next, put the words on a blackboard and have students discuss them. Observe which other words they bring to mind, where to divide the syllables, and the sentence in the book that contained the word. (This enables the students to combine context and phonics.) If the students cannot figure out the word, help them to work through clues, even if you must pronounce the word for them. In doing this activity, it is important not to overwhelm students or keep them from enjoying reading. We often limit students to two to three very important or interesting words per story.

After discussion, have students put each word on an index card. As the pile of cards gets larger, it becomes a visible reminder that they know many long words.

As this activity proceeds, you may want to make it more complex. For example, students can search for big words that fit into categories, such as describing words (or adjectives) like *astonished* and *overbearing*. Students can also look for synonyms. One class collected *staggered*, *evacuated*, and *advanced* for "moved" and *requested*, *communicated*, and *asserted* for "said." Students can collect words with certain prefixes or suffixes. They can collect big words that all contain the same spelling pattern (*checkered*, *checkerboard*, *rechecked*, *checkbook*, *checkroom*). Within a short time, your students will have over a hundred big words. As they list them, they will acquire comfort with multisyllabic words, as well as a store of known words to use in figuring out unknown words.

Modeling Use of Analogies to Pronounce Long Words.

Good readers often use analogies to decode multisyllabic words, just as they use them to decode one-syllable words. When they meet a multisyllabic word, they match patterns in known words to similar patterns in the new word. A student might pronounce *publisher* by using the known words *tub*, *dish*, and *her*. To do this, however, the reader must know how to break the word into parts by looking for already-known chunks.

To model the use of analogies, take a long word and explain to students the strategies you would use to pronounce it. You might write *The dark clouds portended bad weather* on the board. Then read the sentence and, when you come to *portended*, say something like, "I'm not sure I have ever seen that word before. I will read on and see if the sentence gives me a clue." After finishing the sentence, say "Well, I still don't know the word but I can figure it out. I recognize parts of it. I know *or* so *por* is easy. I know the word *tend* and I can add on the *ed* ending. So this word is *portended*. Now what does it mean?" Read the entire sentence again. "I can use context here. I know about dark clouds and rain so I bet that *portended* means the same as signaled or indicated."

You will need to model the use of analogies many, many times before students become comfortable using it independently. Remember to give students opportunities to pronounce big words by making analogies to words they already know. Strategy Snapshot 6.3 focuses on modeling analogies with two third graders.

Breaking Long Words into Syllables.

In order to use known word parts to pronounce unknown words, students must be able to break long words into syllables. Using analogies with a multisyllabic word will not work if you do not know how to divide that word. However, teaching complex syllabication rules is often ineffective for poor readers (Johnson & Baumann, 1984). It has been our experience that work with phonograms and key words is much more profitable.

Shefelbine (1991) suggests that teachers should work with syllable transformations. Syllable transformations illustrate the important difference between open and closed syllables. Open syllables end in a vowel, which takes the long sound (*she*, *go*). Closed syllables

---

Strategy Snapshot 6.3
• • • • • • • • • • • • • •
Using Analogies to Decode Multisyllabic Words

When she came to a multisyllabic word, Deneese valiantly, but vainly, attempted to match letters and sounds, while Melanie would simply stop and say "I don't know." To help both students, Ms. Katz first identified a list of one-syllable words that each girl knew. Deneese and Melanie grouped these words according to the first vowel, putting *grab, black, snail* on the *a* list; *he, scream treat* on the *e* list; *knife, pig, will* on the *i* list; and so on for *o* and *u*. These words were used as models for long, unknown words.

First the teacher wrote a multisyllabic word, such as *republic*, on the board. The teacher then separated the syllables, forming *re/pub/lic*. Denesee and Melanie searched their word lists for model words that had matching vowel patterns, writing the key words underneath *republic*. The match for *re* was *he*; the match for *pub* was *club*; and the match for *ic* was *tic*. The girls first pronounced the known words (*he, pub,* and *tic*) and then transferred these sounds to the new word (*re, pub, lic*). Finally, Ms. Katz presented *republic* in a sentence and the girls used context to determine its meaning. Later in the semester, Ms. Katz began to ask the girls to try to divide the word into syllables for themselves, using their model words as a guide.

---

end in a consonant, and the vowel is given the short sound (*rub, grab,* and *web*). A transformation lesson demonstrates that a minor change in a word or syllable can alter its pronunciation. For example, the teacher writes *su* and guides the students to read this, giving the vowel the long sound. The teacher then transforms the syllable by adding *f*. The students say *suf*, giving the syllable the short sound. A third transformation is *uf* which takes the short sound. Other combinations that teachers can use include (1) *fab, fa, ab,* (2) *ho, hom, om,* (3) *wi, wim, im* (4) *nep, ne, ep,* and (5) *lu, lub, ub.*

Common syllabication patterns are given in Table 6.6 and an informal test for syllabication abilities is given in Table 6.7. (Both tables are at the end of this chapter.)

The Benchmark Program

One instructional package for teaching word analysis is of outstanding quality. The Benchmark Word Identification/Vocabulary Development Program (Gaskins & Downer, 1986; Gaskins et al., 1989) was constructed for use at the Benchmark School, a facility for students with learning difficulties. The program stresses use of context clues and use of decoding by analogy. It employs both mono- and multisyllabic words almost from the very first lessons. The program, which can be purchased, is extremely detailed and provides scripts for daily lessons.

The Benchmark program teaches decoding by analogy through key spelling patterns. The teacher introduces key words for each common vowel pattern and the students practice these words until they know them as sight words. Examples of key words for *o* patterns are *go, boat, job, clock,* and *long*. The students dictate language experience stories containing the key words and repeatedly read them. Students also write the key words and chant each one letter by letter. The words are displayed prominently in the classroom.

Next, the teacher shows how to use key words to identify unknown words, repeatedly modeling the process of comparing and contrasting an unknown word to a key word. For example, the teacher presents a new word in a sentence such as *Jim opened the present with joy.* Pretending not to know *joy*, the teacher thinks aloud, noting that *joy* looks like the key word *boy. Boy* is written below *joy.* The teacher then uses *boy* to pronounce *joy* by saying, "If boy is *boy*, then *joy* is *joy.* Does *joy* make sense in the sentence?" The teacher models checking to see if it fits the context.

As new key words are introduced, these same basic components are employed. Other lesson activities include rhyme recognition, fitting words into cloze sentences, and sorting words into spelling patterns.

The Benchmark Program can be used with students at many different reading levels, and with individuals or groups. The program maintains an emphasis on meaning while teaching students strategies for pronouncing unknown words. (For information write to Benchmark School, 2107 N. Providence Road, Media, PA 19063.)

Assessing Basic Structural Analysis Clues

When readers use structural analysis clues, they break a word into meaningful parts and use these parts to help them both pronounce the word and understand its meaning. In contrast, low-achieving readers are unaware of how structural elements affect meaning.

Miscue analysis provides information about a student's use of structural analysis clues. For example, students who repeatedly leave off word endings are demonstrating a need for analysis in word parts. In addition, informal discussion can provide much insight into use of structural analysis clues.

For compound words, choose a few (*cowboy, steamboat, railroad*) and ask the students if there is anything unusual about them. Request that they tell you how each little word helps in knowing the meaning of the whole word. Asked about *cowboy,* Andy quickly stated that cowboys were boys that rode horses and shoot guns in the movies but he had no idea where cows fit into the picture!

To assess understanding of the meaning of contractions, write the base word on the board and then add the contraction. For example, write *can*; then under it, write *can't.* Ask the student if the two words are different in meaning. If the student seems unsure, place the contractions in two sentences: *I can write my name. I can't write my name.* If the student cannot verbalize the difference in meaning between the two sentences, target the contraction for instructional focus.

For inflectional endings, write both *bird* and *birds* on the board, asking your student to explain the difference in meaning. If the student is unsure, place the words in two sentences: *I have a bird. I have two birds.* Ask your student to explain the difference in meaning.

Teaching Basic Structural Analysis Clues

Many of the guidelines that we suggest for teaching phonics can also be used to teach basic structural analysis. To help students draw a connection between structural analysis elements and reading, ask students to collect words that contain certain word endings. Focus on meaning by telling students how adding endings changes the sense of a word, but do not concentrate on spelling rules for adding endings or forming contractions.

One activity that we have used successfully is called "Making Words Grow." The students take a one-syllable word and try to make it longer by adding inflectional endings, prefixes, or suffixes, and by forming compound words. The student first writes the base word and then, directly under this word, writes a longer word. The third word is written under the second word. It is important to write the base words exactly under one another, for aligning them in this way allows students to see how additional structural elements change the words. Table 6.3 presents an example of Making Words Grow.

Table 6.3 **Making Words Grow**

jump	camp	work
jumps	camps	works
jumped	camped	worked
jumping	camping	working
jumper	camper	worker
jumpy	campsite	workbook
	campout	workbench
		workman
		workshop
		workable

Students enjoy trying to make lists as long as possible. They often willingly go to the dictionary in order to find additional words! Having students highlight the additions in color also helps to illustrate the structural analysis patterns.

We must add one word of caution with regard to inflectional endings. These may pose a problem for speakers of nonstandard dialects and for bilingual students. Since these students may not use inflections consistently in their speech, they may have trouble reading them. When working with such students, the teacher should point out the meaning signified by the inflections, but not be overly concerned about the student's pronunciation. If the student pronounces *Mary's* as *Mary* when reading orally, no corrections should be made. Rather, make sure that the student understands the meaning of the ending (Labov, 1967). Use the informal assessment procedures that we suggested to determine this.

Summary

Readers use a variety of clues to help them recognize words. The clue system that helps with reading fluency is sight word recognition. Three clue systems—context, phonics, and structural analysis—help readers to recognize words accurately. When readers use context clues, they use the meaning of the passage to identify words. Phonics clues help readers match letters and sounds. Structural analysis clues include compound words, contractions, word endings, and prefixes and suffixes.

A teacher can assess use of context by analyzing miscues, interviewing students, and comparing a student's ability to read words in a list with the same words in a passage. The teacher can foster use of context by encouraging students to monitor for meaning as they read. Using cloze passages is also helpful.

Assessment of phonics can also involve miscue analysis. Using pseudo words or nonsense words that illustrate phonics principles is another assessment strategy. Teachers can present phonics instruction using either phonograms or phonics principles.

Effective phonics instruction involves both a focus on words and application in reading. Teachers shouzld model decoding by analogy, or recognizing unfamiliar words by using known words. The combined use of phonics and context can be promoted by cross-checking and a four-step strategy. Students should be made aware of the strategies that they use and be taught to deal with exceptions. Activities for providing practice in phonics include making words to illustrate common patterns, reading books with regular phonics patterns, and, most important, extensive reading.

Phonics instruction should also focus on helping students deal with long words. Students can make long word collections, continue using the analogy strategy, or use "transformations."

Informal evaluation is an effective assessment for basic structural analysis clues. Teachers can teach these clues using the "Making Words Grow" strategy.

Table 6.4   **Useful Phonics Generalizations**

Useful Phonics Generalizations

1. *Single Consonants:* Reading grade level 1
Generally, consonants are dependable in sound. They include *b, d, f, h, j, k, l, m, n, p, r, s, t, v, w, x, y,* and *z. C* and *g* have two common sounds (see item 7).

2. *Consonant Digraphs:* Reading grade level 1
These refer to two consonants that, when together, make one sound. Common digraph are *sh, ch, ck, ph,* and *th* (as in *thy* and *thigh*). *Qu* is sometimes considered a digraph.

3. *Consonant Blends:* Reading grade level 2
These are two or three consonants blended together for pronunciation. Beginning blends include *st, gr, cl, sp, pl, tr, br, dr, bl, fr, fl, pr, cr, sl, sw, gl, str.* Ending blends include *nd, nk, nt, lk, ld, rt, nk, rm, rd, rn, mp, ft, lt, ct, pt, lm.*

4. *Single Vowels, Long and Short Vowels:* Reading grade levels 2–3
Long vowels are sometimes called "free" or "glided" forms. Short vowels are called "checked" or "unglided." Examples are:

Vowel	Short Sound	Long Sound
a	apple	pane
e	egg	teeth
i	igloo	ice
o	pot	home
u	run	use, tuba

Long vowels occur (a) when a vowel is followed by a consonant and an *e*, the *e* is usually silent (e.g., *rate*), and (b) when a vowel ends a word or syllable (e.g., *be, begin*). Short vowels occur when a single vowel is followed by one or more consonants (e.g., *rat*). Words like *rate* are often contrasted to pairs such as *rat*.

5. *"R"-Controlled Vowels:* Reading grade levels 2–3
These include *ar* (car), *er* (her), *ir* (stir), *or* (for), *ur* (fur). Note that *er, ir,* and *ur* sound alike.

6. *Vowel Combinations:* Reading grade levels 2–3
Dependable combinations include *oa* (boat), *ai* (raise), *ee* (bee), *oi* (boil), *aw* (saw), *ay* (say), *ew* (blew), *ou* (loud). Less dependable combinations are *ea* (seat, bear), *ow* (cloud, low), *oo* (boot, look).

7. *Hard and Soft "C" and "G":* Reading grade level 3
Hard and soft sounds are

Letter	Soft Sound	Hard Sound
c	city	cut
g	general	gold

Generally, soft sounds are followed by *e, i,* and *y.* Hard sounds occur elsewhere. These principles are more dependable for *c* than for *g.*

8. *Silent Letters:* Reading grade levels 3–4
When consonant combinations cannot be pronounced together, the second is *usually* pronounced (as in *know* and *would*). However, when the second consonant is *h,* the first consonant is pronounced (as in *ghost*).

Table 6.5   Words for Testing Phonics Generalizations

These nonsense "words" can be used to test phonics mastery. They should be typed in a large typeface or printed neatly and presented in a list format or on individual cards. Students should be warned that they are not real words, when asked to pronounce them.

1. Single Consonants			*2. Consonant Digraphs*	
bam	fep	dif	shap	chep
dup	jit	hak	thip	quen
sut	rez	jer	nack	

3. Consonant Blends			*4. Single Vowels: Long and Short*		
sput	streb	pind	mab	sote	vo
crob	plut	gart	mabe	lib	vom
flug	grat	rupt	sot	lib	
dreb					

5. "R"-Controlled Vowels		*6. Vowel Combinations*		
dar	tor	toat	doil	geet
set	snir	vay	roub	rood
		zew		

7. Hard and Soft "C" and "G"			*8. Silent Letters*	
cit	cam	gast	knas	wret
cyle	ges		gnip	ghes

Table 6.6   Syllabication Guidelines

1. In a compound word, each small word is usually a syllable (e.g., cow-boy).

2. Structural word parts are usually syllables (e.g., re-wind, slow-ly).

3. Vowel combinations and "r"-controlled vowels usually retain their own sounds (e.g., taw-dry).

4. When a single vowel occurs in a multisyllable word:
   a. If it is followed by two consonants, it is generally given its short sound. This pattern may be referred to as VCC: "lit/tle," "ap/ple," "res/cue," "pic/nic." Teach this rule first with double consonants ("lit/tle," "ap/ple"). Then teach different middle consonants ("res/cue," "pic/nic").
   b. If it is followed by only one consonant, (1) the vowel may have its long sound (VCV, as in "li/lac," "tu/ba," "so/lace"), or (2) the vowel may have its short sound (VCV as in "ben/efit," "sev/eral," "mim/ic"). Students should try the long sound first, then the short sound.

5. The letters "le" at the end of a word are pronounced as in "rattle."

Table 6.7   **Informal Test for Syllabication Abilities**

Students may be asked both to divide these words into syllables using paper and pencil and to pronounce them.

1. Compound Words
playdog
freeday

2. Structural Word Parts
stipment
gaiter
repainly

3. Vowel Combinations
tainest
bayter
stirler

4a. Vowel Followed by One Consonant
waman
sowel
fomub
setin

4b. Vowel Followed by Consonants
mattel
fuddot
sandot
dembin

5. "Le" Combinations
rettle
sontle

CHAPTER 7

Improving Word Recognition Fluency

Introduction

In Chapter 6, we discussed word recognition accuracy. In this chapter, we continue our discussion of word recognition by focusing on fluency. Fluency refers to the instantaneous, automatic recognition of words in reading. Words that we read automatically are often called *sight words*. Readers who have an extensive sight vocabulary are able to read accurately, quickly, and with expression (Wilson, 1988).

In this chapter, we first explain the importance of sight vocabulary and fluency. Next, we give methods of assessment. Then, most of this chapter centers around instructional strategies for contextual fluency and the recognition of sight words. The chapter concludes with a description of several programs for developing word recognition.

The Role of Fluency in the Reading Process

Sight words are those words that are recognized in print immediately, without any analysis. Knowing a large number of sight words enables us to read fluently in context. Fluent reading and comprehension work together as students absorb material and read it to others. Most good readers recognize almost all words automatically (LaBerge & Samuels, 1974; Samuels, 1988). Hence they can devote their energies to the meaning of what they are reading.

However, many students with reading problems have difficulty reading fluently. Often, since they do not possess an adequate sight vocabulary, they must labor to decode many of the words in their text. Their oral reading is filled with long pauses, constant repetitions, and monotonous expression. Since their energies are focused on recognizing words, little comprehension occurs.

Students with reading problems need much reading practice if they are to achieve fluent word recognition. Unfortunately, many low-achieving readers do not enjoy reading and avoid it as much as possible. Because they do not read extensively, they cannot develop a good sight vocabulary. In turn, lack of sight vocabulary makes reading more difficult. Thus a vicious cycle develops (Stanovich, 1986). To avoid this negative cycle, we will offer many ideas for making reading an enjoyable, positive experience.

Assessing Word Recognition Fluency

Ways to assess fluency include (1) listening to students read orally, (2) determining reading rate, and (3) timed administration of word lists. All three can be part of the administration of an informal reading inventory. However, the teacher can use these assessment procedures with any text or word list.

Listening to Students Read Orally

A teacher can determine whether or not students are fluent readers simply by listening to their oral reading. Wilson (1988) identifies three problems with fluency.

1. In *choppy reading,* students stumble over words, repeat them, and pause. They treat the text as if it were a list of words.

2. In *monotonous* reading, there is little expression or variation in the rise and fall of a reader's voice. Low-achieving readers who have finally achieved some word recognition proficiency often read in this way. Their lack of expression suggests that they still regard reading as merely pronouncing words.

3. In *inappropriately hasty* reading, students race through the text, ignoring punctuation and sentence breaks. Their goal seems to be to get through the text as quickly as possible, hence they make errors even on familiar words.

Many students with reading problems have a combination of these problems, since fluent reading demands that accuracy, automaticity, and expression work together.

To judge a student's fluency, simply listen to him or her read a text at an instructional or independent level. Using your own common sense and the guidelines given by Wilson (1988), you can determine whether the reading is fluent. You may want to compare audiotapes of a student's reading made at different times to assess improvement. Students often find it motivating to listen to their own tapes. Josh reviewed tapes of his oral reading done at the beginning and end of the semester. He frowned and actually put his head down on the desk as he listened to his first halting and choppy rendition. But when he heard himself reading the same passage several months later, he broke into smiles. In his journal, he wrote, "I sounded real real REAL good!"

Determining Reading Rate

Reading rate in passages is a good indication of fluency. Have the student read a selection at his or her instructional or independent level. As the student reads orally or silently, time the reading, and then calculate words per minute (WPM). To do this, multiply the number of words in the passage by 60 and then divide by the number of seconds it took to read the passage. Table 3.12 (page 63) gives a list of acceptable rates for students reading passages at different levels.

A student's reading rate must be interpreted with some caution. Normal readers show a wide range of acceptable reading rates, even at the same grade level (Carver, 1990). Because of this variability, we recommend that you not compare the rates of individual students with each other. Reading rate also varies across different selections. Most people, for example, read movie reviews faster than they read editorials. Finally, remember that a student can read at an appropriate rate, but still lack expression.

Timed Administration of Word Lists

While our previous two strategies enable us to judge contextual fluency, the timed administration of word lists is used to judge automatic sight *word* recognition. To do this, compare (1) *automatic* recognition (or timed) of isolated words with (2) *total* recognition (or timed plus untimed) of isolated words (both automatic words and those recognized after analysis).

To judge automaticity, give the student a list of words to recognize (such as the ones in the IRI in Appendix C or in Tables 7.2 and 7.3). As the student reads, record performance on a teacher's copy. For each word in the list there are three possible responses: (1) sight or automatic recognition, (2) recognized after hesitation or analysis, and (3) not identified correctly. A word pronounced correctly within one second is marked as an automatic word.

(To judge one second, say to yourself "one thousand." If the student pronounces the word before you are finished, count the word as automatic.) A word recognized correctly, but not automatically, is an analysis word. And, of course, a word recognized incorrectly is unknown.

To compare a student's instantaneous word recognition, compare:

1. Automatic words and
2. Total words known (automatic words plus analysis words).

If a student's total number of words is much larger than the automatic words, the student needs to practice instant recognition of sight words.

Timed administration of word lists can be helpful for assessing sight words; however, remember that reading words in lists is not real reading. (In real life, we do not curl up with a good list of words!) For this reason, your assessment of a student's performance should combine word-list performance with the reading of selections.

Strategies for Developing Fluency in Context

This section describes strategies for improving the ability to read passages with fluency.

Promoting Wide Reading of Easy Text

A large amount of reading is critical to developing fluent reading. As students read to enjoy a story or acquire interesting information, they are unconsciously improving their reading fluency. In addition, they become comfortable with combining all word identification clues to read in context.

Getting students with reading problems to read is a major challenge for their teachers. To do this, teachers must make reading enjoyable, provide regular and daily opportunities to read, and encourage reading at home. To build fluency, students need to read easy books filled with words they can recognize. Teachers should schedule time for reading. Begin by setting aside periods of about 10 minutes, since low-achieving students have difficulty concentrating during long sessions. Then these periods can be gradually increased to 20 or 25 minutes.

It is not always easy for low-achieving readers to choose a book that will foster accurate and fluent word recognition. Students with problems generally select material that is too hard, or they flit from book to book without really reading any of them. To foster better choices, you can read easy books to students and then prominently display the books in your classroom. We find that students often choose these books to read on their own. You can also give the student several books and ask that he or she choose from among them. Or, you can allow the student to reread books or stories from past lessons.

Using Predictable Books

Predictable books, which contain refrains that are repeated over and over, are an excellent source of easy books (see also Chapter 5). Predictable books are invaluable for fostering word recognition because the repeated refrains in the books provide extensive support for word recognition. Since many predictable books are based on classic tales, their rich content interests and motivates children (Holdaway, 1979).

Some predictable books are published in the trade book market, that is, they are intended as children's literature. Table 7.1 presents a list of predictable trade books.

A second type of predictable books is designed to be used in instruction. These books are finely graded into many levels, starting with the reading of pictures. Popular series of predictable books include *The Storybox* and *Sunshine Books* (Wright Company), *Ready to Read* (Richard C. Owens Company), *Traditional Tales* and *City Kids* (Rigby Company). *Mrs. Wishy Washy,* shown in Figure 7.1, is an example of a predictable instructional book from *The Story Box*. Although most of these books tell stories (or are narratives) these companies also publish some excellent informational (or expository) predictable books, including *Infomazing* and *Planet Earth* (Rigby). *Literacy 2000* (Rigby) contains selections of many types of predictable books.

The Reading Recovery program (Pinnell, 1989; Pinnell, Fried, & Estice, 1990), an instructional program for first graders, has done extensive work in evaluating the difficulty of predictable books. In their system, books are divided into 20 different levels, all with-

Table 7.1   **Examples of Predictable Books**

Author	*Title and Publisher*
	Very Easy Books—through beginning first grade level
Burningham, J.	*The School* (Thomas Y. Crowell)
Lindgren, B.	*Sam's Ball; Sam's Cookie; Sam's Lamp; Sam's Teddy Bear; Sam's Wagon* (Morrow)
Martin, B.	*Brown Bear, Brown Bear* (Holt Rinehart Winston)
Shaw, C.	*It Looked Like Spilt Milk* (Harper and Row)
Wildsmith, B.	*Cat on the Mat; Toot; All Fall Down, Toot* (Oxford Press)
	Easy—middle first grade level
Brown, M. W.	*Goodnight Moon* (Harper and Row)
Burningham, J.	*The Blanket; The Baby; The Cupboard; The Dog; The Snow* (Thomas Y. Crowell)
Carle, E.	*The Very Busy Spider* (Philomel)
Hutchins. P.	*Rosie's Walk* (Greenwillow), *Titch* (Macmillan)
Kraus, Robert	*Herman the Helper* (Windmill)
Kraus, Ruth	*The Carrot Seed* (Scholastic)
Tolstoy, A.	*The Great Big Enormous Turnip* (Pan)
West, C.	*Have You Seen the Crocodile?, "Pardon?" Said the Giraffe* (Harper and Row)
Wheeler, C.	*Marmalade's Nap; Marmalade's Snowy Day; Rose* (Knopf)
	More Difficult Books—late first grade level and above
Burningham, J.	*Mr. Gumpy's Outing; Mr. Gumpy's Motorcar* (Puffin)
Carle, E.	*The Very Hungry Caterpillar* (Puffin)
Charlip, R.	*Fortunately* (Four Winds Way)
Emberley, E.	*Drummer Hoff* (Prentice Hall)
Galdone, P.	*The Little Red Hen; The Three Bears; The Three Little Pigs* (Scholastic)
Hutchins, P.	*Goodnight Owl; Happy Birthday Sam; The Wind Blew* (Puffin)
Kraus, Robert	*Leo, the Late Bloomer* (Windmill)
Lobel, A.	*Mouse Soup; Mouse Tales; Frog and Toad Are Friends; Frog and Toad Together* (Harper and Row)
Sendak, M.	*Where the Wild Things Are* (Harper and Row)

Adapted from Peterson, 1988

*Although this table divides trade books into only three levels, the categories mirror the twenty levels used by Reading Recovery to categorize books. Very Easy books, listed above, cover levels 1–5; Easy Books cover 6–12; More Difficult Books cover 13–20.

"Oh, lovely mud,"
said the cow,

and she jumped in it.

"Oh, lovely mud,"
said the pig,

and he rolled in it.

FIGURE 7.1
Mrs. Wishy Washy

Mrs. Wishy Washy, by Joy Cowley, Published by The Wright Group, 19201 120th Avenue NE, Bothell, WA 98021

in the first-grade. Level 1 books contain one or two words on each page and a story heavily supported by pictures. In contrast, Level 20 books have several lines of text per page. Table 7.1 gives examples of predictable books that span a range of these levels.

How can teachers use predictable books most effectively? When introducing a predictable book, begin by paging through it with your students, reviewing pictures and predicting the story line. Next, read the book to your children, modeling fluent reading, and perhaps inviting them to join in the refrains. After reading the book once, you might invite students to join you in rereading it. Experiences with joint readings foster confidence and fluency. Then individual students may reread the book with a teacher's help at troublesome points.

Youngsters will probably need (and want) to review predictable books several times to foster fluency. After reading a predictable book, leave it in a conspicuous place so that students will be able to pick it up and look at it. It is important to create an environment rich in these books.

In addition to their use with primary and lower intermediate-grade students, predictable books also appeal to older students who read on primary levels. We often encourage older students to read these books to younger children.

Assisted Reading

In assisted reading, students read material together with a fluent reader. Although there are several different versions of assisted reading, all support the reader who is struggling with fluent word recognition. Most assisted reading strategies can be used with one individual or a group of students.

There are many reasons why assisted reading is an excellent way to develop fluency. (1) The teacher's support makes reading a nonthreatening activity. (2) Because word recognition efforts are supported by a fluent reader, students can pay attention to meaning and actually enjoy the selection! (3) Assisted reading gives a model of fluent reading. Students are exposed to the way that reading should sound, and have a model to work toward. Too many poor readers are exposed to the halting, choppy reading of their peers. (4) Assisted reading gives much practice reading in context. It also motivates students to read more, since, after joint readings, students often read the very same books independently.

Since the eventual goal of assisted reading is to promote independent reading, it is important that the teacher gradually provide less and less support. In the beginning, teachers may simply read to the students, inviting them to participate and say words when they feel comfortable. Or the teacher may begin by reading an entire selection together with the students. Gradually, however, the teacher's role should be reduced, so that students learn that they can read a new book on their own.

Simultaneous Assisted Reading.

In this assisted reading strategy, the teacher simply reads along with the students. The teacher sets the pace and resists the temptation to slow down to the reading rate of the student, who will always lag slightly behind. When a student meets an unfamiliar word, the teacher pronounces it, and they move on. (If a group is reading with the teacher, few involved in the activity will even notice that one student did not know a word!) There will be times when you will notice a drop in volume at a certain word. You can then mark this word as a possible problem and teach it after the reading is finished.

Simultaneous reading can be changed to meet the needs and levels of your students. Sometimes, the teacher may fade out at key words and phrases to assess whether students can identify them independently. At other times, the teacher may have several students read a page together without teacher assistance. Simultaneous assisted reading is most effective when combined with repeated reading of the same book or story. To foster independence, in each subsequent reading, the teacher participates less and less.

Echo Reading.

Modeling oral reading and asking the students to imitate you is another form of assisted reading (Wilson, 1988). The teacher reads a few lines or a page of text to the students, modeling a fluent pace and effective voice expression. The students imitate the teacher's performance or "echo" the text (B. Anderson, 1981). Echo reading works best for short segments of text and is particularly well suited for beginning readers.

Choral Reading.

In choral reading, a group of students practices orally reading a selection together in order to perform it. The students read the entire selection together or different groups read different parts. Because students find choral reading enjoyable, they willingly practice the word recognition that helps them to give a polished performance. Low-achieving readers enjoy this activity because it gives them the satisfaction of delivering a well-rehearsed, expressive rendition. Choral reading is particularly suited to selections, such as poetry, that contain rhythm and rhyme. We will never forget the heartfelt rendition of "Homework Oh Homework," (by Prelutsky, in *The New Kid on the Block*) delivered by three fifth-grade boys in our Reading Center.

Partner Reading.

In partner reading, students read in pairs, usually alternating pages. This provides extensive reading practice for both students. Partner reading can be a effective way to help students with reading problems develop fluency (Stahl & Heubach, 1993). However, since you want the students to experience success, it is important to have them read the material alone a few times before they read it as partners. This avoids the danger of encountering too many unknown words or becoming frustrated. Often we use other forms of assisted reading with a passage before we ask students to read in partners.

There are many ways to match reading partners. Students enjoy choosing their friends as reading partners. At other times, the teacher can pair students who differ in reading abilities.

In our experience, low-achieving readers of similar ability work well as partners if preliminary support has been provided. Pairing two children with reading problems helps each one to realize that he (or she) is not the only one who has problems with words. Student self-esteem increases through the act of helping another. Danny and Peter became fast friends as a result of consistent partner reading. At one point, Danny confided, "Peter didn't know a word and I helped him. He helps me too. When we read together, we are pretty good readers!"

Simultaneous Listening/Reading.

In this assisted strategy, students listen to tape recordings of material while, at the same time, following along with a book. Simultaneous listening/reading has been used successfully with different age levels (Chomsky, 1978). However, we have found that students sometimes do not follow along in the book, preferring to simply enjoy listening to the tape.

The Neurological Impress Method (NIM).

This read-along strategy (Heckelman, 1969), often abbreviated to NIM, involves the teacher and one student reading together. According to Heckelman, students learn by emulating a fluent reading model. We have found NIM to be particularly effective with reading-disabled adolescents.

In NIM, the student and teacher read orally together. We feel that it is best to begin by reading material at the student's independent level, or material that has been read before. Tell your student not to be concerned about reading accuracy, but to try to read fluently, without looking back. In addition, have the student ignore pictures in the text.

At first, the teacher reads slightly louder and faster. As the student gains fluency and confidence, the teacher begins to read more softly and may even start to lag slightly behind the student. However, if the student encounters difficulty, the teacher should rescue the student in a firm manner. When beginning this procedure, teachers should follow the text along with their finger at the pace of the reading. As the student gains confidence, he or she can assume the responsibility for pointing to the words.

Use of this method may improve oral reading very quickly; however, if no improvement has resulted after six sessions, we suggest you stop. Our experience shows that this method works for some students, but not for all. One fifth-grade student, who enjoyed NIM, improved considerably in reading fluency. Another boy, a seventh grader, had a negative reaction, and we discontinued NIM.

Repeated Readings

In the repeated readings strategy, an individual student rereads a short selection until a certain level of word identification accuracy and fluency is attained (Samuels, 1979). As students read the same selection a number of times, they become more accurate, their reading speed increases, and their reading becomes more expressive (Dowhower, 1987; Herman, 1985; Rashotte & Torgesen, 1985).

To begin repeated readings, give the student a passage of 50 to 200 words at an independent or instructional level. Have the student read the selection orally. As your student reads, record the reading speed and any deviations from the text. Next, discuss any word recognition miscues with your student. Then, over a few sessions, have the student practice the selection until he or she feels capable of reading it fluently. Then have the student read the selection orally again as you record time and accuracy. The process is repeated until a certain accuracy or rate score is reached. At this point, the student moves to another reading selection.

Repeated readings is a flexible strategy that can be adapted to different student needs. To provide more extensive assistance, a teacher can read with the student until he or she feels confident enough to read alone. Or, students can be asked to listen to their own tapes to see if they chunked words into meaningful groups and read with expression.

In choosing material for repeated readings, remember that you need something that will hold a student's interest over several rereadings. If a student is passionately interested in snakes, a selection about reptiles is a good choice. Other selections might include humor, lots of action, or poetry. You can also use readings from the student's content area textbooks or novels, for, in addition to improving word recognition, rereading helps the student to learn the material.

Repeated readings can also be adapted for use with a group (Mossburg, 1989). To do this, read a selection to the students while they follow along in their text. Then, before you read the selection a second time, tell the students that they must follow along very carefully, because you are going to stop at certain places, and they must read what comes next. Read the selection a third time, asking students to take the parts of characters in the text. Then have them read the selection again in pairs.

Our experience in using repeated readings shows that students will not become bored, even if they occasionally complain. Sixth-grade Gregg's tutor used repeated reading in combination with assisted reading. Gregg and his tutor worked for several months on one selection, at times reading together or taking turns on different pages. Occasionally, Gregg complained that repeated readings were "boring." But when the tutor one day omitted repeated reading from the lesson, Gregg loudly objected "I want to do it," he claimed, "because I like how I sound at the end!" As this story illustrates, it is wise to pursue repeated readings on a consistent basis, and not let occasional student complaints turn you away from a powerful technique for developing reading fluency.

The Language Experience Approach

In the language experience approach, students compose personal stories, which are then used for reading instruction. Generally students dictate their stories to a teacher, who records them in writing. Stories can also be written and edited on a computer.

Because students have actually produced these stories, they are anxious to read them. In addition, students can see the direct relationship between speech and reading, for language experience stories are "talk written down." Although the language experience approach is used most widely with younger children (see Chapter 5), it is also effective with older students who are at a beginning reading level.

Many teachers make permanent records of language experience stories. For an individual student, the stories may be printed or typed and collected in a notebook. For groups, the stories may be duplicated so that each student has a copy.

To be most effective, language experience stories should be about experiences that are exciting and of personal interest. A recent firsthand experience such as an unusual event or an exciting television program provides the opportunity to develop a story.

At times, low-achieving students may have some trouble composing stories. Students who encounter this difficulty may be helped to develop stories that they enjoy. Many "wordless" picture books contain amusing stories related without words. Students can "read" and compose captions for such stories. The visual humor in comic strips can also inspire language experience stories. Teachers can eliminate the dialogue "balloons" of the strips, or cut the words out of the strips and have students provide them.

Despite its motivational value, there are some students for whom the language experience approach is not effective. Since stories come directly from fluent oral language, words in a language experience story may accumulate faster than students can learn to read them. Alonzo, one severely disabled thirteen-year-old reader, had to give up learning to read by this approach because his inability to read his own experience stories eventually frustrated him.

Making Oral and Silent Reading Effective

To develop contextual fluency, readers need to have effective and enjoyable oral and silent reading experiences. In this section, we discuss common problems and suggest guidelines for the use of oral and silent reading.

Difficulty Reading Silently.

Since silent reading allows students to process and think independently, it should be used as much as possible with low-achieving students. Despite this guideline, we must admit that students with reading problems often prefer to read orally. As eleven-year-old Jamie often complained, "If I can't read out loud, I don't know what I am reading." There are at least three reasons why students with reading problems tend to avoid silent reading.

1. Beginning readers link reading with oral language, and thus are most comfortable when can they hear what they read. While we must respect the feelings of these beginning readers, we should gently and gradually move students toward silent reading.

2. Many teachers are more comfortable with oral reading because they feel that both they and the students are "doing something." Oral reading also allows teachers to monitor students' word recognition skills. Although some monitoring is valuable, developing independent silent readers is even more valuable.

3. Many poor readers feel that the purpose of reading is to recognize all of the words for a teacher. For these students, reading is a performance rather than an opportunity to learn information or enjoy a story. These students must be convinced that silent reading is an important, adult activity. You might ask them to observe five adult readers to see whether they are reading silently or orally. Such observations generally convince students that silent reading has merit.

Students should be given direct motivation for reading silently. Stress the information or enjoyment that students will gain. If teachers follow silent reading with discussions that focus on the student's personal reactions to the text, students will start to see silent reading as meaningful.

Teachers often ask what to do when students point to words or move their lips as they read silently. Sometimes finger pointing and lip moving can act as an aid that makes halting readers more comfortable. In fact, these actions are normal for primary-grade-level readers. In addition, if reading material is very difficult, individuals of any reading level may revert to using their fingers or lips. However, since finger pointing and lip moving are often signs of frustration, you may check to make sure that the material your students are reading is not too frustrating for them.

If you feel that students need to point their fingers and move their lips in order to feel comfortable, even on easy materials, then it is wise not to interfere with these habits. As students become more fluent readers, these actions will usually disappear.

However if the student simply lip reads or points with a finger from force of habit, these things should be discouraged. First, and most effective, the student can be made aware of the habits, told how they slow readers down, and asked, respectfully, to eliminate them. This simple procedure, plus an occasional reminder, often solves the problem. Finger-pointing can also be eliminated by providing a marker to replace a finger and gradually eliminating the use of the marker. For lip moving, students may be asked to consciously close their lips while reading.

Making Oral Reading Comfortable.

Although silent reading is the preferred mode of reading, oral reading can be an effective way for students to gain reading experience and for the teacher to see how students are dealing with material.

However, students, even those without reading problems, often see oral reading as a negative, performance-oriented experience. College students, telling us about their own schooling, single out oral reading as being stressful and humiliating. They remember quite vividly their feelings of anxiety and shame when they missed a word. One student rather poignantly remarked, "It was only when I did not have to read out loud that I actually began to enjoy reading. Did it have to be that way?" If these are the experiences of successful college students, what must be the experiences of children with reading problems?

There are several ways to make individual oral reading a more positive, meaning-focused experience. (1) Students can practice a selection before being asked to read it in front of their peers. (2) The amount of oral reading should be limited. It is helpful if oral reading serves only a very specific purpose, such as finding information, proving a point, or reading a favorite part. (3) Teachers should remember not to treat oral reading time as a chance to teach phonics. When a student attempts to pronounce an unknown word (and poor readers meet many unfamiliar words), try not to interrupt the reading by saying, "sound it out." The student's repeated attempts to decode the word make him or her, and everyone else reading, lose the meaning of the story. Furthermore, the experience is humiliating.

What should a teacher do if a student doesn't know a word? We suggest that if readers pause or stumble on an important word, the teacher should simply tell them the word and move on. Or the teacher should wait until the end of the sentence and then reread the sentence using the correct pronunciation (Wilson, 1988), at the same time marking the unknown word for later teaching.

Not all mistakes are worth correcting. If a reading mistake involves only a small "function" word (it, the) that does not greatly affect meaning, it should simply be forgotten. By using these guidelines, teachers emphasize that reading is an enjoyable and meaningful experience. This is a crucial understanding for struggling students.

At times, if a student struggles with a word, a peer will laugh or simply call out the correct term. These unkind responses are all too common for low-achieving readers. In fact, poor readers tend to laugh at the errors of other poor readers! You can prevent this by taking a few simple precautions. (1) Never ask children to read alone in front of their peers without practicing first or without providing some support. (2) Teach students to signal when they meet an unfamiliar word (Wilson, 1988). They can tap the book or raise a finger (rather than looking up). If you wish, you can require that the teacher, not the other children, supply the word. (3) Stress that group members are always respectful of each other.

Strategies for Developing Sight Words in Isolation

A sight word is a word recognized instantly, without analysis. How do words become sight words? Each time a reader sees the word *dog* and correctly identifies it, the next recognition of *dog* becomes a little easier and faster. Think of something you learned to do, such as knitting or driving. The early stages were difficult, time-consuming, and often frustrating. But as you practiced, the action became easier and easier, and now you can do it almost automatically, even while thinking about other things. Similarly, each time you accurately identify a word, it becomes easier and easier and, eventually, the word becomes a sight word.

Students with reading problems can best learn to recognize words by reading them in context. However, they may also need additional practice with words in isolation to reinforce automaticity and give them a sense of progress. Practicing individual words is useful for readers at many different levels. A core of sight words enables beginning readers to read easy books and serves as a basis for learning phonics. Reinforcement of sight vocabulary also enables more advanced students to identify the difficult words in their classroom textbooks.

In this section, we first discuss which words should receive additional practice in isolation. Then we suggest some guidelines and strategies for teaching these words.

Choosing Words for Instructional Focus

Lists of frequently used words can help the teacher select words for instructional focus. Table 7.2 shows high-frequency words based on a study of the Dolch Basic Sight Vocabulary, as updated by Johnson (1971). Table 7.3 lists some nouns that can be easily pictured. (These tables are located at the end of this chapter.)

Many high-frequency words are "function words"—words such as *the*, *of*, and *to*. These words, usually articles, prepositions, and pronouns, have little meaning of their own and take on meaning only by acting as connectors for other words. Six-year-old Scott, working on the function words *when* and *then*, sighed and muttered, "These sure aren't fun words like *brontosaurus!*"

Function words are difficult to learn for several reasons. (1) As we have emphasized, they have abstract meanings. (2) They tend to look alike. Words such as *then*, *than*, *when*, *what*, *where*, and *were* are easily confused. (3) Since they tend to have irregular sound/spelling relationships, they often must be mastered as sight words. Because recognition of function words may be particularly troublesome for poor readers, such words deserve special attention. Function words appear so frequently that, if they are not recognized instantly, reading will become uncomfortable and disfluent.

In addition to choosing high-frequency words for teaching, you might select words that are important to your student. At times, these will be the words that appear in a novel your student is reading or are used in the social studies and science texts. At other times, students may want to select words that are important in their lives. Peter, a fourth grader, insisted on learning *Power Rangers*, *tae quon do*, and *karate*.

Guidelines for Teaching Sight Words

Several guidelines will make learning sight words more effective.

Associate Sight Words with Meaning.

This is particularly critical for function words. When readers are simply given word cards and expected to memorize them, learning becomes a rote task that is meaningless. To make this learning more meaningful, have your students write phrases for words on their word cards. For example, they might remember *in* by thinking of the phrase *in the garbage*. Pictures can be cut out, labeled, and placed around the room to illustrate other function words: a can *of* Coke; a fish *in* water; a cat *on* the fence. The students can then be guided to think of the contents of other cans, what else can be *in* water, or *on* a fence.

Practice Sight Words Frequently.

We have already emphasized that words are recognized automatically only after repeated exposures. Practice should include activities both with single words and with reading connected text. Frequent writing, reading, word games, and other word centered activities all provide practice that develops sight word recognition. Poor readers need daily opportunities to read, write, and play with words. Recognizing quickly flashed words also seems to benefit students with reading problems (van den Bosch, van Bon, & Schreuder, 1995).

Keep Records of Progress.

Students with reading problems are motivated by their improvement. Students can keep records or journals of words they have learned. Word banks also can record progress. The one pictured below was made from a shoe box and was used as an alphabetical file for new words. Students can refer to a word bank when they review words, or when they write.

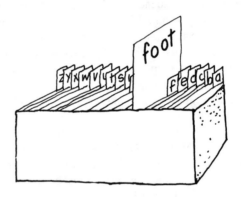

If words are prominently displayed, students will use them more often in their reading and writing. One teacher displayed words on a "word flower," a circle with petals, each one with a sight word. As the student learned more words, petals were added to the flower and, finally, new flowers were created.

Teachers can also demonstrate progress by sorting word cards into three piles: sight words, words that need to be analyzed, and unknown words. Fourth-grade Pat eagerly looked forward to going through his word cards at each lesson. His goal was to get rid of that third pile, unknown words. After each session, Pat filed his three piles separately in a shoe box and took them home for practice. Each time Pat and his teacher went through the cards, he watched the third pile get smaller, giving him visible proof of his improvement. Finally, Pat's third pile disappeared entirely!

Strategies for Focusing on Words

Several strategies provide motivating and important practice in recognizing words. These include word cards, collecting words, word sorts, games, and word walls.

Word Cards.

As we emphasized above, word cards provide one way to practice sight words. The teacher can construct the cards or have the student make them. Word recognition clues, such as a sentence containing the word or a picture illustrating the word, can be placed on the back of the card. Placing collected words on cards is very motivating to poor readers. As the number of word cards increases, they have a concrete reminder of how many words they are learning.

You can use word cards in a variety of ways. Many students enjoy forming sentences from cards. They can also select the word card that correctly fits a missing word in a sentence. Students can collect personal packs of cards to practice at home with a parent or friend.

Collecting Words.

Collecting words that follow certain patterns is another way to practice sight vocabulary. The patterns can emphasize the spelling of a word, its pronunciation, or its meaning. Students can collect words that contain the same letter pattern, such as *cat, bat, sat,* and so on. They can collect words about a favorite topic, such as snake words: *boa, slither, bite,* etc. The collected words are kept in a personal file.

Word Sorts.

In word sorting, students are presented with several words to sort according to different categories. The words are on cards, and the student is asked to sort the words into piles and to give reasons for placing each word in a certain pile.

Strategy Snapshot 7.1
• • • • • • • • • • • • • •
Sorting Words

To start a word sort, Ms. Lessiter gave a group of low-achieving second graders cards containing the words: *sat, mitt, rat, tin, pin, fan,* and *fin.* This was an open sort, and the children chose to sort words by spelling patterns. They first placed the words into four piles: (1) *mitt* (2) *tin, pin, fin* (3) *fan* and (4) *sat, rat.* This sorted the words into the word families *it, in, an, at.* Ms. Lessiter then asked the students to sort into only two piles. The children sorted on the basis of a single vowel, words with an *i* and words with an *a*: (1) *mitt, tin, pin, fin* and (2) *fan, sat, rat.*

Ms. Lessiter then asked the children to sort the words by using the meaning. First, children sorted according to what could be bought. They agreed that a *mitt,* a *pin,* a *fan,* and a *rat* could be bought, and the other words could not. Next they sorted according to what was in their houses. They first decided that all except *sat, fin,* and *rat* could be found in their homes. One of the group members then asked if pet goldfish have *fins.* The children decided they do and placed *fin* in the "home" pile. The group finally sorted according to what they actually owned. The children grouped *mitt* and *pin* together until one student informed the group that she had a *pet rat!* Word sorting was abandoned as the children discussed the joys of such an exciting pet!

The words used for word sorts can come from many sources: words collected by the students, words the students have found difficult, words from textbooks, or spelling words. Words can be sorted according to sound or spelling patterns (Bear, 1994), according to the presence of prefixes or suffixes, or according to meaning. Word sorts are enjoyable and give students with reading problems a sense of control over their language. They also offer valuable experience with letter patterns, sounds, and meanings.

There are two different types of word sorts. In a closed sort, the teacher tells the student how to sort the words. For example, you might tell the student to sort the words *tree*, *run*, *sit*, and *table* by part of speech (nouns and verbs). Closed sorts are often used to practice phonics, since teachers have patterns in mind that they want the students to notice. For example, they might ask students to sort words into *long a* and *short a* piles. In a second type of sort, an open sort, students are free to choose their own categories for sorting. Thus they might choose long words and short words, happy words and sad words, or a phonics pattern. After sorting in one way, students may often want to repeat the sort using other categories.

Sorting words provides many opportunities for students to look at a word and pronounce it accurately. Since low-achieving readers find this gamelike activity both enjoyable and motivating, word sorts can help to increase a student's fund of sight words.

Games.

Games provide another way to practice sight words. They are easily made and can be designed for individual students. One type of game uses a "trailboard" such as that illustrated on page 143.

The game board is made from a 2' x 3' piece of cardboard, laminated or coated with clear adhesive paper for durability. The words to be used are supplied by word cards that are piled on the board, enabling the practice cards to be changed easily. The student rolls dice (or one die), picks up a word from the pile, and moves the number of spaces indicated. If the word can be read correctly, the card is then moved to the bottom of the pack. A few cards, such as "You have been lucky today and may move two spaces," add spice and suspense. These games can be played with a teacher and a student or several students who may wish to practice words independently.

Another game for practicing words is Bingo. Cards are prepared containing the words, and each space is covered as the word is called. If a student (rather than the teacher) calls out the words, the student must then say the word aloud as well as recognize it. Bingo is suitable for group instruction.

Word Walls.

Cunningham (1995) uses a Word Wall for displaying high frequency words and making them easily accessible to the students. A word wall can be placed on a bulletin board or a classroom wall. It is divided into sections for each letter of the alphabet (*a, b, c . . .*). As words are selected for special emphasis, they are placed on the word wall according to their initial letter. These words may be suggested by the teacher or by students. Sometimes they are displayed with a picture or sentence clue; sometimes they are displayed alone. New words are added each week, and sometimes, when a space becomes full, they are taken down. To ensure that you can change words, either attach them on cards or laminate each section for letters (the *a* section, the *b* section) and write words in erasable magic marker.

Students can find, write, spell, and say words from their word wall. The teacher can devise riddles and games using the words. Students or the teacher can compose sentences from words found on the wall. If teachers dictate such a sentence, students then find the missing word. Students can also find all the word walls that, for example, have seven letters, are verbs, or contain an *r*-controlled vowel. In the "I'm thinking of" game, one student gives hints about a particular word on the wall, and the others try to guess it. For example, a student thinking of the word "beautiful" might give the hints that it is an adjective meaning very pretty.

To focus instruction, teachers might want to write words in different colors, using, for example, red for social studies, blue for science, and green for health. Or teachers in resource rooms might assign one color to each of the groups that they see using, for example, green for a 9:30 group and purple for a 10:00 group. Special words, such as function words, might be written in neon marker.

In a very important use, word walls serve as resources for students who have difficulty spelling words. Instead of asking a teacher or struggling for themselves, they simply find the word on the wall. This process reinforces the learning of alphabetical order.

Word walls are an easy way to remind students of important words. A picture of a fourth-grade word wall is shown on page 144.

Mastering Function Words

As we have emphasized, function words, such as *in*, *when*, and *there*, may be particularly troublesome for students with reading problems. The teacher needs to emphasize that context clues can help students to recognize function words. The cloze strategy that we described in Chapter 6 can help to call attention to using context clues. In preparing a cloze passage for function words, simply delete one of every four *function* words from a passage and challenge students to provide these "little" words.

A	B	C	D	E	F	G	H	I
animal awful artful	bird bow beastly	cool cowboy California code comprehension courteous	different D.E.A.R. Dr. Seuss Dr. Mays	extravaganza explorers encyclopedia exaggerate	forget famous flight freedom	Gandhi ghostly glimmer	homespun horrible history	information Indiana iced

J	K	L	M	N	O	P	Q	R
juice juniper	kite kettle	lot lie	Martin mountain Mississippi pronunciation	neighbor notice nevertheless	optioned official outrageous	photosynthesis people Pizza Hut philosophy	queen quizzed	respiratory respect respectful remember

S	T	U	V	W	X	Y	Z	To add:
system Sesame street sullen	tea tattletale Texas telethon too	unknown unicorn unafraid	visa Viking	warrior worry worried wishful	x-ray	yo-yo	zebra	

Highlighting function words in text can also help students to learn them. Teachers can underline words or mark them in "see through" pink, blue, or yellow magic marker. Then ask students to read the text, first silently, and then aloud. Several passages should be used to give students extended practice in recognizing function words over a period of time.

An occasional student with reading problems needs very intensive instruction in function words. Remember that, in this instruction, each function word should be accompanied by a phrase or sentence, since function words contain little meaning by themselves.

If a student finds a few words to be particularly difficult, use the star word approach. Print one word on a large star containing room for little silver stars. Then introduce this as the "star word" of the day. Each time your student says the word correctly, place a little tinsel star on the big star.

Dealing with Reversals

Students with reading problems who are achieving on the first- and second-grade levels tend to reverse certain letters and words while reading. Commonly, they substitute *b* for *d*, *no* for *on*, or *saw* for *was*. In fact, it is not uncommon for emergent and beginning readers to produce backward "mirror writing." Reversals have sometimes been interpreted as a symptom of deep-seated reading problems or even brain dysfunction (Orton, 1937). However, in most cases, reversals simply indicate a lack of experience with literacy. They are seen often in normally achieving children reading at primary-grade levels. In fact, learning-disabled students have been found to make no more reversals than normal readers when both groups of students are reading equally comfortable material (Adams, 1991). Reversals also may occur with teenagers and adults who are just learning to read.

One reason that students make reversals is that reading and writing are the only processes in which symbols change because of their directional orientation. Thus, the only difference between the letters *b* and *d* is that one faces right and the other left. On the other hand, a real-life object, such as a chair or dog, maintains its identify regardless of its orientation in space. A student beginning to read may not yet realize that the orientation of letters and words makes a difference.

When a student with reading problems exhibits reversals, the teacher must decide whether to provide special instruction to eliminate these. If the reversal is only occasional, no special instruction is warranted. If, on the other hand, reversals are frequent and interfere with effective reading, special instruction is needed.

To correct reversals of single letters, concentrate on one letter at a time. For example, to correct a *b*, *d* reversal, first concentrate on *d*. Teachers can make a large chart containing the letter *d*, a memory word (e.g., *dog*), and pictures of words that start with *d*. Accompanying this, several *d* words can be learned by sight. One teacher cut out a 2' by 3' felt *d* and pasted it on a board. The student reinforced the *d* concept by tracing over the letter with a finger. After the concept of *d* has been mastered thoroughly, wait a week before introducing the letter *b*. This "divide and conquer" method is very effective for students with problems. Other methods are:

1. Make flash cards containing confusing words and have students practice recognizing them.
2. Underline the first letter of a confusable word in a bright color, such as red.
3. Have students manipulate letters on a felt or magnetic board to form words that are frequently reversed.

Reversals are further discussed in Chapter 14.

Combining Contextual Reading with a Focus on Words

In this section, we focus on programs that combine several clue systems to help students recognize words.

The Curious George Strategy

The interest created by a captivating book sometimes enables students to read successfully material that is above their previously determined instructional level. A technique we call the "Curious George" strategy has helped children overcome barriers to reading. The method is most useful for small groups of students in the primary grades; it is targeted for those reading between the primer and second-grade levels. Using children's natural enthusiasm for *Curious George* (by Rey) and its sequels and employing many of the techniques described earlier (assisted reading, language experience, and focus on individual words), we have been able to achieve dramatic gains in reading level and enthusiasm.

The "Curious George" strategy has been used informally many times (Richek, 1995; Richek et al., 1989). A documented field study was reported by Richek and McTague (1988). At the end of an eighteen-day period, the experimental Curious George group had, when compared to a control group, increased their comprehension 25 percent and decreased their miscues 65 percent on passages from an informal reading inventory. These differences were statistically significant, and teachers also noticed an increase in enthusiasm for reading and in the ability to write independently. A description of the strategy in action is given below.

In addition to using this strategy with the *Curious George* series, you can use it with the *Clifford the Big Red Dog* (by Bridwell) and the *Harry the Dirty Dog* (by Zion) series. However, the use of a connected series of books is critical to the strategy. Book series are composed of several books that involve the same character or situation. Each book introduces new words, but, more importantly, also repeats words from previous books. The rep-

Strategy Snapshot 7.2

• • • • • • • • • • • • • • •

The *Curious George* Strategy

Instruction was divided into four-day segments of about 30 minutes each. On the *first* day of instruction, the teacher enthusiastically read *Curious George* to the children, while holding the only copy of the book. Next, asking the students to help in reading the book, the teacher and students read together the first 16 pages, in an assisted fashion. Generally, the context enabled students to supply many words and to read with some fluency. Next, there was a focus on individual words. Each child chose five words, and the teacher wrote them on pieces of construction paper. Each child was given a different color. Finally, each child was handed a paperback copy of *Curious George* to take home with his or her five cards, and told to bring the cards and book back the next day.

On the *second* day of instruction, children "showed off" their cards to others, reading them if they could. The teacher then continued with the assisted reading of *Curious George*, pages 17–32. Since they had had the book overnight, the children had generally gained considerable fluency. Next, the children chose five more words, and the teacher wrote them down on individual cards. They again took their personal cards and words home, and were instructed to return them.

On the *third* day of instruction the procedures of the second day were repeated, but the children completed the assisted reading of the book, reading pages 32–48.

On the *fourth* day of instruction, the teacher presented a "book" made from yellow construction paper. Each page contained a picture cut out from a page of *Curious George*. Children took turns dictating the words to accompany the pictures, thus making their own Curious George book.

After completing four days of *Curious George* instruction, the children read sequels, including *Curious George Goes to the Hospital, Curious George Flies a Kite,* and *Curious George Takes a Job,* in the same manner. At first, the process of completing a book took four days, but as children became more confident they took less time.

It is important to let children control their own reading process. For example, at a certain point, some tired of word cards and preferred to spend their time simply reading books. As children moved toward more independent reading, the teacher supplied additional books about Curious George (there are over 30 available). Children also enjoyed writing letters to *Curious George* or writing such personal books as "Curious George and Charita."

etition of words, characters, and situations provides the student with a growing sense of control over reading.

The Multiple-Exposure/Multiple-Context Strategy.

McCormick (1994) describes a method for working with a severely disabled reader involving many exposures to unknown words (Multiple-Exposure) but within a variety of different situations (Multiple-Context). As in the "Curious George" strategy, a series of easy books involving the same characters is used.

The teacher starts instruction using the *Curious George* strategy by reading the story aloud to the children.

The teacher has the student orally read part of the first book in the series, providing and noting the correct pronunciation of inaccurate or unknown words. These unknown words will form the target words presented through multiple exposures and in multiple contexts.

Each lesson has two parts. To extend the student's language abilities, the teacher reads literature selections to the student. In addition, the student practices target words from the book part until they can be pronounced accurately and automatically. To accomplish this, the teacher offers a variety of activities that present the words both in isolation and in context. These include: word cards, matching words to pictures, writing or tracing words, games, reading short sentences, cloze activities, making sentences, and assisted reading. As the student learns the words, the teacher visually demonstrates progress through a chart or graph.

When the target words have been learned, the student reads the first part of the book, and then moves to the next part. The process is repeated as the teacher and student move on to successive books in the series.

Systemwide Improvement Plans for Reading

Two programs, the Reading Recovery Program and Success for All, combine extensive institutional support with effective instruction in word recognition. These two instructional systems provide important clues to the organization and components of effective instruction in reading.

The Reading Recovery Program

This widely implemented and complex program is one of the most successful and influential methods available to deal with students at risk for reading failure (Clay, 1993b; Lyons & Beaver, 1995; Pinnell et al., 1994). Developed in New Zealand by Clay (1993b) and originally distributed in the United States through the Ohio State University (Pinnell, 1989), this program has made a considerable difference in the lives of many children.

The Reading Recovery program provides one-half hour per day of intensive, individual tutoring for first graders who are in the lowest 20 percent of their class. In these lessons, students read easy familiar and unfamiliar books; they write a short story, copy it onto a

HI! WELCOME TO MY READING RECOVERY LESSON

Fluent Writing Practice

Before my 30 minute lesson begins, I get to write some words on the chalkboard. I'm learning to write little important words as fast as I can so I can write them in my stories. It's fun to write on the chalkboard!

Rereading Familiar Books

In every lesson every day I get to read lots of little books. I get to pick some of my favorite stories that I have read before. This is easy for me. I try to read my book like a story and make it sound like people are talking. My teacher says "That's good reading; that's how good readers read."

Taking a Running Record

Now I have to read a book all by myself! My teacher will check on me and won't help me unless I have a hard problem. If I just can't figure out a word or I get all mixed up my teacher will tell me the word or say "Try that again." I read this book yesterday. My teacher helped me work hard to figure out the tricky parts. Now I think I can read it pretty good all by myself!

Letter Identification or Word Analysis (optional)

Sometimes I need to do work on learning about letters or important "chunks" of words. My teacher knows all about the things I need to learn. I like to move the magnetic letters around on the chalkboard; they help me understand what I am learning.

Writing a Story

Every day I get to think up my own story to write in my writing book. I can write lots of the little words all by myself. My teacher likes my stories and helps me work to figure out how to write some of the words. We use boxes and I say the word I want to write slowly so I can hear the sounds and then I write the letters in the boxes all by myself. I like to read my story when I'm done.

Cut-up Sentence

I read the story and my teacher writes it on a long strip of paper. My teacher cuts up my story so I can put it back together. I have to think real hard to get it all back together, then I have to check myself to see if I got it right. Most of the time I do!

New Book Introduced

I like this part of the lesson the best! My teacher picks out a new story just for me and tells me what the story is all about. We look at the pictures and think about what the people and animals say in this book. My teacher also helps me think about some new, important words in my story. Isn't it fun to hear about the story and look at the beautiful pictures before you read it? I think it helps me read the story too!

New Book Attempted

Now it's my turn to work hard again but I like this story and I know my lesson is almost over. When I come to a hard part my teacher will ask me questions to help me think or might show me what I should try to think about or do. My teacher is trying to teach me to do all the things that good readers do. If I have to work real hard on this story we will probably read it again together so I can just think about the story but I'm not sure there is enough time.

Didn't I do lots of work in my lesson today? I hope you learned something too. Bye!

FIGURE 7.2
Reading Recovery Lesson

Mary D. Fried, Columbus Public Schools, The Ohio State University. Reprinted from Sandra McCormick, *Instructing Students Who Have Literacy Problems*, 2nd. Ed. Merrill Press, 1995.

The Cooking Pot, I Am a Bookworm, and *The Seed*, by Joy Cowley. Published by The Wright Group, 19201 120th Avenue NE, Bothell, WA 98021

sentence strip, cut it out, and reassemble it, and they then work with manipulating letters and saying letter sounds. Students are taken through 20 levels of increasingly difficult predictable books, all within the first-grade level. The sequence of a Reading Recovery lesson is given in Figure 7.2. Typically, students stay in the program for twelve to sixteen weeks. At the end of this time, most can read as well as the average student in their class.

Reading Recovery teachers receive a one-year intensive program in instructional techniques and theories, in which they learn how to foster the integration of clue systems in word recognition. Teachers continue to be supervised after training has been completed.

At times, Reading Recovery insights can be adapted to working with older students who are still on beginning reading levels. An adaption called "Reading Rescue" was used by Lee and Neal (1993) to teach a middle-school student who was several years behind.

Success for All

This school-wide program, especially conceived for inner-city environments, has been extremely successful (Slavin et al., 1992). The program involves a school-wide organizational plan in which primary children move to reading groups on their level, where they receive 90 minutes of small-group help. Classroom and special teachers all participate in this instruction, so class size is reduced to about 15. Direct teacher instruction, with *no* "seatwork," consists of language development (reading to students, oral language practice), practicing fluent oral reading, partner reading, reading books containing phonically regular patterns, writing, comprehension, and reading strategy use (Wasik & Slavin, 1993). One-to-one tutoring is used for students in the lowest 25 percent of each school. Parental teams, home reading, and frequent student evaluation provide important support to the program.

Summary

Readers cannot take the time to analyze every word they meet. They must develop a large store of sight vocabulary words, words that they recognize automatically. If we have a large sight vocabulary, we can read fluently. A fluent reader reads accurately, quickly, and with expression. Fluency is an important component of successful reading. If we can recognize words automatically and without analysis, we can pay attention to meaning.

There are three ways to assess fluent reading: listening to students read orally; determining student reading rate measured as words per minute, and timed administration of word lists.

Fluency is best developed as students read connected text. Therefore, teachers must promote wide reading of easy text. The use of predictable books and assisted reading is also effective. In assisted reading, students read material together with a fluent reader, often the teacher. There are various forms of assisted reading: simultaneous assisted reading, echo reading, choral reading, partner reading, simultaneous listening/reading, and the Neurological Impress Method.

Repeated reading is another effective technique for developing fluency; students repeatedly read a text until a desired level of accuracy and fluency is reached.

In the language experience approach, students compose and dictate personal stories which are then used for reading instruction. Students repeatedly read these stories and develop fluency as they do so.

Sight vocabulary can also be developed by focusing on words in isolation. This is particularly important for helping students master high-frequency function words. Students can make word cards, collect words, engage in word sorts, play word games, and construct word walls. Reversals of letters and words are common in all beginning readers, and do not signal neurological problems.

The Curious George Strategy and the Multiple Context/Multiple Exposure Strategy promote the development of fluency within contextual reading. Two successful systemwide programs for reading improvement are Reading Recovery and Success for All.

Table 7.2 **Basic Sight Vocabulary Words**

Preprimer	Primer	First	Second	Third
1. the	45. when	89. many	133. know	177. don't
2. of	46. who	90. before	134. while	178. does
3. and	47. will	91. must	135. last	179. got
4. to	48. more	92. through	136. might	180. united
5. a	49. no	93. back	137. us	181. left
6. in	50. if	94. years	138. great	182. number
7. that	51. out	95. where	139. old	183. course
8. is	52. so	96. much	140. year	184. war
9. was	53. said	97. your	141. off	185. until
10. he	54. what	98. may	142. come	186. always
11. for	55. up	99. well	143. since	187. away
12. it	56. its	100. down	144. against	188. something
13. with	57. about	101. should	145. go	189. fact
14. as	58. into	102. because	146. came	190. through
15. his	59. than	103. each	147. right	191. water
16. on	60. them	104. just	148. used	192. less
17. be	61. can	105. those	149. take	193. public
18. at	62. only	106. people	150. three	194. put.
19. by	63. other	107. Mr.	151. states	195. thing
20. I	64. new	108. how	152. himself	196. almost
21. this	65. some	109. too	153. few	197. hand
22. had	66. could	110. little	154. house	198. enough
23. not	67. time	111. state	155. use	199. far
24. are	68. these	112. good	156. during	200. took
25. but	69. two	113. very	157. without	201. head
26. from	70. may	114. make	158. again	202. yet
27. or	71. then	115. would	159. place	203. government
28. have	72. do	116. still	160. American	204. system
29. an	73. first	117. own	161. around	205. better
30. they	74. any	118. see	162. however	206. set
31. which	75. my	119. men	163. home	207. told
32. one	76. now	120. work	164. small	208. nothing
33. you	77. such	121. long	165. found	209. night
34. were	78. like	122. get	166. Mrs.	210. end
35. her	79. our	123. here	167. thought	211. why
36. all	80. over	124. between	168. went	212. called
37. she	81. man	125. both	169. say	213. didn't
38. there	82. me	126. life	170. part	214. eyes
39. would	83. even	127. being	171. once	215. find
40. their	84. most	128. under	172. general	216. going
41. we	85. made	129. never	173. high	217. look
42. him	86. after	130. day	174. upon	218. asked
43. been	87. also	131. same	175. school	219. later
44. has	88. did	132. another	176. every	220. knew

From Dale D. Johnson, "The Dolch List Reexamined," *The Reading Teacher*, 24 (February 1971), pp. 455–456. The 220 most frequent words in the Kucera-Francis corpus. Reprinted with permission of Dale D. Johnson and the International Reading Association.

Table 7.3   **Picture Sight Words**

1. farm	24. hat	47. garden	70. radio
2. clothes	25. window	48. hand	71. clown
3. money	26. television	49. snow	72. bread
4. water	27. car	50. rain	73. tree
5. grass	28. cookie	51. fire	74. mirror
6. fence	29. apple	52. dish	75. bag
7. stoplight	30. school	53. hair	76. pumpkin
8. bus	31. book	54. children	77. flag
9. balloon	32. chicken	55. lion	78. candle
10. cake	33. nurse	56. world	79. castle
11. duck	34. store	57. watch	80. jewel
12. barn	35. door	58. picture	81. bicycle
13. street	36. doctor	59. shoes	82. baby
14. hill	37. teacher	60. bed	83. sock
15. man	38. egg	61. chair	84. horse
16. house	39. rabbit	62. table	85. ring
17. woman	40. flower	63. spoon	
18. airplane	41. sun	64. fork	
19. train	42. cloud	65. truck	
20. boat	43. shadow	66. bird	
21. dog	44. eye	67. ear	
22. cat	45. mouth	68. skates	
23. telephone	46. nose	69. sled	

Compiled from a survey of widely used basal readers.

CHAPTER 8

Improving Comprehension of Narrative Text

Introduction

Comprehension is the essence of reading; indeed, it is the only purpose for reading. Yet, many low-achieving students are unable to read effectively because they lack critical elements of comprehension. They need to develop strategies that help them become active, competent readers who demand meaning from text.

Focusing on reading comprehension is important, even when a student's primary area of difficulty is word recognition. When students understand what they read, they enjoy it and are motivated to read more. This increased reading results in additional practice in recognizing words. In addition, students who are focused on meaning can use their general understanding of a story to help them recognize difficult words (Anderson, Wilkinson, & Mason 1991).

In this chapter, we describe the general nature of comprehension. We then discuss the comprehension of narrative (or storylike) text, including what it is, how to assess it, and strategies for instruction. The comprehension of expository (or informational) text is addressed in Chapter 9.

General Features of Effective Reading Comprehension

Good readers share subconscious knowledge and attitudes about four important aspects of comprehension.

1. The purpose of reading is comprehension.
2. Comprehension is an active and accurate process.
3. Readers use their background knowledge to comprehend.
4. Comprehension requires higher-level thinking.

The Purpose of Reading Is Comprehension

Good readers know that the purpose of reading is to understand, enjoy, and learn from material. In contrast, students with reading problems often think that reading means recognizing words. Some feel that once they have read all of the words orally, they are finished! To help students with reading problems understand that reading is comprehension you can:

- Always ask students for a comprehension response after they read material. You can use questions, story retellings, or some of the more detailed strategies in this chapter.
- Encourage silent reading. Students who read only orally come to think of reading as a performance. Silent reading helps them to understand that reading is a personal, meaning-focused activity.

Comprehension Is an Active and Accurate Process

As we discussed in Chapter 1, reading is the active construction of meaning. Good readers construct a text in their minds as they read. This text is similar to the text that the author has written, but good readers supply details and draw conclusions not stated in the text. In contrast, problem readers often focus on remembering small details, rather than constructing their own meaning. As a result, low-achieving readers do not monitor their comprehension (Daneman, 1991; Duffy & Roehler, 1987; Paris, Wasik, & Turner, 1991). That is, when they lose the meaning of the material, they do not go back in the text and try to understand. In fact, disabled readers are often unaware that something is wrong. The ability to monitor one's own comprehension and employ "fix-up" strategies is called *metacognitive awareness.*

Reading should be accurate as well as active. Sometimes, when disabled readers come across unfamiliar words, they abandon the actual text and substitute words that have little relation to the text. Some simply construct a story based on just a few words. Teachers can use several strategies to encourage active, yet accurate, reading.

- Interest students in the material before they begin. Tell them what is good or exciting about a story or topic. Discuss the author to show students that stories are written by real people. Draw parallels between the students' lives and the events in a story.
- Remind students to be aware of their own comprehension. If they are lost, they should stop and reread, look at pictures, use context clues to figure out words, or ask for help.

Comprehension Employs the Use of Background Knowledge

Our ability to comprehend is highly dependent on the background knowledge, or schema, we bring to reading (Paris, Wasik, & Turner, 1991). When students understand concepts important to the story, their comprehension increases (Beck, Omanson, & McKeown, 1982; Daneman 1991; Pearson & Fielding, 1991).

Unfortunately, students with reading problems often lack the background knowledge that ensures comprehension. Mike, a fifth grader, read about a boy who found a "skunk," which later turned out to be a mink. Unfortunately, since Mike did not know what minks were, he could not understand that most people had different attitudes toward the two animals. In short, Mike lacked the background information to understand the story.

Since print often deals with more sophisticated concepts than conversation, reading itself helps to build background information needed in school. For example, most of us learned about ancient Greece through school and leisure reading, rather than at the family dinner table. However, since students with reading problems do not read much, they do not learn the many sophisticated concepts needed for success in school (Cunningham & Stanovich, 1993; Snider & Tarver, 1987; Stanovich, 1986).

Even when students with reading problems do have background knowledge, they may not use it effectively (Pace et al., 1989). Some readers underuse their background knowledge and do not summon it to consciousness when they read. Other low-achieving readers overuse their background knowledge (Williams, 1993), letting their personal points of view intrude into their comprehension. To illustrate, Angel, a fourth grader, read a selection about a football game with in which the star player was a girl. Unfortunately, Angel's schema that only boys played football was so strong that he overlooked the information in the text and consistently insisted that *she* was a *he.*

Research shows that increasing students' prior knowledge of a topic improves their reading (Paris, Wasik, & Turner 1991). Many techniques help students to build and use background knowledge:

- Help students build background before they read; gently correct misperceptions.
- If you are teaching in a resource setting, discuss the background knowledge students need to comprehend their regular classroom material.
- Encourage students to modify their own ideas when the text presents new information.

Comprehension Requires Higher-Level Thinking

Higher-level thinking processes are important to story comprehension. Good readers combine their own background information with the information in the text to draw inferences. As they read, they also make predictions, which are confirmed or disproved later in the text. Unfortunately, students with reading problems are often literal readers who do not connect and reason from text in a logical manner. Teachers can foster higher-level comprehension in many ways:

- Ask students inferential and prediction questions, while limiting factual questions. When teachers simply ask more inference questions, students improve in their abilities to draw inferences (Wixson, 1983; Hansen, 1981; Sundbye, 1987).
- Model higher-level thinking skills for students. Low-achieving readers need to see the thought processes underlying skilled comprehension.

Table 8.1 summarizes activities that help to improve students' abilities to comprehend.

Table 8.1   **Activities to Foster Strategic Reading**

Before Reading

Help students relate background information to reading
Build students' background information; gently correct misperceptions
Mention something students might enjoy or learn from the material
Discuss the author

During Reading

Encourage silent reading
Ask students to predict what will happen next
Encourage students to monitor their own comprehension while reading

After Reading

Check comprehension, encouraging active responses
If you ask questions, emphasize higher-level questions and limit literal recall of facts

Comprehending Narrative Materials

Narrative text is one popular and common form of writing. In narratives, stories are told and plots unfold. Narratives have characters and a plot with a sequence of events. While most are fiction (e.g., *Charlotte's Web* by White, *The Cat in the Hat* by Dr. Seuss, "The Three

Little Pigs"), some chronicle real-life events (*My Side of the Mountain,* by George). Narrative text contains some special features.

Narratives Inspire Imaginative Personal Responses

Narratives are written to inspire personal responses (Pearson & Fielding, 1991). Through stories, children and adults leave the limits of their everyday lives and "travel" to the rooftops of London with *Mary Poppins* (by Travers), or to rural Wisconsin in the 1800s in *Little House on the Prairie* (by Wilder). In this way, children learn to represent people, objects, and events in their imagination (Graesser, Golding, & Long, 1991). Thus cognitive growth is fostered by an enjoyable experience.

Good readers become involved in narratives they read. They put themselves in the character's place, asking themselves, "What would I do if I were in this situation?" Students who identify with a character comprehend better and read more (Golden & Guthrie, 1986; Thomson, 1987).

Sadly, some struggling readers have limited experience using their own imaginations and lack these responses to narratives. One group of low-achieving third graders we worked with responded negatively to all types of fiction and anything that seemed unreal. Only after several months of reading and listening to fantasies in books, poems, and stories did they begin to feel comfortable.

To foster personal responses, it is important for students to share their reactions to reading. Adults often do this naturally. Typically, if you tell a friend that you saw a movie, the first question is "Did you like it?" Most children also have strong personal responses to stories, yet teachers rarely ask for their reactions (Gambrell, 1986). When we ask students for personal reactions, we honor their opinions, focus on enjoyment, and raise self-esteem!

To focus on students' personal responses, we often ask students to rate their enjoyment of a story. (We use four ratings: I disliked it. It was OK I liked it. I loved it.) We also ask them if they have anything in common with the story characters or with the situations in a story. When students share responses, they come to realize that others may have differing opinions and experiences.

Narratives Have Story Organization

Narratives are written according to specific forms and include different types, or genres, of materials.

Story Grammar.

Narratives are written according to forms, or "grammars." If you think of a story you read recently, it had characters, a setting, events, and a conclusion. In addition, the characters probably had problems to solve. Students need to be able to:

- Identify important characters
- Identify the setting: time and place
- Recall the major events in proper sequence and separate important events from less important ones
- Identify the problem that the character(s) had to solve and how that problem was resolved

Many narratives also have morals and themes. Fables, for example, are short stories followed by an important moral point. As children mature, they grow in the ability to understand themes and morals.

Good readers implicitly identify story features and use them as a road map to guide their comprehension. In contrast, readers with problems are often unaware of story structure. Research shows that low-achieving students benefit from instruction in story grammar (Idol, 1987; Pearson & Fielding, 1991).

Genres of Narrative Text.

Different varieties of reading materials are called genres. Narrative genres include:

- Realistic fiction, such as tales about children
- Fantasy, including books with talking animals, science fiction, and horror stories
- Fairy tales, folk tales, and tall tales
- Fables
- Mysteries
- Humor, language play
- Historical fiction, set in a period in the past
- Plays
- Narrative poetry, poems that tell stories
- Real-life adventures
- Biographies and autobiographies

To become good readers, students need to gain experience reading many different genres.

Assessing Abilities with Narrative Text

In this section, we give guidelines for measuring general comprehension abilities. These are followed by techniques to help you judge the comprehension of a specific story or book.

Measuring General Comprehension Ability

Many standardized tests of reading contain at least one subtest measuring comprehension. These include the *Woodcock Reading Mastery Test–Revised,* Comprehension Subtest, the *Gates MacGinitie Reading Tests,* and the *Iowa Test of Basic Skills* (see Appendix A). In interpreting these subtests, be aware that a low score on a comprehension subtest does not *always* indicate a comprehension problem. First, a low score on a comprehension subtest may be due to problems with recognizing words in the passage. To check this, look at the student's score on a vocabulary or word recognition subtest from the same general test. If both the vocabulary (or word recognition) subtest and the comprehension subtest are low, it is likely that the student did not recognize the words on the comprehension subtest. In contrast, if the vocabulary (or word recognition) subtest is high, but the comprehension subtest is low, the student's problems are probably specifically related to comprehension.

Second, the actual tasks students are asked to do on comprehension subtests may not reflect what they do in classrooms. For example, in the *Woodcock Reading Mastery Test–Revised* Comprehension Subtest, students read a paragraph orally, and fill in a missing word. In school, however, students must read long stories and answer questions after silent reading. Thus, to interpret test information correctly, it is important to look at the actual items on the test.

One published test, the *Test of Reading Comprehension (TORC)* is specifically designed to measure reading comprehension (see Appendix A). It contains several different subtests, which include vocabulary as well as specific comprehension measures.

Judging the Comprehension of Specific Materials

Can a student effectively comprehend a specific story? In this section, we give two strategies to determine how well a student has comprehended a story: (1) retelling, and (2) questioning. We also describe how these strategies can be used to *improve* comprehension, as well as assess it.

Retelling.

When students retell a story, we gain insight into the text they have constructed in their minds. Retelling shows how a student has mentally organized a selection and what information the student considers important enough to remember. Thus, the teacher observes and analyzes comprehension in action.

To do a retelling, begin by informing the student that he or she will retell a story to you after it is read. Next, ask the student to read the story. When the student has finished, say "Tell me about the story as if you were telling it to a person who had never read it." To avoid undue emphasis on details in a longer story, older students can be asked to summarize rather than to retell.

Do not interrupt as the story is told. When the student has finished, however, you may ask the student to tell more about certain things. This prompting is important for low-achieving readers, since they often know more about a story than they will produce in free recall (Bridge & Tierney, 1981).

Generally, retellings should include:

- the presence of the major character(s)
- the defining characteristics of the characters (good, bad, curious)
- the problem presented by the story
- the solution to that problem (or the end)
- events presented in sequential order
- the ability to include only those events important to the story and exclude unimportant events

Teachers should be aware of some indications that a retelling may be immature:

- referring to all characters as "him," "her," or "they"
- giving a detailed description only of the first page or story segment.

When judging retellings, remember that a student's concept of story structure does not fully mature until the teen years. This means that young students produce unsophisticated retellings.

There is evidence that students who retell stories improve their comprehension (Gambrell, Pfeiffer, & Wilson 1985; Koskinen et al., 1988; Morrow et al., 1986). When teachers give students feedback about their retellings, improvement in comprehension increases, especially for young students.

Asking Questions.

While questioning is perhaps the most common way to assess comprehension, it does have some drawbacks. (1) It does not demand an active response from children. Questions enable teachers to determine whether the student knows what adults consider important to the story. They do not provide information about whether students were able to construct the main events in their own minds. (2) It is difficult to formulate good questions.

If you are going to ask questions, remember the following guidelines:

- Don't spend too much time. Students should not spend more time answering questions than they spent reading a selection! When using questions from a teacher's manual, feel free to eliminate some.
- Do not provide answers to questions as you ask other questions.
- Try to avoid yes/no questions or either/or questions, which have a 50 percent chance of a right answer by guessing.
- Focus on some questions that require long answers; encourage students to explain the reasons for their answers.
- Focus on asking higher-level questions, such as inferences and predictions.
- When one student gives an incorrect answer to a question, work with *that student* to correct that answer, rather than redirecting the question to another student (Crawford, 1989).
- To increase comprehension, students can be encouraged to formulate their own questions (Singer & Donlan, 1982).

Strategies for Improving Comprehension before Reading

The remainder of this chapter focuses on strategies to develop comprehension in narrative text. These strategies are divided according to whether they are used *before, during,* or *after* reading.

In this section, we describe strategies to use before student read. In a classic study, Durkin (1978–9) found that the first part of a reading lesson is the most crucial, yet the most neglected. In this section, we describe three specific activities: (1) building background knowledge; (2) prediction, and (3) reading a selection to students before they read it for themselves.

Building Background Knowledge

Since background knowledge greatly influences comprehension, it is essential to build knowledge of specific concepts in a story before students read it. How can we do this?

Before students read, teachers can provide factual information about key concepts they will meet in a story (Richek & Glick, 1991). Often, teachers can simply read informational material to students. Factual books, such as *The Kids' Question and Answer Book* (edited by *Owl Magazine*), *Mammoth Book of Trivia* (by Meyers), and a children's encyclopedia are good sources for these read-aloud selections. When we read factual material to low-achieving students, we remind them of what they know about a topic and supply them with new facts. We also increase vocabulary, since factual articles mention new vocabulary words that children will meet later in the story they read. Finally, we model the process of summoning up background information before reading.

In one example, before children read "The White Stallion," a story about a heroic horse, a third-grade teacher read aloud a children's encyclopedia article on horses. The article contained unfamiliar facts, and it used words, such as *mare* and *foal*, that the children later found in their story. Objects and displays can also help children absorb background knowledge. In preparation for reading a folk tale about Russia, teachers of at-risk fourth graders brought in Russian nesting dolls, ruble currency, postcards, and books written in Russian.

Students can be actively involved in building their own background knowledge. Rather than simply supplying information, you might begin your lesson by asking them what they know about a subject or topic. Before low-achieving third graders read "The Green Thumb Thief," a story about two child detectives, they listed all of the different detectives they knew about. This dramatically increased their involvement in the story.

Students can also respond actively to information that the teacher presents. For example, to prepare first graders to read a story about a "sleep out," the teacher read *A New True book: Sleeping and Dreaming* (by Milios) to them (Richek & Glick, 1991). Then the students dictated their favorite facts as the teacher listed them on the board.

1. You grow when you sleep
2. Your eyelids flutter when you sleep
3. When you sleep you dream

Predicting and Semantic Impressions

Predicting what a story will be about before they read it gives students an active orientation toward learning and encourages them to use background knowledge. Teachers can simply use prediction or employ a prediction-related strategy called "semantic impressions."

Predicting.

To help students predict, you might list the title of a book or selection on the board and ask students what they think it will be about, or what kind of story it will be. "The Skates of Uncle Richard" will probably involve sports. "How the Duck Learned to Talk to the Pig" probably involves some fantasy.

Students can also predict what a story is about from a list of important story words. For example, after you list the words *witch*, *invisible*, and *wand*, students might hypothesize that the story contains some magic.

Semantic Impressions.

This strategy (McGinley & Denner, 1987) enables children to create their own story, using words that they will later meet in a published story. By writing or dictating their own story, they are actively employing story grammar, using specific vocabulary and drawing on their own background knowledge. Students may write individual stories, or, a class can write a group story.

1. Before children read a story, the teacher writes important words from it on the board in the (approximate) order they appear.
2. Using their own words, students compose a story. The composed stories must use the words in the order that the teacher has given. However, word can be reused. Students may dictate a story to the teacher or write out their own.
3. After the students' story is written, they read the published version of the story and compare the two versions. Often, intermediate and upper grade youngsters like to write about which story they prefer.

In some of our classes, students have become so fond of their stories that they bind them into class books! Two excellent books to use with this strategy are *The Paper Bag Princess* (by Munsch) and, for young children, *Harriet and the Roller Coaster* (by Carlson).

Semantic impressions have been shown to improve comprehension across a wide variety of grade levels, and is particularly effective with low-achieving readers (McGinley & Denner, 1987; Pearson & Fielding, 1991). This valuable method, which can be used with any story or book, encourages students to think like authors and fosters the comparison of stories, a higher-level skill.

Reading a Story to Students

When a story is long or difficult, teachers can read it *to* students before the students read it for themselves. This enables them to learn the story format, sequence of events, and many words in the story before attempting to read independently. Of course, it is important that students later have their own chance to read such stories. Prereading stories to students is particularly effective if they are asked to predict what will happen next as they listen.

Sometimes, simply reading *part* of a story to students is useful. One middle-school teacher reads the first couple of paragraphs of exciting short stories to her students. After their interest has been sparked, students continue to read these stories independently for homework.

Strategies for Improving Comprehension during Reading

Many strategies encourage understanding and enjoyment while students read. In this section, we discuss the Directed Reading–Thinking Activity, using imagery, and Post-it note reactions.

The Directed Reading–Thinking Activity (DR-TA)

The Directed Reading–Thinking Activity (DR-TA) (Stauffer, 1975, 1980) is a prediction strategy that models the processes good readers use to comprehend text. For maximum benefit, DR-TA should be used on a long-term basis, so that students' reading processes can mature.

DR-TA should be used with stories that students have not yet read. Before students see the story, the teacher divides it into sections varying from a few paragraphs to a few pages apiece. Generally, the story is divided into four to six parts, each ending at a natural breaking point. When possible, it is helpful to end sections at the bottom of pages. Teachers need

Strategy Snapshot 8.1
• • • • • • • • • • • • • •
Semantic Impressions

The Paper Bag Princess (by Munsch) is excellent to use with the semantic impressions strategy. In this "twisted" fairy tale, a princess refuses to marry a less than gallant prince. We list these book words:

> *princess*
> *prince*
> *dragon*
> *carried off*
> *chase*
> *bag*
> *forests*
> *fiery breath*
> *meatball*
> *sleep*
> *mess*
> *bum*
> *marry*

Ms. Walega's second-grade class, which included several disabled children dictated this story:

> There once was a *princess* and a *prince*. The prince went to fight the *dragon*. The dragon got past the prince and *carried off* the princess to his cave. The prince *chased* the dragon. The dragon caught the prince in a *bag*. The dragon went into the *forest* with the prince in a bag. The dragon spit his *fiery breath* and made a fire. He ate a magic *meatball*. Then the dragon fell *asleep*. The dragon made a *mess* of his cave because he was real mad. The prince called the dragon a *bum!* The prince *married* the princess and then he killed the dragon.

After they finished, each disabled child in the class was paired with an on-level student and assigned one sentence to illustrate jointly. The resulting book, entitled *The Horrible Dragon*, became part of the classroom library.

Ms. Smith's low-level fourth-grade class (Room 204) produced a somewhat more sophisticated story, which they entitled *The Fire-Breathing Dragon*. After reading the published story, students wrote comparisons:

Kevin: I like 204's story better because it had a happy ending.
Crystal: I like The Paper Bag Princess because I hate the prince and the book has a real author.
Michel: I like Fire Breathing Dragon because it is longer, and we made it.
Katrina: I like Fire Breathing Dragon because it had a lot of activities, and a dragon can't fly, and the prince saved the princess. And boys are supposed to save girls.

not physically divide the text, but just keep the sections in mind. It may take a few days to complete the reading of one story.

To introduce the selection, write the title on the board before passing out the story. Then ask students to predict what will happen based on the title. For example, in one story, entitled "Nate the Great and the Sticky Case" (by Sharmat), fourth-grade resource students predicted that "Something will be stolen," "It's about glue," and "Nate will be stuck somewhere."

Write the individual students' predictions on the board (Richek, 1987). We have found that writing the names of the students next to their predictions increases a feeling of ownership. As each prediction is stated, ask the student his or her reason for making that prediction. For example, the student who predicted that "Something will be stolen" gave as his reason "The title says 'case' and that means a crime, and that's stealing."

After several predictions are written and explained, hand out the story and have students silently read the first section. When they are finished, guide them in reviewing their earlier predictions. Which ones have actually happened in the story? Which might still happen, and should be left on the board? Which need to be revised or erased? Would they like to add any new predictions?

Students then read the next section in the story and, after reading, they again revise their hypotheses. This sequence continues until they have completed the story.

We have found DR-TA to be an extremely motivating strategy, which often stimulates students to read longer selections and to read silently. In their predictions, students naturally combine background information with the clues in the story to anticipate the ending before they actually read it. Readers also begin to use story structure to form predictions.

Using DR-TA is no more time-consuming than reading stories in a traditional manner. Almost any narrative story can be used. In addition, students who are reading novels can make predictions before they begin individual chapters.

However, students with reading problems do not always participate freely in a DR-TA. Some read so passively that they have trouble making predictions. In a group situation, shy students can be encouraged to participate by voting "yes" or "no" on some hypotheses. Including requests for "abstentions" ensures that even the most passive students will take part. When using DR-TA in an individual situation, a teacher can model involvement by making hypotheses along with the student.

When using DR-TA, students should be told not look ahead into a following section in a story. The occasional student who looks ahead should be pulled from a group DR-TA, and asked to sit on the side without making comments. Of course, such students are unconsciously demonstrating that they see reading as "showing off" the right answer rather than thinking about the material. After using DR-TA several times, even these students will come to value the role of their own thinking in reading stories.

When low-achieving readers do their first DR-TA, their predictions are often highly implausible. As they continue using the process, predictions will improve. In addition, as a group of students approaches the end of a story, individuals will start to agree on plausible endings. These are important signs of progress in reading narrative text.

DR-TA is a versatile strategy that can be done in many different ways. At times, you may want to write predictions on the board, and at other times, you may want students simply to give them verbally. Sometimes students who disagree with the author's ending for a story enjoy writing and illustrating their own endings. Other variations are given below.

Strategy Snapshot 8.2
• • • • • • • • • • • • • •
DR-TA in a Low-Achieving Fifth-Grade Class

The thirty-one students in this room used the DR-TA process with the stories in their fourth-grade reading series. The first story used, "Otis's Scientific Experiment" described the adventures of a misbehaving boy who interfered with a class experiment about feeding rats.

We first put the title on the board and asked for hypotheses about the story. The four hypotheses focused on a laboratory with a scientist. Then we passed out the story and asked children to read the first page silently and reformulate their hypotheses. After reading page one, students correctly refocused their predictions on the boy, Otis, and a classroom. However, the students identified the animal as a *mouse* rather than a *rat,* so they were asked to go back and reread. We finished two more sets of predictions on the first day, for pages 2–3 and 4–5 of the story.

As we proceeded, student excitement mounted. More students made predictions, and the predictions became more plausible. We ended the day by taking a vote on the weights of the rats in the story. At the conclusion of the lesson, one student, Perry, copied the predictions from the board for use the next day. (In fact, three other students also copied them, just to ensure accuracy!)

On the second day, Perry recopied the predictions onto the board, and the class did two more prediction segments. Students continued to increase their hypotheses, until there were so many that we were unable to call on all students who wanted to contribute. As the story progressed, students began to agree on their hypothesis for the ending. Thomas, who had been making the others wait because of his very slow silent reading, started to speed up his reading rate.

It was clear to the children that, on the third day, the story would end. Keana and Ryan met us in the hall before school, and asked us whether we could reveal the ending, if they wouldn't tell the others. (We declined to do this!) In class, the ending was finally revealed, to the delight of the children. Ending the story was followed by an in-depth discussion of the clues the author gave about the conclusion, and of other stories that had similar plots.

DR-TA without Justification.

In this activity (Richek, 1987), readers give predictions, but are not asked to supply reasons for them. We began to use DR-TA without justification when we found that many of our students were able to predict, but could not give reasons for their predictions. In fact, when we asked for justification, some became quite uncomfortable. Some low-achieving students may need to use DR-TA without justification before moving on to the more challenging step of supplying reasons.

Silent DR-TA.

In this strategy, students are each given a story with prearranged, written stopping points. Each student reads the selection individually and silently until he or she comes to the first stopping point. Students then *write* their predictions at their desks, without discussing them. Then they read until they come to another stopping point and write that prediction. In the last part of the story the ending is, of course, revealed, and each student can see how close he or she has come to predicting the author's ending.

Silent DR-TA helps older students take responsibility for their own reading and avoids the embarrassment of public discussions (Josel, 1986; Richek, 1987). In addition, making written records of their predictions helps students to monitor their own comprehension. Silent DR-TA motivates students to read silently and respond in writing. After they have completed the story, students look back at their predictions to see how well they caught the clues given in the story.

Using Post-it Notes to Monitor Responses to Reading

The Post-it Note Strategy (Caldwell, 1993a), gives students the opportunity to "talk back" to authors as they are reading silently. The "Post-it notes," pieces of paper with one sticky edge, can be easily placed on text, removed, and reused. Using small notes helps students to pinpoint the precise part of the reading they are reacting to.

The Post-it notes we use contain three graphic messages:

- An exclamation point to indicate that a reader has been surprised by something.
- A "smiley face" to show that the reader likes something that happened in the story.
- A question mark to note a question that the reader has about something in the story.

We generally give each reader three of each type per story or chapter, but we supply more if needed.

As students read silently, they place a Post-it note wherever they meet something in the story that surprises, delights, or baffles them. In this way, they are recording their own reactions to the text. After they read, the Post-it notes make an excellent starting point for discussing a story. For low-achieving students, we often start by discussing the question-mark Post-it notes, next moving to surprising and well liked parts. Students enjoy seeing that others have the same questions and appreciate the same parts as they do.

Making Mental Images

Developing mental imagery in response to reading is an effective way to improve comprehension and interest for students with reading problems (Gambrell & Bales, 1986; Pressley, 1977; Pressley & Harris, 1990). When students form mental images as they read, they combine their background information with the text. Reading becomes more personal and relevant as students construct their unique images. In focusing on their own internal responses to text, students become more willing to read silently. Finally, mental imagery helps students to become comfortable reading text without pictures, because they create pictures in their own minds.

It is both enjoyable and instructive for students to compare their mental images. When students realize that no two people see precisely the same thing, they learn to value personal response in reading (Sadowski, 1985).

We recommend using mental imagery for students aged eight or above. To ensure maximum impact, it should be used on a sustained basis.

Building Readiness for Mental Imagery.
To prepare students for reading activities, first develop the students' abilities to form images while *listening*.

- Ask students to close their eyes and imagine that they are seeing their mother, father, or other adult. Each student, in turn, describes what he or she sees.
- Instruct students to imagine a hot-fudge sundae as you, verbally, build it, giving such clues as "I put in two scoops of vanilla ice cream, I slowly pour hot fudge over the top . . ." Then ask students to describe the colors they see. Then, without describing the container, ask students the type of container they imagine. By imagining something that is not directly described, students develop the ability to build a complete mental picture from partial clues. This is precisely what we do when we make mental images during reading!
- Read short stories to students and ask them to describe their mental images of the characters.
- The book *Hurricane* (by Weisner) is excellent for developing imagery. In this book, a hurricane knocks over a tree. Two brothers use their imagination to incorporate this tree into imaginary scenes, such as a safari and a space ship. After reading it, we ask students to individually tell us what else they could imagine the tree to be. Responses have included a submarine, gym, airplane, raft, tank, and limousine. One fifth grader saw the tree as a castle, and reported seeing dragons, a princess, and birds (because she was up high).

Mental Imagery in Reading.

After forming mental images in listening, students are ready to apply imagery to reading. To do this, simply ask students to read something silently, and then focus on their own mental images.

Imagery can be used at several points in a story. Asking for a mental image after the students have read the first few paragraphs of a story helps them to make the rest of the story more vivid. Teachers may also ask for images at places in the story where students would normally be stopped for questions. Finally, if students have read a story independently, imagery can be used as a follow-up strategy.

Or, when working with imagery, ask students to focus on the most important or exciting part of a story and to describe it. Focusing on only one image helps students to organize their thoughts and avoids confusing or conflicting responses. You might have students close their eyes immediately after reading to hold their images in their minds.

Despite the value of imagery, some students with reading problems find the strategy difficult to use at first. Teachers need to be patient with a student who reports seeing "nothing," on the first day of instruction. Within a week, such readers will often start to image. If students simply list a sequence of events in the story, special attempts should be made to focus on exciting story parts, so that they will become personally involved enough to form an image. Or, you can focus students on imagining what a character looks like.

If students report seeing images that do not match the text, they have probably misread something. Encourage them to reread the material silently and see if their images change. If students consistently misread, break up stories into shorter segments and follow silent reading with oral reading. This focuses the students' attention on the need to read more carefully.

Recently, we used mental imagery to help Bobby, a fourth grader who had poor comprehension and found silent reading difficult. Bobby silently read the first two paragraphs in a story about a snowstorm. When he was finished, we asked him to report his image. At first, Bobby could not report anything, but after rereading the paragraphs, Bobby said he saw snow on the lawn, children building a snowman outside, and a car up the street. This imagery activity made him interact with the text, and his comprehension of the story improved dramatically.

Strategies for Improving Comprehension after Reading

Comprehension strategies that can be used after reading include those that develop a sense of story grammar, encourage a personal response, and connect the literacy experience.

Comprehension Strategies to Develop Story Structure

As we discussed earlier, narratives are usually written according to certain forms, called story grammars. Most narratives contain the elements of *characters, setting* (time and place), and *plot.* The *plot* is generally further broken into a *problem* that a character must solve and different *events* (or *episodes*) that take place in the story. At the end of the story, there is a *solution* or *resolution* to the problem. When students recognize these common elements of narratives, they read with more understanding and are better able to make sense of a narrative.

Since many young children do not have a mature concept of story structure (Appleby, 1978), only a few story grammar activities are suitable for low-achieving primary children. However, these students can develop their skills by *listening* to stories, and then discussing the plot, characters, and setting of the stories.

Story Maps.

Story maps are visual diagrams that show students the elements all stories contain. When students use these maps, they learn to identify the common elements of narrative text. Story grammars are suitable for shorter both stories and novels. A common story frame map contains (1) characters, (2) setting, (3) problem, and (4) solution. To illustrate this, a story map has been filled in for "The Case of the Missing Homework," a story in which Stuey writes his homework in invisible ink, and later cannot find it.

Characters	**Setting**
Stuey	Stuey's classroom
Teacher	Stuey's bedroom
Mother	

Problem	**Solution**
Stuey's homework is not neat	Stuey remembers his neatly done homework was written in invisible ink, and he makes it reappear

A more complex story map, suitable for older students, contains episodes to link the problem and solution (or resolution). It also contains a goal for the character.

Teachers can introduce story maps before students read, and ask them to fill in the frame either during or after reading. Or, give the map to the students after a story has been read, and ask them to identify story elements. Students with reading problems often enjoy working on maps in pairs.

Low-achieving readers often need teacher modeling before they can successfully generalize the features of story grammar. Patient teacher demonstration, followed by discussion, will lead students to using story grammar independently. Remember that story structure is learned gradually and must be practiced consistently over a long period of time.

At times, you will find that students focus on only one part of the story, usually the first part or the most exciting part. To help them refocus on the story as a whole, read a short story to them while placing a story grammar frame on the board or on an overhead projector. As they listen to the story, students should try to fill in the story grammar frame. Then reread the story to them, and have them confirm or revise their story grammars.

As students become more comfortable with story grammar, they will become independent of visual maps. At that point, simply use a story grammar framework to guide comprehension, asking such questions as: "Who was the main character?" "What was the central problem in the story?" Students might also enjoy asking each other these questions.

Problem–Solution Identification.

The identification of the problem and solution to that problem in a story is a shortened form of story grammar that is useful for intermediate and secondary students. To encourage long-term learning we often have students make charts of many stories that they have read, showing the problem of the story in one column and the solution in another.

Since the ability to identify the problem and solution is a sophisticated skill, it requires careful teacher guidance. At first, students may confuse the main problem of the story with the first event. When this occurs, teachers should carefully discuss stories.

Story Pyramids.

Students often enjoy creating their own, personal "pyramids" of stories they have read. In pyramids, they are allowed only eight lines, and may only use a certain number of words per line. Each line must describe something different. If used in a group, the teacher should write the class pyramid on the board for all to see. If used individually, students often like to decorate and illustrate their personal constructions. Pyramids can be used by at-risk readers from kindergarten through high school.

The form of a pyramid is:

- One word naming the main character
- Two words describing the main character (for students in grades three and above, encourage the use of adjectives)
- Three words describing the setting (time and place)
- Four words describing the problem (for students in primary grades who have difficulty with problem identification, substitute "four words describing the first thing that happened")
- Five words describing an important event
- Six words describing another important event
- Seven words describing another important event
- Eight words describing the ending

Students with reading problems have made many creative constructions using the pyramid format. Of course, since a pyramid is a personal response, each pyramid will be a little different. Below are two pyramids from third-grade Title I classes in response to reading "Cinderella."

Cinderella

cute   nice

palace   house   backyard

her mother was dead

stepmother made her sweep floor

she went to the palace ball

she danced with the prince and ran

They got married and lived happily ever after.

Cinderella

nice person

past   palace   house

had mean stepmother

had two mean stepsisters

she could not go to the ball

prince found the glass slipper for Cinderella

After they got married they lived very happily.*

In constructing these pyramids, the children chose the characters, descriptions, and events that were most important to them. However, because a set number of words was needed, they had to manipulate words and combine them creatively. At times, they had to leave out words. This format encourages creative responses, and, in fact, a group of boys in one class insisted on writing an alternative version, using the prince as the major character.

Story pyramids develop many important skills. (1) If students work in groups they naturally tend to discuss the story, an activity that fosters active comprehension. (2) Pyramids give students practice with the major elements of a story (characters, setting, events). Students learn to separate important events from unimportant ones. (3) Students develop language by manipulating and elaborating words to fit into a specified format. (4) Students review vocabulary and concepts mentioned in the story. (5) Building a pyramid is fun! Youngsters look forward to building and displaying their creations.

In intermediate and upper grades, pyramids make excellent alternatives to traditional book reports. Used as a response to independent reading, the pyramid activity does not require much writing, but it enables students to respond actively to their reading. Furthermore, you will always be able to tell if students have read the book.

Comprehension Strategies that Nurture Personal Response

Readers experiencing difficulties often have problems reacting fully to reading. In this section, strategies are given that foster creativity, engagement, and enjoyment, so that low-achieving students can see that reading belongs to them!

---

*Full sentences are given capital letters and periods.

Drama.

Acting out a story immediately involves the reader. As they experience story events from the character's point of view, students with reading problems deepen and improve comprehension (Sebesta, 1993; Wolf & Enciso, 1994). Drama will encourage discussion of a story and foster cooperation and other social skills in your at-risk students.

The "tableaux" strategy is one way to dramatize a story (Purves, Rogers, & Soter, 1990). We have used it effectively at elementary- and secondary-grade levels. In tableaux, students form still lives, or "tableaux," to dramatize story events. To illustrate the scenes, they assume appropriate expressions and body postures. Figure 8.1 shows one scene from "The Little Pine Tree," a story demonstrated by two second graders in front of appreciative classmates. If possible, capture the tableaux on film.

FIGURE 8.1
Tableau of "The Little Pine Tree"

In tableaux, students put themselves physically into the story. They discuss events as they decide which scenes they will act out. Furthermore, since tableaux involve the students "freezing" the scene, events acquire a permanence that they do not always have in the ongoing action of the story. Since these still-lives are silent, at-risk children are able to focus on the story without the distraction of movement and noise.

Tableaux can be done in many formats. In a large class, students can be divided into several groups, and, after listing important events, the teacher can assign one to each group. If there are more students in the group than story characters, some can play houses and trees. For young children, this helps to establish the difference between characters and scenery. More advanced students often enjoy deciding secretly on the scene they will dramatize and asking classmates who watch the tableau to identify it. Secondary students, who are often reading longer material, should be encouraged to pick the most crucial and exciting events to dramatize.

Catch a Rainbow.

Art can be used to foster personal responses to reading. In the Catch a Rainbow Strategy (Richek, 1995) students are asked to represent a story or novel in an artistic form. However, since we want to encourage imagination, they are told that they cannot draw anything recognizable (e.g., people, trees). Instead, they must use *abstract* art, colors, and shapes, to represent the story. In this way, students are freed both from dependence on the illustrations in a book and differences in individual artistic abilities. Because this task requires mature abilities, we usually limit it to students in the fourth grade and above.

After having students read a story, we ask them to represent it in abstract art. We typically give them magic markers. The easy, nonthreatening process takes less than 15 minutes for most students to complete, yet our students never fail to amaze us with the originality of their personal artistic interpretations. In one fourth-grade classroom, each student produced a personal picture after reading "The Code in the Mailbox," about a blind man, Mr. James, who is helped by young Tina. In return, Mr. James teaches Tina to read braille. In a minor incident, Tina becomes angry at her mother for making her stop dyeing a T-shirt.

Anthony used pink and yellow to honor the happiness of the story. But he drew strong lines to indicate that Tina had been annoyed at her mother. (While adults would rarely remember Tina's angry feelings, many students, like Anthony, found this incident meaningful.)

Sean, a student with severe reading problems, represented braille by dots and used circular patterns to indicate "the confusion of blindness." Jagged lines registered Tina's feelings of anger at being interrupted while dyeing her T-shirt. Note how deeply Sean reacted to this story! Catch a Rainbow gives students a chance to express *their* feelings.

It is important that students reflect on their pictures by sharing them. Students can explain their drawing to the class or write captioned explanations for their creations and make them into a bulletin board display.

Character Webs.

In this activity, the name or picture of a story character is placed in the center of a page and surrounded by the traits of that character. Then, incidents from the story that illustrate each character trait are listed. A character web done by a third grader reading the story *Clifford, the Big Red Dog* (by Bridwell) is presented in Figure 8.2.

Skinny Books.

This strategy, most useful for primary children, combines the review of a story with a chance to create a personal version of it. To make a skinny book (Richek, 1995), the teacher needs to obtain two extra copies of the children's reading textbook series. Illustrations are cut from a story that the children have just completed and pasted into a *skinny book*. (Two copies are needed because many illustrations are on the back sides of facing pages.) A front page should be left for a cover.

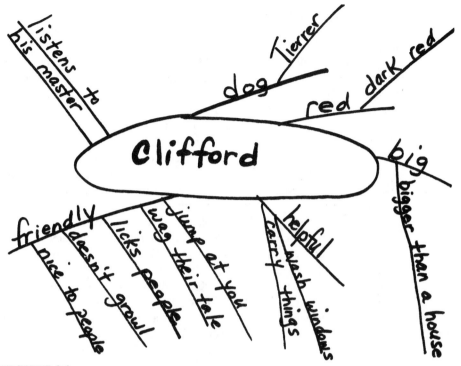

FIGURE 8.2
Character Web of *Clifford the Big Red Dog*

Now the students have an opportunity to become "authors" of the story they have just read by dictating their own text to match the story pictures. Generally, students take turns dictating pages. Individuals may want to sign each page that they have dictated.

One group of Title I/Chapter I third graders made a skinny book of the story "Weekend Ants," which they had read in their regular classroom. Authors Robert, Sherri, Travis, and Chris entitled their skinny book "The Queen That Got Lost." Each student dictated a separate page as the teacher recorded their responses in magic marker. As they summarized the story, they changed it into their own words. These four students proudly carried their skinny book back to their regular class and read it to their peers.

Connecting the Literacy Experience

Students deepen their comprehension as they compare different texts and share their literacy experiences with each other. In this section, we discuss two strategies that help students connect literary experiences: (1) conceptually connected instruction (themes) and (2) genre studies.

Conceptually Connected Instruction (Themes)

In this, students concentrate on one interesting topic, focusing all literacy activities around it. This offers an opportunity to use students' interests for instruction, and it helps them to relate associations from known to unknown material. Thus, a student's interest in football may lead to understanding the business concept of negotiating contracts, bringing law suits, and judging profit margins.

A theme can also lead students to varied types of reading materials. Students may explore football through stories, newspaper activities, score sheets, encyclopedias, books, and manuals. They will be better able to grasp the structure of sophisticated types of text if they deal with familiar topics. The theme approach is particularly successful with students who are quite far behind in reading and need highly motivating instruction.

We have used themes with many students. Elizabeth, a seventeen-year-old reading on a fifth-grade level, decided to research successful women who had, in her words, "made it." Role models were chosen from entertainment, sports, and business. Elizabeth read books, collected newspaper articles, watched TV programs, and listened to audiotapes and compact discs. Her teacher brought in technical terms from the three fields. At the end of three months, Elizabeth had dramatically improved her reading skills.

Edmund, a fifth grader reading on a second-grade level, became interested in Hawaii and volcanoes, collecting many vivid pictures. For homework, his tutor asked him find all the ways pineapples were sold in the supermarket. His results became a written essay featuring 15 different types of pineapples. Edmund also read travel brochures, maps, and social studies textbooks. At the end of instruction, he gave his tutor a fresh pineapple as a gift.

Twelve-year-old Eugene, reading on a third-grade level, was intrigued by the escape artist Houdini. After starting with some easy books, he read through all the books in the school and local libraries. Before another hero replaced Houdini, Eugene had made several trips to the central New York City Public Library.

Sometimes teachers must suggest a topic for a very passive student. In the case of Oneka, a fourteen-year-old student, we chose *food*. She explored the history of popcorn, the taste of egg rolls, and how to eat gyros, incidentally gathering much information about the world.

The theme approach motivates low-achieving students to read a wide variety of reading materials. At the same time, teachers can focus on specific comprehension strategies.

Studying Different Genres.

Studying a genre, such as mystery stories or fairy tales, allows disabled readers to connect and compare their readings. To do this, students should read many examples of one genre, and then compare their common features. For example, Marcus, a sixth-grader who loved watching mysteries on TV, was motivated to read several with his tutor. Marcus made a chart listing how each story contained (1) the crime, (2) the detective, (3) the clues to solve the mystery, and (4) the solution.

Students with reading problems also love to explore fairy and folk tales. Students can chart the features of (1) magic, (2) hero, (3) villain, (4) beginning words (such as "once upon a time"), and (5) ending for each tale.

Students can also compare different versions of one tale. Cinderella has been told in many versions, including *Prince Cinders* (by B. Cole), in which the lead is cast as a picked-on boy. The story of the three little pigs has been published as *The True Story of the Three Little Pigs* (by Szieska), a hilarious revisionist version told from the wolf's point of view, and *The Three Little Wolves and the Big Bad Pig* (by Trivizas), which reverses the usual roles. The Hans Christian Anderson's Tale "The Emperor's New Clothes" has been recast in a school as *The Principal's New Clothes* (by Calmenson).

Students can compare two versions of a tale using a Venn diagram, or two partially overlapping circles. The common portions contain the things that are alike about the two tales. The unique portions list things that appear in only a single tale. Figure 8.3 shows a Venn diagram that Sheila and her tutor constructed for two versions of Cinderella. In exploring and recording differences between these different versions, students gain flexibility in thinking.

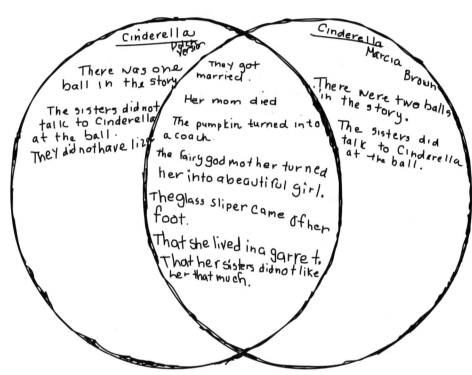

FIGURE 8.3
Venn diagram for Cinderella

Summary

The purpose of reading is comprehension. General features of effective comprehension include (1) realizing that we read to comprehend, (2) realizing that comprehension requires the reader to actively construct a text in his or her mind which accurately reflects the material that the author has written, (3) applying personal background knowledge appropriately to text, and (4) employing higher-level thinking to understand text. Too much teacher questioning discourages active responses to stories.

Narratives, or texts that tell stories, inspire imaginative personal responses. They also have certain organizational factors, including story grammars (characters, setting, plot). They include many different genres, such as adventure, fantasy, and science fiction.

In assessing abilities with narrative text, we can use the comprehension tests on general standardized tests. In addition, we can judge whether a student has comprehended a specific text well by using story retelling and questioning.

Strategies for improving comprehension before reading include building background knowledge, predicting what will be in the story, students' building a semantic impressions story from selected story words, and reading students the story to support comprehension. Strategies for improving comprehension during reading include using the Directed Reading-Thinking Activity (a prediction strategy used while reading), using Post-it notes to mark pleasing, surprising, and puzzling parts of text, and responding with mental images. Strategies for improving comprehension after reading can develop an understanding of story structure through story maps (using characters, settings, events), identifying the problem and solution, and building "pyramids" that retell stories in a format ranging from 1 to 8 words. To nurture personal response after reading, drama (including tableaux still lives), a "Catch a Rainbow" response in abstract art, character webs with visual displays of traits, and skinny books that rewrite stories in students' own words can be used. Finally, the literacy experience may be connected through the study of one theme, or doing genre studies on, say, the characteristics of fairy tales.

CHAPTER 9

Improving Comprehension of Expository Text

Introduction

This chapter deals with the comprehension of expository text, or informational material, such as textbooks used in science, social studies, and psychology. As students move through the grades, the reading tasks that confront them change dramatically. Stories becomes less important and work with expository text, especially school textbooks, increases.

Students are often assigned to read textbooks independently, without supervision. Thus, without any help, students are expected to read a chapter, complete a written assignment, and participate in class discussion. Not surprisingly, many low-achieving readers cannot do these tasks.

In this chapter, we first describe the nature of expository material and discuss why it tends to be more difficult than stories and novels. Next, we provide strategies for assessing the ability to read and study from expository text. Finally, we discuss three kinds of strategies for helping students with reading problems deal with expository material: using background knowledge, monitoring comprehension, and reorganizing or transforming expository text. We focus on developing independent readers who eventually apply these strategies in the absence of a teacher.

The Nature of Expository Text

Expository text conveys information, explains ideas, or presents a point of view.

Types of Expository Text

Expository material is usually organized in one of five ways: (1) sequence or time order, (2) listing, (3) compare–contrast, (4) cause–effect, and (5) problem–solution (Englert & Hiebert, 1984; Horowitz, 1985; Meyer & Freedle, 1984; Taylor, 1992). In addition, most expository text also contains main ideas and supporting details. The ability to recognize and remember these depends to a large degree on the reader's sensitivity to organizational patterns (Baumann, 1986).

1. *Sequence or time order* is often used to present events such as the French and Indian War (in history class) or cell division (in biology class).
2. *Listing* (or description) is used to explain the features of an object or event. Biology textbooks list the features of reptiles, giving their body temperature, reproductive habits, eating habits, etc.
3. *Compare and contrast* involves discussing similarities and differences. A social studies text might compare a congressional system of government with a parliamentary system; a science text might contrast several planets in the solar system.
4. A *cause–effect* pattern outlines reasons for events. The author describes an event (such as the fall of Fort Sumter) with an explanation of what caused the event and the effects that followed from it.
5. Authors using the *problem–solution* pattern discuss a problem and then suggest possible solutions. A history author might discuss the events in a U.S. President's life in terms of the problems he faced and how he solved them.

Skilled adult readers recognize these organizational patterns and use them to facilitate comprehension (van Dijk & Kintsch, 1983). However, it is not always easy to recognize such patterns. Expository materials often do not conform precisely to the patterns we described. Authors may combine two patterns. For example, a listing or description of the battle of Vicksburg may be intertwined with the cause–effect pattern. Or two readers may see different patterns in the same text. An account of how trade goods in the Middle Ages were brought from Asia to Europe could be interpreted as description, problem–solution or sequence.

Difficulties of Reading Expository Text

Expository text presents difficulties for students with reading problems. (1) Recognizing and using the author's organizational patterns is a complex task. (2) Expository text is less personal than narrative text. (3) In reading expository text, students are often required to demonstrate their understanding by taking tests. (4) Expository text usually contains more difficult vocabulary and technical terms than narrative text. (5) Reading expository text often requires extensive background information. (6). Expository text tends to be longer than narrative text. This length may simply overwhelm students with reading problems. (7) The reading level of school textbooks is often well above the frustration level of students with reading problems.

Assessing Abilities with Expository Text

In this section, we present strategies for judging how well students can deal with expository materials. In order to successfully read and remember expository text, students must do three things: (1) use background knowledge, (2) monitor their own comprehension, and (3) reorganize or transform the text in order to remember it. We organize our assessment and teaching of expository text around these three components.

Focusing the Informal Reading Inventory on Expository Text

You can gain valuable insights into a student's ability to handle expository text by adapting the informal reading inventory (IRI) procedure to the student's own textbook.

Choose a passage of 200 to 400 words that has a clearly defined beginning, middle, and end. Duplicate the passage so you will have a copy to write on, but have the student read from the book. Prepare ten questions to ask the student, focusing on important ideas in the passage. (It is unrealistic to expect any reader to remember insignificant details after one reading.)

Have the student read the selection silently and allow him or her to reread the passage or study it for a short time before responding to the questions. When the student is ready, ask the questions. If the student scores below 70 percent, have the student reread the passage orally. This will help you to determine if word recognition difficulties are interfering with comprehension.

To judge the level of the passage, use the comprehension score and, if the student reads orally, the word recognition accuracy score. The guidelines in Chapter 3, Table 3.3, can determine whether this passage is at an independent, instructional, or frustration level.

If the student is at a frustration level for word recognition, we recommend that you do not pursue further assessment or instruction in this textbook. If the student scores at the instructional level for word recognition but at a frustration level for comprehension, you will need to probe further, using the procedures that follow.

Assessing Use of Background Knowledge

Good readers use what they know about a topic to help them understand expository text. One way to determine whether a student does this is to compare performance on familiar and unfamiliar expository texts. Again, use the IRI procedure but choose selections that you think may be familiar to the student and ones that you believe are relatively unfamiliar. To verify this, ask the student to tell you what he or she knows about the topic of the passage.

For example, if the passage is about Roosevelt's New Deal, ask the student for information on "Franklin Roosevelt" or the "New Deal."

Next, have the student silently read a familiar passage and an unfamiliar one. You can expect that students who use their background knowledge as they read will perform better in familiar text. If a student performs equally well in both passages, you should teach the strategies for using background information that are presented later in this chapter.

Assessing Comprehension Monitoring

Skilled readers are continually aware of their own comprehension as they read expository text. In contrast, students with reading problems are often not aware of their comprehension processes, and therefore do not take steps to solve problems that they may encounter in reading.

One way to assess comprehension monitoring is to use an expository passage that the student found difficult. Ask the student to go through the passage and identify "something that you found hard" or "something you didn't understand." After the student identifies these parts, try to determine whether the student actually found this section difficult, or just selected something at random. You might say, "Was it a word that bothered you or a group of words?" "Is there an idea that you did not understand?" If your student tells you that *everything* was hard, reverse this procedure and ask the student to find one or two things that were easier than the rest.

Another way to assess comprehension monitoring is to ask the student to find answers to questions that were answered incorrectly. You can have the student underline the answers to literal questions. However, inferential questions demand that the reader combine background knowledge with the author's clues. For these, ask the student to identify anything in the selection that gives clues to higher-level questions. If the student cannot identify anything, provide the clue and see if he or she can use it to arrive at a correct answer. Going back into the text to correct questions requires active comprehension monitoring. In fact, you will actually be teaching as you assess comprehension.

Assessing Ability to Transform Text for Studying

Many students understand a text they while are reading, but afterward quickly forget it. As a result, they perform poorly on tests. To study effectively, students must transform the text in some way, so that they can remember it. For example, they must reorganize the text to identify and set apart important ideas. Students often use the tools of underlining and note-taking to help in this transformation.

To assess ability to study from text, choose an expository passage and ask the student to take notes as if he or she were studying for a test. You can ask the student to underline or to choose the form of note-taking that he or she prefers. Either method enables you to identify the student who cannot pick out important main ideas, take effective notes, or reorganize the text.

Strategies for Helping Students Read Expository Text

In this section, we focus on strategies that can lead students to read and study expository text independently. The strategies we present are learned slowly and must be used on a long-term basis. As a teacher, you will need to model them repeatedly, encouraging students to verbalize what they are doing, why they are doing it, and how they are proceeding. We suggest that, after choosing a strategy, you stay with it for some length of time. Having students construct bookmarks containing the steps of a strategy also helps. They can tuck these into their content area textbooks.

When teaching students with reading difficulties to deal with expository text, try to use textbooks written at their instructional level. If you must deal with frustration-level textbooks, we recommend that you read the text to the students in four- or five-paragraph chunks while they follow along in their books.

Strategies for Combining Prior Knowledge with Expository Text

Even if we possess only a small amount of knowledge about a topic, we can use this knowledge to read more effectively. When we use our knowledge of a topic as we read, we look for familiar "landmarks." For example, in reading about Theodore Roosevelt, we summon up our landmarks, or background knowledge. We remember when he lived and that he was a soldier, a president, and an environmentalist. We use these landmarks to organize our reading by mentally categorizing information we read in the text under these general topics.

Students with reading problems have two difficulties with background knowledge. (1) They generally have less background knowledge than good readers because they do not read as much. (2) They often do not apply the background knowledge they *do* have to their reading. In fact, they are so used to regarding themselves negatively that they often are not even aware of the knowledge and abilities they can bring to text. These problems are intensified because often content-area teachers assign chapters with little preparation for student reading.

The Expectation Grid.

Constructing an expectation grid is a strategy that students can use independently to prepare for reading expository material (Caldwell, 1993b). Students first learn how to construct an expectation grid in written form. Eventually, however, the formation of the grid becomes a mental exercise that students do before reading.

As a good reader, you probably construct mental expectation grids without even being aware of them. For example, suppose you are about to read an article on a new bill before Congress. Even if you know nothing about the bill, you have certain expectations about the categories of information that you will read in the article. You expect the author to explain the purpose of the bill and describe who is supporting and opposing it. These expectations come from your knowledge of how government works. They are the "landmarks" that allow you to organize your reading.

Students with reading problems can be taught to approach reading with similar expectations. They may know little about the French and Indian War they are studying, but, they often know a lot about wars. Even if this knowledge comes from war movies and the Star Trek TV series, it can help them to form expectations about the categories discussed in their textbook.

To make an expectation grid, students create an organized visual representation of their knowledge before they read. A general topic (war, animals, important people, etc.) is placed in the center of the page and, around this topic, students write categories of information they expect to read about. For example, if the topic is an animal, we can expect that the author will describe the animal's appearance, behavior (movement, noise, temperament, etc.), habitat, and mating habits. Perhaps we will learn about the animal's relationship to man. Do we use it for food or clothing? Is it dangerous to us?

Suppose you are reading about the *ratel*. We suspect that you do not know much about this animal. However, as a skilled reader, you expect the categories of information we have described and you use them to organize your thoughts as you read and recall information.

Figure 9.1 is an example of an expectation grid on the topic of *animal*.

To teach students the use of expectation grids, choose part of a chapter, helping students to preview it by reading headings and looking at maps, graphs, or pictures. This preview will help students to choose a topic for the center of the grid. (Remember that the topic must be a general one such as animal, war, country, etc.) Write the topic on the grid and then model how your knowledge of this general topic allows you to form expectations for the categories of information that will be in the reading.

Let us suppose that your text is an account of the French and Indian War. Put the general topic, *war*, in the center of the grid. Next, ask the students what they know about wars, perhaps from movies, television, or stories of others. Guide them to recognize such categories as who fought the war, where it was fought, causes of the war, effects of the war, who won it, and what weapons were used. Write these categories on the grid.

After you have determined your general categories of information, write *French and Indian War* under *war*. Ask the students what they know about the French and Indian War. Perhaps there are some hints in the text that they learned about during their preview. The students might have information from their own background to add to information from the preview. As students offer what they know about the French and Indian War, have them identify the proper category and write the information on the grid.

Fill in the grid as long as the students have information to offer, but always have them indicate which category their information goes under. You may need to add new categories to accommodate some information.

What if a student offers something that you know is not true? Perhaps a student says that the French and Indian War was between the French and the Indians. If other students

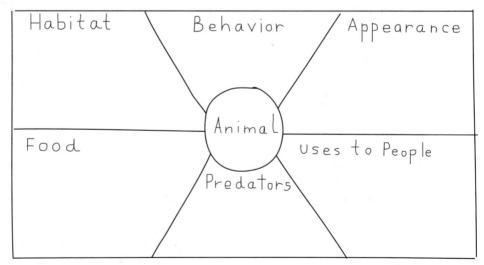

FIGURE 9.1
Expectation Grid for Animal

question this, put a question mark next to the item and indicate that effective learners read to answer questions. However, if no one questions it, simply let it be. You will return to the grid after reading and, at that point, erroneous information can be corrected. We have found that students often can identify incorrect information as they read, and that they are eager to correct their grid after they finish. This opportunity for correction is one of the most valuable features of an expectation grid. They can also use the grid to take notes as they read by adding items to each category.

As you and the students construct an expectation grid, repeatedly explain that this is something they should do by themselves before they read. Tell students that a grid does not need to be written. In fact, the most efficient expectation grid in one that is done mentally.

Table 9.1 presents some general topics with expected categories of information. This is merely meant as a guide, and you should feel free to modify these categories as you and your students see fit. For students in the primary and intermediate grades, we use only two or three categories. It is always a good idea to have a category titled "other" for items of information that do not fit into your chosen categories.

Strategy Snapshot 9.1 and Figure 9.2 (pp. 185) present an example of a class contructing an expectation grid.

Table 9.1   **Topics and Categories for an Expectation Grid**

Animal: appearance; behavior; habitat; mating habits; life cycle; food; predators; used to people.

Plant: type; appearance; habitat; uses; life cycle; enemies.

Important person: achievements, obstacles, personal characteristics; sequence of life; friends or associates; enemies.

Important event: causes; why important; description; people involved; countries involved; sequence; effects.

Country, City or State: location; size, geographical features; government; industry; culture; landmarks.

War: location; time; causes; effects; countries involved; significant events or battles; important people; methods of warfare.

Process: who carries it out; needed organisms; needed materials; end products; possible problems; usefulness.

Government: form of government; structure of government; when established; problems; current status.

The K-W-L Strategy.

This is another strategy for activating prior knowledge before reading expository text and facilitating retention. Like the expectation grid, students can use K-W-L independently. The initials of K-W-L (Ogle, 1986) represent:

K - What I **k**now

W - What I **w**ant to find out

L - What I **l**earned

Steps in using it are given below.

K - What I Know.

Ask students to preview part of an expository selection. Then have them think of everything that they know about the topic. List their responses on the board.

Strategy Snapshot 9.1
• • • • • • • • • • • • • •
Constructing an Expectation Grid

Ms. Scanlon works with a small group of high school students using an expectation grid for their world history text. She helps them preview five pages on how Spanish colonies in the New World gained independence. The students decide that the topic is important event.

She then asks them to describe some important events. Students describe a murder charge brought against a city official, an earthquake, a famine in Africa, a local train wreck, the Super Bowl, and a destructive blizzard. Ms. Scanlon asks them to imagine that they were writing about these events to someone who had never heard about them. What information would they include?

As the students offer information about their chosen event, Mrs. Scanlon guides them to see how descriptions of important events are very similar: they involve people, list specific places, tell why the event was important, describe causes and effects, and list events in order of time (first this happened, next this, etc.). Ms. Scanlon writes the categories: people; location; cause; effects; sequence; why important. She then writes Spanish colonies gain independence under important event and asks the students what they know about the Spanish colonies' fight for independence.

Using the headings from their book preview, students offer the expected information that the colonies had grievances, they were influenced by the American and French revolutions, Haiti gained independence early, and Father Hidalgo began Mexico's struggle. Using pictures, the students add Toussaint L'Ouverture to their grid.

When they run out of preview information, Ms. Scanlon suggests that they think of the American Revolution, leading them to offer the information that war was probably involved, people might have died, and Spain probably fought the colonies. They decide that Spain acted to its colonies like England did to the United States, taxing people and depriving them of rights. Finally, they suggest that colonies formed new governments when they became independent. Ms. Scanlon asks students to identify the category where each piece of information fits.

When the expectation grid is complete, Mrs. Scanlon reminds the students to look for these categories as they read. One student comments that she knew more about the topic than she thought. Mrs. Scanlon gives each student a blank grid and suggests using it for notes during reading. After reading, the students compare their notes and add information to the grid on the board.

Figure 9.2 shows the expectation grid that the students completed before they began reading their text.

Pupils may present some misinformation. For example, while working with a group of low-achieving fourth graders on the State of Washington, we received such "knowledge" as "The President lives there." If they offer such misinformation, you may simply list it, as with the expectation grid, and wait for students to read and correct their knowledge. For students who have many misperceptions, you might want to use the category "What I Think I Know" (instead of "What I Know"). This naturally leads students to correct any misinformation after reading.

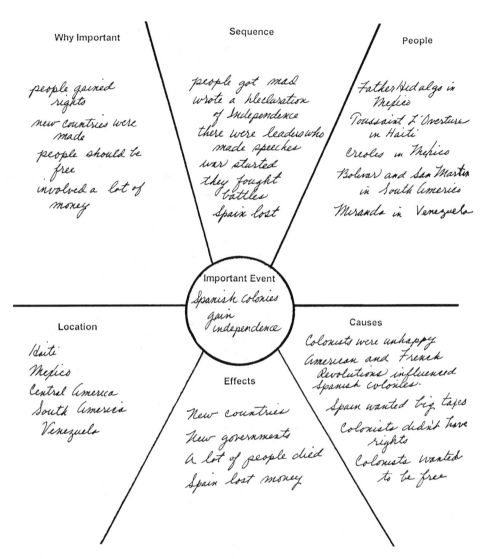

FIGURE 9.2
Expectation Grid on "Spanish Colonies Gain Independence"

After they give information, ask students to examine their pooled information and classify it into categories. The fourth grade class we described above found this direction quite confusing at first. To begin the classification, we had to suggest the category, "mountains." The students were then able to suggest items to fit under this category. Stimulated by this, the students were then able to add categories such as: "work, weather, visiting."

W - What I Want to Find Out.

Ask each student to write down the things that he or she wants to find out or expects to learn. The **W** step is often difficult for low-achieving readers, as they do not have well-developed expectations of expository material. One fourth-grade boy wanted to learn, "Do nice people live in Washington?" a question he would be unlikely to learn from his text. As he experienced K-W-L over a period of several weeks, however, his expectations of text began to mature. Other children wanted to learn things that were not answered in the text but could be answered from other sources. One girl wondered how many people had been injured or killed in the eruption of Mt. St. Helens. Such questions help students realize that learning does not stop with a single textbook, and several learners began to bring in other resources.

L - What I Learned.

Ask students to read the chapter. If the text is at their instructional level, they should read silently. If it is too difficult for them, use assisted reading or read it to them. Then, have each student write down what he or she learned from reading. After recording their learning, students are usually eager to share new knowledge with others.

We worked with the fourth-grade class in social studies for two weeks. Before beginning the text chapter, the children listed all that they knew or wanted to know about Washington. Then daily, as they read each of the four sections of the text, they did a K-W-L sheet for each section. To conclude the unit, the students listed all of the things that they learned about Washington and wrote a composition. Working with K-W-L, the students became more adept at understanding and remembering expository text. K-W-Ls can also be used to write summaries that enhance comprehension (Jennings, 1991).

Both the expectation grid and K-W-L are effective in teaching students to combine their prior knowledge with expository text. The expectation grid begins with general categories and moves to specific items of information. In contrast, K-W-L begins with specific bits of knowledge and moves to the general categories. With careful guidance, both can be used independently and mentally by students.

Strategies for Monitoring Comprehension of Expository Text

Good readers constantly monitor their comprehension as they read. They make predictions, ask questions, and look for prior knowledge "landmarks." If their comprehension falters, they stop reading and attempt to make sense of the text by rereading, identifying what confused them, and possibly using context to identify word meanings. The awareness of one's own mental activities and the ability to direct them is called *metacognition.*

Students with reading problems generally lack metacognition in reading. Since they often do not expect reading to make sense, they let their eyes move over the text and proceed on, unconcerned that they understand almost nothing. This passive orientation toward reading is one reason why low-achieving students have comprehension problems (Jenkins et al., 1986; Johnston, 1984). Brown and Palincsar (1982) have shown that by developing an awareness of monitoring strategies, low-achieving readers can increase their learning. The strategies given below help students both to demand and to obtain meaning from text.

Text Coding.

Text coding (used by Caldwell, 1993c) teaches students with reading problems to recognize and remember (1) known information, (2) newly learned information, and (3) remaining questions. Teaching students with reading problems to recognize these three things is an important first step in teaching them to monitor their comprehension. To make this activity short and concrete, we often teach them to code text, using symbols. (1) Use a plus sign (+) to indicate something the reader already knows. (2) Mark new information with an exclamation mark (!). (3) Mark questions with a question mark (?). To avoid defacing books, place these symbols on small Post-it notes.

Teacher modeling is the best way to do show students how to code text. Remember that you are teaching a *mental* process, one that you would like students eventually to do in their heads, without the aid of written codes. At first, the coding symbols help to make the thinking process visible and bring it to the student's attention. Later, however, you will want the students to do this mentally.

When you teach students to use text coding, begin by getting an oral response. First, read an expository selection to them, stopping periodically to report information that you already knew, information you just learned, and questions you have. Invite the students to join you in talking about what they already knew or something they just learned. Do they have any questions? As you proceed, stop at specific pieces of information in the text, and ask students to respond to them.

We find that low-achieving students tend to say they already knew an item of information when, in fact, they didn't. Refrain from criticizing them in this first stage; as the strategy proceeds, they will become more comfortable identifying new information. If students continue to say that everything was known, you might want to simplify the process by using only two categories: unknown facts, and questions. In addition, students just beginning this process will have difficulties framing questions. Again, their abilities to ask good questions will increase as you model and guide their efforts.

If some students simply echo what their peers say, you might require each student to make a personal decision about text by constructing individual coding cards. Take index cards or Post-it notes and print the coding symbols (+, !, ?) on each side. After giving each student one for each coding symbol, read a segment of expository text to them. Ask them to hold up one of the index cards to indicate whether they already knew this, had just learned it, or had a question. When doing this, you may ask for a student's explanation.

After students have grasped the idea of identifying what they already knew, what they just learned, and what questions they have, move on to a written format. Choose a short segment of expository text and show it to the students. For a large group, you might want to code the text on an overhead. Students in a small group can sit around you and watch as you write the coding symbols on the page. As you read the text, think aloud about what you already knew, what you just learned, and what questions you have. At each item, mark the coding symbols on the text. (You can lightly pencil them in on the page or attach Post-it notes containing !,+,?) The use of written symbols is an important step that makes a mental strategy visible for the students.

As a next step, students should each receive an individual copy of a short text (no more than one page) to read silently and code for themselves in margins or above a line of print. Before students read, the teacher should decide how often they need to react. In the early stages of strategy instruction, or with easy text, we recommend coding each sentence. However, as text gets more difficult, many different items of information can be included in a single sentence, leading to different codes for one sentence. For example, Kenneth coded one sentence by indicating + (already known) for the fact that cicada eggs hatched but ! (just learned) for the fact that the animals from hatched eggs are called nymphs. He also put ? (question) because he wondered why they were called nymphs.

Table 9.2 shows Josh's coding of a paragraph about the cicada.

Table 9.2   **Josh's Text Coding**

        +   !   +   ?
The female cicada lays her eggs in tree branches. She makes tiny holes in the wood and lays her
                +   ?   !
eggs in these holes. The cicada eggs hatch into nymphs. Nymphs are very small and they look
  !   !
like worms. The nymphs crawl down the trees and bury themselves in the ground. They stay in
  !   ?   !   !
the ground for 17 years! They feed on tree roots. During the 17 years, the nymph slowly turns
                                      !
into a cicada. It finally comes out of the ground and climbs into a tree. After it sheds it skin, it
+   ?   !
can fly. The cicada lives on tree leaves and other plants but only lives for 6 more weeks.

Josh's questions, each corresponding to a mark on the paper, were:

How many eggs does she lay?

Why do they call them nymphs?

Why don't they freeze in winter?

Do they hurt the trees?

Coding is a flexible strategy that can be used orally or in writing to guide the understanding of any type of expository text. However, teaching this strategy requires a generous amount of teacher modeling and student response. Students need to verbalize what they are doing, why they are doing it, and how it should be done.

Twelve-year-old Tischa wrote out that she used the coding strategy in this way:

1. If you already knew something put a plus and skip it when you review.
2. If its (sic) new info and you understand it circle a key word and put an exclamation point.
3. If its (sic) confusing put a question mark and reread it or ask somebody.
4. This can help when you read new, hard, and long things.

Nine-year-old Justin explained the coding strategy by writing:

When I read I THINK

- about what I already know

- about what I will learn

- bout what questions to be ansed (sic)

I Love to think!

The Topic/Detail/Main-Idea Strategy.
As they read expository text, competent readers consciously try to determine the main ideas and supporting facts. In doing this, they effectively interrelate facts by forming a core of main ideas, and a cluster of facts around those ideas. This reduces memory load and allows more effective study.

However, constructing main ideas is a complex ability, requiring many component skills (Afflerbach, 1987; Brown & Day, 1983). Since they are often not stated directly in the text, learning to identify main ideas requires careful and systematic teaching over an extended period of time.

In addition, low-achieving students have often formed misconceptions about main ideas, sometimes based on previous instruction. They believe that every paragraph contains a main idea, which is stated in a topic sentence. However, the reality is much more complex. An analysis of social studies texts in grades two, four, six, and eight found that only 44 percent of the paragraphs contained topic sentences. The same study discovered that only 27 percent of short passages in the social studies texts had a topic sentence stating the main idea (Baumann & Serra, 1984).

Students with reading problems also believe that the first sentence in the paragraph is the topic sentence. Asked to take notes on main ideas, Allison cheerfully underlined the first sentence in every paragraph. She then put down her pencil and announced, "I'm all done. It was real easy." In reality, finding the main idea requires hard work and careful monitoring of one's comprehension. As we read, we need to be aware of the topic of the paragraph, what we are learning about the topic and what is the most important statement that the author has made to explain the topic (Aulls, 1986).

The Topic/Detail/Main-Idea strategy is based upon (1) the strategies used by mature readers to construct main ideas and (2) recognition of the organizational patterns of text. As with all expository text strategies, you will need to model the Topic/Detail/Main Idea strategy on a regular basis. In this strategy, students identify (1) the topic of a paragraph, (2) the details of a paragraph, and (3) the main ideas of a paragraph. The main idea often must be *constructed* by the student.

The steps of the strategy are as follows:

1. Read the entire selection.
2. Reread the first paragraph and identify the topic of the paragraph. (The topic is what the paragraph is about). State the topic in one or two words. You can figure out a topic by asking yourself what each sentence is talking about.
3. Now, underline, in your paragraph, each thing that the author tells you about the topic. These are the details.
4. Now that you have the topic and details, check to see if there is a main idea sentence (a topic sentence). Remember that each detail should be connected to this sentence.
5. If you don't find a main idea sentence (and you probably won't), construct one. It helps to ask yourself these questions:

   - Is the author describing something: a person, a thing, a process, or an event?
   - Is the author comparing or contrasting two or more things?
   - Is the author explaining a problem or a solution?
   - Is the author explaining a cause and effect?

As students begin to construct their own main idea sentences, they often use statements such as "The author is describing the cicada's life cycle" or "The author is listing problems with the way we get rid of garbage." These main idea statements provide a good framework for clustering facts.

In modeling the Topic/Detail/Main Idea strategy, we suggest that you duplicate a section of the students' textbook and write directly on the page or use an overhead transparency. You might write the topic in one color and underline the details in a second color. If the paragraph contains a topic sentence, underline it in a third color or use this color to write your constructed main idea sentence. The different colors help students to visualize a strategy that, like the other strategies we have discussed, should eventually be done mentally.

Share with students that not every paragraph contains a main idea. Often several small paragraphs can be joined together to form one main idea unit, or long paragraphs can be split into two main idea units. There are also introductory, transition, and summary paragraphs that do not really contain main ideas. Students often call these paragraphs "get going" paragraphs, "glue" paragraphs, and "bye-bye" paragraphs. Stratgegy Snapshot 9.2 illustrates the topic/detail main idea procedure.

The Think-Aloud Strategy.

In this strategy the teacher models the way that a skilled reader makes sense from text (Davey, 1983). Through displaying their own thinking, teachers show students how good readers actually process text and invite students to use these strategies. The purpose of the Think-Aloud strategy is "to remove the cloak of mystery surrounding the comprehension process" (New Directions in Reading Comprehension, 1987).

To use the strategy, select a short passage that contains unknown words and other points of difficulty. Give the passage to each student, retaining one copy for yourself. Next read the passage aloud, verbalizing, as you read, all of the thought processes you use in trying to make sense of the passage. Davey (1983) suggests that you do these things:

1. Make predictions about topics. Hypothesize what the passage will be about early in the reading and change the predictions if needed. For example, say "The title makes me think that this will be about . . ." or "Now in this next part, it looks like the topic is changing to . . ."
2. Describe any images you form while reading. For example, say "As I read this, I see a sandy beach by the sea . . ."
3. Give analogies to relate the material to your own life or to what you already know about the topic. Say, "This part about how discipline is important to athletes reminds me of how I used to make a schedule to practice the piano."
4. Note confusing points. Say, "I really don't understand what is going on here" or "This doesn't make sense." This is important because it allows students to see that adults, too, have difficulties.
5. Demonstrate the fix-up strategies. These show how to correct misunderstandings. Say, "I think I'll read this passage again and see if this gets clearer" or "I wonder what that word means. The rest of the sentence makes me think it means _____."

After teachers model the think-aloud process several times, students should apply it to their own reading. Have them report on their use of the five strategies you have modeled. They may give their reactions after they have finished reading or after they have read each paragraph. Davey also suggests that students fill out a checklist reporting which strategies they used in reading. Discuss the checklist with students immediately after they read, while the memories of the reading process are still fresh. The checklist in Table 9.3 is adapted from

Strategy Snapshot 9.2
● ● ● ● ● ● ● ● ● ● ● ● ● ●
Topic/Detail/Main Idea Strategy

Ms. Gillman and a small group of fifth-grade low-achieving readers used this selection.

1. The elephant is the largest living animal and one of the most intelligent, and yet elephants are rather easily captured. They are very nearsighted, and so they cannot see anything distinctly unless it is close to them. Hunters take advantage of this to get near to elephants they wish to capture. Even if discovered, a person can escape an angry elephant by getting out of its line of vision.

2. There are two kinds of elephants, the Asian (or Indian) elephant, and the African elephant. Next time you are at the zoo, look at each kind, especially at their ears and sizes. See if you can tell the difference.

3. Both the Asian and African elephants roam about in herds. The leader is usually an older female elephant. When grass becomes scarce in one valley, she will decide when and where to go next. The younger elephants follow her in single file to better grazing land.

4. Members of the herd will often help one another. Once when an elephant was wounded by a hunter, others of the herd helped it to escape. Two large elephants walked on either side of the wounded animal to keep it from falling.

Students first read the entire selection orally together and then reread the first paragraph. Ms. Gillman guided the students to see that each sentence was about elephants so this topic was written in the margin by the first paragraph. They then underlined information about the elephants and looked for a main idea sentence. When one student suggested that the first sentence was the main idea, Ms. Gillman asked if all the sentences talked about the elephant as large, intelligent, and easily captured. They agreed that none of the other sentences mentioned size or intelligence and only the third sentence talked about capture. The group decided that they had to make up their own main idea sentence. They used step 5 of the strategy and decided that the main idea sentence was: "The author is describing elephants." Ms. Gillman asked if the author was describing a particular thing about the elephant. After some lively discussion, the group changed their original main idea sentence to: "The author is describing the elephant's eyesight."

The second paragraph puzzled the students. Ms. Gillman suggested that they skip this paragraph and move on to the next one. She explained that not all paragraphs have main ideas.

The students reread the third paragraph and decided that the topic was elephant herds and they underlined what they learned. However, the students disagreed upon the main idea sentence. Two thought the first sentence a fine main idea sentence because each sentence talked about what the elephants did in herds. Three other students wrote: "The author is describing how the herd acts." Ms. Gillman assured them that both were fine main idea sentences.

The students chose *herd* as the topic of the last paragraph. After underlining what they learned, they all agreed that the first sentence was a good main idea sentence.

Excerpt from "One of the Smartest," New Practice Readers, Book E, 2nd ed., Phoenix Learning Resources, 1988, by permission of publishers.

Davey's model. You can also have students make a bookmark listing the five strategies. This helps to remind them to use the strategy on their own.

Table 9.3   **Think Aloud Checklist**

What Did I Do When I Read?

Made predictions	Yes	No
Formed pictures	Yes	No
Used "this is like"	Yes	No
Found problems in reading	Yes	No
Used fix-ups	Yes	No

Strategies for Transforming Expository Text

In addition to understanding expository text, students must also study and remember what they read, so that they can discuss it and pass tests. Effective studying requires us to do two things: (1) recognize important information and (2) actively process, or transform, it (Anderson & Armbruster, 1984). Taking notes and reconstructing the text in a visual fashion are ways of doing this.

One college student took a course in neuropsychology that involved remembering many details about brain structure and function. To master this very difficult information, the student had to transform it, creating labeled pictures of the brain and making diagrams relating the brain to body parts. She underlined the text, took notes on the underlined parts, and rewrote the notes again. Finally, she mastered the course content. As our example shows, effective studying involves transforming text and changing it into a form that can be remembered.

Teachers generally expect students to study on their own, yet it is difficult to develop the self-guidance and systematic approaches necessary for this independence. Students with reading difficulties need direct instruction in transforming the text so that they can remember it.

The strategies discussed in the earlier parts of this chapter aid in understanding text and recognizing important information. In this section, we discuss different ways of transforming text content into visual diagrams. Constructing these diagrams involves the student in actively processing the information. The diagrams can also be used as study aids.

The Main-Idea Grid.

The Main-Idea Grid can be used as a diagram for taking notes as student work through the Topic/Detail/Main-Idea Strategy (presented earlier in this chapter). After students read and analyze a paragraph, the grid is used to record the *topic, details,* and *main-idea sentence.* A guide is given in Figure 9.3.

The main-idea grid serves several purposes. (1) It acts as a reminder of the comprehension strategy students should be using as they read. (2) It involves students in actively transforming the text. (3) It helps students to take brief notes in their own words. Since space for notes is limited, students must often shorten their writing. (4) It provides a simplified and transformed summary from which students can study. You can give the students copies of the grid to fill in or they can draw their own grid as they go along.

Idea-Mapping.

Idea-Mapping (Armbruster, 1986; Armbruster & Anderson, 1982) visually demonstrates the organizational patterns of expository text and helps students recognize how ideas in a text-

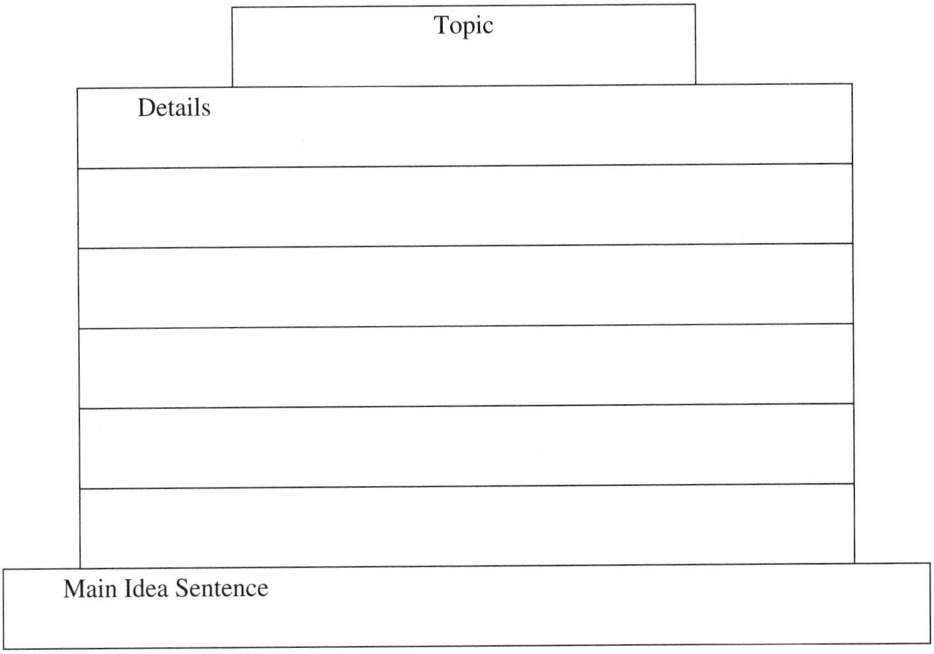

FIGURE 9.3
Main-Idea Grid

book are linked together. Idea-Mapping is based upon the different patterns of expository text that we described earlier in the chapter: sequence or time order; listing or description; comparison–contrast; cause–effect; and problem–solution. Each text structure is represented by a unique idea-map form. The students fill in the map with information from the text. We have simplified and adapted the original idea-maps of Armbruster (1986) and used them successfully with low-achieving readers. Idea-maps remind students to identify patterns of expository organization.

In the early stages of using idea-mapping, we suggest that you identify an organizational pattern for the students and give them the appropriate map to fill in. The next step involves giving them two idea-map choices. The students read the text and decide which organizational pattern best fits; then they fill in the map. Finally, students independently choose which idea-map to use.

We have found that comparison–contrast is an effective map to present first. The items that are to be compared are written in the top spaces. The characteristics of each are written next. If the characteristics are similar or identical, the equals symbol (=) is written between them. If the characteristics differ, the symbol is the equals sign with a line drawn through it (≠). An idea-map for comparing and contrasting deciduous and coniferous trees might look like Figure 9.4.

You can also present the idea-map for Description or Listing in the early stages of teaching the strategy. The item to be described is written in the top space and the descriptive characteristics are listed underneath. An idea-map for describing poison ivy might look like Figure 9.5.

Three other idea-maps represent the expository patterns of Sequence, Problem–Solution and Cause–Effect. The first box of the Sequence idea-map contains the title of the process that is being described. Numbered rectangles connected by arrows indicate that the events placed in each box occur in a set order, as in Figure 9.6.

The Problem–Solution idea-map has a rectangle for the problem connected by an arrow to another rectangle for the solution. Characteristics or comments about the problem or solution are written underneath each. A Problem–Solution idea-map might look like Figure 9.7.

The Cause–Effect idea-map is similar. The cause is written in one rectangle and the effect is written in another. They are connected by an arrow that indicates that the cause precedes or leads into the effect. Again, description or comments about the cause or effect can be written underneath. An example of a Cause–Effect idea-map is given in Figure 9.8.

Idea-maps, like most of the strategies presented in this chapter, take time for students to learn and apply independently. As we mentioned earlier, these expository patterns are not always clear. Two students may choose different idea-maps to represent the same text. Kelly and Amy were reading about the early years of Franklin Delano Roosevelt's presidency. Kelly chose the Sequence idea-map to represent Roosevelt's actions. Amy chose the Problem–Solution idea-map and organized her notes around the many problems faced by Roosevelt and his attempts to solve them.

Of course, students cannot choose just any idea-map. They must choose an appropriate one that fits the text, but variation in choices will occur. Your role is to encourage the students to verbalize why they chose a particular map. We have found that students enjoy sharing their choices with their peers and lively discussion often occurs as students defend these decisions.

In the early stages of instruction, use short segments of text to illustrate idea-maps. Gradually increase the length of the text. As students move into longer text, they often have to use multiple idea-maps. Amy used several Problem–Solution maps to summarize the problems faced by Roosevelt. Kelly divided Roosevelt's early presidency into two Sequence idea-maps, one for each of his first two terms.

Deciduous Trees		Coniferous Trees
Have trunk with bark	=	Have trunk with bark
Vary in size	=	Vary in size
Found throughout world	=	Found throughout world
Have leaves	≠	Have needles
Shed leaves in fall	≠	Remains green in winter
Bear fruit	≠	Bear cones

FIGURE 9.4
Compare–Contrast Idea Map

Poison Ivy
Three leaves
Glossy or dull green leaves
Yellow-white flower
Hairy stem
Grows in woods, roadsides, fence rows
Oil causes skin inflammation
Not harmful to birds

FIGURE 9.5
Description Idea-Map

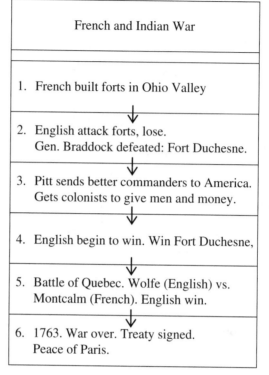

FIGURE 9.6
Sequence Idea-Map

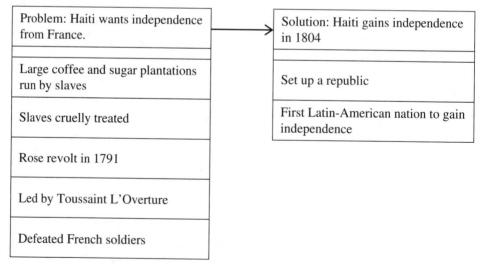

FIGURE 9.7
Problem–Solution Idea-Map

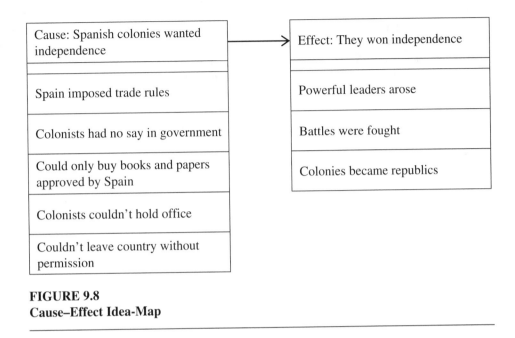

FIGURE 9.8
Cause–Effect Idea-Map

Summary

Expository material refers to informational materials such as school textbooks. Expository material is organized around five basic patterns: sequence, listing, compare–contrast, cause–effect, and problem–solution. Comprehension of the main ideas in a passage is heavily dependent upon recognition of these patterns.

Expository text tends to be difficult, especially for poor readers. Text organization is often unclear. Expository text is less personal than narratives and contains more difficult vocabulary. Students must both understand and remember the content of their textbooks. Poor readers often lack the background knowledge needed to successfully comprehend expository selections.

Successful reading of expository text requires that students activate their prior knowledge before they read, monitor their own comprehension, and develop strategies for reorganizing or transforming text in order to remember it.

Several strategies can be used to assess a student's ability to read expository material. The teacher can adapt the informal reading inventory procedure for use with textbooks. The teacher can assess use of background knowledge by comparing a student's performance on familiar and unfamiliar text. The teacher can assess comprehension monitoring by having the student identify troublesome parts of text. Finally, the teacher can assess a student's ability to reorganize text by having him or her take notes.

Strategies for helping students read expository text should be student centered, that is, able to be used independently by the student. Such strategies take a long time to learn and apply. Teachers need to focus on a single strategy over a long period of time. Teachers should model the strategy and repeatedly ask students to verbalize what they are doing, why they are doing it, and the procedures they are using.

Students can activate their own knowledge of a topic by using the expectation grid and the K-W-L strategy. They can monitor their own comprehension by using Text Coding, the Topic/Detail/Main Idea strategy, and the think-aloud strategy. They can transform the text in order to remember it by using the Main-Idea Grid and idea-mapping.

CHAPTER 10

Improving Language Abilities: Listening Comprehension and Meaning Vocabulary

Introduction

In this chapter, we discuss two important facets of language: listening comprehension and meaning vocabulary. We also suggest strategies that help students with reading problems improve their language abilities. Because reading is language, we cannot read material that is above our language level. Thus, the richer a student's language is, the better he or she will read.

The Importance of Language to Reading

Language abilities are critical to success in reading, particularly after the primary grades. When young children first learn to read, their greatest challenge is to recognize, in print, words that they use in everyday speech. But in the third or fourth grade, high-level words and concepts start to be introduced in school reading. Those students who have a rich language background cope well with this new challenge; those who lack higher-level language do not. Many of the students in our Reading Center have developed problems as the material they have to read becomes more complex.

Researchers find that as students mature, there are increasingly strong relationships between their reading achievement and both listening comprehension (Daneman, 1991; Dymock, 1993) and meaning vocabulary (Anderson & Freebody, 1981; Davis, 1968; Thorndike, 1973).

Causes of Problems with Language

Many low-achieving students lack a solid language base for building reading achievement. There are three major causes of problems with language.

Language Disability and Delay

A problem with language may severely affect reading abilities. Dawn, an "A" pupil in first and second grades, could read words accurately and fluently. She had a highly supportive family that promoted literacy. In third grade, however, she began to fail science and social studies tests. She could not remember new terms, and her parents began to notice that she had difficulty expressing herself. At our Reading Center, Dawn's tutor orally read her social studies text to her. Not surprisingly, Dawn could not summarize, answer questions, or understand key words from the text. This demonstrated that Dawn's reading problem was caused by a language problem.

In some cases, language problems are severe enough to be noticed early, and they affect beginning reading skills. In other cases, like that of Dawn, problems are noticed only as children meet the complex demands of intermediate grade material. Chall (1983b) calls this the "fourth-grade slump." Language disabilities and related problems, such as speech impediments, are further discussed in Chapter 13.

Lack of Reading

Of course, other students with reading problems have had problems recognizing words from the beginning of their reading instruction. Interestingly, these students also tend to have problems developing rich language. In these cases, language problems are actually caused by a lack of difficult reading. How does this happen?

Many difficult words and complex syntactic structures are met only in reading. Therefore, students who read extensively have opportunities to build their meaning vocabularies and learn complex sentence structures. Unfortunately, students who have difficulties recognizing words do very, very little reading, and, therefore, are not exposed to these rich language structures. Thus, many readers who start out with only word recognition problems also eventually develop deficiencies in language (Stanovich, 1986, 1988).

Lack of a Rich Language Environment

A final group of students is not exposed to rich language structures in the home and in other everyday environments. Activities done in a nurturing home, such as reading books, listening to stories, and engaging in the free exchange of ideas, form an important basis for language skills. However, not all families can provide such advantages. Some parents lack the reading skills to foster literacy; others lack time; others do not value such experiences but rather, value obedience and respect from children.

Thomas, a ten-year-old in our Reading Center, had been taught to be quiet and respectful. Before each session, his mother warned him to obey his teacher, and afterwards, she asked if he had been a good boy. Thomas's mother was, at first, baffled by our request that she read to him, since, to her, reading was the responsibility of the child. It took a few months, and attendance at our weekly parent program, until Thomas and his mother became comfortable with the noise and excitement generated as Thomas talked freely and expressively to improve his language.

Assessing Language Abilities

Language abilities can be assessed using both formal measures and informal probes.

Formal Tests

Some formal tests are designed to measure language skills. The *Peabody Picture Vocabulary Test–Revised* (*PPVT-R*) assesses listening vocabulary. In this test, an examiner reads a word and the student chooses one of four pictures to represent that word. The examiner might say "Point to pencil," and the four picture choices might be paper, a pencil, a pen, and a crayon. No reading is involved. In addition, since the student is not required to say any words, the *PPVT-R* is a measure of understanding, or *receptive* vocabulary, rather than *expressive* vocabulary. The test covers ages 2.5 to adult, has norms enabling comparison to a reference group, and comes in two alternate forms.

Informal Measures

Informal measures may also be used to assess language abilities. It is often helpful to determine whether (1) a student's language abilities are more advanced than reading skills or (2) language abilities and reading are at the same level. If a student's language abilities are more advanced than reading, this indicates a need for word recognition instruction, so that the student can learn to read at the language level that he or she can understand. On the other hand, if a student's reading and language are at the same low level, more development of language abilities is needed in order to improve reading. To determine this, a teacher may find whether a reading problem is due to poor word recognition (part of reading) or poor listening level (part of language).

An informal probe of a standardized test allows you to compare reading and language. First, administer a standardized reading test in the regular manner. Then, administer same test by reading it to the student (an informal probe). (1) If the student scores about the same on both the reading and listening versions, a need for language development is indicated. (2) If the student scores better on the listening version than the reading version, student needs to develop more word recognition abilities.

This can be summarized as follows:

Reading and listening equal: language development needed

Listening better than reading: word recognition needed

You may choose to probe only specific subtests of a test. Eric's sixth-grade teacher was interested in whether his difficulties stemmed from poor word recognition or poor language. To find out, Eric was first given the vocabulary subtest of the *Gates MacGinitie Reading Test, Level 4*. In this subtest, he read words and chose synonyms for them. After Eric had taken the vocabulary subtest using this standard administration, the teacher orally read the same subtest to Eric and had him give his answers aloud. If Eric's ability to recognize words had been interfering with his original score, he would have improved his score when the subtest was read to him. Since Eric did not improve his score, his problem was with language, rather than with recognizing words. Using the same procedure for the comprehension subtest of the *Gates MacGinitie*, Eric again failed to improve his score. This further confirmed Eric's need for language development.

In another simple procedure, a teacher can determine how developed a student's language is simply by reading orally to him or her and asking comprehension questions. If a student can comprehend the material, it is within his or her language level. This is the procedure we recommend in Chapter 3. Using an informal reading inventory, we read passages orally to a student to determine a listening (or language) level. We may then compare this with the student's reading level. We can also read school materials to students. As discussed earlier in this chapter, Dawn's tutor read her school materials to her to determine if she had a language problem. When Dawn could not understand them, her tutor concluded that she needed further language development before she would be able to read school materials successfully.

Finally, conversing with a student often gives many insights into a student's level of language and comfort in expressing thoughts. Teachers may learn much from conducting student interviews, talking with students about their interests, or observing language use when students summarize stories and answer questions.

Conditions that Foster Language Learning

Language is all around, as students talk to friends, listen to a teacher, read comics, view videos, and "channel surf" using the TV remote control. From these vast opportunities for communication, how can we select the ones that best enrich the language of students with reading problems? Three principles for selection are (1) give wide exposure to *rich* language, (2) actively involve students, and (3) use both incidental exposure and direct teaching. Since everybody savors the richness of language, teaching it enables your students to enjoy themselves while building an invaluable base for reading.

Language Growth Depends on Exposure to Higher-Level Language

A first priority for improving students' language is to bring high-level language to them. All children hear commands and requests in their everyday lives. However, not all have the rich experiences of listening to detailed verbal descriptions, explaining their own reasoning, or hearing a variety of uncommon words. Similarly, all children study their school texts, but not all get to listen to language-rich books, such as *Tikki Tikki Tembo* (by Mosel) or *To Think That I Saw It on Mulberry Street* (by Dr. Seuss).

The language found in books is richer than that contained in oral language, both in vocabulary (Hayes & Ahrens, 1988) and in grammatical structures (Purcell-Gates, 1986). Books also tend to contain knowledge that is well reasoned and transcends the limits of personal information (Stanovich & Cunningham, 1993). Therefore, in working with students who have reading problems, it is important to use *the language of books.*

It may take patience to foster an appreciation of language-rich books in a student with reading problems, but you will be well rewarded. There is a special magic in seeing an at-risk child enjoy rich language for the first time. After more than a year has gone by, one class still begs us to chant the refrain from *Tikki Tikki Tembo* one more time!

Language Learning Is Active

To gain full control over language, students with reading problems must be comfortable not only listening to and reading the language, but also using it expressively in their own speech and writing. "Doing something" with language gives students stake in their own learning and helps them to overcome the passivity that is a problem for so many low-achieving readers. Language that has been processed deeply, through many different activities, is learned well and used often (Stahl & Fairbanks, 1986).

Students Learn Language from Both Incidental and Direct Instruction

Language instruction can be divided into two types: incidental and direct. In incidental instruction, students absorb meaning vocabulary, grammatical structures, and concepts simply from being exposed to rich language. In direct instruction, students are systematically taught specific words and language structures. Both types of learning improve language abilities.

Most language learning is incidental. For example, research shows that most vocabulary words are picked up through exposure during reading (Anderson & Nagy, 1991; Miller & Gildea, 1987; Nagy, Anderson, & Herman, 1987; Sternberg, 1987) and listening (Stahl, Richek, & Vandiver, 1991). We do not learn an unknown word the first time we are exposed to it. Instead we learn words gradually, needing perhaps 20 or more exposures for full mastery. Dale (1965) found that vocabulary knowledge could be described in four stages of gradual learning:

1. never saw or heard this word;
2. saw or heard it, but don't know it;
3. know it in a sentence; know the meaning vaguely; and
4. know it well.

Over time, and with maximum exposure to language, students learn many words well. Of course, the richer the language that they are exposed to, the more opportunities they will have to engage in incidental vocabulary learning.

Although most language growth occurs through incidental instruction, direct instruction can also help students prepare for success in school. Students with reading problems often must master specific unknown words and concepts before they can effectively read their school assignments. There are many interesting and exciting ways to give these pupils the direct instruction that enables them to have successful reading and studying experiences.

Strategies for Fostering Language: Listening Comprehension

There are many strategies that foster students' language development through listening. These listening activities are nonthreatening, time-efficient, and pay handsome dividends in enjoyment and language growth.

Reading Books to Students

If students cannot yet read language-rich, difficult books, teachers can read these books to them. Through *listening* to reading material containing sophisticated language and structures, students acquire the language proficiency that later enables them to *read* at a high level. We highly recommend reading to low-achieving students at least a few times per week.

Listening to a teacher read is beneficial for students with reading problems. (1) Students absorb higher-level language, build background knowledge, and learn story organization. (2) Students are motivated to learn to read as they become aware of the many interesting things that can be read. (3) Listening to a teacher read is a relaxing activity.

Materials that are above students' reading level, and on the "cutting edge" of their language, will be most effective in fostering language growth. They should contain language that is challenging, but not overwhelming, for students. To build background knowledge, teachers should try to find books that are set in a different time and place or contain elements of fantasy. In addition, they should try to read both short stories and longer books. Reading full-length novels to students helps them to develop comprehension strategies for longer material.

A few suggestions for language-rich books suitable for teacher read alouds for primary grades include *Amos and Boris* (by Steig), *Many Moons* (by Thurber), and *To Think That I Saw It on Mulberry Street* (by Dr. Seuss). For intermediate and upper grades, try *Mrs. Frisby and the Rats of NIMH* (by O'Brien), *Ben and Me* (by Lawson), *North to Freedom* (by Holm), *Sarah Plain and Tall* (by MacLachlan), *In the Year of the Boar and Jackie Robinson* (by Lord), and *The Indian in the Cupboard* (by Banks). Short stories by Edgar Allan Poe, Jack London, Mark Twain, and Sir Arthur Conan Doyle are filled with sophisticated concepts and vocabulary. Students with reading problems also enjoy listening to expository text. We kept one group of Chapter I fourth-graders enthralled as, using the book *Fabulous Facts about the 50 States* (by Ross), we covered one state each session. Finally, books focusing on figurative language, such as *Amelia Bedelia* (by Parish), help to enrich students' language.

When reading to students, do not be alarmed if they don't know the meanings of all the words. If, however, you feel students are uncomfortable or someone asks a question, feel free to stop and explain concepts and words. Young children often like to hear favorites reread. Such rereading enables them to get more from the story and to develop a sense of security.

Reading to students can easily be done at times when they are not at peak energy, such as after lunch or at the end of the day. We recommend that you read for 10 to 15 minutes at one time. At times, however, students get "into" a book, and they may beg you to read longer. Try to stop at a meaningful point, such as the end of a chapter.

The Mega-Cloze Strategy

Developed by Diane Whittier (personal communication, 1993), the Mega-Cloze Strategy is a way to make listening more active, as well as increase prediction skills and knowledge of story structure. In doing daily reading to her class, Ms. Whittier noticed that the attention of her low-achieving students often wandered. To focus them, she took out sentences from the chapter she was going to read and wrote them on strips of paper. She gave each strip to one student, and told the children that she was going to see if they could predict when the sentence each held would appear in the text. Next, she read the chapter. When she came to a sentence that was left out, she gave a signal (such as wiggling her fingers and saying "wiggle"). The students then looked at their strips, and the person who held the right sentence read it aloud.

In preparing a mega-cloze, we generally excerpt one to two sentences per page. To ensure that all students can recognize the words, we have them read the sentences aloud before we start to read the story or chapter. Before you read the story, make sure to mark the sentences you have excerpted in your book; otherwise *you* may forget the sentences the children are responding to!

This strategy can be used with advanced books, such as *A Bridge to Terabithia* (by Patterson) and *Tuck Everlasting* (by Babbitt), or with easier, shorter materials (such as folktales like "The Three Little Pigs"). Older and more able students can predict the sentences without hearing the story beforehand. However, for younger or less able students, we suggest that you first read an entire story to them, and do the mega-cloze activity when you reread it. Several of the groups we have worked with like to do the mega-cloze several times, changing cards each time. To avoid the embarrassment that some students feel when they get a sentence wrong, we sometimes have two students share each card, so they can split the responsibility.

Paired Story Reading

Some teachers feel that their students will not be able to grasp the literary style of classic fairy and folk tales, yet recognize that these are valuable listening experiences. Paired story reading involves easy and hard versions of classic stories (Richek, 1989). It is particularly recommended for students with reading problems in grades one to six.

For this strategy, you need to find both an easier and a more difficult version of the same fairy or folk tale. Collections of fairy tales in easy versions are available, for example, in (1) the *Fairy Stories for Pleasure Reading* (by Dolch) and in (2) the *Fun to Read Fairy Tales* (Modern Publishing Unisystems, Inc.). More difficult versions of fairy tales can be found in Lang's *The Green Fairy Book* (and in the red, yellow, and blue books). Or you can use such single books as *Cinderella* (Perrault, illustrated by Brown) or *Snow White* (Grimm, illustrated by Burkert).

After you have chosen the materials, simply read an easy version of one tale to students on one day (say, "Cinderella" from the Dolch's book) and discuss the story. This will enable them to learn and enjoy the basic plot line. On the next day, read the difficult version of the same tale (such as *Cinderella,* illustrated by Brown). Having the background of the easier tale, the students will enjoy the greater detail and richer language of the harder version. They will also want to compare the slight differences between the story lines of different versions.

Directed Listening–Thinking Activity (DL-TA)

DL-TA parallels the Directed Reading–Thinking Activity (DR-TA) presented in Chapter 8. DL-TA is recommended for primary children who need to develop a sense of story structure and for students of any age who need to improve their language abilities.

In DL-TA, students *listen* to a story being read and predict what will happen next. When reading the story, the teacher stops at several critical points and asks students to predict (Richek, 1987). Freed from the constraints of having to recognize words, students can apply all of their energies to thinking about the story.

It is important to formalize the thinking process of DL-TA just as we do in DR-TA. Thus, when using DL-TA, we carefully write down all of the student's predictions on the chalkboard. This activity encourages a reading response, since students will invariably want to read their own language, as written on the board. (Adaptations of DL-TA suitable for emergent literacy are discussed in Chapter 5.)

Sentence Building

Students with reading problems often have difficulty with sentence comprehension. The Sentence Building Strategy (Richek, 1995) is a creative way to give students practice in creating their own long sentences. Although best suited to a group situation, it can also be used individually.

First write a simple sentence, without punctuation or capitalization, such as

the boy walked the dog

on tag board, word cards, or sentence strips, and put it on the board. You can attach it with masking tape or Plastitac (also known as Funtac). Or, if you prefer, use an overhead projector and transparency sheets that have been cut into small pieces.

Then tell the students that you want them to add to the sentence, with each student taking a turn to make it longer. An important rule, however, is that a student must look at the sentence as it is printed on the board and say the sentence *plus* the addition the student wishes to add. Only then will the teacher put in that student's addition.

The first student might look at "the boy walked the dog" and say "the boy walked the dog to the park." Then the teacher will add to the sentence on the board, changing it from

> **the boy walked the dog**

to

> **the boy walked the dog to the park**

The object is to create a very long sentence. Since students will usually add to the end of a sentence, the teacher should also require that they make additions to the beginning and the middle. The following sentence was created by fourth-grade resource room students:

> **Johnny and the big muscle-bound boy, who had never seen that kind of dog, walked the dog to the park and through the alley, and a girl asked them if she could hold the dog.**

This one was created by fifth- and sixth-grade learning-disabled students in a resource room:

> **Who was the dumb ugly boy with a holey shirt and holey pants who walked the dog all the way home and gave him a bone and gave him some food with water?**

When is a sentence long enough? We ask students to stop building it when they can no longer repeat it in one breath. Since children's breaths increase with age, this permits older students to build longer sentences than younger ones. After a sentence has been finished, you may want to discuss appropriate capitalization and punctuation with the students. Finally, young children in a large class often enjoy each holding one word. Then, as the sentence grows, they get to move to different places.

Developing Verbal Style

Students with reading problems often fear expressing their thoughts and opinions, yet active use of language is essential to building language skills. A few principles, if practiced consistently by teachers, can make pupils feel more comfortable in expressing themselves.

(1) Never interrupt students who are speaking, or allow others to interrupt them. Cultivate your own personal patience and *insist* upon respectful behavior of students toward each other.

(2) Genuinely value students' points of view. This is fostered when we ask students for their opinions. You can model how to express opinions by using phrases such as "I think that . . ." and "It's my opinion that . . ." Often, if you express your opinions in long sentences, students will be inspired to follow your example.

(3) Do not judge the *quality* of what pupils say. Instead, respond to *what* students say, trying not to judge how they express themselves. This gives students confidence to express themselves more fully. Students who feel their language is being judged will be intimidated. In contrast, students who feel that their opinions are valued will be more comfortable talking.

Strategies for Fostering Language: Meaning Vocabulary

Word meanings are critical elements in instruction for students with reading problems. Meaning vocabulary is highly correlated with a student's ability to comprehend, and words themselves embody important concepts that students will meet in reading (Anderson & Freebody, 1981).

In this section, we present (1) direct instructional strategies for introducing and practicing words, (2) ways to encourage incidental vocabulary learning, and (3) helping students to figure out words independently.

Direct Instructional Strategies for Introducing Words before Reading

Knowing key words in a story or book will help students to read more effectively. Even a short introduction of a word helps, since a large part of learning a word is simply noticing that it exists. Have you ever noticed how often you hear a word after you learn it? This is because you have become conscious of the word. The strategies we present are not meant to give students a complete mastery of words before reading, for they will understand the words better after they have read (or listened to) them in a text. Rather, these strategies focus on getting words into use so that students are comfortable enough to read.

Noticing Words.
Simply having students notice words and find them in a story often helps them to gain considerable mastery. To prepare low-achieving third-graders for reading a story, one teacher (K. Voorhees, personal communication, 1994) wrote out each new word for a story on a card. He next passed out these cards, giving one or two words to each child. Then, he read the story to the students and, as he read each word, the child who had that word held up the card. In this way, the children noticed each new word *as it was read in the story,* and were able to use the sense of the text to gain information about meanings. Later, when his students read the story for themselves, they found their personal word(s) in the story.

A neighboring teacher (G. Tate, personal communication, 1994) extended this idea by having students predict, before she read the story to her class, which words would first appear at the beginning of the story, the middle, or the end.

Classifying.
When students classify words into categories, they are actively engaged in using higher-level skills to learn vocabulary. To ensure that students are successful, however, the teacher may have to go over some of the words with the students before they classify. To prepare third-grade children to read the story, "Dragon Stew," words were classified into four categories: (1) king words, (2) cook words, and (3) dragon words. The words were *stew, royal, castle, throne, palace, fellow, rare, fellow, ordinary, stirred, pork, lit, fiery breath, banquet hall, majesty, proclamations, drawbridge, roast, applesauce, sliced, bubbling, vinegar, simmer, onions, gravy-stained, assistant, fanciful.* While doing this, the students' lively discussions about the words helped them to deepen vocabulary learning.

Predict-o-rama.
By classifying words into story grammar categories (see Chapter 8) before they read a story, students become actively involved in learning meanings and predicting story content. To do a Predict-o-rama, list the new words in a story, and then ask students to predict whether each word will be used to describe the setting, the characters, the actions, or the ending. Next, as they read, students can see if these words are used in the way that was predicted (Blachowicz, 1986). If the words are written on Post-it notes, students actually move them after reading, if they need to be reclassified.

Knowledge Rating.

The Knowledge Rating Strategy fosters an awareness of words and gives students control over their own knowledge. The teacher lists the new words for a story and students think about how well they know them. Each student checks one of four categories for each word.

1. I know this word.
2. I know something about this word.
3. I have heard or read this word.
4. I don't know this word.

Students then read the selection, keeping the words in mind and, after reading, the chart is reviewed again (Blachowicz, 1986). Students are delighted to find that they know many words better after they have read them in a story.

Possible Sentences.

This strategy can be used to introduce new vocabulary in areas such as social studies, and science texts (Moore & Arthur, 1981). First give the title of a chapter that the students are about to read. Then write the new words on the board, for example: *molecule, proton, atom, electron, neutron*. Next have students think of sentences that possibly might be true. Each sentence must contain at least two target words. An example would be "A molecule could contain two atoms." Students develop expectations of the chapter as they go through this activity. Then have students read the chapter. After reading, students evaluate the possibly true sentences they have written to see if they are indeed true. They change sentences that are inaccurate, and add other sentences reflecting their new knowledge. This simple strategy combines learning vocabulary with the learning of content material.

Direct Instructional Strategies for Reinforcing Meaning Vocabulary

After words have been introduced there are several strategies that reinforce word meaning by keeping students actively engaged with words.

Display and Vocabulary Picture Cards.

Displaying words they have learned helps students feel a sense of accomplishment and informs others of their achievements. Placing words publicly can also help students to remember them. Eighth-grade Marvin put his words on a colorful web honoring his interest in Spiderman. Other students can use their own personal interests.

Students can become "experts" on some words. In a seventh-grade learning disabilities classroom, all of the words from one book unit were placed on individual small cards, which could be flipped up. Each student was given two words and asked to construct cards for them. On the front, the pupil wrote his or her name, to establish ownership. Inside, the student wrote a definition and a sentence for the word, both of which had to be approved by the teacher. The student who had signed his or her name to the word was an "expert consultant" on the word. All word cards were put on display on the bulletin board. When students wanted to review the words, they went to the board, read the word, and flipped up the chart to check the definition.

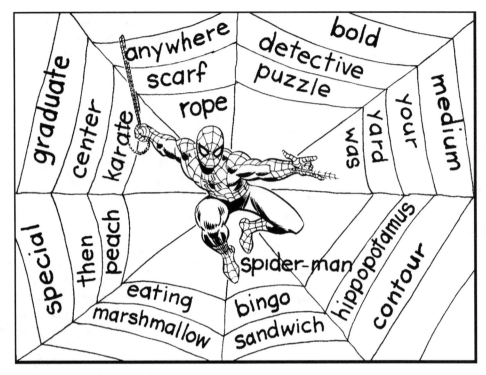

Vocabulary cards featuring picture clues are often effective in reminding students of word meanings. Lansdown (1991) effectively combined picture clue word cards and the "expert consultant" strategies, as shown in Strategy Snapshot 10.1.

The Multiple-Sentence Game.

Students enjoy trying to put a number of their new words into one sentence (Richek, 1994). We recommend this difficult (but exciting) strategy for upper-elementary and secondary students. To do this in a group, prepare a list of target words. Next divide students into small groups and have each group select 3 new words. Groups now exchange words with each other. When each group gets its new list, they must put the words in sentences, trying to use the least number of sentences.

For a sentence with 1 word, they get 1 point.

For a sentence with 2 words, they get 3 points.

For a sentence with 3 words, they get 6 points.

As a teacher, you need to judge the correctness and sense of a sentence before giving credit. Students are allowed to change the form of the word (for example, *slow* to *slowly*). We have observed formerly unmotivated students working on this activity with unprecedented interest, even asking to do it for homework!

Strategy Snapshot 10.1
• • • • • • • • • • • • • • •
Picture Cards and Word Learning

To prepare her 20 at-risk sixth graders to read the difficult novel, *Rascal,* Ms. Lansdown chose 100 difficult *and important* words from the novel and assigned five to each student. The individual student became a "word expert" in these words by preparing cards for each one. On the outside, the word appeared, along with a picture representing it. On the inside was a definition (in the student's own language) and a sentence. The words stayed up on the bulletin board unless the students were using them. When working with them, the students were put in pairs, changing partners each day. For 10 minutes each "word expert" drilled a partner on his or her 5 words, and was drilled on the partner's words in return. Students changed partners for each drill session.

After a week, the students started to read the novel, noticing the words they had been studying as they went along. Ms. Lansdown began to give points, cumulative for the entire class, for finding the words, either in the book, other reading materials, or nonprint sources (radio, TV, speech). In three weeks, the class had almost 1,000 points.

The excitement of learning these words was matched by the enthusiasm students felt in being able to read *Rascal* with considerable proficiency. As an ending project, Ms. Lansdown tested the students on all 100 words, and this class of low-level readers averaged 97 percent. A month later, their proficiency had not slipped. A student word card for *perpetually* is below.

Automaticity.

To fully master words, students need to recognize them quickly. Spending a few minutes a week having students say words quickly, rapidly supply definitions, or quickly compose sentences are good ways to foster automaticity. In one program, Beck, Perfetti, and McKeown (1982) had students quickly answer "yes" or "no" to statements containing vocabulary words. Examples were:

> A philanthropist steals money.
>
> A hermit lives by himself.
>
> A novice is still learning.

Fostering Incidental Vocabulary Learning

As we have mentioned, most meaning vocabulary is learned in an incidental fashion, through listening and reading. In this section, we focus on strategies that help students learn words from their environment.

Modeling Difficult Words in Speech.

If teachers consciously try to use "million dollar words," students will unconsciously absorb them. Employ words that challenge students to expand their vocabularies. Encourage them to ask the meanings of these words and, thus, to take control of their own learning. For example, in a noisy fourth-grade Chapter I class, the teacher said, "I find this noise onerous and burdensome." Fascinated by the words, the pupils immediately quieted down and requested the meaning of this intriguing statement. The teacher wrote the words on the board and discussed them. Teacher use of challenging vocabulary takes little additional time, yet exposes students to many words. One teacher (K. Voorhees, personal communication, 1994) used a million-dollar word every day for his low-achieving third-grade students. Each child had to use the word at least once during the day. Favorites included *dogmatic* and *eccentric*.

Word Collections.

Collecting different types of words increases students' interest in meaning vocabulary. A class of low-achieving fifth graders collected *soft words* (*whisper, slipper*), *green words* (*grass, lime*), and *happy words* (*ecstatic, birthday*), placing them in individual canisters. Students also collect synonyms for the overused word *say*, such as *whispered, muttered, shouted, exclaimed*, and *announced*. Other students have collected expressions. One intermediate class's collection of expressions containing the words *gold, green*, and *black*, included several figures of speech, like "golden years," "golden egg," "green-eyed," "green thumb," "black belt," and "black hole." Your students will become quite creative in thinking up categories they would like to pursue.

Relating Words to Students' Environments.

Words become interesting when they relate to the lives of students (Richek, 1987). Students can look up the meanings of their names in "How to Name Your Baby" books. Car names often intrigue older students: *Chevrolet* was a famous car racer; *Cadillac* was the French explorer who founded Detroit; *Seville* and *Granada* are names of cities; *Mustang* and *Pinto* are types of horses. Other students enjoy discussing the reasoning behind the names of common household products, such as Tide, Wisk, Mr. Clean, Cheer, Vanish. Common foods, such as *hamburger, frankfurter, tomato, banana,* and *tea* have origins on other languages. Students may use them to practice dictionary skills as well as to gain geographical knowledge.

The "Ears" Strategy.

This combines listening to books with an effort to raise children's awareness of words. First, select a story to read, which should contain several difficult words. Next, draw a picture of an ear and duplicate it several times. Then, each student is handed a personal word, on an ear, that appears in the story. To ensure that pupils will recognize these words, the teacher should pronounce them before the story begins. The teacher then reads the story and, each time a child hears her or his word, the child holds it up. Recently, we did this with a group of 16 disabled third graders. After reading the classic story "Rapunzel," most of the students could give substantial information about each of 18 difficult words.

Using Strategies to Figure Out Unknown Words

In this section, we describe some strategies that students can use to figure out word meanings independently.

Using Context Clues.

Most good readers use the sense of the surrounding sentence, or context clues, to learn new words. Students with reading problems will also profit from learning to use context. Although the context will not always define a word thoroughly, it is effective in giving many clues to meaning Gipe (1980). However, the process of gaining meaning from context is not easy for many problem readers. To build vocabulary in this way, they must be encouraged to take risks and to make "intelligent hypotheses." (We often use these very words to encourage our students.)

To help students to use context clues, we put words in a sentence context, and ask students to read them and think about the underlined word. An example might be: "Because John *dawdled,* he arrived late." We then ask students to hypothesize about what this word might mean. Finally, one student looks the word up in the dictionary to determine the exact meaning.

Josel (1988) dramatically demonstrated to low-achieving eighth graders that they used context clues to determine meaning. First, she gave them a list of words (taken from a novel) to match to definitions. Since the list contained words such as *etesian* and *clamorous,* few students could match any correctly. Next, she presented sentences from the book that contained these words (such as "We are sailing before the *etesian,* which blows from the northwest.") and asked students to define the words. Students found they were able to define the majority of the words. This activity demonstrated the helpfulness of context clues in determining word meanings.

After students have become comfortable with context clues, ask them to use these clues consciously as they are reading. First, list new words from a selection students are about to read. Then have students read the selection. When they finish reading, go back to the words, asking students what meanings they hypothesized from the context. It is handy for the teacher to write down the location of the words in the text, so that the class can easily find the words for discussion. If questions remain, the class can consult a dictionary to clarify meanings. This procedure models the way that good readers combine context clues and dictionary skills.

Students with reading problems can also be taught that, when they come to a word they don't know, they should substitute a word or phrase that makes sense. The substitution is likely to be the definition of the unknown word. For example, in the sentence "Because prices were going up, we decided to *defer* buying a car until next year," many students would substitute the phrase *put off* or the word *delay*. These are, in fact, approximate definitions of "defer."

Using Prefixes, Suffixes, and Roots.

The structural parts of words are helpful in giving students with reading problems effective clues to meaning. These include prefixes, suffixes, and roots.

Suffixes, or word endings, are very common in written English, and they provide valuable clues to recognizing long words. However, students with reading problems often ignore word endings and need to practice focusing on them. Since suffixes are relatively easy to teach, a small amount of effort can dramatically increase the ability to recognize long words. In Chapter 6, we gave guidelines for teaching the easiest suffixes (*s, ed*); here, we give strategies for more advanced ones.

Many suffixes change the part of speech of a word. Examples of this are *identify-identification* (verb becomes a noun) and *comfort-comfortable* (noun or verb becomes an adjective). Table 10.1 lists some of the most common suffixes in English and their approximate grade levels (Richek, 1969). Since almost all students have some familiarity with suffixes, it is not necessary to teach them one at a time. Instead, simply teach students to be aware of suffixes as they read in context.

Table 10.1 **Graded List of Suffixes**

First Grade		Second Grade	
er, est*	bigger, biggest	able	serviceable
s, es (plural)*	ponies	al	seasonal
s (possessive)*	Jane's	ing	singing
s (third person)*	she dances	ly	slowly
ed (past)*	waited	ness	bigness

Third Grade		Fourth Grade		Fifth Grade	
y	cherry	ish	childish	ance	insurance
tion	relation	ive	impulsive	ity	serenity
ist	violist	ful	beautiful	ent	excellent
ic	angelic	ency	presidency	age	postage
ize	idolize	ery	slavery	an	musician
ment	contentment	ous	famous		
		ate	activate		

*These are inflectional suffixes. Other suffixes are derivational.

Three activities are useful for helping students to use suffixes.

(1) Select a short text, and ask students to underline each suffix that they find. Provide the hint that some words contain two or even three suffixes. (We find words like ill-ness-es and publish-er-s in third- and fourth-grade materials.) Once students have

completed this task, review it with them. Few students catch *all* of the suffixes, and they will enjoy finding out about the less obvious ones, such as *hurry/hurried*.

(2) In a slightly more difficult task, students listen to (rather than read) a text read by the teacher. Each time they hear a suffix, they tap a table. For some words, they must tap two or three times. Since this requires intense attention, it deepens students' understanding of suffixes. Our older students often enjoy using newspaper articles.

(3) Select one word and see how many different words students can make from it using suffixes. For example, from the word *sleep* they may make *sleeping, sleepily, sleepless*, etc.

Students can also increase their facility with suffixes by collecting words with suffixes and keeping notebooks of suffixed words that they meet in reading. Have students put a different suffix on the top of each page of a blank notebook. As they encounter words with this suffix, they simply enter them in the book. Below, a list displayed by Ramiro, a fifteen-year-old student reading on a sixth-grade level, is given.

In addition to suffixes, difficult words include many *prefixes* (word beginnings) and *root words* (the main part of the word). Many English prefixes and roots descend from Greek and Latin. Because both prefixes and roots contribute basic meaning to the words they form, students can use them for vocabulary building. Examples of prefixes that affect word meaning are *pre* (before) and *trans* (across); examples of such roots are *port* (to carry) and *script* (to write). Students who know the meaning of a root such as *script* have valuable hints to the meanings of such words as *postscript, prescription, scribe,* and *inscription.* A list of useful roots and prefixes (Richek, 1969) is given in Table 10.2.

Table 10.2

Useful Prefixes and Roots

Prefixes			*Roots*		
anti	antifreeze	against	astro	astrology	stars, heavens
aqua	aquarium	water	auto	automation	self
ante	antedate	before	micro	microscope	small
endo	endoderm	inner	aque	aqueduct	water
ex	exoderm	outer	bio	biosophere	life
ex	ex-president	former	dent	dentist	teeth
geo	geography	earth	dict	dictate	word
im	impossible	not	equi	equivalent	equal
non	nonparallel	not	itis	bronchitis	illness
post	posttest	after	graph	biography	write
pre	pretest	before	ling	linguistics	language
re	rewind	again	mid	amid	middle
semi	semisweet	sort of	ortho	orthodontist	straight
sub	subterranean	below	phobia	claustrophobia	fear
tele	television	far	phon	phonics	sound
trans	transistor	across	polit	political	politics
un	undo	not	script	scripture	writing
			sonic	resonant	sound
			spec	spectator	sight
			therm	thermometer	heat
			viv	vivid	life

Numbers

mono, uni	1	oct	8
di, bi	2	non	9
tri	3	dec	10
quadr, tetr	4	cent	100
quint, penta	5	milli	1/1000
hex, sex	6	kilo	1000
hept, sept	7	hemi	1/2

Word history adds variety to the study of word parts. For example, the word part *uni* is descended from Greek, and the many words that incorporate *uni (unicycle, universe, unity, unicorn)* are derived from Greek. The word *astronaut,* formed in the 1950s is derived from the Greek elements *astro* (or star) and *naut* (or sailor).

Using the Dictionary.

The dictionary gives students independence in learning word meanings; however, it should not be overused as an instructional tool. Students with reading problems find looking up word meanings tedious, and if they can learn words through other means, they should be encouraged to do so. Furthermore, dictionary definitions are often more difficult than the word itself. Finally, since dictionaries do not teach correct usage, sentences using words and discussions of words should accompany dictionary study.

Research has shown that dictionary definitions, even those from children's dictionaries, are very difficult to understand (McKeown, 1993). For this reason, we suggest that, when students ask you what a word means, you tell them, rather than requiring them to look up the meaning in a dictionary.

Even though it does not provide a complete vocabulary program, the dictionary does have many uses. It provides definitions, offers a means to distinguish among definitions, gives a key for pronunciation, and supplies the different forms of a base word. Dictionary skills, organized from less to more advanced are

1. *Alphabetizing words.* The use of the first letter in a word is taught first, followed by a second letter, third letter, and so on.
2. *Locating words.* This includes opening the dictionary to the correct half or quarter to locate a word and using key words to determine if a word is on a page.
3. *Using the dictionary pronunciation key.*
4. *Determining the correct dictionary entry for different word forms.* For example, the word *slowly* should be looked up under the word *slow*.
5. *Determining which of several definitions should be used in a particular context.*
6. *Determining the historical origin of a word.* (Usually only advanced dictionaries provide this information.)

Creative games help students to learn effective dictionary use.

1. *Making dictionary sentences.* Students can open the dictionary to a given page and try to construct the longest sentence possible using words from that page (Moffett & Wagner, 1983). Words such as *the*, *and*, *is*, *if*, and *I* may have to be added.
2. *Drawing pictures of words found in dictionaries.* Students can record the page where they found a word and draw a picture of it. Other pupils must then find the word in the dictionary.
3. *Seeing who can locate a word in the dictionary using the fewest opening "cuts."* This exercise helps students to locate words quickly.

Remember that different dictionaries are helpful for students at different levels. Young disabled students may need a primary level or intermediate dictionary. Older students can profit from college- or adult-level dictionaries.

Using Poetry to Develop Language

Using language in playful, imaginative ways helps students with reading problems enjoy and appreciate it. Poetry is an effective language form for this, for in this medium, sounds and word arrangements assume a special importance. We have had enormous success using poetry to foster language and personal growth. Since poetry invites students to memorize and recite it, it is an excellent way to build expressive language skills.

Simply reading and allowing students to react to the work of outstanding children's poets helps them to explore language and ideas. Kutiper and Wilson (1993) found that narrative poetry, which tells a story, is most popular. Students like poems that contain strong rhyme, rhythm, and humor. Familiar experiences and animals are popular poetry topics. Some of the most popular children's poetry books are:

The New Kid on the Block, by Prelutsky

Where the Sidewalk Ends, by Silverstein

A Light in the Attic, by Silverstein

If I Were in Charge of the World, by Viorst

Of course, you may have your own personal choices. For example, *Hailstones and Halibut Bones* (by O'Neill), a book of nonrhyming poems, each reflecting a color, became a favorite of several classes of low-achieving third graders. In reading *The Giving Tree* (by Silverstein), a short book with a poetic story, one teacher cried along with her fourth-grade students. When working with poetry, read poems that *you* enjoy!

Shapiro (1994) provides many easy ways to encourage students to explore poetry. She urges you to make poetry books and poems readily available on a poetry shelf, or in a poetry corner. Poetry is an oral medium, and it is *meant* to be read aloud. To set a mood, poetry can be read at a certain time, perhaps at the beginning of an instructional session. Or, once a week, you can have a poetry reading. Students can also form a group poetry circle.

Poetry can be effectively shared through the teacher's oral reading. Make sure that you practice beforehand, so that you read smoothly and with interpretation. Students will often want to read the poem aloud after you finish it. As you will see, a poem takes on a different interpretation with every individual who reads it.

Students also enjoy reacting to poetry. They can share experiences that remind them of the poem. They can discuss what they liked or disliked in the poem. Or, of course, they can discuss their favorite parts, rhymes, or words.

Shapiro (1994) has invited students to copy favorite poems into a poetry journal. This is an educational experience, for as they copy poems into a journal, students realize that poets use lines and spaces for a variety of effects. They also begin to learn how poets use rhyme, rhythm, and repetition.

Students who become involved in poetry may wish to give readings of favorite poems. They can perform in choral readings, with partners, or individually. Students should always have the option of memorizing the poem or reading it. Some poetry is particularly useful for performing. For example, *Joyful Noise: Poems for Two Voices* (by Fleishman) contains parts for two voices in rhythmic, nonrhyming poetry. Of course, since fluent, expressive oral reading is the essence of reading poetry, this activity will help to improve reading fluency. Remember that students with reading problems may need much practice before they become comfortable performing.

Art and writing are also effective mediums for responding to poetry. After we shared "Homework Oh Homework" (from *The New Kid on the Block,* by Prelutsky), each child in a low-achieving fourth-grade room drew a response to the unpopular topic.

Summary

Language is the basis of all reading, and we cannot read language that we cannot understand. Language development is particularly important to reading in the intermediate and upper grades. Causes of problems with language include language disability and delay, a lack of reading (since reading is the source of much language growth), and a lack of exposure to rich language in the environment.

Language abilities can be assessed through formal tests, such as the *Peabody Picture Vocabulary Test–Revised* or through informal measures, such as comparing listening level and reading level on a standardized test or IRI.

Conditions that foster language include exposure to high-level language, active responses in learning, and direct teaching as well as incidental exposure to rich language in listening and reading.

Strategies for fostering listening comprehension include reading books to students; the Mega-Cloze, in which students supply missing sentences from books read by the teacher; paired reading of easy and harder versions of one story; the Directed Listening–Thinking Activity, in which students listen to a story and predict what will happen; building sentences on the board from a short sentence; and encouraging students to employ advanced verbal styles.

Direct instructional strategies for fostering meaning vocabulary before reading include noticing words that appear in text; classifying words into categories; Predict-o-rama, or classifying how words will be used in a story; knowledge rating, or rating one's knowledge of words; and possible sentences, or composing possibly true sentences before reading. Direct instruction for reinforcing meaning vocabulary include making word cards with pictures, fitting a multiple number of words into one sentence, and practicing responding to words quickly. Incidental vocabulary growth can be fostered by the teacher's modeling of difficult words in speech, collecting words of different types, relating words to students' environments, and holding up "ears" containing words when the teacher reads a story.

To figure out unknown words independently, students can use context clues (the sense of a sentence); prefixes, suffixes, and roots (structural analysis); and the dictionary. Since dictionary definitions are difficult for students, this tool should not be overused.

Reading and Writing

Introduction

During the last twenty years, research has shown that there are strong ties between reading and writing (Tierney, 1990). In this chapter, we discuss the writing process and give many strategies to foster its development. We also share some instructional strategies that help students connect reading and writing. Finally, we present suggestions for teaching spelling and handwriting.

The Importance of Teaching Writing

Why should a reading teacher focus on writing? The process of writing is highly related to the process of reading, since readers and writers are both constructing—or composing—meaning. In reading, we construct meaning from the author's text; in writing, we compose or construct meaning as we create text. Since reading and writing are closely related, reading helps students write better and writing helps students read better (Stotsky, 1983).

In emergent literacy, writing helps students understand that print progresses from left to right and from the top of the page to the bottom. In beginning reading, writing provides students with the practice they need to pay attention to individual words and helps them match letters and sound in words (Clay, 1993a).

At all levels, practice in writing increases the understanding of how authors compose text (Goodman & Goodman, 1983). Tierney (1990) interviewed students and found that those who identified themselves as authors viewed reading in a new light. These students expressed more enthusiasm for both reading and writing, and they read more critically. They viewed reading as a resource for new ideas and information for their writing.

Students also use writing to clarify their understanding of what they read. When they make written responses to reading, they increase comprehension (Jennings, 1991; Moffett & Wagner, 1983; Wittrock, 1984). Writing can help students master information in science, social studies, and other subjects (Mayher, Lester, & Pradl, 1983).

Using writing in instruction offers important sources of success and motivation for students with reading problems. Students just learning to read may write, or dictate, messages, and read their *very own words*. Freed from the burden of trying to determine what another author meant, these students now have an opportunity to create, read, and display their own meanings.

For more advanced students with reading problems, writing can be used to deepen comprehension responses and to stimulate more reading. These students enjoy the permanence of making responses to books they have read in writing, which can be referred to later and shared with others. In addition, students who identify a topic to write about are often motivated to use reading as a way to find information.

Writing Instruction

Many instructional strategies can be used successfully with students who have reading problems. In doing these, students learn that we write for different purposes and for different audiences. For example, we use lists to organize our lives and letters to communicate with friends and family. We use reports to convey information; we publish books to share our thoughts with the public.

In this section, we first describe the writing process, a general strategy that students may use as they develop thoughts into finished written pieces. We then explore three more specific types of personal writing: written conversations, personal correspondence, and personal journals.

The Writing Process

In recent years, teachers have used the writing process to help students become joyful, proficient composers of text. In this process, we recognize that there are several stages of composing, which range from a first idea to the creation of a formal product. In completing these stages, students in our Reading Center have come to write more easily and naturally. They have also become proud authors of written pieces that are now part of our library.

Selecting Topics.

Topic selection is a key feature of good writing. Students are more willing to write if they choose what to write about. In shaping their content, they also think about the audience who will listen to or read their piece.

At first, students tend to do personal writing about their own experiences. Topics may include someone they know, a special event, or themselves. Ideally, students should select their own topics; however, low-achieving readers often have little confidence in themselves as writers. Teachers can help these students by asking them to make lists of people who are special to them. While students are creating their lists, we write our own list on the board:

Special People

Granddaddy

Mother

Betty, my sister

Dad

Tom, a friend from junior high

Next, we share our list with the students, explaining briefly why we chose these people. Finally, we encourage students to share their lists. Then, we ask students to choose one person to write about. While students write about their topic, we write about ours. When beginning the writing process, you may want to stop periodically to support students in their efforts.

Of course, some students may wish to write reports or letters rather than doing personal writing. Because we value topic selection, we honor these choices.

Writing Drafts.

After topic selection, students begin writing drafts. Encourage your students just to write what comes to mind about their topics. Students need not worry about spelling, punctuation, or the other mechanical aspects of writing as they draft their thoughts.

You may devote several writing sessions to topic selection, drafting, and responding positively to students' writing. This helps students develop the habit of writing on a regular basis and builds their confidence.

Making Revisions.

As ideas become clearer, writers revise their pieces. Mature writers do this constantly, making many insertions, deletions, and other changes. However, students with problems in reading and writing are often reluctant to revise. Sometimes, just writing a draft has required extensive effort, and making revisions seems overwhelming.

There are several strategies teachers can use to encourage revision. First, teachers can model revision in dictated stories and in their own work, so that students view this as a natural part of the writing process. Share one of your unfinished pieces, and ask students for suggestions. Use their responses to make changes in your own writing, and share the revised version with students in the next lesson.

When students meet to share their drafts, revision is often fostered through suggestions. Writers may find that others have questions about things that are unclear or suggestions for improvement. However, sharing drafts should also be a positive experience. First have students identify something they like about the draft that is being shared. Only after this should they ask questions and make suggestions.

For your most reluctant revisers, we suggest transforming an existing text into another genre. For example, you might alter a fairy tale from its narrative version to create a play. In this process, students must revise the text to create a script. After trying this with well-known stories, they are usually better able to write their own stories.

Editing.

When students are satisfied with content, they are ready to deal with mechanics (spelling, punctuation, and grammar) so that someone else can easily read their piece. It is important not to overburden students with changes. Guidelines that foster editing include (1) focus on items that can be changed immediately, (2) limit suggestions to items that have been presented in instruction, and (3) make no more than three suggestions to younger students and no more than five to older students.

Make notes about items that cannot be changed easily, and save these for later instruction. Direct instruction that deals with revision or editing concerns can be given as short "minilessons" during writing time.

Publishing.

When the editing process is complete, the writing is ready to be shared with a wider audience. Graves (1994) refers to this as "publishing." Publishing may occur as a book is bound and shared with the class or placed in a classroom library. It may consist of a presentation, a bulletin board display, or even a puppet show. As the writing process develops, students' contributions will fill your literacy environment.

Evaluation of Writing.

In guiding students to improve their writing, we must be able to evaluate their pieces. The evaluation of writing should focus on several levels, including the content, the organization of ideas, the structure, and the mechanics. By evaluating each, we gain a broad overview of a student's writing capabilities. To permit organized evaluation, start with the most general level—the content—and work toward the most specific—mechanics.

First, and most important, is a focus on content, the ability of the student to communicate thought. We ask two questions about the student's piece: (1) Does this student have an understanding that writing is a means of communication? (2) Does this student use writing effectively to express his or her ideas?

Next, we focus on the student's ability to organize ideas. For students in the beginning stages of writing, organization may consist of the ability to write information in sentences. Later, we evaluate primary students' ability to present ideas in sequential order. For intermediate-level writers, we evaluate abilities to organize related ideas into paragraphs.

For more mature writers, we evaluate the ability to organize paragraphs and sections of papers by related ideas.

Next, we evaluate structure, the ability to use different writing forms, or genres, appropriately. For students in the beginning stages of writing, we focus on sentences and grammatical structure. For intermediate students, we judge paragraph structure as well. For older students, we focus on the characteristics of specific formats, such as essay or thesis.

After a selection of writing has been evaluated for content, organization, and structure, we focus on the mechanics. These include spelling, punctuation, and proper use of capitalization.

From this evaluation, we can make decisions about a student's instructional needs on several different levels. These can include, for example, aspects of writing as broad as how to write a letter, or as narrow as using an apostrophe.

Evaluation leads us to two instructional decisions. First, we decide what the student should correct to make his or her writing more easily read by others. This decision depends on the level of the student's reading ability. In addition, we limit our areas to ones that the student has been taught previously. The second decision is what the student needs to learn next in instruction. From the second decision, we formulate instructional plans and present "minilessons"—short lessons focused on different aspects of writing.

Written Conversations and Personal Correspondence

In this strategy, developed by Carolyn Burke (S. Anderson, 1984), two students, or a student and a teacher, sit beside each other and communicate. The partners cannot speak; writing is the only communication allowed. If one person's message is unclear, the partner must ask for clarification in writing. Using this activity on a regular basis helps students learn to record their thoughts in writing.

We often use this strategy in our Reading Center as a way of "catching up on the news" with students. Instead of *asking* how things are going, the teacher *writes* a greeting and question to the student; the student, in turn, responds in writing. We use different colored pens or pencils and date each page.

Some teachers like to have both partners writing at the same time. Other teachers prefer to have participants use one paper and take turns writing. Each session can include two or three exchanges.

If a teacher and a student form a partnership, the teacher can model correct spellings and grammatical structures in his or her responses. Over several weeks, we often notice significant improvements in student's writing. Figure 11.1 presents an example of a written conversation between a teacher in our Reading Center and her student.

Of course, students also enjoy forming partnerships with each other. When two students are paired, they may form friendships, sharing interests and everyday experiences with the partner.

In a variation of written conversations called *personal correspondence,* students are assigned a penpal to communicate with over a longer period of time. Partners may be in the same school, but it is best if they are not in the same class. This is an especially nice activity to establish cross-grade partnerships. The older students' writing models the patterns the younger students need to learn, while older students become more aware of making their writing clear for their younger penpals. Students should never be allowed to hand their correspondence to their penpals. The teacher can serve as the "mail carrier" or a student can be assigned the job.

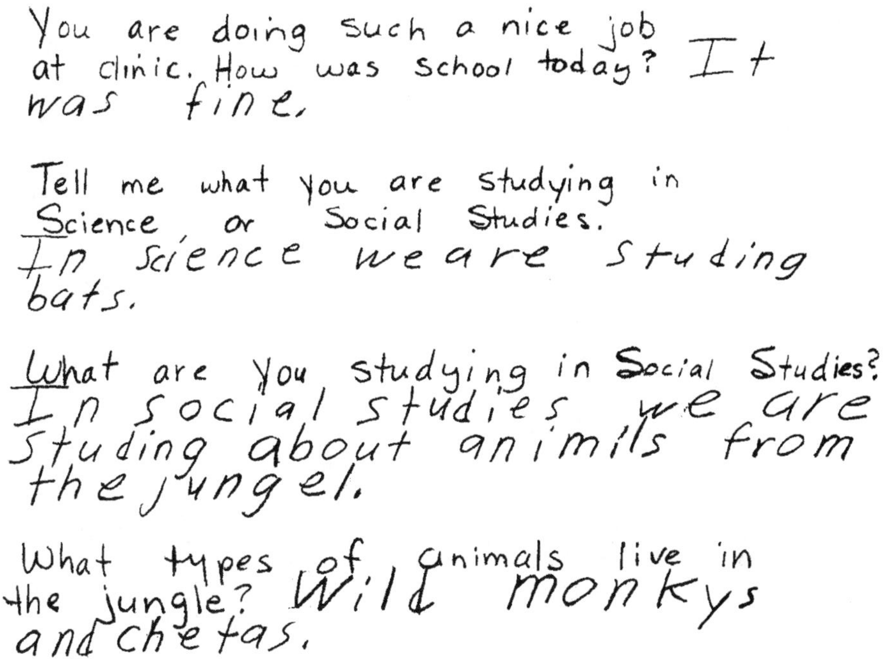

You are doing such a nice job
at clinic. How was school today? It
was fine.

Tell me what you are studying in
Science, or Social Studies.
In science we are studing
bats.

What are you studying in Social Studies?
In social studies we are
studing about animils from
the jungel.

What types of animals live in
the jungle? Wild monkys
and chetas.

FIGURE 11.1
A Written Conversation

Personal Journals

In personal journals, students reflect on events or experiences, much as we do in diaries. In doing this, they practice recording personal experiences in writing. Usually, journals provide day-to-day records of events in our lives and how we felt about them.

When students maintain personal journals, they form a record of their own thoughts and feelings, which they can later read. To begin, each student needs a personal journal, usually a notebook of lined paper. Students may want to create a title for their journal or decorate it. Time is set aside (usually at least a few periods a week) to record personal thoughts in journals. We generally ask students to write only on one side of a page.

After writing, a few students may choose to read their reflections to their classmates, and ask for their responses. In addition, the teacher can collect journals, read them, and write responses. However, students may not want to share all of their journal entries. To preserve privacy, students can simply fold a page in half, lengthwise, to cover it; the teacher should not read folded pages. In responding to journals, teachers should be careful not to correct grammatical and spelling errors, as this undermines the student's confidence and may lessen the amount of writing. Instead, try to respond personally to the content of the student's message. You may correctly spell words the student originally misspelled by using them in these responses.

Sometimes, students with reading problems have such low self-esteem that they lack the confidence to maintain journals. They often feel that their lives are not important enough to deserve recording. Teachers can help students overcome this problem by modeling journal writing.

Students with reading problems sometimes have difficulty thinking of journal topics. To help them, we often supply one category for each of the first six journal writing sessions and ask them to "brainstorm" a list within this category. Then, they choose one idea from their list and write about it. Topics might include: favorite places, special people, favorite stories, things I like to do, things I don't like to do, things that make me angry, and things I do well. To help them keep a record of these ideas, students create an "Ideas to Write About" page, divided into six sections, in their journals.

After you have engaged in journal writing using this technique six times, students are ready to choose their own topics without guidance. Then, if students have trouble thinking of a topic, suggest they use one of the topics from their "ideas" page.

Strategies for Integrating Reading and Writing

In this section, we discuss ways to incorporate writing into reading instruction. We include strategies for responding to narrative and expository text. Students need opportunities to reflect about their reading and to respond to it thoughtfully. Writing their thoughts about materials they are reading helps students to organize the ideas presented in the text and increases their comprehension (Doctorow, Wittrock, & Marks, 1978). As they formulate these responses, they also improve their writing skills.

Writing in Response to Narrative Text

There are many motivating formats that students with reading problems can use to respond to stories. These include scripted stories, rewritten stories, and reading response journals.

Scripted Stories.
Patterned, or scripted, writing is a good strategy for emergent and beginning readers. In this technique, the teacher shares a predictable book or poem with students. Then the students write their own version, altering the author's version slightly. This activity gives them the security of a writing "frame" that they can use to form their own, personalized response. One good book to use is *Brown Bear, Brown Bear, What Do You See?* (by Martin). In this book, each page contains a refrain such as "Brown bear, brown bear, what do you see? I see a blue bird looking at me." This is illustrated by the work of a first grader in our Reading Center, who used the same pattern with the words *Al* and *vet*.

Scripted writing encourages students to use their imaginations and practice words they meet in reading as they build their own confidence as writers. Good books to use for scripted writing include *Goodnight, Mr. Fly* (by Jacobs), *Polar Bear, Polar Bear* (by Martin), and *Alligator Pie* and *Jump Frog, Jump* (by Lee). Useful poems are contained in *Beneath a Blue Umbrella, Poems by A. Nonny Mouse, Zoo Doings,* and *Laughing Out Loud* (by Pretlutsky), *Honey, I Love* (by Greenfield), *The Pocketbook Book of Ogden Nash* (by Nash), *Sing a Soft Black Song* (by Giovanni), and *The Big O, The Missing Piece, Where the Sidewalk Ends,* and *A Light in the Attic* (by Silverstein).

Rewritten Stories.
Having students rewrite stories is invaluable in providing a model for story structure, enhancing language development, and comprehending text. This activity can be used along

Book cover from *Brown Bear, Brown Bear, What Do You See?* by Bill Martin, Jr., copyright 1970 by Harcourt Brace & Company, reproduced by permission of the publisher.

with comprehension strategies, such as the Directed Reading–Thinking Activity or Story Grammar (see Chapter 8).

After your students have read a story, you may ask them to re-create it in their own words. Young children who have difficulty with the mechanics of writing may prefer to dictate a story version that is written down by the teacher. Older students are usually able directly to write their own version. In creating their own rewritten version of a story, students need to reflect upon the structure of the story they have read. There are several ways you can provide guidance for this activity.

(1) Use a story grammar and have students identify a character, setting, problem, and events. Then have students construct the story around these elements. In doing this, stu-

dents often create their own written "story grammar" containing these elements, and use it to guide them as they create their own stories.

(2) Students can tell or write about a story they have read, but take another point of view. To model this, you might use *The True Story of the Three Little Pigs* (by Sciesza), which retells the classic fairy tale from the wolf's point of view. Then students can create their own versions of classics, for example, rewriting "Snow White" from the stepmother's perspective.

(3) Students can rewrite by assuming a role within a story they have read. Lauren, a sixth grader in our Reading Center, read the book *If You Grew Up with George Washington* (by Fritz) and then rewrote it, casting herself as the main character. A selection from the resulting book, "If you Grew Up with Lauren Lang," is shown in Figure 11.2.

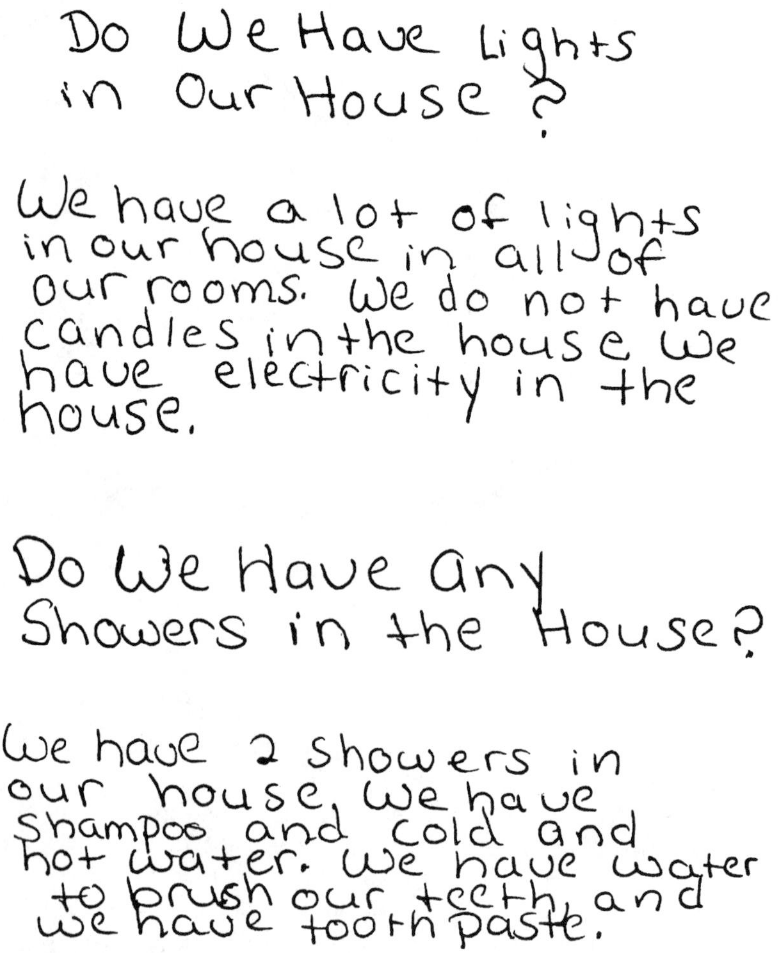

Do We Have Lights
in Our House?

We have a lot of lights
in our house in all of
our rooms. We do not have
candles in the house. We
have electricity in the
house.

Do We Have any
Showers in the House?

We have 2 showers in
our house. We have
shampoo and cold and
hot water. We have water
to brush our teeth, and
we have toothpaste.

FIGURE 11.2
A Rewritten Story of "If You Grew up with Lauren Lang." Adapted from "If You Grew up with George Washington."

We've all read stories with disappointing or surprising endings. Students may be asked to write their own endings to such stories. After reading "The Garden Party" (by Mansfield), Karen, a high school student, wanted to change the ending. The ending she wrote is:

> I think Laura would have said, "Isn't life a learning experience?" The reason why I think Laura would have said this is because Laura has learned that life isn't always joy and happiness, but pain and sorrowful.

Karen uses her new ending to gain further insight into the story:

> I think Laura also learned about her own life. She has lived a sheltered life. Now she realizes that people don't have to dress nicely to be good. She realizes this when she apologizes for her hat.

Reader Response Journals.

A reading journal is used to write personal reactions to reading. Reading journals provide opportunities to connect reading to our own experiences.

These journals can also provide teachers with valuable feedback about students' understanding of ideas presented in text. When students respond to a story in writing, the teacher can tell whether or not they understood the story (Farr et al., 1990).

To introduce reading journals, we recommend you start by writing about something you and your students have read together, such as a short story. Try to connect the story to the students' own experiences. Students also like to use reading journals as opportunities to critique stories. At times, we have asked students to give "stars" to something they have read in their journals, ranging from one ("I hated it") to four ("I loved it"). Then, beneath the stars, we ask them to explain why a chapter or story received this rating.

Teachers may also ask students to write about their favorite characters. Asking students to write about why they think the author had a character act in a certain way helps to make them more aware of how authors create stories. This awareness helps students when they write their own stories. Keeping a record of their own reaction to a character's development in a reading journal fosters literary appreciation.

Some teachers write responses to students' reading journals, making them into *reading dialogue journals*. Through these written responses, teachers can enhance a student's understanding, correct misunderstandings, offer a different perspective, or simply share a mutual appreciation for a story.

Writing in Response to Expository Text

In this section, we present strategies for responding, in writing, to the expository (or informational) texts students read. In using these written responses, students are able to absorb, organize, and reflect upon information more effectively and fully.

Learning Journals.

In a learning journal, teachers ask students to write the most important things that they learned from a content area, such as social studies or science. Students may respond to a chapter in a textbook, an encyclopedia article, or a teacher's lecture. Students are also free to ask questions in their journals and, if a teacher notices a misunderstanding, he or she may clarify it for the student. Learning journals are especially helpful in content areas (Giacobbe, 1986). By asking students to describe what they learned, teachers can see which concepts need reteaching. In this way, writing can help content area teachers teach diagnostically. Figure 11.3 presents a sample of a learning journal entry by a student in our Reading Center. This entry was written in response to a science article about peccaries.

Raft.

This strategy helps students to develop imaginative responses by assuming different roles and tasks in writing (Santa, Havens, & Harrison, 1989). RAFT stands for

THE PECCARY

Today I read about a peccary. I read that peccaries eat thorns, weeds, roots, cactus, and nuts. They live in Arizona, Texas, New Mexico, North America, South America, and Central America. The paper said they make sounds like a dog. They look like a pig and on their neck it is white and then it turns brown.

FIGURE 11.3
Robin's Learning Journal Entry

Role - who is writing

Audience - who is being written to

Format - the type of writing being done

Topic - what is being written about

Each of these four parts of writing can vary. For example, a role may include any character or object that has been studied. Students may write from the point of view of a participant in a historical event or of a cell in a biological function. In addition, any other character or object can form an audience. A student may write to another cell or to a historical figure on the opposing side. Formats can also vary. Students can write a letter, poetry, an invitation, a television script, a telegram, or a complaint. Finally, students can choose any one of a number of topics to write about.

One middle-school teacher of at-risk students was having difficulty teaching the scientific concepts of matter. To enliven this subject, she asked each student to choose one of three roles: a solid water molecule, a liquid water molecule, or a gas molecule. Students were also free to choose their audiences, formats, and topics. One student, for example, chose to be a liquid water molecule writing to the cloud from which he had come. His format was a letter, and the topic concerned what it felt like to be in a raindrop. The RAFT activity dramatically increased learning and enthusiasm in this science classroom.

Teachers may assign RAFT tasks or let the students choose them. The more varied the RAFT choices, the more students will develop an appreciation for other points of view and possibilities. Santa, Havens, and Harrison (1989) suggest that teachers avoid the word *write,* using more precise words, such as *describe, convince,* or *explain,* in assignments. These terms encourage students to be more precise in their writing and to develop the ability to write persuasively.

Here is a RAFT example from a third-grade student in our Reading Center.

Role - Curious George

Audience - Alex, a monkey friend from the zoo

Format - Letter

Topic - What happened after Curious George left the zoo

> Dear Alex,
> I left the zoo and I hijacked a bus to find the man with the big yellow hat's house. I did not know how to find the man with the big yellow hat's house. So I went to the police station instead. I got to ride in the police car. They took me to the zoo. Please write to me at Lincoln Park Zoo.
> Your friend,
> Curious George

At times, students can do only part of a RAFT. Figure 11.4 shows a low-achieving fifth-grade student assuming the *role* of an American officer in the American Revolution.

Writing with Poetry

When students write poetry, they use language actively and express themselves in imaginative ways. However, it is very difficult for students with reading problems to write

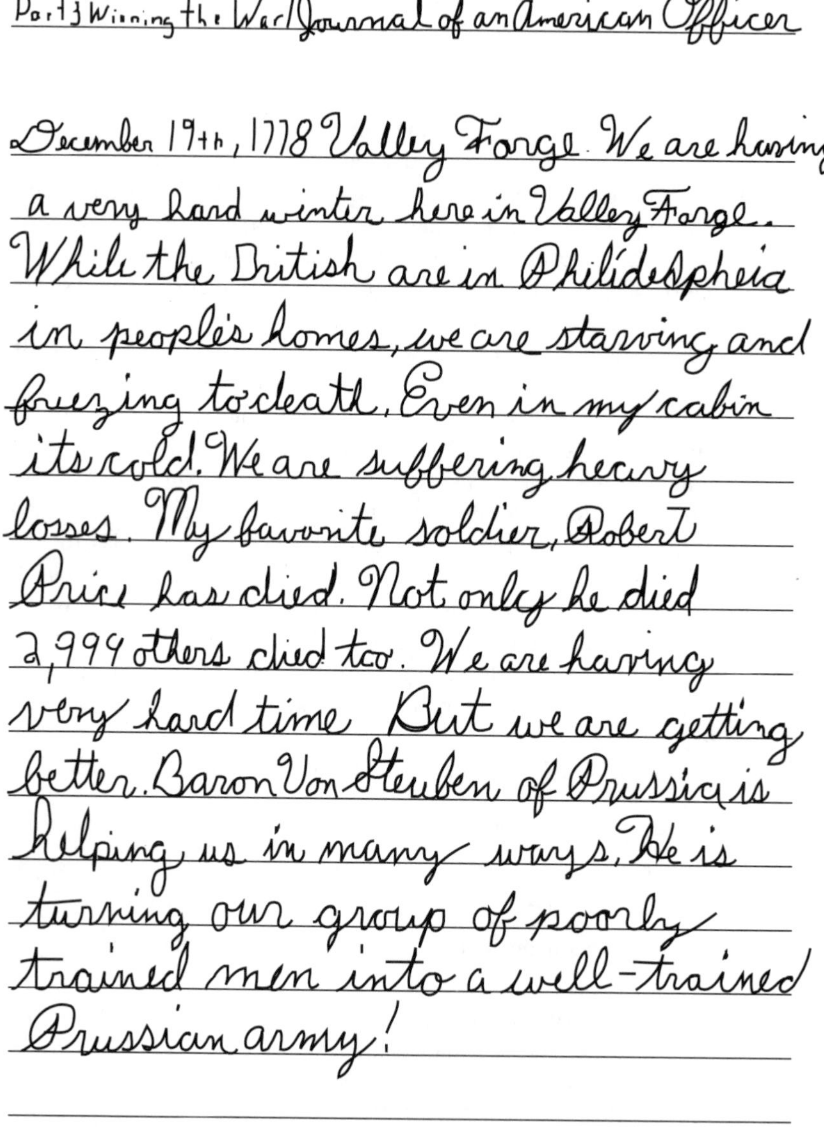

Part 3 Winning the War/Journal of an American Officer

December 19th, 1778 Valley Forge. We are having a very hard winter here in Valley Forge. While the British are in Philiddspheia in people's homes, we are starving and freezing to death. Even in my cabin its cold. We are suffering heavy losses. My favorite soldier, Robert Price has died. Not only he died 2,999 others died too. We are having very hard time. But we are getting better. Baron Von Steuben of Prussia is helping us in many ways, He is turning our group of poorly trained men into a well-trained Prussian army!

FIGURE 11.4
Murray's Diary Journal Entry on "Winning the War"

rhyming poetry, since imposing rhyming patterns on one's thoughts requires almost professional-level skill. For this reason, we recommend that you encourage writing poetry without rhymes.

Students with reading problems often feel most comfortable creating poetry from structured formats. Character poems provide a high comfort level as well as an opportunity for getting acquainted. One of the formats our Reading Center students enjoy is presented in Table 11.1

Table 11.1   **The Character Poem**

Format for Character Poem	*Jennifer's Character Poem*
First name	Jennifer
Three words describing yourself	Shopper, athlete, pretty
Sister/brother/daughter/son of …	Sister of Steven
Who likes …	Who likes birds and baseball
Who fears …	Who fears the dark
Lives in …	Lives in Chicago
Last name	Smithers

In Strategy Snapshot 11.1 on page 234, teacher Mary Welch uses the poetic formats of haiku and rap to help Eddie, a disabled high school student, record his interests.

Recently, in a third-grade class with many at-risk students, we shared "Sarah Cynthia Sylvia Stout Would Not Take the Garbage Out," a poem by Shel Silverstein from *Where the Sidewalk Ends,* about the fate that befell a child who refused to take out garbage. We asked students to describe what they thought garbage would be like, using each of their five senses. We created a class book, consisting of five pages, one for each sense.

Examples of what garbage *felt* like included:

It's gooey around you

Gook

Mashed potatoes

Mud

Yuck

Nasty stuff

A soft chicken

The class book was decorated with illustrations by several students and placed in the classroom library.

Computers and Writing

Word processing, the use of the computer in writing, is one of the most effective and widely used applications of computer technology. Using a keyboard, students with reading problems can write without worrying about handwriting and revise without making a mess of the written document.

Advantages of Word Processing

Word processing, the writing tool of the contemporary classroom, has many advantages for students (MacArthur, Schwartz, & Graham, 1991).

Strategy Snapshot 11.1
• • • • • • • • • • • • • •
Eddie Writes Poetry

Mary Welch (Shapiro & Welch, 1991) used poetry to motivate and instruct Eddie, a fifteen-year-old boy classified as severely learning disabled and reading five years below his grade level. He wrote character poems of different forms. Eddie extended his expertise into haiku, a poem of three lines, using the following format:

Line 1: What or who (5 syllables)
Line 2: Feeling, action, or description (7 syllables)
Line 3: A summative phrase (5 syllables)

Eddie wrote about his favorite motorcycle:

Harley Davidson
Ride into the setting sun
Stay with their design.

Eddie also wrote raps:

Harleys are cool, especially when they're blue
They look so fine, all of the time
When I go for a ride, everybody wants a ride
If I say no, you'll say go!
So bye-bye, it's time to fly

To help Eddie use his interest in music to improve his reading, Mary used *The Poetry of Rock* (Goldstein, 1969), which features the lyrics to popular songs. One of the best outcomes of Eddie's program was his growing sense of power as he taught Ms. Welch important facts about cars and motorcycles.

1. Students can easily produce neat, error-free copies in a variety of formats.
2. The visibility of a computer screen and anonymity of printed text encourages students to write collaboratively.
3. The editing power of the computer eases the physical burden of correction and revision.
4. Typing is easier and neater than handwriting, for students with motor problems.
5. Spell checkers and thesauruses facilitate writing on many computers.

Studies indicate that students with learning problems prefer the use of the computer to handwriting. However, teacher instruction is needed to aid inexperienced writers in using the potential of the computer to facilitate revision (MacArthur, Schwartz, & Graham, 1991).

Word Processing Programs

Many excellent word processing programs are available for students at all levels. The type of computer (hardware) must match the word processing program (software). Most schools use Apple and Macintosh at the elementary levels, and Macintosh or IBM (or IBM compatible) at the secondary level.

Several programs allow students to combine graphics and text, creating electronic books. The computer screen becomes equivalent to the printed page, giving students electronic tools for writing and illustrating stories. Mead (1995) and others suggest many excellent programs. *Children's Writing and Publishing Center* (Learning Company) is an easy desk-top publishing software program. *Story-Maker* (Bolt, Beranek, and Newman) allows students to draw illustrations or select from a pool of prepared graphics, and includes large type. *Bank Street Storybook* (Mindscape) gives a sophisticated, yet easy to use, illustrations program. *Kidwriter*'s (Gessler) choice of pictures and easy use make it excellent for primary children. In *Co:Writer* (Don Johnson), to help the student, the computer suggests a next word from a partial sentence the student has written. *Write: Outloud* (Don Johnson) is a talking software package that speaks words as the student writes.

Keyboarding or Typing Skills

In order to effectively use a word processing program, students must learn to "keyboard." Students need special instruction in typing on the computer keyboard, for it is better to learn the correct finger positions than to develop the bad habit of using a hunt-and-peck method. In general, the earlier keyboarding skills can be taught, the better. Teachers have found that third or fourth graders are able to learn these skills effectively. Easy programs for learning keyboarding include *Typing Tutor III* (Scholastic Software), *HypeType* (CompUnique), *PAWS (MECC), Master Type* (Mindscape), and *Alphabetic Keyboarding* (Scholastic Software).

Developing the Ability to Spell

To make their writing more easily read by others, students need to learn to spell. Spelling is best developed by practice; daily writing experiences develop good spelling abilities. This writing should be done for genuine purposes and specific audiences, rather than just being writing "exercises" (Gentry & Gillet, 1993). In addition to writing, however, many students with reading problems need more direct instruction in spelling.

Spelling is challenging for many people, even some who read well. Students who have reading problems are almost always poor spellers. Spelling is certainly more difficult than reading. The context, structural analysis and meaning clues that help us to read a written word are not present when we want to spell it. In reading, we can sometimes substitute a word for an unfamiliar one and maintain meaning for the text. In spelling, only one pattern of letters is accepted as correct; no substitutions are allowed. Finally, there is not always a consistent correspondence between spoken sounds and written forms in English.

Reading, writing, and spelling are closely related. Learning letter–sound associations in reading helps us to use them in spelling. As children read, they repeatedly see words spelled correctly. As their reading and writing develop, students learn regular sound–letter patterns, which they use to read new words and to spell (Henderson, 1985; Wong, 1986).

Spelling Development

Just as children go through stages when learning to talk, when beginning reading and writing they go through stages in learning to communicate in print. Much research has focused on the concept of "invented spelling." For example, Read (1971, 1975) has documented that preschool children use the sounds of letter names to write words before formal instruction. Children follow similar sequences as they learn to spell, although they may go through stages at different rates (Henderson, 1981).

Drawing and Scribbling.
Children in early stages of literacy may draw pictures to communicate ideas. As they become aware that adults communicate through lines and squiggles on paper, they begin to do so too.

Precommunicative Stage.
When children become aware that writing uses letters, they begin to make strings of letters. There may be no connection to letter sounds or names. Instead, children simply write letters they have seen in their environment, such as a cursive $\mathcal{K}$ made the way it appears on a cereal box. Adults usually cannot usually read what children have written at this stage. In fact, children themselves cannot reread what they have written unless it is read immediately.

Semiphonetic Stage.
When children become aware that letters are associated with sounds, they begin to use letter names to help them in their writing. They may write only one letter (usually the first sound) to represent an entire word. Frequently, one string of letters, without spaces, represents an entire sentence, or several sentences. While children can often reread what they write, it is difficult for teachers to do so.

Phonetic Stage.
Once children understand what words are, they can identify sounds within them. At the phonetic stage, students write all the sounds they hear in words. While these "invented" spellings may not look like the English spellings, they are systematic and phonetically correct. Students at this stage still use letter names to determine which letters to write, but each sound is represented, and adults can often read them.

Transitional Stage.
As students receive reading and writing instruction, they become aware that print represents visual characteristics of words as well as sounds. For example, rather than writing the *r* that they hear for the last syllable in *letter*, they now begin to use *er*, visually representing this syllable in the conventional English way. Frequently, students will overgeneralize patterns. After students learn the word *enough*, they may overuse the letters *gh* to represent the *f* sound in other words. Most students now separate words by spaces. Often students in the transitional stage become reluctant to take risks in writing, using only words they know how to spell.

Conventional Stage.
In this stage, students use all aspects of print to represent words. They know that letters represent specific sound patterns. They are also aware that some patterns differ from the typical English letter–sound correspondence.

Spelling Assessment

Teachers can learn a great deal about students' word knowledge by analyzing samples of their writing. However, students with reading problems often choose only familiar words in their writing. For this reason, spelling tests provide valuable tools for analyzing students' word knowledge. Schlagal (1989) developed a *Qualitative Inventory of Word Knowledge,* which includes specific patterns students are likely to encounter from grades one through six. Table 11.2 presents this test.

Table 11.2   Schlagal Qualitative Inventory of Word Knowledge

Level 1	Level 2	Level 3	Level 4	Level 5	Level 6
1. girl	1. traded	1. send	1. force	1. lunar	1. satisfied
2. want	2. cool	2. gift	2. nature	2. population	2. abundance
3. plane	3. beaches	3. rule	3. slammed	3. bushel	3. mental
4. drop	4. center	4. trust	4. curl	4. joint	4. violence
5. when	5. short	5. soap	5. preparing	5. compare	5. impolite
6. trap	6. trapped	6. batter	6. pebble	6. explosion	6. musician
7. wish	7. thick	7. knee	7. cellar	7. delivered	7. hostility
8. cut	8. plant	8. mind	8. market	8. normal	8. illustrate
9. bike	9. dress	9. scream	9. popped	9. justice	9. acknowledge
10. trip	10. carry	10. sight	10. harvest	10. dismiss	10. prosperity
11. flat	11. stuff	11. chain	11. doctor	11. decide	11. accustom
12. ship	12. try	12. count	12. stocked	12. suffering	12. patriotic
13. drive	13. crop	13. knock	13. gunner	13. stunned	13. impossible
14. fill	14. year	14. caught	14. badge	14. lately	14. correspond
15. sister	15. chore	15. noise	15. cattle	15. peace	15. admission
16. bump	16. angry	16. careful	16. gazed	16. amusing	16. wreckage
17. plate	17. chase	17. stepping	17. cabbage	17. reduction	17. commotion
18. mud	18. queen	18. chasing	18. plastic	18. preserve	18. sensible
19. chop	19. wise	19. straw	19. maple	19. settlement	19. dredge
20. bed	20. drown	20. nerve	20. stared	20. measure	20. conceive
	21. cloud	21. thirsty	21. gravel	21. protective	21. profitable
	22. grabbed	22. baseball	22. traffic	22. regular	22. replying
	23. train	23. circus	23. honey	23. offered	23. admitted
	24. shopping	24. handle	24. cable	24. division	24. introduction
	25. float	25. sudden	25. scurry	25. needle	25. operating
			26. camel	26. expression	26. decision
			27. silent	27. complete	27. combination
			28. cozy	28. honorable	28. declaration
			29. graceful	29. baggage	29. connect
			30. checked	30. television	30. patient

From *Reading Psychology: An International Journal*, vol. 10 (3), p. 230, R.C. Schlagel, "Constancy and Change in Spelling Development," published by Taylor and Francis, Washington, D.C. Reproduced with permission. All rights reserved.

We recommend that you begin one level below the student's instructional reading level and continue until the student scores below 50 percent. The highest level at which the student scores 50 percent or above is the student's spelling instructional level. Generally, the spelling level lags slightly behind the reading level. Responses of emergent spellers to the grade one list will enable you to determine whether a child is at a semiphonetic, phonetic, transitional, or conventional stage.

For all students, an analysis of errors on the Schlagal test can help a teacher to plan spelling and phonics instruction. In analyzing the Schlagal inventory, compare your student's responses to the correct spellings of the words. Look for patterns in your student's errors to determine instructional needs. For example, if your student consistently uses initial and final consonants correctly, but has problems with medial consonants, include those in your plans. If your student uses short-vowel patterns correctly, but spells all long-vowel patterns with a final *e*, plan instruction that focuses on long-vowel patterns.

Spelling Instruction

There are many different formats and strategies that can be used for spelling instruction.

Spelling Workshop.
Gentry and Gillet (1993) recommend a workshop approach to teaching spelling similar to that used in teaching the writing process. This approach includes several steps.

(1) To foster ownership, students select their own words to study for a week. These words may be selected from their writing folders or they may be words from stories or topics being studied. Young children should select only four or five new words. Older children may choose ten or more. In addition, teachers may add words for study based upon student needs or, sometimes, the class may decide to focus on a specific pattern (such as a word ending.)
(2) Students keep their own records as they progress through the week's activities. They may also monitor their progress on end-of-week tests, selecting missed words for another week's study. They may keep a spelling log to record their new words.
(3) Students work together to learn their words. They may play games, work on common patterns, practice with each other to improve visual memory, and help provide feedback for each other.

Visual Memory.
In spelling, students need to visualize patterns in words. This becomes even more important in later spelling development, as they must visualize root words to help them in spelling derivatives (e.g., *nation, nationality, nationalize*). There are many ways to develop visual memory.

In tactile writing, students use their fingers to trace words cut from felt, sandpaper, or other textured paper. This is a good way to help very disabled students remember words and patterns. Using these, you can ask students to trace words within one word family (*rate, mate, skate*).

The look-cover-write-check strategy has been used successfully for years. The steps include:

- Looking at a spelling word.
- Covering the spelling word.
- Visualizing the covered word in your mind.
- Writing the spelling word from memory.
- Checking your writing with the uncovered spelling word.

Visualizing words and writing them allows students to learn words independently. It also avoids the useless step of merely having students copy words.

Cunningham (1995) suggests the use of *Word Walls* to support students' spelling and writing. Teachers can write the words being studied on word cards and attach them to the wall, ordered according to their beginning letter. Word walls are helpful both in giving students ideas for writing and in supporting their spelling. Encourage students to visualize words and try to write them before they look at the wall. For a more complete discussion of word walls, see Chapter 7.

Structural Patterns.

Students need to develop an awareness of root words and combining affixes to create more complex words.

Compound words provide a good introduction to structural patterns. Gentry and Gillet (1993) suggest beginning with a compound word from a story or content area lesson. For example, reading the book *Snow* (by Keats) can serve as a springboard to a lesson on such compound words as *snowfall*. Then you can brainstorm words to combine with *snow* to create other compound words (*snowbank, snowmobile*).

Students can also study root words and how we add prefixes and suffixes to create derived words. To explore such spelling patterns, students can create lists of words that end with *-tion, -ic,* or *-ence* or begin with *anti-* or *pre-*.

Gentry and Gillet (1993) describe a variation of the game *Concentration* that helps students focus on root words and derivatives. To play this game, write sets of derived words on cards. One set might include *confide, confidence, confidential, confidante.* Another set could be *remind, remember, memory, reminisce.* To play the game, students try to make words of related pairs (for example, *remind* and *reminisce*).

Handwriting

Despite the growing popularity of computers, the physical act of handwriting remains basic to many school and life activities. A student with difficulties in handwriting is greatly hampered. Many students who do not read well also suffer from problems that result in poor handwriting. These include poor eye–hand coordination, deficient motor development, and limited spatial judgment (Lerner, 1993). Since our writing system is adapted to right-handed students, those who are left-handed often have difficulties.

Most children begin writing in manuscript (or "printing"), which is relatively easy to construct and similar to the typeface in printed material. Students learn cursive writing in second or third grade. Even students without reading problems sometimes have difficulty making the transition from manuscript to cursive writing. Cursive letters are complex, requiring a greater variety of lines, curves, loops, and transitions.

Many teachers report easier transitions from manuscript to cursive writing using the D'Nealian method of writing instruction in beginning stages. In this method, students are taught to write in manuscript, but the manuscript letters are written at a slant and the end strokes end in upward curves rather than straight lines. However, in D'Nealian, there is a greater difference between the appearance of their written words and the printed words in books.

Some simple suggestions, if practiced regularly, may help improve handwriting.

1. Have students practice on chalkboard before using paper. They can make large circles, lines, geometric shapes, letters, and numbers with large, free movements using the muscles of arms, hands, and fingers.
2. Some students need to trace printing and writing. Make heavy black letters on white paper and clip a sheet of onionskin (thin) paper over the letters. Have students trace letters with crayons or felt-tip pen.
3. Put letters an transparencies and project the image on an overhead projector on a chalkboard or large sheet of paper. The student can then trace over the image.
4. Guide students verbally as they write. For example, say "down, up, and, around" as children form letters.
5. Since writing is a matter of habit, monitor proper posture and ways to hold writing implements. Students may need lines on a desk to show them how to position paper.

Summary

Reading and writing are similar processes that involve composing. Writing strengthens reading by giving insight into spelling for emergent readers, by helping students to understand how text is organized, and by serving as a springboard to reading as students need to collect information about the pieces they compose.

Writing instruction can involve the writing process: selecting topics, writing drafts, making revisions, editing, and publishing. In this process, students choose and develop their own topics, and are not evaluated on mechanics until near the end of the process. To evaluate writing, focus, in this order, on content, organization, structure (the ability to use genre properly), and mechanics. Other writing strategies include written conversations (or conversing in writing), personal correspondence with another student, and journals that record personal reactions.

Students may also integrate reading and writing by using writing to respond to reading. There are many responses to narrative text. In scripted stories, they use the format of a published book to make their own book; rewritten stories feature the students' own rewriting or changed endings; reader response journals involve written reactions to reading. Responses to expository text include learning journals, in which students record their learning and ask questions, and RAFT, in which a student assumes a role, audience, format, and topic. Students can also explore imaginative aspects of writing by composing poetry, although rhyming poetry should be avoided.

The use of computers for word processing has freed students to experiment in writing, write more freely, and transcend the limits of messy handwriting.

Spelling ability involves several stages, including drawing and scribbling, the precommunicative stage, the semiphonetic stage, the phonetic stage, the transitional stage, and the conventional stage. These stages should not be interpreted as mistakes, but rather as natural processes in spelling development. Spelling lists give insights into assessment. Spelling instruction includes a spelling workshop, visual memory strategies, and learning structural patterns.

Handwriting, particularly in cursive style, may be difficult for students to master.

Literacy in a Diverse Society

Introduction

One of the important strengths of American society is its diversity. In this chapter, we address the instruction of students who come from a wide variety of backgrounds. We give effective strategies to foster cooperation between reading instruction, home, and community. To conclude, we address the special needs of adolescent and adult students, whose life experiences give them a special perspective on literacy.

Bilingual and Limited English Proficient Speakers

In our pluralistic society, increasing numbers of students come from homes where a language other than English is spoken. Many of these students speak Spanish; currently over 15 percent of students in the United States are identified as Hispanic. In fact, it is expected that by 2020, 25 percent of children in the United States will be of Hispanic descent (Gersten, Brengelman, & Jiménez, 1994). Since Spanish is spoken by so many individuals, it is useful to know features in Spanish that contrast with English. A short list of such differences is given in Table 12.1.

Although Spanish is the second most commonly spoken language in the United States, many other languages are also used. After English, the ten most widely spoken languages in the United States are: Spanish, Vietnamese, Hmong (from South East Asia), Cantonese, Cambodian, Korean, Laotian, Navajo, Tagalog (from the Philippines), and Russian. Immigration into the United States and the number of students who speak English as a second language is increasing dramatically (National Center for Education and Statistics, 1994). According to data from the U.S. Department of Education, there are approximately 2.3 million students with limited English proficiency in the United States. This is an increase of nearly 1 million students since 1984.

The field of bilingual education meets the challenges faced by *minority language* students, or students who do not speak English as a native language. In 1994, Congress passed Title VII, the reauthorized Bilingual Education Act, which is part of the Improving America's School's Act.

The primary purposes of the Bilingual Education Act programs are to facilitate the learning of English in all areas of the curriculum, while strengthening the development of the language and cultural skills necessary for the United States to compete effectively in a global economy (Office of Bilingual Education and Minority Languages Affairs, 1994; Improving America's Schools Act, 1993). If there is a concentration of students who speak a first language other than English in a school, bilingual teachers must be provided. If a school simply has a few students, or has students from many different languages, ESL (English as a Second Language) instruction must be given. Provisions are developed to assess abilities in English that facilitate proper placement.

Students who are bilingual understand and use two languages. For most students in the United States, one of these languages is English. Research shows that bilingual abilities are associated with higher levels of cognitive attainment (Cummins, 1989; Hakuta & Garcia, 1989). The duality of languages does not hamper overall language proficiency or cognitive development for bilingual students.

However, some students who speak languages other than English are not actually bilingual, or fluent in two languages. Instead, these students have limited English proficiency (LEP), and experience difficulty in understanding and using English. Some speak only in

Table 12.1 **Differences Between Spanish and English Languages**

Phonological	***Fewer vowel sounds***
	no short *a* (hat), short *i* (fish)
	short *u* (up), short double *o* (took)
	or schwa (sofa)
	Fewer consonant sounds
	no /j/ (jump), /v/ (vase),
	/z/ (zipper), /sh/ (shoe), /ŋ/ (sing),
	/hw/ (when), /zh/ (beige)
	Some possible confusions
	/b/ pronounced /p/ — *cab* becomes *cap*
	/j/ pronounced /y/ — *jet* becomes *yet*
	/ŋ/ pronounced as /n/ — *thing* becomes *thin*
	/ch/ pronounced as /sh/— *chin* becomes *shin*
	/v/ pronounced as /b/ — *vote* becomes *boat*
	/y/ pronounced as /j/ — *yes* becomes *jes*
	/sh/, /sp/, /st/ pronounced as /esk/, /esp/, /est/ — *speak* becomes *espeak*
	/a/ pronounced as /e/ — *bat* becomes *bet*
	/i/ pronounced as /ē/ — *hit* becomes *heat*
	/e/ pronounced as /i/ — *heal* becomes *hill*
	/u/ pronounced as /o/ — *hut* becomes *hot*
	/ōo/ pronounced as /ōo/— *hut* becomes *hot*
Morphological	*de* (of) used to show possession — *Joe's pen* becomes *the pen of Joe*
	mas (more) used to show comparison — *faster* becomes *more fast*
Syntactical	use of *no* for *not* He no do his homework
	no *s* for plural my two friend
	no auxiliary verbs She no play soccer.
	adjectives after nouns The car blue.
	agreement of adjectives the elephants bigs
	no inversion of question Anna is here?
	articles with professional titles I went to the Dr. Rodriguez.

Adapted from: C.A. O'Brien, *Teaching the Language-Different Child to Read*. Columbus, Oh: Merrill, 1973.

their native language; others use both English and their native language but still have considerable difficulty with English.

Research shows that gaining proficiency in a language requires sufficient time. A student may acquire conversational English in six months, but still lack the language to support the complex demands of academic work in English. In fact, it may take two or more years to develop these higher-level skills (Cummins, 1989).

If a second language is perceived positively in the student's environment, learning will be enhanced. Often, however, a second language such as English is used only in school and thus is of little value in everyday life. Or a second language may be associated with people who are hostile. The more knowledge and empathy a teacher possesses toward a student's personal background and cultural heritage, the more effective English instruction will be (Hakuta & Garcia, 1989; Moll & González, 1994).

Exposure to English is important. If students use English frequently, they will learn it more easily. Thus, students benefit most from exposure to people who communicate fluently and naturally in English.

Some minority language children also have learning or language problems. If a language disorder is present in the primary language, it will also be present in the second language (Carrasquillo & Baecher, 1990; Langdon, 1989).

Approaches to Teaching a Second Language

In this section, we describe widely used current approaches toward teaching LEP students: the native language approach, the sheltered English approach, and in addition, we discuss ESL, bilingual education, dual language, and immersion.

Native Language.
In this approach, students are taught complex academic content in their native language first, so that they can understand and discuss challenging material without the added demand of constantly having to translate or express ideas in a second language. Once the student learns the information in his (or her) native language, it can be transferred to English (Gersten, Brengleman, & Jiménez, 1994). Underlying this view is the belief that it is not possible to read in a language one does not know. If reading involves the act of understanding complex written material, a student must have a well-developed understanding of the language of that material.

Sheltered English.
This approach introduces English more rapidly, teaching it, in large part, through reading and content-area instruction. The goal of sheltered English is for students to learn English while they develop academic and cognitive abilities in areas such as comprehension and problem solving. For this reason, schooling often takes place in English. Merging English language instruction with systematic instruction in social studies and science can accelerate academic and conceptual English language vocabulary. Reading in English is used as a method for developing English language competence. When students are given an abundance of high-interest story books in English, their progress in reading and listening comprehension increases at a rapid rate (Gersten, Brengleman, & Jiménez, 1994).

English as a Second Language (ESL).
Using this approach, students learn English through carefully controlled oral repetitions of selected second-language patterns. This approach is often used in schools in which children come from many different language backgrounds, and it is not feasible to provide instruction in all native languages.

Bilingual Education.

In this method, students use their native language during part of the school day and the second language (English) during the other portion of the school day. The objective of bilingual programs is to strengthen school learning through the native language, gradually adding a second language. In this way, students will come to recognize and respect the importance of their native culture and language in American society. In the bilingual method, academic subjects are usually taught in the native language and the student receives oral practice in English.

Dual Language.

When two language groups of students attend the same school, each group can learn the other's language. To do this, children are placed together, and instruction is done in both languages.

Immersion.

Here, students are "immersed" in, or receive extensive exposure to, the second language. In fact, where there is no formal instruction for a person learning a second language, this is usually what occurs naturally. Individuals simply learn English as they live daily in the mainstream of an English-speaking society. Immersion is widely employed with schoolchildren in Canada, where it is used to teach French to English-speaking children by enrolling them in French-speaking schools (Genesee, 1985).

There is limited research evidence on how different instructional methods affect students *with reading problems* whose native language is not English. However, it is evident that teachers must be particularly sensitive to the needs of these students. Teachers need expertise both in teaching reading and in teaching minority language students (Ortiz, 1988).

Effective Classroom Settings for LEP Students

How many sad stories we have of past generations of immigrant children who felt lonely and lost in classrooms that did not respect their rich heritages! Many were forbidden to speak their native languages. Others were made to feel ashamed of their families. Fortunately, in today's schools, we recognize and celebrate language and cultural differences.

The school settings in which students spend so much time should, of course, reflect their cultural backgrounds. We present several strategies as examples of ways to make classrooms and materials reflect the diversity of student backgrounds in our schools (Garcia & Malkin, 1993):

(1) Encourage minority language students to use their first language around the school, even when they are not receiving instruction in it. For example, books in the classroom and library, bulletin boards, and signs can be in your students' native language. Students can also help each other. Jerzy, a child who spoke Polish, was made a helping partner to Irena, a child who had just immigrated from Warsaw. This increased the self-esteem and language skills of both students.
(2) Display pictures that show people from various backgrounds and communities, showing people from culturally diverse backgrounds at work, at home, and in leisure activities.

(3) Develop units for reading and language arts, using literature from a variety of linguistic and cultural backgrounds that reflect the diversity in U.S. society. In Table 12.2, at the end of this chapter, we present a bibliography of books suitable for students from many different backgrounds. Students of *all* backgrounds enjoy reading them but, of course, they are especially important for the self-esteem of students in the groups they feature.

(4) Be sensitive to your own speech and nonverbal communication. Since cultural norms vary, it is surprisingly easy to communicate biases that you do not intend.

(5) Use seating arrangements and class organization to encourage students to try new ways of interacting and learning. Students from different cultural groups enjoy sharing ideas and experiences. This is best fostered if students have a variety of opportunities in which to sit, talk, and work with others.

Instructional Practices for Teaching Reading to LEP Students

Reading is based on language. Thus, to read in English, students must understand the English words and sentence structures they meet in books. It is *not* acceptable for students to simply pronounce words that they do not understand, for this is reading without meaning. Students who are limited in English should be free to learn sophisticated information and concepts in the language they are most comfortable using. Information and abilities can be learned in any language, and transferred to another (Hakuta, 1990).

On the other hand, since reading is connected to listening and speaking, reading done in English may be used to strengthen all language abilities in English. If students have some proficiency in English, reading English books will further all English language skills.

Below, we give ways that reading and language acquisition may support each other in instruction. Remember that a student's culture must always be respected.

Using English Books.

English language reading can be an excellent medium to improve general mastery of English. When students learning English are given an abundance of high-interest story books in English, their progress in reading and listening comprehension increases at almost twice the usual rate (Gersten, Brengleman, & Jiménez, 1994).

When using this strategy, you may need to focus on books that supply repetition in language structures. For example, predictable books (see Chapters 5 and 7), which repeat refrains over and over, are excellent for learning English. Similarly, attractively illustrated books, in which pictures support the text, are excellent for students. Well-known folk tales and fairy tales with familiar plots are also useful. Allen (1994) suggests several other helpful books for students learning English. To develop concepts, use *The Toolbox* (by Rockwell); *Circles, Triangles, and Squares; Over, Under, Through, and Other Spatial Concepts;* and *Push-Pull, Empty-Full: A Book of Opposites* (by Hoban); *Bread, Bread, Bread* (by Morris); *People* (by Spier); and *Growing Vegetable Soup* (by Ehlers). Books that invite talk include *A Taste of Blackberries* and *The Biggest House in the World* (by Lionni); *Nana Upstairs, Nana Downstairs* (by De Paola); and *The Story of Ferdinand* (by Leaf).

Students who are more advanced in English language skills profit from using books focusing on language use, such as *Amelia Bedelia* and its sequels (by Parish), which feature common idioms in amusing situations, and *Many Luscious Lollipops* and its sequels (by Heller), which focus on parts of speech, such as adjectives, nouns, and adverbs. Finally, the increasing number of books written in two languages (see Table 12.2) allows students to match their native language patterns with corresponding English ones.

Opportunities to Use English.

Minority language students must be given many opportunities to move from learning and producing limited word translations and fragmented concepts to using longer sentences and expressing more complex ideas and feelings. As you engage students in increasingly complex reading and writing experiences, check to make sure that they understand the concepts you are teaching. Teachers should use redundant language, relatively simple sentences, and physical gestures as prompts (Gersten, Brengleman, & Jiménez, 1994). In one method, Total Physical Response (Asher & Price, 1969), nonverbal gestures foster active learning of a second language. As you work with children, be aware of the need to provide the background information that helps them to understand the concepts and language you present.

Opportunities to use more complex English vary according to the level of students. In one kindergarten class of Russian-speaking children, a game of "Simon Says," complete with gestures, provided active response to English. At a more advanced level, a third-grade bilingual Spanish class listened to the hilarious "twisted" fairy tale, *The True Story of the Three Little Pigs* (by Scieszka) in both English and Spanish, and then acted it out. Later that year, the class listened to *Charlotte's Web* (by White) read in English, chose their favorite words, and then matched these words in Spanish.

Using Conversation about Books to Foster Natural Language Usage.

In fostering a discussion of a story, the teacher can ask such questions as: "What do you think this story will be about?" "What do you think will happen next?" "Why do you think that?" "Tell me more about . . ." "What do you mean by . . . ?" Encourage students by giving them time to respond. In addition, students may respond in pairs, making the activity less threatening. Conversation about personal reactions to stories are excellent for giving meaning-based practice in using English. Students enjoy discussing their favorite characters and the best parts of a story. To aid them, the teacher may list helpful English adjectives on the board.

Using Language-based Approaches.

Approaches based on using students' language to connect reading, writing, and speaking are excellent for teaching students English in a natural setting. Students can dictate language experience stories (see Chapters 5 and 7) that use their own experiences and language. Thus, in reading them, students are using familiar language to master English reading skills. Stories might include words both in English and in the students' native language.

Whole language methods (Goodman & Goodman, 1979; K. S. Goodman, 1992), which foster a natural use of all language systems together, are also excellent for developing English (Chamot & O'Malley, 1994). There are many activities consistent with a whole language approach. Students may, for example, learn to read the print in their environment using TV guides and advertisements as reading material. When reading books, authentic children's books are preferable to the tightly controlled, artificial language often found in reading textbooks. Role playing and drama are excellent for fostering language use. Students may also enjoy poetry, in which they explore rhythm and rhyming patterns in English. Finally, personal writings, especially those that reflect the children's own culture, are valuable. Teachers may want to use the writing process to create a literate environment (see Chapter 11).

Using Cooperative Learning.
Small cooperative groups allow students to interact with peers while doing schoolwork assignments. Cooperative learning creates opportunities to use language in a meaningful and nonthreatening way. It draws on primary language skills while developing English language skills, promotes higher-order cognitive and linguistic discourse, and fosters peer modeling and peer feedback. Of course, teachers must serve as facilitators to guide these cooperative peer groups.

Fostering Home–School Collaboration.
It is important to establish communication with the parents, the home, and other family members such as siblings. More can be accomplished when the school and home work together. Parents should be contacted frequently to communicate students' successes as well as the problems their child encounters. Remember that parents often have valuable information and insights that can be useful in the teaching process. Families can also make valuable contributions to school programs. In one fourth-grade bilingual room, two mothers sewed all the costumes for 36 fifth-grade children who sang Venezuelan songs. In helping the school's celebration, parents, school staff, and students gained a sense of community involvement.

Collaboration in the School.
To help foster the education of linguistically diverse students, there is a need for collaboration among school personnel. Classroom teachers, reading teachers, special education teachers, instructional support staff, and administrators should work together to meet the needs of children. We recommend that school staff, as well as students, share their knowledge of other languages and cultures. This is a first step in fostering the understanding that adds richness to American life and education.

Teaching in Today's Multicultural Society

With each year that goes by, our society becomes increasingly multicultural. We have been immeasurably enriched by the many different groups of people, each bringing unique contributions, that form our current population. This diversity enables us to respond vigorously and flexibly to new challenges. Furthermore, as new groups add their strengths and established ones maintain their heritage, we become a society increasingly rich in cultural resources.

We are called upon to accommodate the diversity that is woven into the fabric of our society, and yet, our schools have not fully met this challenge. Minority-group children have not achieved historically as well as children from the dominant, middle-class culture. Minorities have lagged behind considerably in rates of graduation from high school (Garcia, Pearson, & Jiménez, 1994). Finally, these children are overrepresented, in proportion to the population, in programs providing special services.

As teachers, we need to offer to all students the best instruction we can. Several understandings will help us in this effort.

Views of Reading

Not all people view literacy, and literacy learning, in the same way. In fact, a student's family may view reading very differently than does a teacher. Literacy teaching in American schools is often formulated on the basis of middle-class culture, and expects children to have the kinds of experiences that middle-class, English-speaking parents have traditionally provided. These are, in fact, very much like the experiences that are usually provided in school.

For example, middle-class parents frequently read stories to their children (often at bedtime) and discuss them. Through these efforts, children become aware of what a book is, how to handle it, how print and speech match, and the structure of a story. Such experiences are also common school activities in kindergarten and first grade. Similarly, middle-class parents frequently ask their children questions for which the parents already know the answer. This is, again, an experience frequently repeated in school, when a teacher is questioning children about material they have read (Garcia, Pearson, & Jiménez, 1994; Heath, 1981, 1983).

However, these types of interactions are not common to all families. For example, Heath (1983) found that, in one community, storybook reading was uncommon; in another community, story reading was done, but not with the adult–child interaction that fostered the ability to handle books. In both these communities, people pursued other reading activities, such as reading the Bible, mail, recipes, TV guides, word searches, and crossword puzzles. Although these are valuable activities, early experiences with books in school tend to mirror the middle-class child–parent reading interaction, and children unfamiliar with it may be unprepared for key elements of school instruction.

Literacy experiences that do not reflect commonly held views of schooling may, nevertheless, enrich language, cognitive skills, and reading. Moll and González (1994) describe several working-class families that shared valuable information and respected heritages in pursuing hobbies and small business projects. At times, schools were able to use this knowledge to enhance their curricula. For example, many students in one community near the Mexican border were involved in trans-country trips dealing with the sale of candy. The school used this to form a unit on candy, including its nutritional content, a comparison of U.S. and Mexican candy, sugar processing, and the marketing of candy. In an African American community, the school tapped the resources of a father, employed as a gardener, who possessed a wealth of knowledge about musical and theatrical performance. This man wrote and produced an original musical, which was performed by students. In addition to a focus on performing skills, the school created units on the acoustical properties of sound, construction of various instruments, and ethnomusicology (Hensley, 1994).

It is important for teachers to remember that children come to school with different experiences, and to honor those which children have already had, while providing those the children have not had.

Views of Language

Cultural differences are also seen in styles of verbal interactions. In studies done in two countries, Cazden (1988b) found that children from some lower-class cultures were not encouraged to speak in an extended fashion until they had developed enough competence to "hold their own" on whatever topic adults were discussing. Thus, while some parents treasure every word of a child's "baby talk," listening to and responding to it, other parents discourage children from using it.

Since many children are not encouraged to display extended language use at home, they may not feel comfortable expressing themselves at school. Cazden (1988a,b) found that some children did not want to talk or answer questions until were certain they were correct. Thus, they were often afraid to offer opinions or engage in conversations in class. In the children's view, a good child was a *quiet* child.

The lack of willingness to talk did not mean that children had nothing to say. Cazden (1988b) notes that both middle-class and lower-class children possessed similar amounts of information about objects presented to them. However, because of clash in cultural styles and lack of experience in talking about objects, lower-class children needed to be prompted twice as much as middle-class children before they would verbalize what they knew. This study has important implications for teachers. As Cazden (1988a,b) found, children may not always be willing to express what they know; thus, teachers may underestimate the extent of their knowledge. In building language and reading skills, it is important to encourage children to express themselves and, at the same time, to realize that they may be reluctant to do so.

In addition to using language differently, students whose home experiences do not mirror school experiences may not know how to act or react in school. They may have no experience with how to behave in halls, how to play at recess, how to treat books, or how to organize themselves for instruction. Delpit (1988) calls this the "power code"—norms that are often unspoken and untaught, but which children in the mainstream culture learn from their parents. Teachers sometimes need to carefully explain to children and families the types of behavior that are expected in school. They may also need to explain the curriculum they are using, and why they are using it.

Views of Instructizon

Different cultures see the schooling experience, and the role of teachers, differently. In some cultures, the teacher is venerated as an authority whose power and authority is not to be challenged (Delpit, 1988). In mainstream American schools, however, we tend to see a teacher as a helper and guider of children. Contemporary mainstream instruction is often focused on hints and indirect teaching, rather than on direct correction of errors.

Reyes (1992) noted several conflicts between the concept of a teacher for the Spanish bilingual classes she studied, and the way mainstream students see teachers. These differences were a source of confusion and frustration for both bilingual students and teachers. For example, in their journal writing, bilingual students made many spelling errors (as do all children writing in journals). The teacher's method of correction was to respond to the child by writing back in the journal, using a misspelled word over again, but this time spelling it correctly. To one teacher's amazement, the students never followed her spelling models. When, at the end of the year, students were asked about the teacher's corrections, they answered that they did not realize that the teacher's respellings were corrections. The students said that if their teacher wanted to correct their spelling, why not simply tell them so ("¿Porqué no me lo dijo?")? In other words they valued, and expected, direct instruction. In the same way, Reyes noted that when children were asked to choose a book and read silently, bilingual students seemed lost, and simply wandered around the room. Even direction from classmates did not help them to make book choices. Instead they seemed to expect, again, direct teacher instruction in choosing and using books.

Views of Language Differences

Many children who are not in the mainstream culture talk in nonstandard ways, either because they speak a nonstandard dialect, or because they speak a language other than English as their native language. Language differences are very powerful in determining our judgment of other people. At times, we tend to judge people who speak differently from us harshly.

In fact, however, all dialects of English are linguistically sound ways of communicating. For example, Black English Vernacular (spoken by some African Americans) is a fully formed dialect of English, with its own rules and vocabulary (Labov et al., 1968), and is particularly rich in vocabulary. Many standard English words have originally come from this dialect. In addition, the dialect has a very highly developed set of verbal games. It has been shown that proficiency in playing "The Dozens," one verbal game, predicts the ability of students to comprehend figurative language (Delain, Pearson, & Anderson, 1985). Students who speak this dialect should not be judged to have verbal problems any more than should children who speak any other form of English.

In the same way, it is sometimes difficult for teachers to judge students who speak a language other than English. A year ago, we were visiting a school in Chicago with a friend from Hungary. In this school, we met a nine-year-old Hungarian child, recently arrived in the United States, who was described as shy, unhappy, and a problem for his teacher. When our friend talked to him in Hungarian, however, she discovered an outgoing, confident child who was quite artistic and familiar with many modern artists.

Reyes (1992) claims that many instructors unconsciously feel that legitimate instruction takes place only in English, and that using another language is viewed as a deficient learning experience. Such a view is, of course, contrary to United States laws and policies on bilingual education, which specify that children should, for some years, receive instruction in their strongest language.

Steps toward Understanding

What steps can we, as teachers, take to make our programs havens where children can share their linguistic and cultural contributions, and can achieve in ways that help them attain the jobs and futures they deserve? Cazden (1986) suggests that relatives (such as grandparents) and community members who work, visit, or donate time to a school can help bridge important gaps between minority and mainstream cultures. Later in this chapter, we describe several successful programs we have implemented using community volunteers. We have found that these volunteers can relate successfully to the children, while helping them understand the expectations of the mainstream culture. Our volunteers were particularly helpful when misunderstandings occurred.

We also advise teachers to explain fully their expectations and routines when working with all students. Such topics as how to choose a book, what happens during quiet time, how to take turns, and how to listen to a teacher read a story may need explicit instruction.

Finally, students need to make and share contributions from their own cultures. We have had several successful experiences with African American children writing raps that summarize their learning in American history and science, as well as novels.

In one school setting, each child in a fourth-grade bilingual classroom was paired with a child in an English-monolingual second grade. Each child taught 5 words on different topics (say, sports, food, or Mexico) in that child's first language, to his or her partner, and engaged in much animated conversation. Thus, English-speaking children learned Spanish words, and Spanish-speaking children learned English words. This culminated in the second-grade's participation in the annual bilingual celebration of the school, as well as the communal breaking of a very stubborn piñata to celebrate the holiday Cinquo de Mayo.

Families from different cultures can often share experiences and feelings in writing. The Montgomery County Public Schools (Maryland) serves many minority language children. In one classroom, children's older brothers and sisters were asked to write the story of how their families came to America (or to Maryland) (S. Clewell, personal communication, 1987). We believe the response of this fifth-grade boy echoes an important promise to all of us.

My Family's Trip to America

This story all began when my family was in the war suffering. Lots of people were pushing and shoving. They pushed and shoved because they wanted to escape from the Communists. If they were caught, they would die or would be their prisoner and would be put in jail. The jail is a dark, damp dreary dungeon. Most were killed by gun shots. My family came to America. My mom and dad came from Vietnam. Freedom is what my father and mother came for. They chose the right place, America. They were glad they made it.

Working with Parents

Parents are key to the development of a child's attitude about and preparedness for reading. When the child fails to learn to read, the parents experience feelings of frustration and anger. How can we help parents to aid and encourage their children?

First, the teacher should talk regularly to parents of children with reading problems. Devoting time to understanding the needs of these families is important, for it shows your willingness to help. We have found that parents who realize how hard the teacher is trying will often match the teacher's efforts by reading with their children at home or buying them books. Of course, in these encounters, it is important to be respectful of parents' perspectives. In fact, by listening to the parent's experiences with their children, we often gain information that is important to our instruction.

In addition to communicating with parents, you may want to offer other forms of support.

The-Read-to-Me-I'll-Read-to-You Program

In this program (S. Shapiro, personal communication, 1988), a child places two books in a large envelope. One is to be read by the parent to the child; the other is to be read by the child to the parent. Primary children are expected to engage in 15 minutes of personal reading and to listen to a parent read for an additional 15 minutes. For older children, the time is extended to 20 minutes. To verify that the reading has occurred, a form is provided for the parent to list the books, the number of minutes spent reading, and to sign.

In this program, parents become participants in the reading process. The program also acquaints parents with a variety of reading formats. Parents may read a high-level book to their child, providing language development. Parents and children may read different books at the same time, silently, each enjoying a private reading experience. Or parents and children may read the same book and then discuss it after reading. Parents may read a book to a child and the child can "echo read" each page that the parent has read. Parents and children can also take turns reading the same book, or read them as plays, taking parts. We often provide very easy books and tapes to parents who are uncertain of their own reading abilities.

Parent Workshops

Being the parent of child with a reading problem can be a frustrating and discouraging experience. Parents need to share their feelings and experiences with others, perhaps getting useful ideas from them. They also need information about the best placement for their child and their rights under the law. Perhaps most important, parents need to share positive literacy experiences they have had with their children.

For a number of years, we have been conducting workshops for parents. The workshops meet once per week for about 10 sessions. Frequently they are held during the time when the children are being taught in our Reading Center. During the workshop sessions, parents share experiences and ideas with each other, often developing close relationships. Our parents have asked for information concerning laws on special education and educational placement. They have also sought ways to foster reading in their child.

What specific ideas do we use with parents? Often we ask parents to bring a favorite book that they remember reading when they were children (Jennings et al., 1993). The books they bring are easy and entertaining. This activity demonstrates that children will want to learn if the books they are encouraged to read are easy and fun. We also have asked parents to remember the affectionate experiences they and their own parents shared during reading and discuss ways to foster these happy experiences with their own children.

We share special books with parents. One semester, the parent leader showed the beautiful book *On the Day You Were Born* (by Frasier). In the following weeks, many parents read this book to their children. At the end of sessions, we had a final celebration in which parents read a description of the actual day their own individual child was born. While most of descriptions were given by mothers, two were given by fathers.

As the previous example shows, we also encourage our parents to write. This deepens their own understanding of literacy and helps them to understand how difficult writing can be for children. Parents come to understand the nature of the writing process and how spelling and punctuation should be a last step in writing, rather than the first step. At the end of each semester, a piece of writing from each child and participating parent is bound into a joint Reading Center book and is read at a final celebration. Each parent and child receives a copy of this joint book as a memento of a positive experience.

The leaders of the parent workshops also share strategies that parents can use with their children. Typical strategies (L. Chenault, personal communication, 1993; S. Ali, personal communication, 1994–5) have included:

- Making family message boards to encourage literacy
- Reading a favorite book over again
- Displaying books in theme baskets (e.g., Halloween, Spring)
- Suggestions on how to choose books at libraries and bookstores

- Taking field trips that support what your child is studying
- Modeling thinking about what you know about a topic before you read
- Modeling thinking about what you learned after you read
- Listing places to purchase discount children's books

Ada (1988) reports similarly successful experiences with Spanish-speaking parents in communities that included many migrant workers. Parents were delighted to record, in Spanish, their positive family experiences.

Adolescents with Reading Problems

Adolescence (the thirteen- to twenty-year-old age range) is a well-documented of period of social, emotional, and physical change. Adolescents must resolve conflicts between a desire for freedom and security as they are torn between wishing for independence and yet not being ready for the responsibilities of full adulthood. They must cope with rapid physical changes in growth, appearance, and sexual drive. Peer pressure greatly affects adolescents, as they seek group acceptance and are increasingly aware of how their peers are doing. All these characteristics of adolescence present challenges that may negatively affect learning (Hammechek, 1990; Kerr, Nelson, & Lambert, 1987).

Characteristics of Adolescents with Reading Problems

Teenagers with reading problems not only have difficulty in school, but they must also cope with the normal challenges and adjustments presented by adolescence. Trying to deal with this combination creates special burdens for teenagers.

1. *Passive learning.* Adolescents with reading and learning problems have often developed an attitude of "learned helplessness" and dependence (Ellis et al., 1991). They wait for teacher direction.
2. *Poor self-concept.* Low self-esteem and other emotional problems result from years of failure and frustration (Smith, 1992).
3. *Inept social skills.* Adolescents with academic problems often have difficulty making and keeping friends during a period when friendships and peer approval are important (Vaughn, 1991; Bryan, 1991).
4. *Attention deficits.* Poor attention and concentration are common in teenagers who read poorly (Lerner, Lowenthal, & Lerner, 1995). Since long periods of concentration are required for high-school work, attention problems are quite serious.
5. *Lack of motivation.* After years of failure, many teenagers feel that they are "dumb" and that their efforts to learn will be useless. Adolescents can learn only if they are motivated and can attribute success to their own efforts (Zigmond, 1990).

Special Considerations at the Secondary Level

Schools often fail to meet the needs of adolescents with reading and learning problems. For example, only 50 percent of learning-disabled students (many of whom have reading problems) receive high-school diplomas (U.S. Department of Education, 1994). Students who drop out of school often face grim futures in the streets.

Secondary students with academic problems face new challenges, as demands for excellence in education have led to increased requirements (in mathematics, foreign languages, science) for high-school graduation. Students with learning problems are no longer sheltered from the demands of the regular curriculum, but are expected to meet many of the same requirements as all other students. Over three-fourths of all states now require that high-school students pass minimum competency tests before receiving their diplomas.

Finally, many content-area secondary school teachers are not oriented to working with low-achieving readers. Focusing on their specializations, such teachers have not been trained to adjust their specialized curricula in mathematics, French, or physics to the student with reading problems. For this reason, a major task of the high-school reading specialist is to help the content teachers understand and deal with the needs of low-achieving students.

There are many options that reading teachers can suggest to help disabled students. If the student has a severe reading problem, it might be possible to tape lessons. At times, books recorded for the blind can be made accessible to nonreaders through local libraries. During examinations, students might be allowed to give answers orally, to tape answers, or to dictate answers to someone else. Students who do write could be allowed additional time. Convincing high-school teachers to modify their programs for special students is an essential element of a reading specialist's job, one requiring considerable skill in interpersonal relationships.

Components of Effective Secondary Programs

Zigmond (1990) has identified four effective program components.

1. *Intensive instruction in reading and mathematics.* Many students with reading problems continue to require instruction in basic skills.
2. *Direct instruction in high-school "survival" skills.* Training may be needed for successful functioning in a high school. "Behavior control" helps students learn how to stay out of trouble in school. "Teacher-pleasing behaviors" allow students to acquire behavior patterns (look interested, volunteer responses) that will make teachers view them more positively. Strategies such as organizing time, previewing textbooks, taking notes from a lecture or text, organizing information, and taking tests are needed for academic success (Zigmond, 1990).
3. *Successful completion of courses.* Students with problems may cut classes, come late, and not complete assignments. Empathetic, caring teachers and counselors can foster course completion. Success in grade nine is particularly critical for high school (Zigmond, 1990).
4. *Planning for life after high school.* Adolescents with reading problems need to prepare for a successful transition to higher education or the world of work.

Adults with Reading Problems

For many individuals, a reading disability is a lifelong problem, one that does not disappear when schooling has been completed. In this section, we consider the problems of reading-disabled adults.

Adult literacy presents an ever-growing challenge. Some adults with problems in reading have dropped out of school and now find themselves blocked from employment. Others may be employed but want to advance in their jobs or enhance their personal skills. Some have been denied opportunity because they lived in countries that did not provide a free education. Yet other adult learners are concerned with learning to speak and write in English. Finally, some have continuing literacy problems, sometimes associated with learning disabilities.

Postsecondary and College Programs

Postsecondary education includes community colleges, vocational–technical training, and colleges. Programs in a variety of settings at a growing number of colleges and other postsecondary institutions serve adult learners with reading problems.

Accommodations have been triggered by Section 504 of the Rehabilitation Act (P.L. 93-112) (1973), which requires educational institutions receiving federal funds to make reasonable accommodations for students who are identified as having a disability. Many such individuals suffer from reading problems.

How can we help adult students in postsecondary education deal with academic demands? Some suggestions are:

1. Give course syllabi to them 4–6 weeks before class begins and discuss them personally.
2. Begin lectures and discussions with systematic overviews of the topic.
3. Use a chalkboard or overhead projector to outline lecture material, orally reading what is written on the board or transparencies.
4. Use a chalkboard or overhead projector to highlight key concepts, unusual terminology, or foreign words.
5. Clearly identify important points, main ideas, and key concepts orally in lecture.
6. Give assignments in writing and orally; be available for further clarification.
7. Provide opportunities for student participation, question periods, and/or discussion.
8. Provide time for individual discussion of assignments and questions about lectures and readings.
9. Provide study guides for the text, study questions, and review sessions to prepare for exams.
10. Allow oral presentations or tape-recorded assignments instead of requiring students to use a written format.
11. Modify evaluation procedures: include untimed tests, wide-lined paper for tests, and alternatives to computer-scored answer sheets.

Needs of Adults with Reading Problems

Although some adults are lucky enough to get higher education, many adults with severe reading problems have great difficulty finding their niche in the world. They have trouble working, socializing, and even coping with daily tasks. Many adults with reading problems have ingenious strategies for avoiding, hiding, and dealing with their problems.

A man whose wife had died a few years before was caught in the social dating whirl. He would routinely enter a restaurant with his lady friend, put down the menu, and say, "Why don't you order for both of us, dear? Your selections are always perfect." This man hired professionals to handle all of his personal matters, including his checkbook. His friends attributed his actions to wealth, never suspecting his inability to read.

Instructional Programs for Adults

Adults who seek help with their reading problems are likely to be highly motivated to learn and to demand an explanation of the goals and purposes of their programs. This commitment enables them to succeed.

More and more adults seek help that goes beyond the basic stages of literacy. As a result, the field of adult literacy has expanded its original responsibilities from basic functional literacy to a high technical level (approximately twelfth-grade reading level) (Chall, 1987, 1994).

Some instructional options for adult programs are:

(1) *ABE and GED Programs* provide Adult Basic Education (from elementary levels through eighth grade) and a high-school level education with a General Education Diploma. Both the ABE and GED are funded by the *federal* government and require group instruction. Approximately two-and-a-half-million adults are enrolled in them (Gottesman, 1994).

(2) *Literacy Volunteers of America,* a private organization training volunteers to work with adults, serves the needs of over 52,000 people. Instruction is individual and programs are aimed toward the illiterate and semiliterate adult. A component for teaching English as a second language is available.

(3) *Laubach Literacy Action* is the U.S. division of Laubach Literacy International. Frank Laubach, a missionary, developed a program to teach literacy to people worldwide. This program uses volunteers and currently serves over 150,000 adults. Materials, including initial instruction in a pictorial alphabet, are available through New Readers' Press.

(4) *ESL adult literacy programs* concentrate on English as a Second Language. Federal funding comes from the Adult Literacy Act, currently serving over one million limited-English adults. As more immigrants enter the United States' work force, ESL services are expected to increase (Newman, 1994).

Adults with reading problems express wishes for developing a wide variety of life skills. Needs include social skills, career counseling, developing self-esteem and confidence, overcoming dependence, survival skills, vocational training, job procurement and retention, reading, spelling, management of personal finances, and organizational skills. Help in coping with jobs was expressed particularly strongly.

Summary

The diversity of American culture is one of its most important strengths. An increasing number of students speak English as a second language. Approaches to instruction for bilingual and limited-English-proficient students include teaching complex concepts in the student's native language; Sheltered English with carefully sequenced content-area instruction; ESL (teaching English as a second language) with controlled pattern repetition in English; bilingual education, instruction in two languages; dual language, two groups of students learning each other's language; and immersion, or full exposure without instruction. Effective classroom settings honor students' native cultures and do not unconsciously communicate bias. Instructional practices for teaching reading to LEP students include using interesting

English books; a language-rich English environment; using instructional conversation about content areas; connecting reading, writing, speaking, and listening; using cooperative learning, and fostering home–school collaboration.

Families from different cultures hold views of reading, language, and instruction that may not reflect the dominant views of society. For example, some people respond to the teacher as an authority figure, and are uncomfortable with informal and indirect learning. Language differences should not be interpreted as reflecting inferiority.

Parents can cooperate with the school in many ways.

Adolescents with reading problems add academic difficulties to the difficult adjustment that is typical of their age group. Instruction should reflect concern for their future. New laws have increased the number of adults in postsecondary school and college. In addition, the number of adults who wish to learn English is increasing. Adults are goal-oriented in their learning.

Table 12.2 **Multicultural Children's Books**

African and African American

Afrobets Series, S. Willis Hudson   Preschool concepts (colors, shapes, numbers) presented with African animals, artifacts, and everyday objects.

A is for Africa, I. Onyefufo   Photographs in alphabet book provide a stunning view if life in a Nigerian village.

Amazing Grace, M. Hoffman   Can an African English girl play Peter Pan in a school play? This story concerns racial awareness and self-esteem.

Mary Had a Little Lamb, S. Hale (illus. by B. McMillan)   Photographs of an African American Mary offer a unique interpretation of this classic nursery rhyme.

The People Could Fly, V. Hamilton   Anthology of 24 folktales focus on the Black Experience in the southern U.S.

Pink and Say, P. Polacco   In this true story, a black Union soldier nurses a wounded Confederate soldier.

Native American

Dancing with the Indians, A. S. Medearis   African American author tells of her ancestors' participation in a Seminole Indian celebration.

Encounter, J. Yolen   Set in 1492, a Taino Indian child recounts the visit of Columbus, highlighting differences between Native American and Europeans.

Ikomi and the Boulder, P. Goble   Lively trickster tale explains why the Great Plains are covered with rocks and bats and have flat faces.

Knots on a Counting Rope, B. Martin, Jr., & J. Archambault   Wise grandfather helps a Native American boy to face his blindness.

Maii and Cousin Horned Toad, S. Begay   Navaho fable explains why coyotes stay away from horned toads.

Sunpainters, Baje Whitethorne   According to Navajo legend, the sun must be repainted after an eclipse.

Hispanic

Un Cuento de Queztalcoatl, M. Parke & S. Panik   Part of the Mexican and Central American Legends series in which each of several tales is told (in separate short books) in English and Spanish. This, the tale of the ball game, tells of a game among the Aztec gods.

Diego, J. Winter   The life of the famous muralist Diego Rivera is depicted in simple bilingual text with artwork that mirrors his own.

Everybody Has Feelings, C. Abery   A bilingual (Spanish/English) exploration of people and their feelings.

First Day of School, M. Deru   Young foxes, hunting for chickens, make friends with them instead.

Let's Go (Vamos), E. Emberley   This book explores the four seasons in bilingual text.

Moon Rope, L. Elhert   Peruvian folktale (Spanish/English) about why there is a moon features a fox.

Radio Man, A. Dorros   A child of a migrant worker family (Spanish / English), sends a message to his friend via a radio. Text is bilingual.

Asian

Baseball Saved Us, K. Mochizuki   A Japanese American boy interned during World War II, finds solace in baseball.

The Dragon's Robe, D. Nourse   A Chinese girl weaves a beautiful silk robe to save her father's life.

Grandmother's Path; Grandfather's Way, L. Vang & J. Lewis   Lore and legends of the Hmong Southeast Asian tribe (Hmong/English)

Jar of Dreams, Y. Uchida   Rinko, a Japanese American girl, tells about her family life in California.

The Little Weaver of Thai-Yen Village, Tran-Khanh-Yuyet   One of the Fifth World Tales Series, in Vietnamese and English. A Vietnamese girl comes to the United States for an operation. Other books in this series feature different Asian groups.

Momma Do You Love Me?, B. Joosse   An Eskimo child questions mother about "What if I . . . ?" Many Eskimo terms are explained.

This list was compiled by Susan Ali.

CHAPTER 13

Factors Related to Reading Disability

Introduction

This chapter explores the factors related to a student's ability to read. We discuss both (1) environmental factors and (2) factors within the individual. Environmental factors include the home, school, social, and cultural groups. Factors within the individual include emotional factors, intelligence, language factors, and physical factors. We introduced many of these factors in Chapter 2. In this chapter, we give theoretical information and research to extend your knowledge. In addition, we describe more advanced assessment tools.

It is important to remember that factors relate to reading in multiple and complex ways. Even if a factor is present, it may not affect a student's reading. For example, many students with difficult home lives are excellent readers. In an extensive investigation of correlates of reading disabilities, Robinson (1946) concluded that poor reading was generally the result of several factors, all interacting with each other. As research modifies our understanding of reading disabilities, knowledge is still evolving about the exact relationship between each factor and reading performance.

Environmental Factors

The different environments in which students live and grow have a strong impact on their desire and ability to learn. Important environments include the home, the school, the social group, and the cultural milieu. How does each one affect reading?

The Home Environment

The home, a child's first environment, is the foundation for tremendous cognitive growth and development. The experiences that occur during the critical first five or six years of life are powerful influences upon a child's intelligence and language.

Parents provide emotional well-being as well as intellectual stimulation. A crucial interaction known as "bonding" takes place during the early months of infancy and becomes the basis for later emotional health. Bonding depends upon a successful interactive relationship between the mother (or primary parent figure) and the infant (Bowlby, 1969). The early development of the ego and self-concept are also dependent upon the support and encouragement of parents. Studies that compare good and poor readers show that students who experience success are much more likely to have a favorable home environment (Chall, Jacobs, & Baldwin, 1990; Gollnick & Chin, 1990; Levine & Havighurst, 1992).

Parents are also very important in stimulating a love for reading. Parents who read to children, take them to libraries, and buy books as presents teach children to value reading. Parents who read themselves provide a role model for literacy. The parent's role continues to be crucial even after the child enters school.

Youngsters who experience difficulty learning to read are in special need of satisfying family relationships. Parents can alleviate some of the psychological and emotional consequences of reading failure by what they do in the home environment. They can provide love, acceptance, and other opportunities for success.

Sadly, today's children come from increasingly difficult environments. Census figures show that 27 percent of all children under the age of 18 live with a single parent who has never married (U.S. Census Bureau, 1994). It is predicted that 80 percent of children born to unwed mothers will live in poverty (Jouzaitis, 1994). In addition, it is estimated that 60 percent of all Americans born in 1984 will spend some time living in a single-parent household before reaching age eighteen (Jouzaitis, 1994; Norton & Glick, 1986). Understandably, children in such households may be under stress, and feel too burdened to cope with school demands.

The School Environment

Since youngsters spend a substantial portion of their waking hours in school, their experiences and relationships in the school environment profoundly affect their lives. For the poor reader, school experiences are too often unhappy ones (Brophy, 1988).

Interactions within the School.
Students with reading problems often have unsatisfactory relationships with adults in their schools. Studies show that poor achievers tend to be perceived negatively by teachers, teacher aides, and principals. In fact, adults form negative impressions of students with learning problems after viewing them on videotape for only a few minutes (Pearl, Donahue, & Bryan, 1986). Teachers identify these students as aggressive and lacking self-discipline. Low achievers receive little praise or acknowledgment from teachers, and are likely to be criticized (Good, 1983; Keogh, Tchir, & Windeguth-Behn, 1974). These findings have serious implications for students with reading problems.

Instructional Factors in Reading Problems.
As we have emphasized in Chapters 2 and 4, instruction that does not meet a student's needs can be an important factor in a reading problem. Immature children who are given formal reading instruction before they can profit from it may become frustrated and develop reading problems (Olson, 1989). Other students do not receive sufficient instruction in critical skills, and thus they fail in the initial stages of learning. For example, Stanovich (1988a,b) has demonstrated an important link between phonological awareness and early reading; if this critical skill is not learned by first grade, reading in all following grades will be affected. Finally, low-achieving students often do not read enough to become better readers (Johnston & Allington, 1991).

The Social Environment

Successful interactions with friends should provide many satisfactions and opportunities to gain confidence. Unfortunately, a sizable body of evidence shows that social unpopularity tends to accompany school failure. Poor achievers are often rejected or ignored by their classmates and are uninvolved in extracurricular activities (Pearl, Donahue, & Bryan, 1986).

Students with reading problems tend to have problems in interactions, exhibiting poor social perception skills (Bryan, 1991; Vaughn, 1991). When children develop normally, they learn social skills in a casual and informal manner. Through incidental experiences, they learn appropriate ways of acting with people: what to say, how to behave, and how to "give and take" in a human situation. However, students with learning problems are sometimes not sensitive to social nuances, and they may be unaware of how others interpret their behavior.

Often students with reading problems are unable to accommodate themselves to another person's point of view. Because they fail to consider the needs of other people, their chances for successful social interaction with peers are reduced (Wong & Wong, 1980). These authors suggest that role-playing games, in which one person is made to adopt the viewpoint of another person, may help to improve social relationships.

In contrast to normal achievers, low-achieving students tend to overestimate their own popularity (Bryan, 1991). They seem unable to recognize their own social shortcomings and have difficulty relating to peers in a social setting.

The Cultural Environment

The population of North America is a composite of hundreds of different ethnic and cultural traditions. In today's society, we see ever-changing patterns of immigration and movement as new groups of people add their cultural riches to our schools. A few decades ago, it was assumed that Americans would all be assimilated into the "melting pot" of the dominant culture. Since then, we have witnessed a new effort to value and maintain diverse cultural traditions. One of the greatest challenges our schools face is to provide an excellent education to students of all cultures, whatever their geographical origin, socioeconomic status, or language.

Since a significant portion of American families live below a specified poverty level, it is important to be aware of the possible effects of poverty on students' academic performance. Although individuals with incomes below the poverty level come from diverse backgrounds, they tend to have certain similarities. Because they are necessarily concerned with basic survival needs, parents are likely to have less energy to devote to their children's development. As a consequence, children from these families often must care for themselves at a very young age and may come to school with relatively limited background experiences (Carnegie Corporation, 1994; Levine & Havighurst, 1992).

Sometimes students reject the traditional values of the school and identify with subcultures in which values work against academic learning. This trend is particularly evident when adolescents join "gangs." The reading achievement of gang members is often substantially below that of other students, despite a high degree of verbal skills, leadership qualities, and intelligence in gang members (Labov et al., 1968). Cultural differences, particularly those arising from a culture of poverty, may lead to intense suspicion and discomfort with those individuals perceived to be in the dominant culture.

These generalizations do not, of course, hold true for all low-income students. In many poor families, education is cherished, the values of the school are upheld, and family members are encouraged to read and achieve. The opportunity to progress from poverty to economic security is a fundamental promise of democratic nations.

Assessing Environmental Factors

In Chapter 2, we presented interviews and questionnaires as tools for gathering information about environmental factors. In this chapter, we add a discussion of systematic observation, a sophisticated tool for assessing the environment. Systematic observation is a useful method of assessing student behavior and interaction with many different environments, both social and academic. Even short observations can provide valuable information, since they provide objective evidence about behavior.

The key to behavioral observation is to identify and describe clearly behaviors that are being observed. The observation should not consist of value judgments, such as "Amy caused trouble." A written observation is a careful recording of actual behaviors; for example, "Amy walked up to Mary's desk and tore up Mary's spelling paper." The cumulative records of many observations provide a basis for making diagnostic decisions and planning instruction.

Many different systems can be used for observing behavior (Wallace & Larsen, 1978). These include time sampling, event sampling, and the anecdotal record.

1. *Time Sampling.* This method enables the teacher to observe the length of time a student persists in certain behaviors. Generally, one type of behavior, such as maintaining attention, is chosen for analysis. The teacher records the number of times the behavior occurs and the length of time it persists during the observation period.

2. *Event Sampling.* Here, a specific type of event is chosen for recording. The observer tries to record the event in as much detail as possible each time it is observed. Event samples often last several days.

3. *The Anecdotal Record.* In this system, the student is observed throughout an extended period of time, and all incidents of particular interest are described in detail. Many different types of activities can be recorded in the anecdotal record, since it is meant to give the "flavor" of a student's activities.

Emotional Factors within the Individual

Low-achieving students, particularly those with a long history of failure, often have accompanying emotional problems that impede learning. Sadly, emotional problems tend to increase as a youngster moves up through the elementary years and enters adolescence.

Sometimes it is hard to determine whether a problem is the result of an underlying emotional disorder or if emotional problems have developed because of the reading disability. Silver and Hagin (1990) suggest it may be of little value to try to determine whether the learning failure or the emotional problem is the primary precipitating factor. A more constructive approach is to help the student experience success in reading which, in turn, will build feelings of self-worth and confidence. Accomplishment in reading then becomes a kind of therapy. A therapeutic approach to the teaching of reading can build confidence, establish self-esteem, and capture the pupil's interest (Roswell & Natchez, 1989). On the other hand, students with very severe emotional disorders may need psychotherapy or counseling (Silver, 1992) before reading will improve.

Emotional Responses to Reading Problems

No one personality type describes all low-achieving students, for students react to learning problems in different ways. Some failing readers evidence no emotional problems, others display a variety of disordered psychological behaviors (Bryan, 1991; Cohen, 1986; Roswell & Natchez, 1989).

Learning Block.

If learning has been a painful experience, the student may simply block it. In this way, the student keeps pain and distress out of the reach of consciousness. Learning blocks often can be overcome when reading is taught in interesting and nonthreatening ways and students begin to enjoy learning.

Nine-year-old Maria developed an emotional block against books. Whenever the teacher brought out a book her response was, "I told you I can't read a book." To solve this problem, the teacher copied all the words from one picture book and taught them, one word at a time, without showing Maria the source. After all the words were mastered, the teacher presented the book to Maria who, of course, at first refused to read it. However, when the teacher demonstrated that Maria could read any word in the book, she overcame her fear and went on to read that book, and others.

Hostile–Aggressive Behavior.

Pupils with reading problems may become hostile and overly aggressive to compensate for feelings of inadequacy. Students who appear to be tough, ready to fight, and even delinquent may be seeking a sense of accomplishment that they are unable to find in school. Antisocial behavior can be a manifestation of students' anger and frustration with academics, and with the failure of others to understand them. Often such students display less hostility when they are taught in small groups or individually, and when their problems receive earnest attention from teachers.

Learned Helplessness.

Avoiding failure can be an important goal for some disabled readers. To make sure that they do not fail, students may refuse to try. Thus they avoid stress through withdrawal and apathetic behavior. Such students may become very passive, refusing to complete assignments, participate in class discussions, or read. They need to be encouraged to take risks (such as guessing at words they are not sure of) and to learn that a certain amount of failure is an unavoidable and acceptable part of living. When instructing these students, teachers should tell them what they will be learning and why they are learning it. Encouraging and rewarding students for "guessing" may also be helpful.

In some cases poor achievers cannot accept personal responsibility for learning, even when they are successful. *Attribution theory* suggests that such students attribute their success and failure to the teacher who is in charge of the learning situation and has caused the learning to occur (Bryan, 1991). These students need more personal involvement and responsibility in the learning situation.

Low Self-esteem and Depression.

Understandably, students who have been subjected to continual failure develop a low opinion of themselves. They display a negative self-image, poor ego development, and a lack of confidence. The problem often deepens as students become older and realize that they are not meeting society's expectations (Bryan 1991; Weinberg & Rehmet, 1983).

A self-defeating "what's the use" attitude may result in an overall depression. Such students need to know that they are accepted as they are, and that the teacher understands their problem and has confidence that they can learn. Every instructional success must be emphasized for these students.

Anxiety.

Anxious students are never sure of their abilities and are afraid of making a mistake and being reprimanded. Stress clouds their lives, draining their energy and ability to concentrate on learning. Anxious students need reassurance that they can learn.

Assessing Emotional and Behavioral Factors

Teachers who are aware of students' emotional responses are more effective in teaching them to read. Usually, an informal assessment of emotional factors is sufficient for the purposes of the reading diagnosis.

Occasionally it may be necessary to refer a student to mental health specialists (such as psychiatrists, psychologists, or social workers) for further evaluation and possible psychotherapy or counseling. Such referrals are needed when emotional problems are so severe that they interfere with reading progress and the student has made little growth over a long period of instruction.

One useful informal assessment measure that can be used by a reading teacher is the *sentence completion activity.* In addition, information from interviews (see Chapter 2) provides useful information about the student's emotional status.

The sentence completion activity is a series of beginning sentence fragments that the student completes, such as "I like _____." In finishing these sentences, students often provide insights into their thoughts and feelings. The activity can be administered orally or in writing. A sample sentence completion form is given in Table 13.1. In interpreting results, however, bear in mind that it is only an informal measure. Although it may suggest ideas about student attitudes, these hypotheses should be verified further through interview, observation, and perhaps the administration of formal measures.

Intelligence: The Potential for Learning

The factor of intelligence provides an estimate of the student's capacity or potential for learning and for reading achievement. Teachers cannot help but notice differences in their students' abilities to learn. In the process of instruction, it is easy to note that one student grasps the lesson very quickly; another student learns the lesson in an unusual or unique way; a third student has great difficulty "catching on."

Our notions about the nature of intelligence and its measurement have changed over the years and are continuing to evolve. Among the questions studied by the scientific community is "What is intelligence and how much can it be changed?"

Definitions of Intelligence

For centuries, philosophers and scholars have attempted to define intelligence, yet theories about its nature continue to be controversial. Intelligence has been defined as the capacity to understand the world and the resourcefulness to cope with its challenges (Wechsler, 1975). As generally used, however, intelligence refers to an individual's cognitive or thinking abilities, or to the child's potential for acquiring school skills. In fact, most intelligence tests have been validated by comparing them with school performance.

Since a persons's intelligence cannot be observed directly, what we call intelligence is inferred through responses in a test situation. These responses are used to explain intellectual differences among people in their present behavior and to predict their future behavior. The "IQ" is a score obtained on an intelligence test, which reports performance on the test questions in relation to peers of the same age. (See Chapter 15 for a discussion of IQ tests.) It is obvious, however, that intelligence encompasses more than what is measured

Table 13.1 **Sample Sentence Completion Form**

1. I like _____.

2. Eating _____.

3. I am happiest when _____.

4. School is _____.

5. My greatest fear is _____.

6. I wish I could _____.

7. There are times _____.

8. My mother _____.

9. My father _____.

10. Sometimes I wish _____.

11. I sleep _____.

12. When I dream _____.

13. I want to _____.

14. One thing that bothers me is _____.

15. Sometimes I hope _____.

16. I think I will never _____.

17. Other people are _____.

18. One thing I don't like is _____.

19. I feel sorry for people who _____.

20. My mind _____.

21. Most of the time _____.

22. I try to _____.

on an intelligence test. It also includes the capacity to learn, the total knowledge a person has acquired, and the ability to adapt to new situations and environments.

Some theories of intelligence postulate that it consists of several different components. A student may indicate high capacity in one component (i.e., verbal abilities) but low aptitude in another (i.e., spatial abilities). The Wechsler series of intelligence tests, such as the *WISC III* (*Wechsler Intelligence Scale for Children – Third Edition*) provides scores on two major components: verbal intelligence and performance intelligence. The Kaufman test,

K–ABC (*Kaufman Assessment Battery for Children*) divides intelligence into sequential and simultaneous processing. Yet another theory of intelligence (Gardner, 1985) postulates seven factors: linguistic, musical, logical–mathematical, spatial, bodily kinesthetic, sense of self, and sense of others.

Can a Person's Intelligence Be Changed?

A major question concerning intelligence has been "Is a persons's intelligence determined by *heredity* (the result of one's biological makeup) or by *environment* (the result of one's personal experiences)?" Research shows that both heredity and environment contribute to a person's cognitive abilities. A complex sequence of interactions between heredity and environmental factors occurs during the development of an individual's intelligence. Although heredity may account for much of the variance in intelligence, the child's environment also contributes a substantial portion (Slavin, 1991).

Scientists are finding that the human brain is literally shaped by experience and develops more fully in enriched environments. The human brain grows rapidly during the first few years of life. Trillions of connections (or synapses) form, linking the billions of neurons to make complex thinking possible. Neural pathways that are not used disappear forever. Eventually the brain no longer is plastic, but becomes hard-wired, and the neurological structure that has been established will serve the individual for life. In this way, a child's environment actually influences the number of brain cells formed and the connections that are made between them (Carnegie Corporation, 1994). Thus, the child's home and social environments, the level of health care and nutrition, and school learning experiences all can influence intelligence.

A child's mental abilities can change significantly under favorable conditions. Studies of preschool at-risk children show that intelligence test scores are highly modifiable at this level and can increase substantially when children receive early intervention (Berrueta-Clement et al., 1985). Improvements in cognitive ability can also occur in adolescents. Feuerstein's (1980) work with mentally retarded adolescents demonstrates that intelligence can be modified at all ages and stages of cognitive development.

Basic to the teaching profession is the conviction that the ability to learn is present at all stages of development and that teachers play a vital role in the teaching/learning process. As teachers, we make a very important difference.

Cultural Bias in the Measurement of Intelligence

Intelligence tests have been criticized because of cultural bias. Studies show race and class differences in IQ scores; students from middle-class homes score higher than children from lower-class homes. It is also argued that intelligence test items do not match the experiences that minority and lower-class children have in their cultural environment (Levine & Havighurst, 1992).

In the landmark legal case, *Larry P.* v. *Riles* (1979), the court ruled the IQ testing is racially and culturally discriminatory when used as the sole criterion for placing children in classes for the mentally retarded. However, in a later case *PASE* v. *Hannon* (1980), the court ruled that there was little evidence that the items were biased. The issue of bias in assessment through the use of intelligence tests continues to be debated in both the courtroom and academic research.

Using Intelligence Tests to Determine the Existence of a Reading Disability

In Chapter 3, we defined a reading problem in terms of the difference between the student's appropriate reading level (usually a student's grade placement) and the student's actual achievement. In addition, intelligence test scores are sometimes used to determine whether a student has a reading disability. Using this method, we determine whether there is a significant discrepancy between the student's *potential* for reading achievement (as measured by an intelligence test) and the student's actual reading performance. A large gap or discrepancy between reading potential and reading achievement indicates a reading disability, because the student has the potential to read much better.

In calculating a discrepancy, (1) an intelligence test, such as the *WISC III* (*Wechsler Intelligence Test for Children–Third Edition*), is used to measure potential and (2) a standardized reading test is used to measure current reading achievement. (The *WISC III* and other tests of intelligence are discussed in Chapter 15, Formal Tests). In calculating a discrepancy, we determine a *reading expectancy* level and compare it to *current reading achievement.*

One method to calculate a discrepancy is the *reading expectancy age* method (Harris & Sipay, 1985). This uses a mental age (MA) to calculate whether a reading problem exists. To obtain MA from the IQ, use the formula:

$$MA^* = \frac{IQ \times CA}{100}$$

Once we obtain the MA, we can calculate the reading expectancy:

$$REA \text{ (reading expectancy)} = \frac{2MA + CA}{3}$$

*In this formula, MA (mental age) and CA (chronological age) should be expressed in years and tenths (rather than years and months).

The formula gives a reading expectancy age. To convert from an expectancy *age* to an expectancy *grade* (REG), subtract 5.2.

We can illustrate the reading age expectancy formula thus: Marion is 10-0 years old and she has an IQ of 120. We first calculate that her MA is 12.0 years. Using the REA formula, we can see that she has a reading expectancy age of 11.3 and a reading grade expectancy of 6.1 (11.3 – 5.2). If Marion's current level of reading is 3.0, she would have a 3.1 year discrepancy.

$$REA = \frac{2(12.0) + 10.0}{3} = 11.3$$

$$REG = 11.3 - 5.1 = 6.1$$

$$\text{Discrepancy = Reading Expectancy − Reading Achievement} = 6.1 - 3.0 = 3.1$$

Table 13.2, based upon the Harris and Sipay formula, will help you to avoid doing calculations. If you know the IQ and CA of a student, the reading expectancy grade can then

Table 13.2   Reading Expectancy Grade Levels

	IQ Score															
	70	75	80	85	90	95	100	105	110	115	120	125	130	135	140	145
6–0	—	—	—	—	—	—	—	1.0	1.2	1.4	1.6	1.8	2.0	2.2	2.4	2.6
6–3	—	—	—	—	—	—	1.0	1.2	1.5	1.7	1.9	2.1	2.3	2.5	2.7	2.9
6–6	—	—	—	—	—	1.1	1.3	1.5	1.7	2.0	2.2	2.4	2.6	2.8	3.0	3.2
6–9	—	—	—	—	1.1	1.3	1.6	1.8	2.0	2.2	2.4	2.7	2.9	3.1	3.4	3.6
7–0	—	—	—	1.1	1.3	1.6	1.8	2.0	2.3	2.5	2.7	3.0	3.2	3.4	3.7	3.9
7–3	—	—	1.1	1.3	1.6	1.8	2.0	2.3	2.5	2.8	3.0	3.2	3.5	3.7	4.0	4.2
7–6	—	1.0	1.3	1.6	1.8	2.0	2.3	2.6	2.8	3.0	3.3	3.6	3.8	4.0	4.3	4.6
7–9	1.1	1.3	1.5	1.8	2.0	2.3	2.6	2.8	3.1	3.3	3.6	3.8	4.1	4.4	4.6	4.9
8–0	1.2	1.5	1.7	2.0	2.3	2.5	2.8	3.1	3.3	3.6	3.9	4.1	4.4	4.7	4.9	5.2
8–3	1.4	1.7	2.0	2.2	2.5	2.8	3.0	3.3	3.6	3.9	4.2	4.4	4.7	5.1	5.3	5.5
8–6	1.6	1.9	2.2	2.4	2.7	3.0	3.3	3.6	3.9	4.2	4.4	4.7	5.0	5.3	5.6	5.8
8–9	1.8	2.1	2.4	2.7	3.0	3.3	3.6	3.8	4.1	4.4	4.7	5.0	5.3	5.6	5.9	6.2
9–0	2.0	2.3	2.6	2.9	3.2	3.5	3.8	4.1	4.4	4.7	5.0	5.3	5.6	5.9	6.2	6.5
9–3	2.2	2.5	2.8	3.1	3.4	3.7	4.0	4.4	4.7	5.0	5.3	506	5.9	6.2	6.5	6.8
9–6	2.4	2.7	3.0	3.4	3.7	4.0	4.3	4.6	4.9	5.2	5.6	5.9	6.2	6.5	6.8	7.2
9–9	2.6	2.9	3.2	3.6	3.9	4.2	4.6	4.9	5.2	5.5	5.8	6.2	6.5	6.8	7.2	7.5
10–0	2.8	3.1	3.5	3.8	4.1	4.5	4.8	5.1	5.5	5.8	6.1	6.5	6.8	7.1	7.5	7.8
10–3	3.0	3.3	3.7	4.0	4.4	4.7	5.0	5.4	5.7	6.1	6.4	6.8	7.1	7.4	7.8	8.1
10–6	3.2	3.6	3.9	4.2	4.6	5.0	5.3	5.6	6.0	6.4	6.7	7.0	7.4	7.8	8.1	8.4
10–9	3.4	3.8	4.1	4.5	4.8	5.2	5.6	5.9	6.3	6.6	7.0	7.3	7.7	8.1	8.4	8.8
11–0	3.6	4.0	4.3	4.7	5.1	5.4	5.8	6.2	6.5	6.9	7.3	7.6	8.0	8.4	8.7	9.1
11–3	3.8	4.2	4.6	4.9	5.3	5.7	6.0	6.4	6.8	7.2	7.6	7.9	8.3	8.7	9.0	9.4
11–6	4.0	4.4	4.8	5.2	5.5	5.9	6.3	6.7	7.1	7.4	7.8	8.2	8.6	9.0	9.4	9.8
11–9	4.2	4.6	5.0	5.4	5.8	6.2	6.6	7.0	7.3	7.7	8.1	8.5	8.9	9.3	9.7	10.1
12–0	4.4	4.8	5.2	5.6	6.0	6.4	6.8	7.2	7.6	8.0	8.4	8.8	9.2	9.6	10.0	10.4
12–3	4.6	5.0	5.4	5.8	6.2	6.6	7.0	7.4	7.9	8.3	8.7	9.1	9.5	9.9	10.3	10.7
12–6	4.8	5.2	5.6	6.0	6.5	6.9	7.3	7.7	8.1	8.6	9.0	9.4	9.8	10.2	10.6	11.0
12–9	5.0	5.4	5.8	6.3	6.7	7.1	7.6	8.0	8.4	8.8	9.2	9.7	10.1	10.5	11.0	11.4
13–0	5.2	5.6	6.1	6.5	6.9	7.4	7.8	8.2	8.7	9.1	9.5	10.0	10.4	10.8	11.3	11.7
13–3	5.4	5.8	6.3	6.7	7.2	7.6	8.0	8.5	8.9	9.4	9.8	10.2	10.7	11.1	11.5	12.0
13–6	5.6	6.0	6.5	7.0	7.4	7.8	8.3	8.8	9.2	9.6	10.1	10.6	11.0	11.4	11.9	12.4
13–9	5.8	6.3	6.7	7.2	7.6	8.1	8.6	9.0	9.5	9.9	10.4	10.8	11.3	11.8	12.2	12.7
14–0	6.0	6.5	6.9	7.4	7.9	8.3	8.8	9.3	9.7	10.2	10.7	11.1	11.6	12.1	12.5	13.0
14–3	6.2	6.7	7.2	7.6	8.1	8.6	9.0	9.5	10.0	10.5	11.0	11.4	11.9	12.4	12.8	13.3
14–6	6.4	6.9	7.4	7.8	8.3	8.8	9.3	9.8	10.3	10.8	11.2	11.7	12.2	12.7	13.2	13.6
14–9	6.6	7.1	7.6	8.1	8.6	9.1	9.6	10.0	10.5	11.0	11.5	12.0	12.85	13.0	13.5	14.0
15–0	6.8	7.3	7.8	8.3	8.8	9.3	9.8	10.3	10.8	11.3	11.8	12.3	12.8	13.3	13.8	14.3

Chronological Age (in years and months)

This table gives reading expectancy grade level. If the intelligence score or chronological age falls between two values, use the closest one. For students over fifteen years of age, use the 15.0 chronological age value.

be found by noting the intersection of the chronological age with IQ. For students over fifteen years of age, use 15.0 as the chronological age. If the CA and IQ fall between two values on a table, use the closest value. For convenience, the expectancy *grade* level (rather than *age*) is reported directly.

Language Development

Language has been recognized as one of the greatest of human achievements—more important than all the physical tools invented in the last ten thousand years. Language permits human beings to speak of things unseen, recall the past, and verbalize hopes for the future.

Reading is an integral part of the language system of literate societies. The student's ability to express and receive thoughts through oral language provides the foundation for reading; in other words, reading is based upon language development. Not surprisingly, some students with reading problems have underlying problems with language. In this section, we describe the many different components of language.

Written and Oral Language

Our language is an integrated system linking the *oral* language forms of listening and talking to the *written* language forms of reading and writing. As children mature, language plays an increasingly important part in the development of thinking and the ability to grasp abstract concepts. Words become symbols for objects, classes of objects, and ideas.

As children gain competence using language in one form, they also build knowledge and experience with the underlying language system, which is carried to learning language in another form. Thus, oral language provides a knowledge base for reading and writing. Similarly, practice in writing improves both reading and oral language. One philosophy of reading instruction, whole language (Goodman, 1992; Goodman & Goodman, 1979), is based on a recognizing the interrelationships of listening, speaking, reading, and writing, and promotes these connections in teaching.

Receptive and Expressive Language

There is an important distinction between receptive language (understanding through listening or reading) and expressive language (using language in speaking and writing). Usually, people's expressive abilities exceed their receptive ones. That is, they understand more words than they use in speech and can read more words than they can write.

At times, a student may appear to have poor language abilities because he or she engages in little conversation or gives one-word replies to questions. However, oral expressive language can be influenced by a student's comfort level. Therefore, it is important to consider the student's language abilities in both receptive and expressive oral language.

Systems of Oral Language

Linguists have shown that there are four different systems involved in our oral language: (1) *phonology* (the sounds of language), (2) *morphology* (meaningful elements within words), (3) *syntax* (the grammatical aspects of language), and (4) *semantics* (the vocabulary of language). Students with reading problems may exhibit difficulties in one of these linguistic systems.

Phonology.

This refers to the sound system of a language. Oral language consists of a stream of sounds, one after the other. Each individual sound is called a *phoneme*. There are important differences in the ways speakers of different languages think about phonemes. For example, in English the /b/ and /v/ sounds are two different phonemes, or sounds. In Spanish, in contrast, they are simply variations on one phoneme. These differences make the mastery of English difficult for students whose native language is not English, just as Spanish or French is difficult for native English speakers.

Young children have difficulty in producing certain speech sounds, or phonemes. Typically children do not complete full articulation development until about the age of eight. Late-maturing consonant sounds include *r, l, ch, sh, j, th* (as in *thy* and *thigh*), *s, z, v,* and *zh* (as in pleasure). Young children who have not mastered these sounds in speech may have difficulty distinguishing them in reading.

In developing the ability of *phonological awareness,* children learn to recognize that words are made up of phonemes or sounds. This ability is closely related to success in beginning reading (See Chapter 5). Auditory discrimination, the ability to hear distinctions between phonemes (for example, to recognize that *big* and *pig* are different) is another problem area for some disabled readers (Wiig & Semel, 1984).

As we discussed in Chapter 6, our phonics system, which links spoken sounds and written letters, is not completely regular. For example, the letter *c* represents two different sounds, as in the words *city* and *cat*. Although the English alphabet has only 26 letters, the average American English dialect contains 46 sounds.

Morphology.

This system refers to meaningful units (or morphemes) that form words or word parts. For example, the word *walked* contains two morphemes: *walk* and *ed,* a morpheme that signals the past tense. Other examples of morphemes are *s* (game*s*) and *re* (*re*wind). Many students with reading problems have deficits in morphological development (Wiig & Semel, 1984; Vogel, 1974). We refer to the ability to recognize different morphemes, when they appear in reading, by the term *structural analysis* (see Chapters 6 and 10).

Syntax.

This system, also known as grammar, governs the formation of sentences in a language. For example, in English a well-formed sentence has a subject and a verb (e.g., *Jane walks*). Further, sentences are combined by using conjunctions, such as *Jane walks and Jane runs.*

Children do not acquire syntactic ability passively. Rather, they construct syntactic rules for themselves. For example, a young child who says *he goed* for the past tense of *go* is using the rule that the past tense is formed by the addition of *ed,* even though the child is overgeneralizing this rule. Although most basic syntactic structures are acquired by the age of six, some growth in syntax continues through the age of ten. Development of the ability to understand very complex or difficult sentence patterns may continue even throughout the high school years. Since syntactic abilities continue to develop through the school years, teaching sentence comprehension is important to reading instruction. Table 13.3 presents examples of difficult sentence types.

Vocabulary or Semantics.

This system refers to the acquisition of word meanings. Compared with other languages, English has a very large vocabulary. The complexity and rich variety of English words makes the mastering of English vocabulary a lifelong task.

Factors involved in mastering English vocabulary include:

1. *Size of vocabulary.* The number of words that students can use or understand.
2. *Knowledge of multiple meanings of words.* Words such as "plane" and "cold" each have several meanings.

Table 13.3 **Difficult Sentence Types**

Category	Example
Passive sentences: reversible°	John was given the pen by Mary.
Out-of-order time sequences*	Move a yellow bead, *but first* move a red one. Move a yellow bead *after* you move a red one.
Relative clause construction	John, *who is in the second grade*, is learning to read. The man *standing on the corner* is nice.
Appositives	Mr. Smith, *the postman*, is very nice.
Complement structures	*The fact that Steve is silly* worries Meg. *Steve's being silly* worries Meg. *For Steve to be silly* worries Meg. Steve asked Meg *what was worrying her.*
Delayed reference in sentences†	John promised Mary to go. John asked Mary what to feed the doll.
· Anophoric, or reference structures	John saw Mary and *he* said hello. John saw Mary and said hello.
Sentence connectives	*If you don't* do this, I will go. *Unless* you do this, I will go.

°The nonreversible sentence *The ball was dropped by the boy* would be easier.

*The construction *Move the yellow one and then the red* would be simpler because it occurs in time order.

†In these cases, *John* does the action of going or feeding the doll. In a sentence such as *John told Mary what to feed the doll, Mary* feeds the doll. The latter type of sentence is easier to comprehend.

3. *Accuracy of vocabulary meaning.* Children may overextend or underextend the meanings of words. For example, in an overextension, a small child may call all four-legged animals "dogs."

4. *Accurate classification of words.* In classifying words, "red," "blue," and "green" all belong to "colors."

5. *Relational categories of words.* Relational words include prepositions (under, over, besides, to, from); comparative terms (good-bad, better-worse, lighter-darker); time elements (yesterday-today-tomorrow); and terms of human relationship (mother, aunt, grandmother).

Since vocabulary is highly related to reading achievement (Anderson & Freebody, 1981), limited vocabulary development can seriously hamper reading.

Speech Problems and Language Disorders

Because reading is an integral part of the language system, underlying problems with language can affect the ability to read. Two types of language problems are speech problems and language disorders.

Speech Problems.

Children display three kinds of speech problems: (1) *articulation problems* (the inaccurate production of sounds), (2) *voice disorders* (improper pitch or intonation), and (3) *stuttering* (breath or rhythm problems). Although there is a somewhat higher incidence of speech problems among low-achieving readers, speech problems do not necessarily lead to reading problems. Nevertheless, students who exhibit speech difficulties should be referred to a speech-language specialist for further evaluation and, if needed, therapy. If a speech problem is noted, hearing acuity should be tested, for sometimes a hearing impairment is the cause of a speech problem. Students with speech problems can be embarrassed when asked to read orally, and therefore oral reading should be avoided for them.

Language Disorders.

Language disorders refer to the slow or atypical development of receptive and expressive oral language. The child with a language delay is slow at talking, poor in vocabulary development, and may have difficulty in learning to formulate sentences. Language delay is often a forerunner of later difficulty in reading (Wiig & Semel, 1984). If a reading teacher suspects an underlying language disorder, a speech-language specialist can provide further evaluation and treatment.

Nonstandard Dialects

Many students in our schools have a personal language that differs from the standard language of school instruction. A nonstandard dialect is a language pattern used by a subgroup of the speakers of a language. There are many dialects in American English. For example, speakers from New York City, Boston, Montreal, and certain Southern states often speak a characteristic regional dialect. Some students raised in certain specific cultural groups speak a dialect of English used in their environment, such as Appalachian or a dialect referred to as Black English Vernacular (BEV). To illustrate the differences between one such dialect of English and the dialect that is generally considered to be "Standard English," the features of BEV are given in Table 13.4.

Table 13.4   **Features of Black English Vernacular**

Phonological or Sound Changes

Category	Examples
When two or more consonants are at the end of a word, one may be omitted.	*Test* is pronounced like *tes.*
	Bump is pronounced *bum.*
"R" may be omitted.	*Fort* is pronounced like *fought.*
"L" may be omitted.	*Toll* is pronounced like *toe.*
Short "i" and short "e" are pronounced the same before some consonants.	*Pin* is pronounced like *pen.*

Syntactic or Grammatical Changes

Category	Examples
The possessive may be omitted.	That's Molly('s) book.
The verb *to be* may be omitted.	He('s) downstairs; they('re) there.
The past-tense ending may be omitted.	He walk(ed) to the store yesterday.
The third-person-singular ending may be omitted.	She think(s) he is very nice.
Contractions signaling the future may be omitted.	He('ll) be there soon.
A "be" construction to indicate ongoing action may be inserted.	I *be* going there on Thursdays.

Linguists who have studied American dialects conclude that all dialects, regardless of their cultural associations, are logical, rule-based systems of English (Labov et al., 1968;

Wolfram, 1969). In fact, the BEV dialect has made many important contributions to standard English. Although dialects may differ, all English speakers share common underlying language forms. Students who speak nonstandard English can learn to read texts in standard English without changing their speech patterns.

When assessing and instructing students who speak nonstandard dialects, teachers should be aware of some pitfalls. First, constant correction of a students' oral language is damaging to a student's self-concept. A barrier between the student and teacher may form, reducing verbal output in the classroom. This has destructive effects, since students who do not want to talk will not be able to develop rich language. Second, dialect differences should not be mistaken for cognitive deficits or disorders in language development. As we mentioned above, there *are no deficient dialects of English.*

Bilingual and Limited-English-Proficient Students

In Chapter 12, we discussed the growing number of students in the United States and Canada who speak English as a second language. It is important that these students master English while maintaining their first language and their cultural heritage. Specific strategies to do this are given in Chapter 12.

Assessing Language Development

Frequently used formal tests to assess language development are described in Chapter 15. In addition, a student's listening level provides an informal estimate of how well that student can understand language. The ability to comprehend oral language through listening is sometimes used as an informal measure of a student's receptive language abilities and reading potential. A high listening level indicates that a student understands language well and has potential to read at a high level. A low listening level indicates that a student needs language development. In Chapters 3 and 13, we give methods for determining a listening level on an informal reading inventory and on a standardized test.

Physical Factors

Good health is important to learning. In this section, we describe a variety of physical factors that can affect reading problems.

Hearing Impairment

Since the ability to acquire reading skills may be severely affected by even moderate or temporary hearing loss, it is recommended that pupils be screened for *auditory acuity,* or the ability to hear sounds. It should be noted that *auditory acuity* is different from the ability to work with or distinguish sounds.

Hearing loss has several causes: (1) childhood diseases, such as scarlet fever, meningitis, mumps, or measles; (2) environmental conditions, such as repeated exposure to loud noises; (3) congenital conditions, such as malformation of, or injury to, the hearing mechanism; (4) temporary or fluctuating conditions, due to allergies, colds, or even a buildup of wax in the ears; (5) maternal prenatal infection (including rubella); (6) middle ear infection or problems; (7) certain medications (such as amino glycosides and some diuretics).

Screening for Hearing Impairment.

Hearing acuity is measured in two dimensions: frequency and intensity. Frequency refers to the ability to hear different pitches or vibrations of a specific sound wave. The pitches are actually musical tones; the higher the tone, the higher the frequency. Since different sounds of our spoken language have different frequency levels, a person may be able to hear sounds clearly at one frequency, but not at another.

Intensity refers to the loudness of a sound and is measured in terms of decibels. The louder the sound, the higher the intensity or decibel level. How loud does a sound (or decibel level) have to be before a person should be able to hear it? A person who can hear soft sounds at 0 to 10 decibels has excellent hearing. Students who cannot hear sounds at a 30 decibel level (or higher) are likely to encounter some difficulty in school learning.

The audiometer is an electronic instrument for measuring hearing acuity. In screening for a hearing loss, students wear headphones and sit with their backs to the examiner. The examiner produces a tone on the machine and asks the subject to raise a hand when a tone is heard. For screening, the audiometer is usually set at one frequency level, and the examiner determines how loud (or intense) the sound needs to be before the student can hear it. The right and left ears are tested separately for each frequency. It is extremely important that screening take place in a quiet room.

An audiogram showing the results of an audiometric hearing test is illustrated in Figure 13.1. Students who cannot hear frequency sounds at the preset level of 30 decibels at one or more frequencies should be referred to a hearing specialist for further testing. The pupil whose audiogram appears in Figure 13.1 showed a 40 decibel loss at 2000 frequencies and 4000 frequencies in the right ear and was therefore referred to a hearing specialist.

If auditory screening indicates a hearing problem, students should be referred to an audiologist (a nonmedical specialist in hearing) or to a otologist or an otolaryngologist (medical specialists in hearing). Although the audiometer is a good device for screening, only a specialist trained in measuring and treating hearing difficulties can make a final determination of the extent and nature of a possible hearing impairment.

Alleviating Hearing Problems.

Medical specialists can also take measures to alleviate a student's hearing problem. At times, medication or tubes in a child's ear can alleviate clogged passages and improve hearing. At other times, children can be fitted with hearing aids.

Sometimes students pass the audiometric screening test, yet still have hearing problems. One little girl had a sporadic hearing loss due to allergies, but since her visits to the pediatrician came after the allergy season, the hearing problem went undetected for years. Although the hearing problem was eventually cleared up, she had missed some important early language growth, and her difficulties in reading continued into the later grades. Thus, if a reading teacher even *suspects* a hearing loss, the student should be referred to a professional for continued monitoring.

Even moderate loss in the ability to hear may substantially affect the ability to read. A hearing loss impedes communication with teachers and peers, making it difficult to function in class. Students may have difficulty learning phonics because they do not hear certain sounds. A low-frequency hearing loss (500–1500 Hz) may cause difficulty with vowel sounds; high-frequency losses (2000–4000 Hz) may cause difficulty with consonant sounds that continue, such as /s/, /z/, /j/, /v/, /th/, /sh/, and /ch/.

The most devastating effect of a hearing loss is that it prevents normal language development. When children cannot hear adequately, they are deprived of the communication
necessary for normal language acquisition and growth. Their vocabulary, grammar, and verbal thinking processes often remain poorly developed and their language skills may be inadequate to acquire higher-level reading skills.

Visual Impairment

The ability to see clearly is obviously critical to the reading process. However, the relationship between reading and vision is complicated. A particular visual impairment may
impede reading in one individual, while another person with a similar problem may be able
to read effectively.

Types of Vision Problems.

There are several types of visual impairment of concern to the reading teacher. These include
myopia, hyperopia, astigmatism, binocular vision problems, and color perception.

Myopia or *nearsightedness* is the inability to see objects at a distance. Myopia is caused
by an elongated eyeball that focuses visual images in an improper way. Although the problem of myopia is not highly related to reading difficulty (Robinson 1946), myopia can make
it difficult to see objects such as the blackboard. A substantial portion of the population is
myopic; the condition often begins between the ages of nine and twelve. Myopia is usually correctable with eyeglasses.

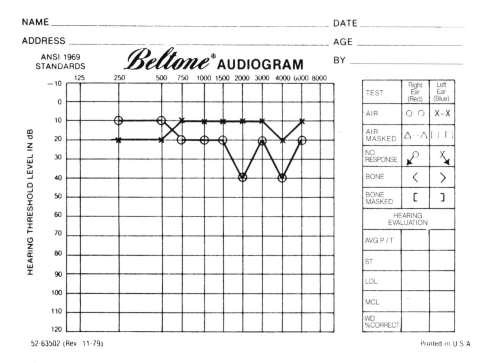

FIGURE 13.1
A Sample Audiogram
Reprinted with the permission of Belltone Electronics Corporation.

Hyperopia or *farsightedness* is the inability to see objects clearly at nearpoint (that is, 13 inches or less). In children, it is often caused by an eyeball that is too short to permit focusing. Children are typically hyperopic until they reach the age of seven or eight; thus, primary-grade textbooks generally contain large print. If hyperopia is a continuing problem, it can be corrected with lenses. Since reading is done at nearpoint, hyperopia can affect the ability to read.

An *astigmatism* is the blurring of vision because of irregularities in the surface of the cornea. This condition is generally correctable with lenses.

Binocular difficulties refer to the inability to focus both eyes on the same object, and is one of the most complicated of visual functions. Both eyes focus together easily on an object that is far away, but as that object moves closer, the eyes must turn inward to maintain their focus. If the eyes cannot focus together, a double image may result. This condition is not tolerated well by the brain, and the image of one eye may be suppressed, possibly leading to a deterioration of that eye. In severe cases, the eyes appear to be crossed. Binocular vision problems may blur vision and also cause the reader to become easily fatigued. Thus they can interfere with reading.

Unfortunately, binocular vision is not as easily correctable as other visual problems. Three strategies used to correct binocular problems are (1) surgery (often used to correct a "cross-eyed" condition), (2) corrective lenses in eyeglasses, and (3) visual exercises to strengthen eye muscles. Opinions differ among eye specialists about the value of visual exercises as a treatment in overcoming binocular difficulties (American Academy of Pediatrics, 1992; Wesson, 1993).

Color perception is also a part of vision. A small portion of the population, usually male, is unable to perceive color. *Color blindness,* which may be limited to a few colors, is not associated with reading problems. In addition, a set of controversial new treatments focuses on the glare that is experienced by some individuals during reading. This problem is often called *scotopic sensitivity.* To eliminate this glare, colored overlays or lenses may be provided. Although some have reported decreased problems in reading, this controversial treatment has had somewhat inconsistent results (Bruce & Evans, 1993; Ward, 1992; Fletcher & Martínez, 1994). Nevertheless, it remains one treatment option for possible visual problems.

Screening for Visual Impairment.

Students with reading problems should be screened for possible visual difficulties. An adequate visual screening should test, at least nearsightedness, farsightedness, and binocular visual functioning. As with the hearing tests that are used by the reading teacher, visual tests given by schools or teachers are intended only for screening purposes. Students who do poorly on a visual screening test should be referred to an ophthalmologist (a physician who specializes in eye problems) or to an optometrist (a nonmedical eye specialist) for further testing. Vision tests that can easily be administered by a teacher include the *Keystone Telebinocular Vision Tests* and the *Orthorater* instruments.

Neurological Dysfunction

All learning, including learning to read, is neurologically based. The reading process is a complex human task, requiring an intact and well-functioning brain and central nervous system. It should not be surprising that a dysfunction in the central nervous system can interfere with learning to read. Today, knowledge about the brain and its relationship to learning is rapidly expanding. Theories about the relationship of neurological function to reading performance, current research on neurological dysfunction, and the condition of dyslexia are discussed in Chapter 14.

Gender Differences

For reasons that are not entirely clear, more boys than girls exhibit reading problems in American schools. In fact, boys commonly outnumber girls in special reading and special education programs. At least three reasons have been proposed for the preponderance of boys with reading and learning problems.

1. *Heredity.* There is some evidence that a reading disability may be caused by a sex-linked gene that affects more boys than girls (Lubs et al., 1993).
2. *Maturation.* Since boys are less physically mature than girls at the age of beginning reading instruction, they may not have developed certain skills that aid in reading, such as the ability to pay attention and the ability to manage pencils and books. Some researchers have also hypothesized that males are more prone to injury while in utero, before they are born (Nass, 1993).
3. *School environment.* The school environment may affect boys and girls differently. The U.S. primary-grade classroom is traditionally female oriented, employing women teachers and rewarding behaviors such as being neat and quiet. In other cultures, boys actually exhibit superior reading ability (Gross, 1978; Preston, 1979), suggesting that sex differences may be due to cultural or other factors in instruction rather than to hereditary or maturational differences.

Since more boys than girls are likely to be in special reading classes, it is important to make these boys feel welcome and happy in the reading environment.

Despite the fact that boys outnumber girls in remedial programs, disabling conditions can also be found in girls. One such hereditary problem is *fragile x syndrome,* which creates cognitive and learning difficulties (Hagerman et al., 1992).

Other Physical Problems

Good physical health is an important basic condition for learning. The pupil who is listless, tires easily, and cannot maintain attention may have an underlying medical problem. Prolonged illness, especially if accompanied by high fevers and long periods of absence from school, can also contribute to a reading problem.

General Health and Nutrition.

Nutrient deficiency in infancy or early childhood has been shown to result in anatomical and biochemical changes in the brain. Early malnutrition impairs growth, both of the body in general and of the central nervous system in particular (Martin, 1980). Other health concerns include problems of nutrition, rheumatic fever, asthma, lack of sleep, biochemical imbalances, and endocrine problems. A general physical examination is often recommended as part of a complete assessment for reading problems.

Injuries and Illnesses that Affect the Brain.

Concussions, or swelling of the brain, can affect cognitive functioning. Concussions are often caused by injuries. If a brain injury results in unconsciousness, a student has experienced a concussion. In addition, some illnesses, such as spinal meningitis and brain tumors, can destroy cognitive functioning.

Controversial Medical Conditions.

Some students with reading problems receive medical or medically related treatments, which are purported to alleviate their educational problems. Since teachers may be asked to provide feedback to physicians or parents about students, it is important to be aware of both the underlying conditions and the therapies.

1. *Hypoglycemia.* This condition, a deficiency in the level of blood sugar, is thought by some to cause learning problems. Treatment consists of controlling various elements in the student's diet (Runion, 1980).
2. *Allergies.* Other authorities feel that allergies, which are caused by both the diet and the environment, can cause learning difficulties. Treatment consists of the removal of the element causing the allergy (Crook, 1977; Rapp, 1979). The precise relationship of allergies to the learning process is yet to be determined.
3. *Medication therapy.* Many students with learning problems, particularly those with attention deficit disorders (ADD) are prescribed medication intended to control hyperactivity, increase attention span, and reduce impulsive behavior. Widely used medications include Ritalin, Dexedrine, Librium, and Cylert. Levinson (1984) has also suggested the use of anti-motionsickness medication. There is some difference of opinion about the effectiveness and safety of these drugs, and therefore it is very important to monitor their effects closely. Teachers are an important resource for providing feedback to physicians.
4. *Food additives.* One of the most widely discussed and controversial theories on the negative effects of food additives is that of Feingold (1975), who points out that artificial flavors, colors, and preservatives are used increasingly in the American diet. Feingold's treatment consists of the removal of foods that contain additives and the inclusion of certain natural foods. However, a panel of experts at the National Institutes of Health concluded that there was insufficient evidence to recommend this diet for treating childhood hyperactivity (Silver, 1986).

Reviewing many of the medical and biomedical treatments for learning problems, Silver found their effectiveness to be unproven. He concluded that the treatment of choice for reading problems is the best educational instruction available, taught by a well-qualified and sensitive teacher.

Summary

There are a number of factors that may be related to a student's reading disability. Environmental factors include the home, school, cultural, and social environments.

The home is the child's first environment where the critical learning of the early years occur. The school environment is another important system for the student, one that is often difficult for students with reading problems. Students with reading disabilities tend to have difficulty in their social environments. The cultural environment is another system that affects attitude and interest in reading. Methods for assessing environmental systems include three systems of observation.

Factors within the individual include emotional factors, intelligence, language, and physical factors.

Emotional problems influence reading achievement. Opinions differ about the need to treat emotional problems prior to the treatment of reading problems. Among the emotional problems exhibited by poor readers are emotional blocks, hostility–aggressiveness, learned helplessness, low self-esteem and depression, and anxiety. Emotional factors may be informally assessed using the sentence completion activity.

Intelligence refers to the potential for learning. There are several definitions and components of intelligence, but most intelligence tests measure scholastic aptitude. While much of what is called intelligence is inherited, a child's intelligence can be dramatically influenced by environmental conditions. In general, the teaching profession assumes that the environment, including teaching, can make a difference.

There are separate components or abilities that make up intelligence. The *WISC-III* has subtests that are useful for gathering information about different substandard abilities. This test yields scores for verbal and performance intelligence. The *K-ABC* measures simultaneous and sequential processing. A discrepancy between estimated potential for reading based on intelligence and actual reading level can be used to determine if a reading disability exists.

The child's language is an important factor related to reading disability. Language includes oral language (listening and speaking) and written language (reading and written).

There are four oral language systems: (1) phonology (the sound system of language), (2) morphology (the system of expressing meaning through word parts), (3) syntax (the sentence structure or grammatical forms of language), and (4) semantics or vocabulary (the words in language). Studies show that some students with reading disabilities have difficulty with one or more of these linguistic systems. Speech problems and a language disorder can affect the learning of reading. Some children with reading disability have an underlying language disorder. Nonstandard English should not be interpreted as language inferiority.

Physical factors are also related to reading disability. Hearing impairment, including a mild or temporary hearing loss, can affect language learning and learning to read. The audiometer is used to screen for a hearing loss. Visual impairment is also related to reading disability. Visual problems include myopia, hyperopia, astigmatism, poor binocular vision, and perhaps color sensitivity. Teachers can screen for visual impairment.

There are many other physical factors related to a reading disability. Neurological problems may be a factor for some severely disabled readers. Research suggests that these students have central nervous system dysfunctions. Reading difficulties are more common in boys than girls. Causes may be genetic, maturational, or cultural.

Other physical problems related to reading are health and nutrition. Many disabled readers receive medical and medically related treatments, including drug therapy, control of food additives, and treatment for hypoglycemia and allergies. Teachers should be aware of such conditions and the students who are receiving such treatment.

· ·

Severe Reading Disabilities

Introduction

In this chapter, we consider the problems of students who have extreme difficulty acquiring even the most basic reading skills, students who struggle for years with first-grade books. Who are these students and how can we help them? In the first part of the chapter, we consider the characteristics of these very disabled students. We then present an overview of special strategies for teaching them.

Characteristics of Students with Severe Reading Disabilities

The severe difficulties that some students in our schools encounter in language learning, in learning to read, and in literacy proficiency are rooted in a variety of causes.

Dyslexia: The Baffling Reading Disorder

Some otherwise normal individuals have extreme difficulty learning to read. They seem to have a condition, sometimes known as *dyslexia,* that is an unusual type of severe, inborn reading disorder. These individuals have puzzled the educational and medical professions for years. Many individuals with this condition are intelligent in other ways, and may, in fact, even be gifted in mathematics and art. However, despite the best of teaching and nurturing, reading is often a lifelong problem. Dyslexia has been the focus of research in many disciplines, including reading, special education, neurology, psychiatry, psychology, learning disabilities, speech and language, and optometry. Adults who have suffered from dyslexia can long recall the anguish of trying to cope with this mysterious condition in a world that requires people to read (Lerner, 1993).

Brain Research Studies on Dyslexia.

Accumulating research on the brain offers strong confirmation that dyslexia is due to a neurobiological abnormality in brain function. Brain studies offer several kinds of evidence about the neurobiological nature of dyslexia. Researchers have uncovered evidence that dyslexic individuals have a different anatomical brain structure (Galaburda, 1989). Furthermore, they have unique characteristics in brain function (Duane, 1989; Duffy, 1988; Hynd, 1992; Zametkin et al., 1990). Finally, evidence suggests that dyslexia is genetic or an inherited trait (Smith, 1992).

The brain research studies on dyslexia that have received most attention are: (1) the postmortem anatomical studies of the brain tissues of dyslexic individuals, (2) research using the new machines and technologies (Flowers 1993), and (3) genetic studies of learning disabilities (Lubs et al., 1993; Lyons, Newby, Recht, & Caldwell, 1991; Smith, 1992).

Postmortem Anatomical Brain Studies of Dyslexic Individuals.

In the ongoing research on dyslexia at Harvard Medical School's Department of Neurology, Beth Israel Hospital, Boston, neuroscientists are conducting postmortem studies of the brain tissues of dyslexic individuals. Many of these subjects were young men who met sudden death in circumstances such as motorcycle accidents. Currently the brain tissues of eight dyslexic persons—6 male and 2 female—have been studied.

Remarkably, all eight cases show the same abnormality in brain structure. The area in the brain known as the *planum temporale* is located in both the left and right hemispheres, and this area in the left hemisphere is the center of language control. Typically, the planum temporale is asymmetrical; that is, it is larger in the left than in the right hemisphere. (In most individuals, language functions are controlled in the left hemisphere.) In the dyslexic brain, however, the planum temporale is symmetrical; it is similar in size in the right and left hemispheres (Duane, 1989; Galaburda, 1989). This research provides strong evidence that dyslexia has a neurological basis that is related to a difference in brain structure.

Brain Studies Using the New Machines and Technologies.

Several new technological innovations allow scientists to study the active, living brain, rather than studying it through autopsy. These studies provide additional support for the findings of the autopsy research. The new technologies include MRI (magnetic resonance imaging), BEAM (brain electrical activity mapping), CT (computed tomography), and PET (positron emission tomography).

The MRI (magnetic resonance imaging) is the most recent advance in neuroimaging. It is a device that converts signals into a sharp image on a video screen. The MRI generates images of multiple sections of the brain, indicating the shape and location of various brain structures. Research with MRI scans shows that the frontal region of the brains of children with dyslexia and severe learning disabilities is symmetrical and smaller than in normal individuals (Hynd, 1992). The researchers draw an analogy to a poorly functioning radio: the brains of children with dyslexia do not efficiently pull in or analyze signals.

The BEAM (brain electrical activity mapping) is a procedure to monitor brain wave activity. BEAM technology is a major advancement of the older EEG (electroencephalogram) procedures. In the BEAM procedures, computers convert and map electrical brain waves that subjects produce in response to sounds, sights, and words. Duffy (1988) found major differences in electrical activity produced by the brains of individuals with dyslexia. Differences have been found in the left hemisphere, in the medial frontal lobe, and in the occipital lobe (the brain's visual center).

Computerized tomograph (CT) is a scanning radiological technique that painlessly and safely allows visualization of brain structures. The CT scans brain structure, not brain activity. Research with CT scans show that dyslexic individuals have atypical development of left hemisphere structures (Rosenberger & Hier, 1980). Consistent with other findings, CT research shows that the dyslexic brain differs in structure from a normal brain.

Positron emission tomography (PET) has been one of the most successful research approaches to studying brain deficiencies in attention deficit disorders. (This disorder is discussed later in this chapter.) PET is a technological device that permits the measurement of metabolism within the brain.

The research of Zametkin et al. (1990) demonstrates that the metabolism of individuals with attention deficit disorders is different from that of normal individuals, with less cerebral glucose metabolism in individuals with ADD.

Genetic Bases for Dyslexia.

The research on the genetic basis for dyslexia includes family and twin studies carried out over the years (DeFries and Decker, 1982; DeFries et al., 1991; Smith, 1992). An extensive study of 250 families and 1,044 subjects has shown strong evidence that the tendency for severe reading disabilities is inherited. The theory of a genetic, sex-linked basis for dyslexia is further supported by studies that show that more than four times as many boys as girls are impaired in reading (Vellutino, 1987). Strong evidence for a dyslexia gene, found on chromosome VI, has been found in three studies (Cardon et al., 1994).

Brain Injury Research.

Some of the strongest evidence that dyslexia is a neurological disorder comes from the severe reading problems caused by surgical procedures or accidental injury. For example, individuals who have strokes or accidents affecting different areas of the brain may experience different types of acquired dyslexia, including *deep* dyslexia (an inability to process letter–sound relationships) or *surface* dyslexia (an inability to recognize visual symbols) (Berninger et al., 1991).

Psychological Processing and Dyslexia.

Researchers have found that students with extreme difficulty in learning to read also have some problems in two basic psychological processes.

In the first, students have great difficulty in *phonological processing,* or phonemic awareness (Blachman, 1994; Torgesen, Wagner, & Rashotte 1994). That is, students cannot understand the sound structure of English words, including the fact that spoken words consist of sounds. Such students cannot identify the component sounds in a whole word, cannot take blend sounds together to form spoken words, cannot identify the first (or last) sound in a spoken word, and cannot understand rhyming patterns. Although many students with reading problems have problems with phonological processing, the problems of dyslexics, or severely disabled students, are often resistant to change (Blachman, 1994) and require extensive instruction. Many suggestions for assessing and developing phonological processing are given in Chapter 5.

Rapid Automatized Naming (RAN), the ability to identify rapidly flashed symbols, has also been identified as a problem in severe reading disabilities (Badian, Duffy, Als, & McNaulty, 1991; Blachman, 1994; Wolf, 1991). Strategies to improve automaticity include using a computer (see Chapter 4), working on fluent word recognition, and gaining more reading practice (see Chapter 7).

At one time, many people believed that the psychological processing deficits of dyslexics were primarily visual in nature. Thus, characteristics such as reversals of letters and words were considered important. However, recent research has shown that deficits of dyslexics are probably auditory (Aaron, 1993), and that even reversals may have an auditory basis. Both phonological processing and rapid automatized naming are believed to have underlying auditory components (Torgesen, Wagner, & Rashotte, 1994).

Determining Dyslexia.

Despite the widespread agreement that some individuals have severe and unexplainable reading difficulties, assessing the condition of dyslexia is complex and controversial. In fact, the definition and criteria for identifying dyslexia can vary considerably.

Although many researchers identify dyslexia as a very serious reading disability, others simply define it as a discrepancy between intelligence scores and reading scores. Finally, some use the term to refer to *all* students who are behind in reading. These professionals feel that differences among types of readers are not well substantiated (Kamhi, 1992; Siegel, 1992). If used, these last two definitions would include underachievers whose poor reading scores may be due to excessive absences, low motivation, lack of preparation from the home environment, or poor teaching.

The definition of dyslexia has been debated for over 50 years, and controversy will probably continue. However, most professionals dealing with problem readers agree that a "hard core" of reading disabled students does, indeed, exist. Increasing medical evidence shows that this disability has a basis in the brain, in neurological functioning, and in psychological processing (Blachman, 1994; Lerner, 1993).

At-Risk Students

A considerable number of students are at risk because of the lack of a sound home and social environment. At-risk students, particularly those living in poverty, figure prominently among severely disabled students (Wood & Algozzine, 1994).

Students born into single-parent homes plagued by poverty and characterized by lack of education are also likely to develop physical problems that lead to reading disabilities. These problems include fetal alcohol syndrome, drug dependence at birth, exposure to malnutrition and smoking during mother's pregnancy, lead exposure, premature birth, child abuse, and lack of early cognitive and language stimulation. It is estimated that one-third of our nation's children are at risk for school failure before they enter kindergarten.

A wide-ranging study of the Carnegie Corporation of New York (Chira, 1994) indicates that millions of our nation's infants and toddlers are so deprived of medical care, loving supervision, and intellectual stimulation that their growth into healthy and responsible adults is threatened.

Such students often have problems in the early childhood years, from birth through age three, which are critical in the development of the brain. Research on brain development suggests that any attempt to maximize intellectual growth must begin during the first three years of life. Research summarized by the Carnegie Corporation of New York (1994) shows that:

- Brain development before age one is more rapid and extensive than previously realized.
- Brain development is much more vulnerable to environmental influence than suspected.
- The influence of early environment on brain development is long lasting.
- Environment affects the number of brain cells, connections among them, and the way connections are wired.
- Early stress has a negative impact on brain function.

In other words, a healthy, nurturing, stress-free environment actually nurtures intelligence. Sadly, many at-risk students lack this environment and, hence, are especially prone to develop severe reading disabilities.

Many at-risk students receive instruction through supplementary instructional programs supported through Title I (formerly Chapter I) of the Elementary and Secondary Education Act, reauthorized by the U.S. Congress in 1994. The purpose of Title I legislation is to supply education to at-risk students from low-income homes.

Title I grants, which are distributed through school districts, serve students whose academic performance is below grade-level criteria (as determined by the state or local education agency) and who attend a school which has enough low-income children to warrant funding. Schools that are eligible for Title I funds provide supplementary instruction oriented to achieving high standards. As of a 1994 report, over 75 percent of the students in Title I received reading instruction (Garcia, Pearson, & Jiménez, (1994).

In many low-income area schools, programs for students with learning problems are supported predominantly through Title I funds. As of 1994, the program served 7 million students. Recent revisions of Title I rules encourage programs that serve all students in a low-achieving school, urge professionals to help students within the regular classroom setting (rather than in a "pull-out situation"), and require that schools develop written policies to include parents in programs.

Students Identified as Learning Disabled and Attention Deficit Disordered

Students who have been identified as having two disabilities—(1) learning disability and (2) attention deficit disorders—are likely to have reading problems. Since these students may need special reading services, we describe them in more detail.

Learning Disabilities.

A learning disability is one type of special education classification that receives funds under the provision of IDEA (Individuals with Disabilities in Education Act, 1995), the Federal Special Education Act. One-half of students served under IDEA, a figure comprising 4 percent of U.S. schoolchildren, are identified as learning disabled. The legal definition of specific learning disabilities is:

> a disorder in one or more of basic psychological processes involved in using language, spoken or written, which may manifest itself in an imperfect ability to listen, think, speak, read, write, spell, or to do mathematical calculations. The term includes such conditions as perceptual handicaps, brain injury, minimum brain dysfunction, dyslexia, and developmental aphasia. The term does not include children who have learning problems that are primarily the result of visual, hearing, or motor handicaps, of mental retardation or emotional disturbance, or of environmental, cultural, or economic disadvantage.

IDEA also requires that students with learning disabilities exhibit a discrepancy between potential and academic achievement.

In the above definition, a learning disability is explained as a problem in using language. Since reading is one aspect of language, it is not surprising that 80 percent of students with learning disabilities suffer from reading problems (Lerner, 1993). Furthermore, many severely disabled readers are classified as learning disabled.

The Individuals with Disabilities Education Act (IDEA), is federal legislation, reauthorized in 1995, mandating that individuals with disabilities, ages three to twenty-one, have the right to a free, appropriate, public education (FAPE). Under this act, students with disabilities, including those with learning disabilities, are entitled to an individual educational program (IEP). Specific provisions of IDEA and the IEP process are found in Table 14.1.

Increasingly, students with learning disabilities, as well as other categories of special education students, are served in regular classroom. In fact, many schools are using an *inclusion* model, which states that *all* children, including those with disabilities, should be instructed in regular classrooms within neighborhood schools. Thus, students with all types of disabilities, both severe and mild, are being placed in regular classrooms. Inclusion supporters feel that students with disabilities are best served through experiencing mainstream society and having integrated social opportunities. Inclusion receives support in the "Least Restrictive Environment" provision of the IDEA law. At times, however, it may be difficult to accommodate children with severe disabilities in the regular classroom setting. As a result, inclusion has become the one of the most controversial issues in education (Kauffman, 1993).

Attention Deficit Disorder (ADD or ADHD).

ADD is defined as a chronic neurobiological condition that is characterized by developmentally inappropriate attention skills, impulsivity, and, in some cases, hyperactivity. It is estimated that 3–5 percent of the population, or 2 million students, could be classified as having ADD (Parker, 1992). Although ADD is not currently one of the categories of special education served under IDEA, it has been recognized by the U.S. Department of Education (1991) as a condition that may need special services.

ADD affects all areas of children's lives. At home, a child may resist going to bed, refuse to eat, or break toys during play. At school, students have trouble completing work and miss valuable information because of their underdeveloped attention capacities. They talk out of turn and get into trouble. Such behaviors also hinder their ability to make and

Table 14.1   Provisions of the Individuals with Disabilities Education Act (IDEA)

Categories: specific learning disabilities, seriously emotionally disturbed, mental retardation, hard of hearing, deaf, speech or language impaired, visually impaired, seriously emotionally disturbed, orthopedically impaired, other health impaired, autistic, deaf–blind, multihandicapped, and traumatic brain injured.

IEP Process and Provisions: Each student must have a written *individualized education program* (IEP), developed as follows:

(1) *Referral* for those potentially in need of special educational services.

(2) *Assessment.* A multidisciplinary team gathers information and develops an IEP within 30 days of initial referral. The IEP indicates long-range goals, short-term goals, objectives, and suitable instructional placements. It states dates for initiation, anticipated duration of services, and evaluation. Related services (e.g., speech therapy, social work services) may also be specified.

Participants in the IEP meeting must include a school representative, the student's teacher, parents, the student (when appropriate), and other professionals (e.g., social workers, advocates, lawyers). The parents and school personnel must sign an agreement to the IEP before it can be put into effect.

(3) *Implementation and evaluation.* The plan is implemented. Goals are evaluated annually, and a complete evaluation is done every 3 years.

Procedural safeguards. Parents must be given written consent to evaluation and IEP provisions. They have a right to all information collected. Assessment must be conducted in the student's native language, and findings must be reported in the parents' native language. Evaluation procedures must be free of racial or cultural bias; the student's confidentiality must be respected.

Parents and students can challenge decisions with a "due process" hearing. If parents (or the school) disagree with the findings of this hearing, they are entitled to a higher-level hearing. Further challenges require a civil action law suit.

Placement for Instruction. *Continuum of Alternative Placements* states that schools are to establish an array of educational placements (regular classes, resource rooms, special schools) to meet the varied needs of students with disabilities. *Least Restrictive Environment* (LRE) states that the IEP team must foster, to the extent appropriate, the education of disabled students with nondisabled students.

keep friends (Lerner, Lowenthal, & Lerner, 1995). Many have academic problems that are difficult to overcome (Schiller & Hauser, 1992).

The American Psychiatric Association (1994) established criteria for classifying children as ADD in *DSM IV* (*Diagnostic and Statistical Manual of Mental Disorders*). Three subtypes of ADD have been identified: (1) ADHD,IA. primarily inattentive subtype, (2) ADHD,HI. primarily hyperactive-impulsive subtype, and (3) ADHD, combined subtype.

In order for a diagnosis to be valid, six symptoms of inattention must be present. The symptoms must have started by age 7, have lasted for 6 months, and have been present in two or more situations. Finally, the child must experience clinically significant distress or impairment in social, academic, or occupational functioning.

Students with ADD may be served in two ways. First, if they have also been identified as needing special education services, they may be served under the IDEA law. Otherwise, the provisions of Section 504 of the Rehabilitation Act, broad Civil Rights legislation, entitle ADD students to special accommodations in a regular classroom so that their learning may not be impeded.

Instructional Options for Severe Reading Disabilities

In this section, we outline ways to teach students with severe reading disabilities. As noted, researchers have begun to identify specific causes for extreme, or "hard core," reading disability. However, professionals find that many of the same teaching strategies that are successful with all low-achieving students are also successful with severely disabled students (Vellutino, 1987). When working with severely disabled readers, strategies must be used more intensively and more slowly, for severely disabled students need much direct, explicit instruction and frequent monitoring of progress (Roswell & Chall, 1994).

In this section we give additional methods for dealing with severely disabled students. These deal with teaching prerequisite (or psychological processing) abilities, adapting a standard method, special remedial approaches, teaching to different learning styles, and direct instruction.

Building Auditory and Visual Prerequisite Abilities

Most students, even very disabled ones, have auditory and visual abilities that are well enough developed to enable them to read. If further work in these is needed, we suggest first using an emergent literacy approach, which combines reading and writing with teaching underlying abilities.

Stemming from a learning-disabilities perspective, some published tests, such as the *Detroit Test of Learning Aptitudes,* are available for assessing auditory and visual perception. However, a number of studies have found training in auditory and visual skills to be unproductive (Allington, 1982; Kavale & Forness, 1987; Vellutino, 1987). Therefore, we do not recommend such training.

Adapting Standard Reading Methods to Severe Disabilities

Methods or materials designed for teaching reading in the regular classroom often can be modified for use with severely disabled readers. These require few specialized materials, and allow much flexibility in instruction.

In using this approach, it is especially important to avoid situations in which the student learns one method in the regular classroom and a very different method from a reading teacher.

Your student may acquire skills at a very slow pace, particularly at the beginning phases of instruction. Ronnie, a boy in our Reading Center, spent ten weeks learning eight sight words. Although this seems very slow, it was a remarkable achievement for Ronnie. In fact, these were the first words that he had been able to learn and retain. Because progress may be painstaking, it is particularly important to highlight every success, charting or graphing progress on the road to reading.

Effective adaptations of standard reading methods can be made for (1) sight word strategies and (2) phonics methods.

Selecting a Method.

To select the most appropriate method for an individual student, Roswell and Chall (1994) advise that the teacher (1) administer informal and formal diagnostic tests and (2) give informal trial teaching sessions. The diagnostic tests provide an estimate of strengths and weaknesses in various components of reading. The informal trial lessons help to find methods and materials that are acceptable to the student.

Roswell and Chall (1994) have developed a complete assessment instrument, *Diagnostic Assessments of Teaching with Trial Teaching Strategies (DARTTS)*, which measures reading potential, determines reading strengths and weaknesses, and provides informal trial teaching sessions. This battery is further described in Appendix A.

In addition, a diagnostic word learning lesson can help determine the student's comparative abilities in learning through sight or phonics. In this task a nonreading student learns two sets of words, with five words presented as sight words and five words present as phonics words. By comparing performance on these two tasks, the teacher can judge the student's learning strengths. A sample word learning task with directions is presented in Table 14.2. A student who learns better through the sight word task might be instructed using a sight or language experience method. For a student who does better on the phonics test, employ a phonics teaching strategy first. In addition to learning about achievement on the two tasks, the process of watching students learn by different methods provides many diagnostic insights.

Table 14.2   Diagnostic Word Learning Task

1. *Sight word task:* Words are "house," "children," "boy," "farm," "wagon."
   a. Print the words carefully on cards.
   b. Go through each word. Read it to the student, use it in a sentence, point out visual features of the word ("children" is long; "boy" is short, etc.).
   c. Mix up cards. Present five trials of the word, with the words mixed after each trial.
      (1) for the first three trials, pronounce incorrect words for the student and use them in a sentence.
      (2) For the last two trials, do not correct incorrect responses.
   d. Mark results of all trials on the form below.
2. *Phonics word task:* Words are "at," "bat," "cat," "rat," "fat."
   a. Print the words carefully on cards.
   b. Present the "at" card first; pronounce this word for the student.
   c. Mix up cards. Present five trials of the word, with words mixed after each trial.
      (1) For the first three trials, pronounce incorrect words mixed after each trial.
      (2) For the last two trials, do not correct incorrect responses.
   d. *Response form:* Mark correct or incorrect.

Sight Word Task Trial	1	2	3	4	5
house					
children					
boy					
farm					
wagon					

Phonics Task Trial	1	2	3	4	5
at					
bat					
cat					
rat					
fat					

Adapted from Barr, 1970.

Adapting a Sight-word Method.

The sight word method involves teaching students to recognize the visual form of words instantly, without further analysis. In using this approach with severely disabled students, words should be selected with care. In general, long words are harder to learn than short words, although an occasional long word adds interest. Concrete words are easier to learn than abstract words. For example, the student's name, parts of the body, the name of the school, and so on are far easier to learn than function words, such as *the*, *when*, or *to*.

The words selected for instruction should also be varied in shape or configuration and in length to avoid visual confusion. Move carefully from words to sentences to books. For guidance in this, refer to McCormick's (1994) ME/MC method (see Chapter 7). Words should also be reviewed many times to firmly establish them in the student's memory. Be careful to use standard manuscript writing for all teacher-made materials. Since severely disabled readers may focus on very small differences, they may be confused by a letter *d* with a "tail" attached.

Adapting a Phonics Method.

Adaptations for phonics methods that are suitable for severely disabled readers can be classified into two groups: (1) *synthetic phonics* and (2) the *analytic (or linguistic)* approaches.

In the *synthetic* method, the student first learns individual letter sounds and then how to blend letter sounds or groups of letter sounds into a whole word. For example, the student learns the individual sounds for *r*, *a*, and *t*. Then the student learns to blend these sounds into the word *rat*. The synthetic method requires that student to learn certain phonics rules, such as the rule that would guide the reader to pronounce *rat* and *rate* differently.

The concept of synthetic phonics is often difficult for the severely disabled reader to grasp at first. Before instructing through a synthetic approach, teachers should make sure the student possesses needed skills, such as phonological awareness. However, once basic phonics concepts are mastered, the student often gains rapidly in reading performance. Sample materials that use this approach include the *Key Text* reading series (Economy Company).

Although intense effort is required, this method works for some severely disabled readers. Betty, an intelligent thirteen-year-old, had a long history of reading failure, but she was anxious to learn. Her teacher taught her the sounds of the consonants, followed by the sounds of long and short *a*, and rules for using them, in a tedious process that took several months. Once these initial steps were mastered, however, progress was much faster. In fact, she learned the other vowels quite easily and, in her second six months of instruction, Betty demonstrated gains of over two years.

In the *analytic* method, students learn whole words that contain regular phonics patterns. Words are never broken apart, but by presenting the words over and over again in patterns (or word families), such as *at*, *bat*, *cat*, or *run*, *sun*, *fun*, the student begins to form generalizations about sound regularities. This method is similar to the *analogy* method presented in Chapter 6. Books using the linguistic approach are based upon patterns of word families, resulting in text such as:

- Dan ran the fan.
- Can Dan fan Nan?
- The pet is wet.
- Is the pet wet?

An important prerequisite skill for learning analytic phonics is the skill of rhyming. Often older severely disabled readers prefer analytic phonics because it gives them considerable independence. Materials that have featured this approach have included the *Sullivan Program,* the *Merrill Linguistic Readers,* the *SRA Reading Program* and the *Phonic Remedial Reading Lessons* (Kirk, Kirk, & Minskoff, 1985). While the first three present words in context, the *Phonic Remedial Reading Lessons* present organized word drills.

Ten-year-old Billy was a nonreader who was taught analytic phonics for several months. His initial learning rate was one word family per week for four weeks, and two families a week thereafter. Billy's teacher controlled the word families carefully so that they would not be too similar. After each word family was learned, it was presented in a story. The words from the word family were at first color coded (for example, one family was written in yellow and another in red). Billy's independent reading was done with books containing rhyming words, such as Dr. Seuss's *Hop on Pop* and *Green Eggs and Ham.* He also created his own book of word families, featuring one, with many example words (e.g., *ight, ake*), on each page.

Differences in Learning Styles

Not all people learn in the same way. Differences in temperamental styles have even been observed in infants and young children (Thomas & Chess, 1977). Some babies are alert and responsive; others are irritable or passive. Some researchers and practitioners have suggested that teachers adjust instruction to the learning styles of students (Carbo, Dunn, & Dunn, 1986). They feel that if the learning style of the student is at odds with the style required to succeed in the classroom, serious learning problems can occur. In this section, we review possible options for doing this.

One view of learning styles involves psychological processes. For example some students might learn best by listening (an auditory learning style), some by looking (a visual learning style), some by touching (a tactile style), and some by performing an action (a kinesthetic style). Adults, too have preferred ways of learning. Some adults learn best by listening to an explanation; others know that to learn something they must read about it or watch it being done; still others learn best by writing or going through the actions themselves.

Reflecting these differences in prerequisite abilities, the suggestion that there are "auditory" and "visual" learners was made several years ago by researchers in learning disabilities, and has received some renewed support (Beattie, 1994). Some have put forth the theory that students with stronger visual processing skills will learn better through sight word/language experience methods, and that students with stronger auditory processing skills learn best through phonics methods (Johnson & Myklebust, 1967). This theory is often called the aptitude–treatment interaction.

Although appealing from a commonsense viewpoint, researchers have not found differences in modes of processing to predict reading success by different methods (Allington, 1982; Robinson, 1972). In fact, Caldwell (1991) found that the amount of reading done by disabled students, rather than their "auditory" or "visual" aptitude, determined reading progress. For this reason, we suggest you use trial teaching, rather than prerequisite skills, to determine instructional methods for severely disabled students.

Carbo and her associates (Carbo, Dunn, & Dunn, 1986) have postulated eight different learning styles for students, and, for each, have unique instructional suggestions.

Although many of the teaching suggestions Carbo gives are valuable, the research establishing learning styles has received serious challenges (Stahl, 1988).

Styles of learning may also be *active* or *passive*. Efficient learning requires an active and dynamic involvement in the learning process. Active learners organize information, ask themselves questions about the material, and compare new information to what they already know. They are motivated and have a desire to learn (Brown & Campione, 1986).

Students with passive learning styles lack interest in learning, possibly because of frustrating past experiences. Not believing that they can learn, these students become passive and dependent, a style that is often called "learned helplessness." Passive learners wait for the teacher to do something to lead them to the learning, instead of taking the initiative. In effect, they expect to be "spoon fed," step-by-step.

Until research issues can be further clarified, teachers may consider learning styles one option that may explain some severe reading disabilities, but they should not rule out other options.

Multisensory Methods

Multisensory methods are built upon the premise that stimulation of several sensory avenues reinforces learning. The student may see a word to be learned, say the word, hear the word, and write the word. Several specialized methods use this approach, including VAKT, the Fernald method, and the Orton–Gillingham method. Although multisensory methods can be valuable first steps, they are often slow. For this reason, they should only be considered if adaptations of standard methods do not work, or if severely disabled students need to reinforce certain difficult words or concepts. Three classic applications of multisensory teaching of reading are *VAKT,* the *Fernald Method* (Fernald, 1943/1988) and the *Orton–Gillingham Method* (Gillingham & Stillman, 1970).

VAKT.

This technique uses four senses: *visual, auditory, kinesthetic,* and *tactile* senses (hence, the name VAKT). Students learning a word *see* the word, *hear* the teacher say the word, *say* the word themselves, *hear themselves* say the word, and *feel the muscle movement* as they trace the word. The activity utilizes tracing a word in teaching. The student traces the word with a finger in contact with the paper. To increase the tactile and kinesthetic sensation, sandpaper letters, sand or clay trays, and finger paints have been used for tracing activities.

The Fernald Method.

Over 50 years ago, Grace Fernald (1943/1988) developed a multisensory approach for extremely poor readers that simultaneously involves four sensory avenues: visual, auditory, kinesthetic, and tactile, plus the language experience approach. Because progress may be very slow, the method is generally used only when other methods have failed. The student learns a word as a total pattern, tracing the entire word and thereby strengthening the memory and visualization of the entire word. The words to be learned are selected by the student. The method consists of four stages. Students start learning words with stage 1; once this is mastered they move on to stage 2, and so on.

Stage 1.

At the beginning of stage 1, the student selects a word that he or she would like to read. Then

1. The word is written on large cards or paper (in manuscript or cursive script) in chalkboard size using crayon. While writing, the teacher says the word.
2. Using one or two fingers, the student traces over the word while saying each part of the word as it is traced.
3. The tracing is repeated until the student feels that the word can be written (or printed) from memory.
4. The student tries to reproduce the word from memory without looking at the word. As the word is written, it is again pronounced in parts.
5. If the student cannot write the word correctly, the tracing procedure is repeated.
6. After the word is written correctly from memory, it is filed in an alphabetical word file box.

No errors are permitted. If the student makes a mistake he or she is stopped and told to begin the process again. Any activities that break up word learning are discouraged.

After several words are learned, students begin to appreciate their powers to read and write words. At this time, they start to write their own stories. Words to be learned are now identified as those needed to write these stories.

Stage 2.

When the teacher feels that students no longer have to trace words for learning, they are ready for stage 2. The method for word learning differs from stage 1 in two ways: (1) the words may be presented on smaller cards (e.g., index-sized cards) and (2) the tracing stage is eliminated. In stage 2, the word is printed (or written) on a file card. The student looks at it, says it (emphasizing its parts), and then attempts to write it while saying it without looking back at the original. Words may continue to be taken from the student's stories, and students continue to use a file box of words.

Stage 3.

In this stage, students begin to read from actual texts, and the words to be learned are drawn from these texts. Students are permitted to read whatever they desire. Index cards are no longer used; rather students learn words directly from text. When new words are encountered, the student looks at the word on the printed page and tries to write it from memory. Words learned are again filed into the word bank.

Stage 4.

In this stage, the student is able to read a word in text, say it, and remember it without the crutch of writing from memory. Students are encouraged to figure out unknown words by associating them with known words or by using context clues. Only words that the student cannot "figure out" are written down for further review. Since the identification of unknown words should precede reading, Fernald suggests that students survey material they read to locate and figure out unknown words. If additional unknown words are encountered during reading, teachers are advised to supply them for students rather then to interrupt the meaning-gaining process.

The Orton–Gillingham Method.

The Orton–Gillingham method, a multisensory approach for teaching reading, is an outgrowth of Samuel Orton's neurological theory of language disorders (Orton, 1937). Over 50 years ago, Orton, a physician who specialized in children with language and disorders, worked with a teacher, Anna Gillingham, to develop a multisensory, synthetic phonics approach using direct instruction. The approach is associated with the Orton Dyslexia Society, which is dedicated to finding causes and treatments for dyslexia.

Today, there are several variations of the Orton–Gillingham method. *Project READ*, an application of the Orton–Gillingham method in the public schools, reported significant gains in reading achievement (Enfield, 1988). *Alphabetic Phonics* is an expansion of the method (Cox, 1986). Another version, the *Slingerland Method* (Slingerland, 1981), provides an extensive set of materials. In the *Recipe for Reading* (Traub & Bloom, 1978), the method is accompanied by twenty-one supplementary readers.

The original Orton–Gillingham (Gillingham & Stillman, 1970) method is a highly structured approach requiring five lessons a week for a minimum of two years. The initial activities include learning letters and sounds, learning words, and using words in sentences.

Letter names and sounds are learned through six sensory associations. These are: visual–auditory (V-A), auditory–visual (V-A), auditory–kinesthetic (A-K), kinesthetic––auditory (K-A), visual–kinesthetic (V-K), and kinesthetic–visual (K-V). Instruction takes place in three phases:

Phase I

1. A visual and auditory (V-A) association with the letter name is established. The teacher shows a card with a letter on it and says the letter name, which the student repeats. In saying the letter, an A-K association is made. This step is the foundation for oral reading.
2. When mastery of the letter name has occurred, a visual and auditory association with the sound is developed. The teacher says the sound while exposing the card, and the pupil repeats it. This also involves V-A and A-K associations.

Phase II

The student develops the ability to relate the sound to the letter name. The teacher, without showing the card, makes the letter sound, and the pupil tells the name of the letter. This is the basis for oral spelling.

Phase III

1. The letter is printed by the teacher and its construction explained. The student then traces over the original, copies it, and, finally, writes the letter from memory while averting eyes from the paper. This association is V-K and K-V.
2. The teacher says the sound and the pupil writes the letter that has that sound, thereby developing the A-K association.

After learning letter–sound associations, the student learns to *read words*. This starts by blending letter sounds and spelling the words. The initial words taught contain two vowels, "a" and "i," and eight consonants, "b," "g," "h," "j," "k," "m," "p," and "t." The blended words follow a consonant–vowel–consonant pattern (CVC), and blending occurs by pronouncing the first consonant and vowel together (*ra*) and then adding the final consonant (*rat*). These words are commercially distributed on colored cards, and they are known as the student's "jewel case." Sample jewel case words are *bat*, *hip*, *bib*, and *job*. After these words are mastered, words containing other letters are added.

After a basic set of words has been learned, the words are *combined into sentences* and stories, and the student learns to read these. Reading continues to be taught by a phonics method and combines spelling and dictation exercises.

Direct Instructional Methods

Direct instruction, based upon behavioral theories of learning, is concentrated on explicit instruction on tasks and skills to be learned. Direct instruction (Rosenshine & Stevens, 1986) is academically focused and teacher controlled. It involves the direct teaching of basic skills by using a structured sequence, clear goals, and continuous evaluation. The instruction allows immediate feedback to students, teaching a skill until mastery is achieved.

Based upon work by Engelmann and Bruner (1974), *DISTAR* combines direct instruction with systematically taught phonics. Research reviews reported by and Becker and Carnine (1980) show *DISTAR* to be effective. The program consists of Books I and II of the *SRA Reading Mastery* basal reader series. It is a highly structured decoding program, requiring a very specific step-by-step procedure and emphasizing drill, and repetition. (There are, in fact, three types of *DISTAR* programs: one for language, one for arithmetic, and one for reading.)

Reading Mastery Program: DISTAR contains both isolated drills and instructional reading. It follows a behavioral management approach, progressing in small steps, and uses specified teacher praise as reinforcement. Directions are so specific that words are actually supplied for the teacher.

In *DISTAR,* pupil instruction is given in small groups for thirty-minute periods, five times per week. Skill mastery in the program is measured by criterion-referenced tests. If a student has not mastered the skill, special additional lessons are provided.

DISTAR uses a synthetic phonics approach, and the students are first taught the prerequisite skill of auditory blending to help them combine isolated sounds into words. In addition, the shape of some alphabet letters is modified so that they provide clues to the letter sounds. A sample of these materials appears in Figure 14.1. The special alphabet of *DISTAR* is gradually phased out as the students progress.

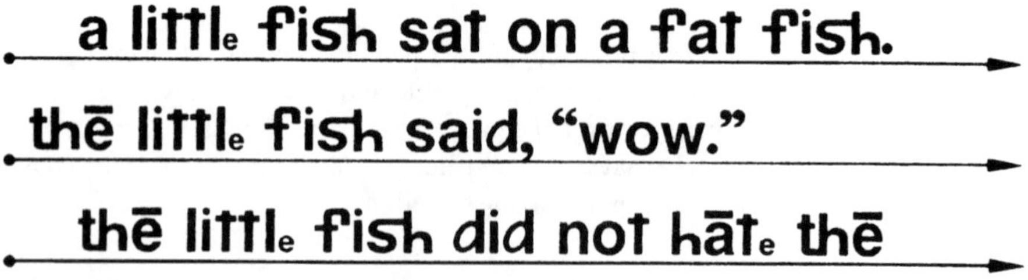

a littlₑ fish sat on a fat fish.

thē littlₑ fish said, "wow."

thē littlₑ fish did not hāTₑ thē

From DISTAR READING I by Siegfried Engelmann and Elaine C. Bruner 1974, 1969. Science Research Associates, Inc. Reprinted by permission of the publisher.

FIGURE 14.1
The DISTAR Reading Alphabet

Summary

Students have severe difficulties in learning to read for a variety of reasons. The condition known as dyslexia is an unusual type of severe reading disorder that has baffled and intrigued the professional community. People with dyslexia have extreme difficulty recognizing letters and words and interpreting the printed language. Recent brain research studies show that dyslexic individuals have differences in brain structure and brain functioning.

Many students in our culturally diverse society are at-risk for reading failure because of environmental conditions, extreme poverty, or lack of a stimulating home environment. Recent research on brain development indicates that the most important brain growth occurs in the ages from birth to age three. Many at-risk students are served by federal Title I programs.

Students with learning disabilities and attention deficit disorders may suffer from severe reading disabilities. Learning-disabled students are covered by the IDEA law. ADD students are entitled to the protection of Section 504 of the Rehabilitation Act. There are three subtypes of ADD students.

Even though there are many causes of severe reading disabilities, similar methods for teaching these students can be effective with many of these children. There are several useful methods to teach severely disabled readers. Students may learn needed strategies for emergent literacy. We do not, however, advocate teaching visual and auditory processing skills.

Standard reading methods can also be adapted for the use of severely disabled students. Both sight word and phonics methods can be used. Learning styles form another instructional avenue, although research matching children's learning styles to instruction has been challenged.

Multisensory methods use several sensory avenues to reinforce learning. The VAKT method, the Fernald method, and the Orton–Gillingham method are effective with students who have severe reading disabilities. Direct instruction is concentrated explicit instruction focusing on reading tasks and skills to be learned. A reading program built upon the direct instruction philosophy is *DISTAR*.

CHAPTER 15

Assessing Reading Achievement: Formal Measures

Introduction

In this chapter we discuss the *formal* tests that are used for assessing students. Discussions of informal measures appear much earlier in the volume (in Chapter 3 and many following chapters) because increasingly teachers find that informal and authentic assessment methods, such as informal reading inventories, trial lessons, curriculum-based assessment, and structured observations, offer immediately usable and practical information about students.

However, information from formal tests is also needed for a comprehensive evaluation. Formal testing supplies many types of usable information to professionals. (1) Formal tests are the best way to compare your student to others of the same age or grade level. (2) Formal test information is more familiar to other professionals, such as psychologists and physicians, than informal testing results. (3) Formal tests help teachers to make objective decisions about a student's performance. (4) Formal tests best fulfill legal requirements of testing required by local, state, school, and federal laws and policies. A very complete picture of a student's reading is obtained by combining the information gained from both informal and formal measures.

This chapter first presents an overview of formal tests. Then, several different types of tests, including tests of general reading assessment, tests of diagnostic reading assessment, and tests of intelligence are discussed. Many additional tests are listed and described in Appendix A.

We hope that this information will serve as a guide to help you choose, administer, and interpret tests. However, for further information, refer to the *Mental Measurement Yearbook* (Kramer & Conoley, 1992). This fine resource contains extensive reviews of many different tests. The Buros Institute also publishes a descriptive list of tests in *Tests in Print* and has published guides to reading tests called *Reading Tests and Reviews.*

Some formal tests have been criticized for a lack of authenticity in (1) assessing only short passages and words and (2) testing skills in an isolated format. It is important, however, to note recent trends in creating longer passages for students to read, and for integrating more authentic reading tasks into formal testing. For example, the *Iowa Test of Basic Skills* (Houghton Mifflin) now includes longer passages for reading. New assessment tools also provide ways to combine formal and informal assessment. The Psychological Corporation has published an *Integrated Assessment System* that provides formal assessment of a collection of student work (portfolio) and authentic tasks.

Overview of Formal Tests

Formal tests include a broad class of instruments that are commercially produced, formally printed, and published. They also have specific procedures for administration and scoring (Bauman & Murray, 1994). Two types of formal tests are norm-referenced and criterion-referenced tests.

Norm-Referenced Tests

Most formal tests are *norm-referenced* (also called *standardized*). This means that there are statistics (norms) for comparing the performance of a student to a large sample of similar students (the norm sample). Norm-referenced tests are developed carefully using a norm sample—a large number of students who are representative of the general population. The test is given to each student in the norm sample, and norms are established to determine, for example, how well the average fourth grader does on the test. This permits you, as a teacher, to compare the fourth grader you are testing with the fourth graders in the norm sample. To assure that your student's scores can be compared with the norm sample, it is essential that procedures for test administration, scoring, and interpretation be strictly followed.

Criterion-Referenced Tests

Some formal tests are *criterion-referenced.* In this type of test, a student's performance is compared to a specific standard or criterion (rather than to the norm sample). This test determines whether a student has mastered certain competencies or skills. For example, can the student recognize *ing* endings or find the main idea in a paragraph? Criterion referenced tests are useful because they provide a means of accountability that can be related to the curriculum. For example, a teacher can determine whether, after the concept of the main idea has been taught, a student has mastered it.

To understand the difference between a normed and a criterion-referenced test, we can draw an analogy to another area of learning: swimming. In norm-referenced terms, a child can be tested in swimming and judged to swim as well as the average nine-year-old. In criterion-referenced terms, a child is judged on the basis of certain accomplishments, such as putting one's face in the water, floating on one's back, and doing the crawl stroke. In other words, criterion-referenced tests measure mastery rather than grade level, or they *describe* rather than *compare* performance.

Bias in Testing

Tests should be fair in representing student performance and should be free of racial or cultural bias. The content of the test should represent the experiences and values of all groups taking the test. For example, a reading test should not contain vocabulary, pictures, or stories that are unfamiliar to certain populations taking the test. As discussed in Chapter 13, formal intelligence tests, in particular, have been subjected to the criticism of cultural bias.

Ethical Considerations

In using formal tests for assessment, professionals must comply with basic professional standards. If professionals from different disciplines are involved in assessment (i.e., educators, psychologists, counselors, social workers, medical specialists), each must abide by the standards of his or her own profession. All must maintain the confidentiality of the student, keep complete records, and follow standard testing criteria. The International Reading Association has published guidelines to guide the administration of tests in reading.

Scores on Normed-Referenced Tests

The scores on norm-referenced tests indicate how an individual student has performed compared to students of the same grade or age level who are in the norm sample. After a teacher gives a test, the teacher determines a *raw score,* which is usually the number correct on the test. Raw scores are then converted into *derived scores,* which can be used for interpreting the student's performance. Derived scores on norm-referenced reading tests can be reported as standard scores, reading grade scores, percentiles, normal curve equivalents, and stanines.

Many scores on reading and other academic tests are based upon a normal curve distributions of scores. In this distribution (shown by the "humped curve" in Figure 15.1) most

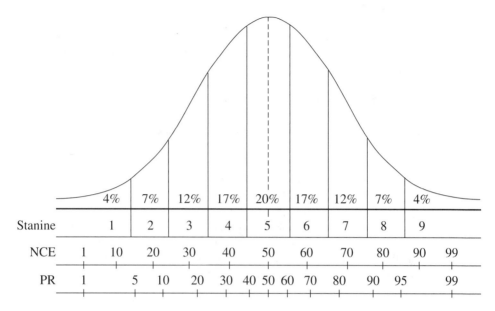

FIGURE 15.1
Relation among Stanines, NCEs, and Percentiles

Reproduced from Gates-McGinitie Reading Tests, Manual for Scoring and Interpretation, Level 4 © 1989. The Riverside Publishing Co. Reprinted with permission of the publisher. All rights reserved.

scores fall in the middle, creating a "hump." However, some high and low scores fall at the upper and lower ends of the curve. In other words, most scores are average, but some are very high or low. The more extreme (high or low) the score, the less frequent it is.

The highest point on the curve is the *mean* (or average) point. The "area" within each vertical division represents the percent of people in it. As you can see, the closer to the mean a division is, the more individuals are in it.

Standard Scores.
Some formal tests report *standard scores,* which refer to scores in which the mean and the standard deviation (which is a measure of variations) have been assigned preset values. For example, in the *Weschler Intelligence Scale for Children III (WISC III),* the mean is set at 100, and the standard deviation at 15.

Reading Grade Score.
This score indicates how well a student reads in terms of grade level. For example, a score of 4.5 (the fifth month of the fourth grade) indicates that the student correctly answered the same number of questions on this particular test as the average pupil in the fifth month of the fourth grade. Reading grade scores do not indicate an absolute performance; they indicate how the student performed in relation to the students in the norm sample population.

Percentiles (PR).
These describe the student's performance in relation to others in the same age group or grade. Percentiles can be understood as a rank within 100, expressed in numbers from 1 to

99. A percentile rank is the percentage of students that scored lower than the student being tested. For example, a percentile score of 57 indicates that this student scored higher than 57 percent of the comparison group and lower than 42 percent. The fiftieth percentile indicates the median (or middle) score. The highest percentile is 99 and the lowest is 1. The higher the percentile, the better the student's performance.

Equal distances in percentiles, however, do not indicate equal difference in raw score points. Since many scores center near the mean, the difference between the fiftieth and sixtieth percentiles may be only a few raw score points, whereas the distance between the eightieth and ninetieth percentiles often represents a great many raw score points on the test (see Figure 15.1).

Normal Curve Equivalent Scores (NCE).

NCE scores are similar to percentiles in that they have a range from 1 to 99, and a mean of 50. They differ from percentile scores because they have been transformed into equal units of reading achievement. For example, the difference between the fiftieth and sixtieth NCE and the eightieth and ninetieth NCE is the same in raw point scores. Figure 15.1 shows the distribution of NCE scores in comparison to percentiles.

Stanines.

The stanine score ranks pupils from 1 to 9. The lowest stanine score is 1, the median stanine is 5, and the highest is 9. Stanine scores are assigned so that the results represent a normal distribution. Thus, in an average class, most students will receive stanine scores of 4, 5, or 6, and a few will receive stanine scores of 1 or 9.

The name "stanine" is a contraction of "standard nine" and is based on the fact that the score runs from 1 to 9. Stanines are normalized standard scores with a mean of 5 and a standard deviation of 2. Figure 15.1 shows the percentage of students in each stanine, in each 10 NCE units, and compares these with percentiles.

Standardization, Validity, and Reliability

Which norm-referenced tests are the best? In judging the value of a norm-referenced test, teachers should consider the test's standardization, validity, and reliability.

Standardization.

To standardize a test, it is given to a large representative group of students (the norm sample). Based on data derived from this norm sample, then, inferences are made about other students who take the test. When selecting a test, teachers should consider whether the norm sample was large enough to establish stable performance norms. In addition, the characteristics of the individuals who comprise the norm sample is important. Did the norm sample include representatives of the students who are being tested? If the norm sample group is not considered representative, some school districts develop their own local norms.

Validity.

Validity refers to whether a test measures what it is supposed to measure. There are at least two types of validity: (1) content validity, and (2) criterion validity. Content validity involves inspecting the test to see whether the items are valid for testing purposes. For example, a valid reading comprehension test would probably contain passages with questions. In contrast, a comprehension test that required the student to match words would have question-able content validity.

Criterion validity refers to how the test compares with some other aspects of achievement. Most norm-referenced reading tests provide information about the comparison of performance on the reading test with some aspect of school achievement (for example, grade-point average). The comparison is usually done in the form of a statistical correlation. This correlation may range from +1.0 (a high positive correlation) to –1.0 (a very negative correlation). For acceptable criterion validity, the correlation should be *positive and high* (generally at least .70).

Reliability.

Reliability refers to the stability of test scores. If a test is reliable, the person will receive the same score on repeated testings. To be useful for making decisions about an individual, a test must have high reliability. Salvia and Ysseldyke (1995) feel that acceptable reliability for a test depends on the situation. If test scores are reported for groups of students for general administration purposes or screening, a reliability score of about .80 is acceptable. For individual decisions about students, such as placement in a Title I/Chapter I class or in special education, the reliability of the test should be .90.

There are two forms of reliability: (1) test–retest reliability and (2) internal reliability. In test–retest reliability, the test is given to a group of students two times. Then the scores are correlated to determine whether individual students perform about the same on the first and second administrations. In internal reliability, items within a test are compared with each other. In one form of internal reliability, split-half reliability, a group of students' scores on one half of the test items is correlated with performance on the items from the other half.

Tests of General Reading Assessment

Tests of general reading assessment are used to evaluate a student's general level of achievement as well as to determine the general areas of reading strengths and weaknesses. Types of tests that are used in the general reading assessment phase include (1) group survey tests, (2) individual survey tests, (3) normed oral reading tests and (4) literacy tests.

Group Survey Tests.

Survey tests are norm-referenced tests that are used to assess the student's reading level. Both group survey tests and individual survey tests are used for this purpose.

Group survey tests are the most commonly used tests in the schools. They are generally used once per year to assess student progress in reading and other academic subjects, to identify those who may have problems, or to evaluate the success of a program. Examples of group survey tests for reading are the *Stanford Achievement Test*, the *Iowa Test of Basic Skills*, the *California Reading Test*, and the *Gates–MacGinitie Reading Tests*. These are designed for testing a group of students in a class, but they are also useful for testing individual students. All standardized group reading tests permit us to compare a student's score to scores in large norm samples.

A group survey test is actually a series of tests at different levels. The different levels are suitable for students at different grade levels. In addition, each level usually has a few equivalent forms (e.g., Form A and Form B). Since the two forms are normed similarly, the scores on the two forms can be compared. If Form A is given during an initial assessment and Form B is given after a period of instruction is completed, the student's progress can be evaluated easily.

Despite their excellent statistical properties, group survey tests have some limitations for use with students with reading problems:

(1) *Out-of-Level Tests.* Students with reading problems must be given test levels that are appropriate for their reading level but not for their age level. For example, an eighth grader reading at a second-grade level will find the eighth-grade test to be too hard, but the second-grade test too "babyish."

(2) *Inability to measure school-related tasks.* Over a period of years, many strides have been made in making these tests better reflect the actual type of reading students do in school. However, the tests continue to measure more discrete tasks, such as reading single words and relatively short passages. For this reason, it is important to supplement information from standardized tests with informal measures that assess such abilities as reading whole stories and taking notes.

(3) *Limits of a Formal Situation.* Some students "freeze" on standardized tests. In addition, because they require a standard procedure, formal tests do not allow teachers to observe student performance closely and to probe a student's responses. Informal assessment, with its ability to adjust situations to a student's needs, may give far more information.

A description of a few tests that are widely used for students with reading problems gives examples of group survey tests that the reading teacher is likely to encounter.

The *Stanford Diagnostic Reading Test (SDRT)* is intended for use with lower achievers and contains more easy items than most survey tests at the same levels. The four levels of the test are red, green, brown, and blue; at each level, the test contains two forms. Phonics abilities are tested at all levels of the test. The red level, for grades 1–2, tests auditory discrimination, basic phonic skills, auditory vocabulary, word recognition, and comprehension. The green level, for grades 3–4, tests auditory discrimination, phonetic analysis, structural analysis, auditory vocabulary, comprehension, and reading rate. The brown level, for grades 5–6, tests phonetic analysis, structural analysis, auditory vocabulary, comprehension, and reading rate. Finally, the blue level, for grades 9–12 and community colleges, tests phonetic analysis, structural analysis, word meaning, word parts, comprehension, reading rate, and scanning and skimming. The test is well standardized, and reports many different types of norms for students.

In addition, the *SDRT* contains a criterion-referenced section called Progress Indicators. All of the test items measuring a certain skill are added together and a criterion is given for mastery of that skill.

The *Gates–MacGinitie Reading Tests, Third Edition,* is another standardized reading test often used with low-achieving students. The test comes in nine levels: Readiness, Pre-Reading, Level 1 (for upper grade 1), Level 2, Level 3, Level 4, Levels 5–6, Levels 7–9, and Levels 10–12. The readiness, prereading, and grade 1 levels have one form, Levels 2 through 10–12 have two forms. Level 1 through Level 10–12 tests contain two subtests, vocabulary and comprehension. In the vocabulary test, which has a 20-minute time limit, students match isolated words to one of four pictures (at lower levels) or to one of four synonyms (at higher levels). In the comprehension subtest, which has a 35-minute time limit, students read short passages and either match them to one of four pictures (at lower levels) or answer multiple choice questions (at higher levels). This well-standardized test is used widely in Title I programs.

Individual Survey Tests.

Individual survey tests, which are used widely in assessing students with reading problems, are designed to be administered to a single student. As survey tests, they give general information about reading scores rather than a detailed analysis of reading. In fact, many of these tests also include information about areas such as mathematics and spelling.

Individual survey tests usually consist of one level that is suitable for a wide range of reading abilities. Since an individual survey test might cover grades 1 through 9, it would be suitable for an older reader who is reading at a primary-grade level. Individual survey tests are usually standardized, so they permit valid comparison with a norm sample.

Through careful observation, the teacher can obtain diagnostic information during the process of giving a survey test. For example, the teacher can note whether the student hesitates or recognizes words instantly and whether the student uses decoding methods.

The actual reading tasks that students perform vary greatly from test to test. Many of the test authors use considerable ingenuity to make their tests brief or to use a multiple-choice format. Unfortunately, such methods may lead to tests that do not measure the authentic ability to read. Before using a test, the teacher should inspect the actual items to determine exactly what they require the student to do. The name of the test, or of its subtests, may not reflect the content.

Four widely used individual survey tests are the *Wide Range Achievement Test, 3rd edition,* the *Slosson Oral Reading Test,* the *Peabody Individual Achievement Test,* and the *Kaufman Test of Educational Achievement.*

The *Wide Range Achievement Test, 3rd edition (WRAT-III),* comes in two forms and has three subtests: reading, spelling, and arithmetic. The reading subtest assesses skills in letter recognition, letter naming, and pronunciation of words in isolation. A grade level is obtained by having students read individual words orally. The *WRAT-III* is widely used because it is short and convenient. However, isolated word reading does not provide a comprehensive assessment of a person's reading abilities (McCormick, 1995; Salvia & Ysseldyke, 1995). We recommend that the *WRAT* be used only for very initial assessment.

The *Slosson Oral Reading Test (SORT)* is another test of reading based solely upon word lists. Similarly, it should not be used as a reliable measure of reading level but only as a very initial reading screening device. Since both the *WRAT-R* and the *SORT* are short, usually taking less than 10 minutes, they are perhaps overused. Both should be supplemented by other measures.

The *Peabody Individual Achievement Test–Revised (PIAT-R)* is a norm-referenced, individually administered test designed to provide a wide-range screening measure of academic achievement in six content areas: mathematics, reading recognition, reading comprehension, spelling, general information, and written expression. Two subtests assess reading, and a "Total Reading" score on the *PIAT-R* is obtained by combining scores of the Reading Recognition and Reading Comprehension subtests.

Reading Recognition is measured through oral reading of words in isolation and, for beginning items, matching letters and naming capital and lower-case letters. The Reading Comprehension subtest contains 81 multiple-choice items assessing skill development in understanding what is read. After reading a sentence the student must indicate comprehension by choosing the correct picture out of a group of four. The Reading Recognition and Reading Comprehension subtests are interrelated, and a student cannot take the Comprehension subtest unless a score of 18 or above is achieved on the Reading Recognition subtest.

The *PIAT-R* also has subtests for mathematics, general information, and written expression. The standardization of the *PIAT-R* is considered good, and its reliability and validity is considered adequate for making important educational decisions about students (Salvia & Ysseldyke, 1995).

The *Kaufman Test of Educational Achievement (KTEA)* is an individually administered norm-referenced multiple-skill achievement test that can be used with students in grades 1 through 12. It comes in two quite different versions: the Comprehensive Form and the Brief Form. The Comprehensive Form contains five subtests, two of which are Reading Decoding and Reading Comprehension. The other subtests are Mathematics Applications, Mathematics Computation, and Spelling. In the Reading Decoding subtest, students identify letters and then read phonetic and nonphonetic words. In the Reading Comprehension test, the student must first respond through gestures or oral statements to directions in printed sentences. For the rest of the test, the student reads passages and answers questions. The Brief Form contains Reading, Mathematics, and Spelling subtests. The Reading subtest of the brief form has features of both the Reading Decoding and Reading Comprehension subtests described above.

The *KTEA* is considered acceptable in terms of standardization and reliability. Teachers need to check the curriculum they are teaching to determine whether the *KTEA* meets their needs (Salvia & Ysseldyke, 1995).

Normed Oral Reading Tests

Normed oral reading tests, like informal reading inventories (see Chapter 3), contain graded passages for oral reading. However, unlike informal reading inventories, these tests include statistical norms. This provides another way to obtain a general reading assessment that compares your student to others in a normed sample.

Several normed tests of oral reading are available through commercial publishers—for example, the *Gilmore Oral Reading Test* and the *Formal Reading Inventory*. In Chapter 3, we discuss oral reading assessment and the rich diagnostic opportunities oral reading tests provide. The *Qualitative Inventory–II* has been particularly highly rated (Taylor et al., 1995). The test inventory in Appendix A includes a description of several tests of oral reading.

Literacy Tests

Literacy tests are often used for the general reading assessment of older students with reading disabilities. An increasing awareness of the problems of adult illiterates has led to a number of tests that measure the ability to read functional material for everyday living. Materials on these tests measure such skills as reading traffic signs, menus, and bills. Some literacy tests are norm-referenced; others are criterion-referenced.

Criterion-referenced tests are appropriate for use when the teacher wishes to determine whether a person possesses the specific skills to function in society. Literacy tests are described further in the test inventory in Appendix A.

Diagnostic Reading Tests

Diagnostic reading tests yield more specific information than general survey reading tests. They provide a more detailed analysis of specific reading strengths and weaknesses. Two kinds of tests are described in this section: (1) diagnostic reading batteries and (2) diagnostic tests of specific areas of reading. Both are listed in Appendix A.

Diagnostic Reading Batteries

A diagnostic reading battery consists of a group of subtests, each of which assess a different component of reading. It offers useful information for obtaining a profile of the student's reading in several areas, such as oral reading, phonics, sight vocabulary, and comprehension. As with all tests, teachers should examine the subtests to make sure that they actually test the skills they describe.

Typically, diagnostic batteries are more suitable for beginning readers. Although they sample several components of reading, there tends to be more emphasis on emergent literacy and word recognition than on comprehension or word meaning.

Since diagnostic batteries often do not contain extensive reading passages, we suggest that, to obtain best information, they should be used in conjunction with other tests of actual reading and comprehension. Sometimes it is useful to administer only the sections of these batteries that are relevant to a particular student, rather than to administer the entire battery. Three widely given diagnostic batteries are the *Woodcock Reading Mastery Test–Revised,* the *Gates–McKillop–Horowitz Reading Diagnostic Test–Revised,* and the *BRIGANCE Diagnostic Inventory of Basic Skills.*

The *Woodcock Reading Mastery Test–Revised (WRMT-R)* is a widely used reading diagnostic test that measures individuals from a beginning reading level through that of an advanced adult. It is available in two forms (Form G and Form H) both of which are accompanied by a comprehensive and well-organized test manual. Form G contains all six subtests and Form H contains the four reading achievement tests.

In Form H, the four basic reading achievement subtests of the *WRMT-R* are (1) Word Identification, (2) Word Attack, (3) Word Comprehension, and (4) Passage Comprehension. These four subtests may be combined to obtain a full-score reading performance assessment.

In the Word Identification subtest the student reads single words aloud. In Word Attack, the student sounds out nonsense words. The Word Comprehension test requires the student to perform three separate tasks with vocabulary: providing antonyms, providing synonyms, and completion of analogies for a word (e.g., day is to night as up is to _____). The words used in the word comprehension test are divided into general reading, science and mathematics, social studies, and humanities. In the Passage Comprehension subtest, the student orally fills in a missing word in a paragraph.

Form G also contains two subtests for beginning readers: (1) a visual–auditory test, in which children are assessed on their ability to associate words to picturelike symbols, and (2) a test of letter identification.

The *WRMT-R* contains many useful features and teacher aids. However, the ability to read in context is measured only in the reading comprehension subtest. Furthermore, this subtest requires only oral reading and, as a response, asks the student to fill in a word. This task is somewhat different from the silent reading and responses to questions that most students are required to do in school.

Figure 15.2 details the structure of the test. The *WRMT-R* is considered appropriately and adequately normed, and evidence for reliability and validity is good (Salvia & Ysseldyke, 1995).

The *Reading Diagnostic Tests* (by Gates, McKillop, & Horowitz) are a diagnostic battery with eight distinct parts, as can be seen in the scoring sheet shown in Figure 15.3. The battery contains an oral reading inventory with an analysis of oral reading, a test of

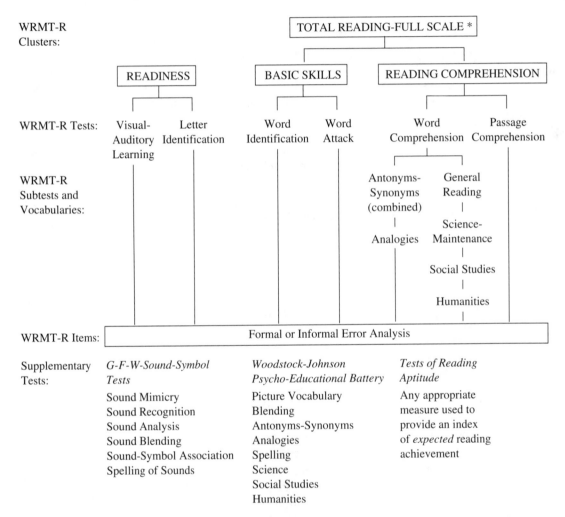

FIGURE 15.2

Structure of Information Included in the Total Interpretation Plan of the *Woodcock Reading Mastery Test–Revised*

PUPIL RECORD BOOKLET

Gates • McKillop • Horowitz
READING DIAGNOSTIC TESTS
SECOND EDITION

ARTHUR I. GATES
Professor Emeritus of Education

ANNE S. McKILLOP
Professor of Education

ELIZABETH CLIFF HOROWITZ
Adjunct Assistant Professor of Education

TEACHERS COLLEGE, COLUMBIA UNIVERSITY

Pupil's Name _____ School _____ Date _____

Age____ Birthday_____ Grade_____ Examiner_____ Teacher_____

Age, Grade, Intelligence
Chronological Age _____

Grade Corresponding to
Chronological Age _____

Actual Grade _____

Intelligence Testing:
Name of I.Q. Test _____

Date Administered _____

I.Q. _____

READING AND OTHER TEST SCORES

			1	2	3
			Raw Score	Grade Score	Ratings ( )( )
Name of Test		Date Given			
1 _____					
2 _____					
3 _____					

READING DIAGNOSTIC TESTS

	Raw Score	Grade Score	Ratings ( ) ( )		Raw Score	Grade Score	Ratings ( ) ( )
Oral Reading				**Knowledge of Word Parts: Word Attack**			
Analysis of Total Errors				Syllabication			
Omissions				Recognizing & Blending Common Word Parts			
Additions				Reading Words			
Repetitions				Giving Letter Sounds			
Analysis of Mispronunciations				Naming Capital Letters			
Directional Errors				Naming Lower-Case Letters			
Wrong Beginning				**Recognizing the Visual Form of Sounds**			
Wrong Middle							
Wrong Ending				Vowels			
Wrong in Several Parts				**Auditory Tests**			
Accent Errors				Auditory Blending			
Total Mispronunciation Errors				Auditory Discrimination			
Reading Sentences				**Written Expression**			
Words: Flash				Spelling			
Words: Untimed				Informal Writing Sample			

FIGURE 15.3
Scoring Sheet for the *Gates–McKillop–Horowitz Reading Diagnostic Tests*

reading sentences, flashed (automatic) words, untimed words, word attack, recognition of vowels, two auditory perception tests (blending and discrimination), and written expression. The oral reading test consists of one continuous passage that increases in difficulty, and there are only thirty words on any specific grade level. The grade placement score is based solely on oral reading, as no comprehension questions are asked. In addition, auditory perception-emergent literacy abilities and word recognition are emphasized. The inclusion of spelling and writing subtests reflects an integrated language philosophy. The battery was normed on only 600 students, which is a small sample compared with most survey tests.

The *BRIGANCE Diagnostic Inventory of Basic Skills* is another widely used set of diagnostic batteries. There are five different batteries (see Test Inventory in Appendix A). We describe the *BRIGANCE Diagnostic Inventory of Basic Skills* (grades Pre-K–6).

The *BRIGANCE Diagnostic Inventory* is a criterion-referenced test that does not include norms. The test covers a wide range of skills in emergent literacy/readiness, reading, language arts, and mathematics. The topics covered by the reading section are shown in Figure 15.4. Section B contains graded oral reading passages in the form of an informal reading inventory, which includes assessment of word recognition accuracy and word recognition fluency ("oral reading level" and "oral reading rate") and comprehension. Sections A, C, and D assess very specific reading skills in word recognition and vocabulary.

II. READING

Test	Title	Test	Title	Test	Title
A. Word Recognition		C-2	Initial Consonant Sounds Auditorily	C-14	Common Endings of Rhyming Words
A-1	Word Recognition Grade Level	C-3	Initial Consonant Sounds Visually	C-15	Suffixes
A-2	Basic Sight Vocabulary	C-4	Substitution of Initial Consonant Sounds	C-16	Prefixes
A-3	Direction Words			C-17	Meaning of Prefixes
A-4	Abbreviations	C-5	Ending Sounds Auditorily	C-18	Number of Syllables Auditorily
A-5	Contractions	C-6	Vowels		
A-6	Common Signs	C-7	Short Vowel Sounds	C-19	Syllabication Concepts
B. Reading		C-8	Long Vowel Sounds	**D. Vocabulary**	
B-1	Oral Reading Level	C-9	Initial Clusters Auditorily	D-1	Context Clues
B-2	Reading Comprehension Level	C-10	Initial Clusters Visually	D-2	Classification
B-3	Oral Reading Rate	C-11	Substitution of Initial Cluster Sounds	D-3	Analogies
				D-4	Antonyms
C. Word Analysis		C-12	Digraphs and Diphthongs	D-5	Homonyms
C-1	Auditory Discrimination	C-13	Phonetic Irregularities		

FIGURE 15.4
BRIGANCE® Diagnostic Inventory of Basic Skills—Reading Section
Reprinted with the permission of the publisher, Curriculum Associates, Inc., North Billerica, MA 01862.

A student's performance on any subtest of the *Brigance Diagnostic Inventory* can be directly translated into an instructional objective. For example, if a student does not "pass" the Long Vowel Subtest, the test provides a specific instructional objective.

> When presented with one-syllable words having the patterns "consonant, vowel consonant, and final e" or "consonant, double vowel, consonant," the student will pronounce the vowel(s) with a long sound. He will be able to perform this task for _____ (quantity) of the five vowels. (p. 54)

Performance on a subtest may be immediately transferred to into a specific goal. This feature makes the *Brigance Diagnostic Inventory* valuable for formulating the Individualized Education Program (IEP) of a student who has been identified as needing special education services.

Diagnostic Tests of Specific Areas

Tests of specific areas concentrate on an in-depth evaluation of a specific area of reading. They are particularly useful in gathering very detailed information about one area of reading, such as the student's abilities in phonics. Diagnostic tests of one area can be group or individual tests, and they can be norm- or criterion-referenced tests. One example is the *Test of Reading Comprehension*. These tests are described in Appendix A.

Measuring Intelligence

Perhaps no concept has provided more controversy in education than the measure of intelligence. Heated public debate periodically erupts on the nature of intelligence, its role in achievement, and the role of culture in intelligence. This important measure is used in making decisions about who is entitled to special education services and, in some instances, who should be classified as reading disabled (see Chapter 13). For this reason, we devote a special section to the measurement of intelligence.

The full concept of intelligence is much richer than what is actually measured by intelligence tests. Intelligence includes mechanical ability, street knowledge, creativity, and social skills. However, most intelligence (IQ) tests simply predict whether an individual is likely to do well in schoolwork, especially in learning tasks with highly verbal content (Salvia & Ysseldyke, 1995). Therefore, intelligence tests can be best regarded as measures of scholastic aptitude.

An IQ score, in part, reflects a student's background. Intelligence scores are also affected by a student's comfort with the testing situation. Thus, we cannot measure *intelligence* with absolute accuracy. Nor do we know how much a particular student might ultimately achieve. Intelligence tests measure only the current potential for learning; future potential is unknown. In summary, IQ must be interpreted in a judicious manner.

Teachers should remember that the content of these tests and the validity of their scores have come under serious criticism. An IQ test cannot give a definitive or permanent rating of a student's mental ability. Thus, teachers should be alert to the many other sources of information about students, including behavior in class, independence in living, and interests and accomplishments outside the school setting.

Using Intelligence Test Information in Reading Assessment

The purpose of obtaining information on a student's cognitive abilities and aptitude for learning is to help the teacher better understand the reading problem. The intelligence test information can be used to (1) assess a student's current potential, (2) analyze a student's component cognitive abilities, and (3) observe the student's behavior during the testing situation. Each of these uses is discussed below.

Assessing a Student's Potential.

As we described in Chapter 13, information from an intelligence test can help the teacher determine whether a student has the potential to read better than he or she does at present. To illustrate this use, in evaluating Ellen, we find that her intelligence test score indicates a potential for reading which is much higher than her present reading achievement level. This discrepancy between potential and performance shows she has the cognitive ability to read much better than she does at present. In contrast, in evaluating Mark, we conclude that although he is reading poorly, he is actually doing fairly well in relation to his potential for learning. Mark, however, will still benefit from reading instruction suited to his individual needs.

When evaluating a student with suspected learning disabilities, federal law (Individuals with Disabilities in Education Act–IDEA) requires the evaluation team to consider whether the student has a severe discrepancy between the potential for learning and the current level of performance. Methods for determining the discrepancy are discussed in Chapter 13.

Analyzing a Student's Component Cognitive Abilities.

Intelligence is more than a single general factor. The component theory of intelligence suggests that it comprises many separate abilities (Sternberg, 1985). In addition to providing an overall general score (IQ score), many tests of intelligence contain subtests and subscales that measure different (or component) cognitive functions. These tests help us analyze the student's strengths and weaknesses in learning aptitude. Several methods are used in determining cognitive patterns in students with reading and learning problems (Breen, 1986).

1. *Comparison of subscales.* The subscales contained in some intelligence tests allow us to compare cognitive abilities. The widely used Wechsler Intelligence Scales (including *WISC-III, WPPSI-R, WAIS-R*) classify subtests as either verbal tests or performance tests. The *Kaufman Assessment Battery for Children* identifies sequential and simultaneous processing.
2. *Evidence of subtest scatter and variability.* Some intelligence tests, such as the *Wechsler Intelligence Scales for Children–Third edition (WISC-III)* and the *Woodcock–Johnson Psycho-Educational Battery–Revised Test of Cognitive Abilities,* and the *Kaufman Assessment Battery for Children* contain subtests which tap differing abilities. A significant scatter among subtest scores, with a student doing well in some subtests and poorly in others, suggests variability in cognitive functioning. However, authorities caution against the overinterpretation of subtest scatter (Taylor, Partenio, & Ziegler, 1983).

3. *Recategorization of subtest scores to ascertain unique cognitive patterns.* Some analysts suggest that subtest scores be regrouped or clustered to provide insight into the student's cognitive functioning. Different methods for regrouping have been advocated. Bannatyne (1974) suggests regrouping the subtests of the *WISC* into four areas: spatial ability, verbal conceptualization ability, and acquired knowledge. Kaufman (1981) uses factor analysis to regroup *Wechsler Intelligence Scale for Children–Revised (WISC-R)* subtests into clusters of verbal comprehension, perceptual organization, and freedom from distractibility.

The scoring system of the *Woodcock–Johnson Psycho-Educational Battery–Revised– Tests of Cognitive Ability* enables the tester to group individual subtests to obtain general clusters of cognitive factors, including verbal ability, reasoning, perceptual speed, and memory (Breen, 1986).

Subtest clustering has come under some criticism. Kavale and Forness (1987) point out problems in the research underlying such clustering. Although they view this type of research as promising, they suggest that more investigation is needed before clusters can be used with confidence.

Observing a Student's Behavior.

Testers have the opportunity to observe students as they take intelligence tests. The tester can observe which activities the student enjoys, which activities are frustrating, and how the student goes about doing tasks. For this reason, examiners watch carefully as students use problem-solving strategies to perform the many different tasks on an IQ test.

Types of Intelligence Tests

Instruments that assess intellectual ability can be divided into two types: group tests and individual tests. Group tests are designed to be given to several students at a time, and they are sometimes routinely administered as screening devices to identify those pupils who are different enough from average to warrant a more thorough examination. A drawback of group intelligence tests is that they often require students to read, making the IQ score dependent upon reading ability. In addition, they do not provide in-depth information (Salvia & Ysseldyke, 1995). In general, then, more credence is given to individual intelligence tests than to group tests.

Individual tests must be given to an individual student. Some individual intelligence tests must be given by a trained examiner, and often this person is the school psychologist. Although other individual tests can be given by a reading teacher, these also require training in administration and scoring.

A listing and brief description of tests of intelligence and potential are presented in the test inventory in Appendix A. Some individual intelligence tests that are frequently used in a reading diagnosis are discussed below.

The *Wechsler Intelligence Scale for Children–III (WISC-III)* is one of the most frequently administered individual intelligence tests. It must be administered by a trained examiner, usually the school psychologist. However, in diagnosing a student's reading problem, teachers can make good use of the information obtained in the *WISC-III* by examining subtest scores, as well as the scores of the Full IQ, Verbal IQ, and Performance IQ. The test covers ages six to sixteen. (Other Wechsler tests cover younger and older individuals; see Appendix A.)

The *WISC-III* is particularly useful for measuring component subskills of intelligence. The test yields a Verbal IQ score, a Performance IQ score, and a full IQ score. There are thirteen subtests: six verbal and seven performance. A full score is obtained by giving five verbal subtests and five performance subtests.

Verbal Scale
1. *Information:* answering information questions.
2. *Similarities:* noting how two things are alike.
3. *Arithmetic:* solving timed problems.
4. *Vocabulary:* defining words.
5. *Comprehension:* dealing with everyday situations and abstract issues.
6. Alternate Test: *Digit Span:* repeating digits forward and backward.

Performance Scale
1. *Picture Completion:* Determining missing items.
2. *Coding:* matching and writing symbols and numbers.
3. *Picture Arrangements:* sequencing pictures to "tell a story."
4. *Block Design:* Duplicating a pictorial design with red and white blocks.
5. *Object Assembly:* fitting puzzle pieces together.
6. Alternate Test: *Mazes:* finding the way through a maze.
7. Alternate test for coding only: *Symbol Search:* searching to see if a target symbol appears on a "search" group.

The examiner converts the raw score on each subtest to a standard (or scaled) score. The average standard score is 10. By comparing the various subtest scores, the patterns in the components of mental functioning may be revealed. Students with learning problems exhibit somewhat more "scatter," or differences among subscales, than normal learners (Kaufman, 1981). In addition, students with reading problems tend to have higher scores in performance IQ than verbal IQ (Moore & Wielan, 1981).

The *Woodcock–Johnson Psycho-Educational Battery–Revised* is an individual test that can be used for a wide range of ages. There are two parts: (1) Tests of Cognitive Ability and, (2) Tests of Achievement (mentioned earlier in this chapter). The test can be administered by teachers and is designed so that a discrepancy analysis can be developed by comparing aptitude and achievement scores. It uses subtest clusters for interpretation and a computer program is available to assist the scorer.

Our interest here is with the first part, the *Tests of Cognitive Abilities.* The Standard Battery of the cognitive subtests consist of seven tests:

- *Memory for Names:* Auditory–visual tasks in which the individual learns the names of nine pictures of space creatures.
- *Memory for Sentences:* The ability to repeat orally presented sentences.
- *Visual Matching:* A timed assessment of skill in identifying two identical numbers in a row of six numbers.
- *Incomplete Words:* Words with one or more missing phonemes that the student is to identify.
- *Visual Closure:* The identification of visual stimuli in distorted or incomplete pictures.

- *Picture Vocabulary:* The ability to identify pictured objects or actions.
- *Analysis–Synthesis:* The ability to analyze the parts of an equivalency statement and create a new one.

The supplementary battery of the Cognitive Tests consists of another fourteen subtests.

The achievement part of the *Woodcock–Johnson Psycho-Educational Battery–Revised* consists of fourteen achievement subtests, which test four academic areas: reading, mathematics, written language, and knowledge. (Two subtests are the same as those in the *Woodcock Reading Mastery Test–Revised.*) The scores of the *Woodcock–Johnson–Revised* can be combined into seven cognitive factor clusters, four scholastic aptitude clusters, two oral language clusters, and three total scores.

The *Slosson Intelligence Test–Revised (SIT-R)* is an individual test and can be administered by teachers. This relatively short screening test includes many items that appear in the Stanford–Binet Intelligence Scale (see the test inventory in Appendix A). The test yields a single IQ score. It covers a wide age range of ages, but norms are based on a relatively small sample.

The *Kaufman Assessment Battery for Children* contains two processing scales that can be combined into a Mental Processing Scale. A nonverbal scale can also be included in assessing intelligence. In addition to these scales, which measure cognitive functioning, an Achievement Scale measures school achievement. Two of the subtests in the achievement test measure reading.

The subtests of the basic cognitive battery relevant to school-aged children include:

Sequential Processing Scale
- *Hand Movements:* recreating a sequence of taps the examiner makes;
- *Number Recall:* repeating digits;
- *Word Order:* pointing to silhouettes of common objects in the order that was named.

Simultaneous Processing Scale
- *Gestalt Closure:* completing and describing an inkblot drawing;
- *Triangles:* assembling triangles to match a design;
- *Matrix Analogies:* selecting a picture or design to complete a visual analogy;
- *Spatial Memory:* remembering where pictures were arranged on a page;
- *Photo Series:* organizing and sequencing photos that illustrate an event.

The test is also available in a shortened form, called the *Kaufman BIT.* The Kaufman scales are considered adequate in reliability and validity.

Interpreting Intelligence Test Scores

Modern intelligence scores are reported as deviation scores, as a student's score is compared with the scores of a norm group. IQ score is based upon the concept of a normal curve, as shown in Figure 15.5. An IQ of 100 is designated as the mean for each age group. As shown in Figure 15.5, approximately 34 percent of the population will fall within one standard deviation below the mean and 34 percent of the population will fall within one standard deviation above the mean.

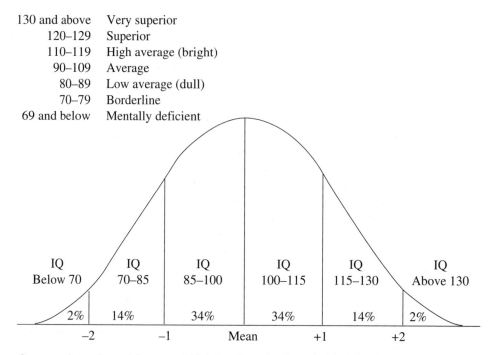

130 and above	Very superior
120–129	Superior
110–119	High average (bright)
90–109	Average
80–89	Low average (dull)
70–79	Borderline
69 and below	Mentally deficient

•Scores are clustered around the mean, which is the tallest point. A standard deviation (SD) is a number (e.g., in the WISC-R it is 15). A child scoring one standard deviation above the mean, if the mean is 100 and the standard deviation is 15, would score 115. A child scoring two standard deviations above the mean would score 130. The percentages show what percent of the population is included in any standard deviation. For example, 34 percent of the people score between zero and one standard deviation below (or above) the mean. Two percent of the population scores between two and three standard deviations below (or above) the mean.

FIGURE 15.5
Distribution of *WISC* IQ Scores on a Normal Curve

To illustrate, on the *WISC-III,* one standard deviation is 15 points. Therefore, 34 percent of the population will score between 85 and 100, and 34 percent of the population will score between 100 and 115.

Intelligence ranges for the *WISC-III* are shown below. Teachers will find them useful for reporting results of this IQ test to parents. If tests other than the *WISC-III* are used, the test manual should be consulted for the IQ range for those tests. Although almost all IQs have means of 100, there is some variation in the standard deviations reported.

In addition, *WISC-III* scores can be interpreted as follows:

130 and above	Very superior
120–129	Superior
110–119	High average (bright)
90–109	Average
80–89	Low average (dull)
70–79	Borderline
69 and below	Mentally deficient

Summary

Formal tests are published tests meant to be administered according to prescribed procedures. Some are norm-referenced, and compare students to a norm sample. Others are criterion-referenced, and determine whether a student has achieved mastery. Formal tests that allow us to compare students to others of the same grade and age are familiar to professionals, permit objective decision making, and are required by some laws.

Scores on norm-referenced tests derive standard scores from raw scores, generally using means and standard deviations. Scores include reading grade score, percentiles, normal curve equivalents (NCEs), and stanines. Normed tests should have an adequate standardization sample, good validity (testing what is supposed to be tested), and reliability (stability of scores).

Tests of general reading assessment include survey tests (both group and individual), normed oral reading tests, and literacy tests. Diagnostic reading tests include batteries of specific skills and tests of individual areas.

Intelligence tests can be used to estimate a student's potential for school achievement, although this can change with appropriate conditions. Patterns of scores and behavior during testing also give insight into learning. Widely used intelligence tests include the *WISC-III, Woodcock–Johnson Psycho-Educational Battery, Kaufman Assessment Battery for Children* (and short form), and the *Slosson Intelligence Test.* IQ test scores are distributed on a normal curve distribution.

Appendix: Table of Tests

The following table presents tests frequently used in reading diagnoses. Many of these tests are described in the text of this book. This table includes tests of physical factors, intelligence and cognitive processing, language development, general achievement, reading tests: survey and diagnostic, and informal reading inventories. For each test, we have included the name of the test, its publisher, the ages or grades for which it may be used, levels included, a description of its contents, the scores yielded by the test, the estimated time needed for administration, and whether special training is needed to administer the test.

Tests of Physical Factors

Audiometer
Beltone Electronic Corporation
Maico Hearing Instruments
Used as a screening test to determine students' hearing threshold for series of tones at various frequencies and decibels. Results are graphed on an audiogram. *Individual administration:* 10–20 min.

Keystone Vision Screening for Schools
Keystone View Company
Comprised of two parts. Four-part rapid screening measure includes near-point and far-point items. Comprehensive measure includes fourteen subtests which test eye posture, binocular imbalance, binocular depth perception, color discrimination, usable binocular vision, and near-point and far-point acuity. Eyes tested separately and in coordination. Yields ratings of unsatisfactory, retest, and satisfactory. Provides analytical summary for reporting results. *Individual administration:* 10–15 min.

Orthorater
Bausch and Lomb

Contains twelve subtests that screen for binocular action of the eyes, nearpoint and farpoint vision, depth perception, and color discrimination. Norms are available for job-related activity. An adapted version may be used with children. *Individual administration:* 15–20 min.

Snellen Chart
American Optical Company

Consists of a wall chart containing rows of letters gradually decreasing in size in each descending row. The letters are read at a distance of twenty feet, testing only farpoint vision. *Individual administration:* 2–3 min.

Tests of Intelligence and Cognitive Processing

Detroit Tests of Learning Aptitude–3 DTLA–3
Ages 6–17
Stoelting Company

Provides detailed profiles of students' abilities and weaknesses. Used to diagnose learning disabilities. Includes eleven subtests: word opposites, design sequences to measure visual discrimination and memory, sentence imitation, reversed letters, story construction, design reproduction from memory, basic information, symbolic relations, word sequences, story sequences, and picture fragments. Provides an overall composite score and six domain composites: verbal, nonverbal, attention-enhanced, attention-reduced, motor-enhanced, and motor-reduced. Provides standard scores, percentiles, and age equivalents for subtests and composites. *Individual administration:* 50–120 min.

Kaufman Intelligence Tests
American Guidance Service, Inc.
Kaufman Assessment Battery for Children (K–ABC)
Ages 2.5–12.5

Includes 16 subtests. Sequential processing scale includes hand movements, number recall, and word order; child must arrange stimuli in sequential or serial order. Simultaneous processing scale includes magic windows, face recognition, Gestalt closure, triangles, matrix analogies, spatial memory, and photo series; requires integration and synthesis of information. Achievement scale includes expressive vocabulary, faces and places, arithmetic, riddles, reading/decoding, and reading/understanding; measures child's ability to apply processing skills to learning situations. Provides standard scores and percentile ranks; grade equivalents provided for arithmetic and reading subtests. *Individual administration:* 35 to 85 min. Special training needed for administration.

Kaufman Brief Intelligence Test (K–BIT)
Ages 4–90

Includes verbal and nonverbal subtests. Verbal subtests include expressive vocabulary and definitions. Nonverbal subtest requires students to solve problems using pictures and abstract designs. Provides verbal, performance, and composite IQ scores. *Individual administration:* 15 to 30 min. Requires graduate training in measurement to administer.

Kaufman Adolescent & Adult Intelligence Test (KAIT)   Ages 11–85+

Includes core and expanded batteries. Core battery consists of two scales: crystallized and fluid. Crystallized scale includes auditory comprehension, multiple word meanings, and word completion when provided a meaning clue. Fluid scale includes rebus learning, using codes, and using logic to solve problems. The expanded battery includes design memory, identifying famous people, using previously learned rebuses to "read," and auditory recall. Provides fluid, crystallized, and composite IQ scores. *Individual administration:* core battery, 60–90 min. Special training needed for administration.

Slosson Intelligence Test–Revised (SIT–R)
Ages 4–18
Slosson Educational Publishers

Designed to measure verbal intelligence in six areas: vocabulary, similarities and differences of objects or concepts, comprehension of common sayings, quantitative skills, and auditory memory for repeating sequences forward and backward. Yields a single quantitative index of intelligence. Norming samples and descriptions of norming procedures considered inadequate. Useful only as a screening device. *Individual administration:* 15–20 min.

Stanford–Binet Intelligence Scale, Fourth Edition
Ages 2–adult
Riverside Publishing Company

Consists of 15 subtests grouped in four areas: verbal reasoning, quantitative reasoning, abstract/visual reasoning, and short-term memory. Verbal reasoning includes vocabulary, absurdities, and verbal relations. Quantitative reasoning includes number series and equation building. Abstract/visual reasoning includes pattern analysis, copying, matrices, and paper folding and cutting. Short-term memory includes bead memory, memory for sentences, memory for digits, and memory for objects. Yields standard age scores for four areas and a composite IQ score. *Individual administration:* 60 to 90 min. Special training needed for administration.

Wechsler Intelligence Scales
The Psychological Corporation
Wechsler Intelligence Scale for Children, Third Edition (WISC–III)
Ages 6–16.11

A widely used individual measure of children's intellectual ability. Includes 10 core subtests and 3 supplemental subtests. Verbal subtests include: information, similarities, arithmetic, vocabulary, comprehension, and digit span (supplementary). Performance subtests include: picture completion, coding, picture arrangement, block design, object assembly, and symbol search and mazes (supplementary). Yields performance, verbal, and total standard scores and IQ. *Individual administration:* 50 to 70 min. Special training needed for administration.

Wechsler Preschool and Primary Scale of Intelligence–Revised (WPPSI–R)
Ages 3–7.3

Includes 12 subtests. Verbal subtests include: information, comprehension, similarities, arithmetic, vocabulary, and sentences (supplementary). Performance subtests include: picture completion, block design, object assembly, coding, mazes, and geometric design (visual recognition and discrimination for younger children and drawing of figures for older children). Yields verbal, performance, and full-scale standard scores and IQ. *Individual administration:* 75 min. Special training needed for administration.

Wechsler Adult Intelligence Scale–Revised (WAIS–R)
Ages 16–74

Includes 11 subtests. Verbal subtests include: information, comprehension, similarities, arithmetic, vocabulary, and digit span. Performance subtests include: picture arrangement, block design, object assembly, coding, and picture completion (supplementary). Yields IQ scores. *Individual administration:* 75 min. Special training needed for administration.

Woodcock–Johnson Psycho-Educational Battery–Revised
Ages 2–90+
Riverside

Includes tests of cognitive ability and achievement.

Test of Cognitive Ability

Cognitive battery comprised of a standard battery and a supplemental battery. Standard battery consists of seven subtests: memory for names, memory for sentences, visual matching, incomplete words, visual closure, picture vocabulary, and analysis–synthesis. The Early Development Battery consists of memory for names, memory for sentences, incomplete words, visual closure, and picture vocabulary. The supplementary battery consists of: visual–auditory learning, memory for words, cross out, sound blending, picture recognition, oral vocabulary, concept formation, delayed recall to test memory for names, delayed recall to test visual–auditory learning, reversed numbers, sound patterns, spatial relations, listening comprehension, and verbal analogies. *Individual administration:* Early Development Battery, 30–40 min.

Tests of Achievement

Standard battery includes letter-word identification, passage comprehension, calculation, applied problems, dictation, writing samples, science, social studies, and humanities. Supplemental battery includes five subtests: word attack, reading vocabulary, quantitative concepts, proofing, and writing fluency. Provides individual test scores and cluster scores, standard scores, and age and grade equivalents for K–16.9. *Individual administration:* 30–40 min.

Tests of Language Development

Comprehensive Receptive and Expressive Vocabulary Test (CREVT)
Ages 4–17
Riverside
Consists of two subtests. In the expressive vocabulary subtest, students provide definitions of words pronounced by examiners. In the receptive vocabulary subtest, students point to pictures of words pronounced by examiners. Pictures are color photographs rather than line drawings. Two equivalent forms. Provides standard scores, percentiles, and age equivalents. *Individual administration:* 45 min.

Goldman–Fristoe Test of Articulation
Ages 2–16+
American Guidance Service, Inc.
Measures students' ability to articulate consonant sounds in initial, medial, and final positions. Includes three subtests: Sounds-in-words which requires students to identify pictures; Sounds-in-sentences, which measures sound production as students engage in connected speech; Stimulability, in which examiners pronounce words previously mispronounced by students to determine if they can correctly produce modeled sounds. Sounds-in-words and stimulability subtests yield percentile ranks. *Individual administration:* 30–60 min.

Peabody Picture Vocabulary Test–Revised (PPVT–R)
Ages 2.5–Adult
American Guidance Service, Inc.
Measures receptive vocabulary. Each item consists of four pictures; administrator pronounces a stimulus word and student points to corresponding picture. Consists of two equivalent forms. Yields standard scores, percentile ranks, stanines, and age equivalents. *Individual administration:* 10–20 min.

Test de Vocabulario en Imagenes Peabody (TVIP)
Ages 2.5–18
American Guidance Service, Inc.
Based on the *PPVT–R,* for Spanish-speaking and bilingual students. Manual available in English and Spanish. Provides standard scores, percentile ranks, and age equivalents. *Individual administration:* 10–15 min.

Test of Adolescent Language (TOAL–3)
Ages 12–24
Riverside
A comprehensive evaluation for adolescents and adults. Consists of ten subtests to measure listening, speaking, reading, writing, spoken language, written language, vocabulary, grammar, receptive language, and expressive language. Yields standard scores. *Individual administration:* 40–60 min.

Tests of Language Development, Primary and Intermediate (TOLD–2)
American Guidance Service, Inc.
Assesses understanding and use of spoken words, grammar, pronunciation, and ability to distinguish between similar-sounding words. *Individual administration:* 40–60 min.

TOLD–2, Primary
Ages 4–8.11
Includes seven subtests. In the picture vocabulary subtest, students point to pictures of words pronounced by examiners. In oral vocabulary, students provide definitions of stimulus words. Grammatic understanding measures ability to understand syntactic structures. Sentence imitation requires repetition of complex sentences. In grammatic completion, students provide the last words in sentences. In words discrimination, students identify pairs of similar words as the same or different. Word articulation measures ability to pronounce individual words. Provides standard scores, percentile ranks, and age equivalents for subtests as well as listening, speaking, semantics, syntax, and phonology. *Individual administration:* 40–60 min.

TOLD–2, Intermediate
Ages 8.6–12.11
Subtests include: generalizations, malapropisms, and vocabulary to assess understanding and use of spoken words, sentence combining, word ordering, and grammatic comprehension. Yields standard scores and percentile ranks. *Individual administration:* 40 min.

Tests of Word Finding
Riverside
Test of Word Finding (TWF)
Ages 6.6–12.11
Includes six sections: picture naming of nouns, picture naming of verbs, sentence completion naming, description naming, category naming, and vocabulary comprehension. Measures both speed and accuracy. Yields standard scores and percentile ranks. Includes grade norms for grades 1–6. Provides suggestions for analyzing gestures, extra verbalizations, and substitution types. *Individual administration:* 20–30 min.

Test of Adolescent/Adult Word Finding (TAWF)
Ages 12–80
Companion test to TAWF, with similar subtests. TAW includes a 40-item brief test. Yields standard scores and percentile ranks, with grade norms included for grades 6–12. *Individual administration:* 20–30 min.

Test of Word Knowledge (TOWK)
Psychological Corporation
Assesses knowledge of figurative language, multiple meanings, conjunctions, transition words, receptive vocabulary, and expressive vocabulary. Core Battery consists of two receptive language and two expressive language subtests. Includes supplementary sub-

tests. Provides raw scores, standard scores, receptive composite scores, expressive composite scores, total scores, age equivalents, percentile ranks, normal curve equivalents, stanines, and means.

Level 1
Ages 5–8
Subtests include expressive vocabulary, word definitions, receptive vocabulary, and word opposites. Supplementary subtest, Synonyms, included for 6- to 8-year-olds. *Individual administration:* 25–30 min.

Level 2
Ages 8–17
Subtests include word definitions, multiple contexts, synonyms, and figurative use. Supplementary subtests include word opposites, receptive vocabulary, expressive vocabulary, conjunctions, and transition words. *Individual administration:* 40–65 min.

Tests of Overall Academic Achievement

BRIGANCE Inventories
Curriculum Associates
Provides assessment in: readiness, speech, word recognition and placement, oral reading, reading comprehension, listening, word analysis, reference skills, graph and maps, spelling, writing, and mathematics. Criterion referenced, helpful in developing IEPs. Software for writing IEPs and monitoring student progress available for both IBM and Macintosh. *Individual administration:* 15–90 min.

BRIGANCE Diagnostic Inventory of Early Development–Revised
Ages Birth–7
Includes 11 skill areas: preambulatory motor, gross motor, fine motor, self-help, speech and language, general knowledge and comprehension, social and emotional development, readiness, basic reading, manuscript writing, and basic math.

BRIGANCE Diagnostic Comprehensive Inventory of Basic Skills
Grades Pre-K–9
Includes assessment in 22 skill areas: readiness, speech, word recognition, oral reading, reading comprehension, listening, word analysis, reference skills, graphs and maps, spelling, writing, and math.

Brigance Diagnostic Inventory of Basic Skills
Grades K–6
Assesses strengths and weaknesses in fourteen skill areas: readiness, word recognition, reading, word analysis, vocabulary, handwriting, grammar and mechanics, spelling, reference skills, math placement, numbers, operations, measurement, and geometry.

Brigance Diagnostic Assessment of Basic Skills, Spanish Edition
Grades K–8
Includes ten major areas: readiness, speech, word recognition, oral reading, reading comprehension, word analysis, listening, writing and alphabetizing, numbers and computation, and measurement.

Brigance Diagnostic Inventory of Essential Skills
Grades 6–Adult
Assesses strengths and weakness of secondary students in three academic areas. Reading/Language Arts includes word recognition, oral reading, reading comprehension, word analysis, writing, and spelling. Math includes numbers, number facts, computation, measurement, metrics, and math vocabulary. Study skills includes reference skills, schedules and graphs, and forms. Life skills assessments include food and clothing, money and finance, travel and transportation, and communication and telephone skills. Rates abilities in applied skills, such as health and attitude, responsibility and self-discipline, job interview preparation, communication, and auto safety.

California Achievement Tests
Grades K–12
CTB/Macmillan/McGraw-Hill
Organized into three broad areas: Reading/Language Arts, Mathematics, and Supplementary Content Areas. Each level includes two equivalent forms. Also provides a locator test to determine appropriate levels for administration. This allows examiners to test students on performance levels rather than grade placement levels. Yields percentile ranks, stanines, grade equivalents, normal curve equivalents, and scale scores. Also provides curriculum referenced scores. *Group administration:* time varies.

Iowa Tests of Basic Skills and Tests of Achievement and Proficiency
Riverside

Iowa Tests of Basic Skills (ITBS)
Grades K–8
Basic battery measures vocabulary, reading, writing, listening, mathematics, and study skills. Supplementary subtests measure science and social studies. Two forms available at each level. Yields raw scores, standard scores, grade equivalents, national percentile ranks, stanines, and normal curve equivalents. Both norm and criterion referenced.

Iowa Test of Achievement and Proficiency
Levels 15–18 Grades 9–12
Subtests include listening, writing, reading comprehension, written expression, using sources of information, spelling, capitalization, punctuation, usage, language organization, letters and themes, mathematics, science, and social studies. *Group administration:* time varies.

Kaufman Test of Educational Achievement
Grades 1–12
American Guidance Service, Inc.

Comprehensive Form
Consists of five subtests: reading decoding, reading comprehension, mathematics applications, mathematics computation, and spelling. Provides individual subtest scores and composite scores by grade or age, percentile ranks, stanines, normal curve equivalents, and age and grade equivalents. *Individual administration:* 30–75 min.

Brief Form
Consists of three subtests: mathematics, reading, and spelling. Provides norm-referenced subtest scores and a battery composite. *Individual administration:* 20–30 min.

Peabody Individual Achievement Test–Revised (PIAT–R)
Ages 5–18
American Guidance Service, Inc.
Consists of 6 subtests: general information, reading recognition, reading comprehension, spelling, mathematics, and written expression. Written expression consists of two levels, Level I for K–1, and Level II for Grades 2–12. Provides standard scores, age and grade equivalents, percentile ranks, normal curve equivalents, and stanines. *Individual administration:* 60 min.

Stanford Achievement Test Series
Grades K–Community College
Psychological Corporation
Consists of three measures: the Stanford Early School Achievement Test (SESAT), the Stanford Achievement Test (SAT), and the Test of Achievement Skills. Basic battery can be used to assess reading, mathematics, and/or listening comprehension. Norm and criterion referenced. *Group administration:* Times vary.

Wechsler Individual Achievement Test (WIAT)
Ages 5–19
American Guidance Service, Inc.
Comprehensive Form
Consists of eight subtests: basic reading, mathematics reasoning, spelling, reading comprehension, numerical operations, listening comprehension, oral expression, and written expression. Provides age and grade-based standard scores, composite scores, percentile ranks, stanines, normal curve equivalents, and age and grade equivalents. *Individual administration:* 30–75 min.

Screener Form
Includes basic reading, mathematics, reasoning, and spelling. Provides scores comparable to comprehensive form. *Individual administration:* 10–18 min.

Wide Range Achievement Test–Revised (WRAT–3)
Ages 5–75
Riverside

Consists of three subtests: reading, which includes recognizing and naming letters and pronouncing printed words; spelling, which includes copying letters, writing one's name, and printing words; and arithmetic, which includes counting, reading numerals, and oral and written computation. Two equivalent forms. Provides raw scores, standard scores, percentile ranks, and grade equivalents. *Individual administration for reading; small group administration for spelling and arithmetic:* 15–30 min.

Reading Tests: Survey and Diagnostic

Diagnostic Assessment of Reading with Trial Teaching Strategies
Grades 1–12, Adult
Riverside
Diagnostic Assessments of Reading

Identifies strengths and weaknesses in reading through six areas: word recognition, word analysis, oral reading, silent reading comprehension, spelling, and word meaning. Identifies students' reading levels. *Individual administration:* 20–30 min.

Trial Teaching Strategies

Provides a series of teaching sessions to identify most effective methods and materials for individual students. Provides three reading levels: potential, instructional, and independent. Criterion referenced. *Individual administration:* 30 min.

Formal Reading Inventory
Grades 1–12
Pro-Ed

Consists of four forms: Students read Forms A and C silently, and Forms B and D orally. Each form contains thirteen graded passages. After reading each passage, students answer five multiple-choice questions. Miscues in the oral reading passages are categorized according to their similarity to the target words by meaning, function, or graphic/phonemic. If miscues fit more than one category they are scored as multiple sources; self-corrections are also recorded. Scores include a silent reading comprehension quotient, percentiles for silent reading comprehension, and oral reading miscue classification. Forms B and D are identical to the passages in the Gray Oral Reading Test. Examiners may use the manual from this test to determine an oral reading comprehension score. *Individual administration:* 15 min.

Gates–MacGinitie Reading Test
Grades K–12
Riverside

Measures vocabulary and reading comprehension. Yields standard scores, grade equivalents, stanines, percentile ranks, grade equivalents, and normal curve equivalents. Readiness, prereading and grade 1, one form; levels 2 through 10–12, two forms.

Level PRE: Pre-Reading Evaluation
Grades K.5–1.5
Subtests include literacy concepts, reading instruction relational concepts, oral language concepts and linguistic awareness, and letters and letter–sound correspondences. *Group administration:* 85–105 min.

Level R: Beginning Reading Skills
Grades 1.0–1.9
Subtests include initial consonants and consonant clusters, final consonants and consonant clusters, vowels, and use of sentence context. Provides norms tables for grades 1.0–2.5. *Group administration:* 55–70 min.

Levels 1–2
Grades 1.4–2.9
Subtests include vocabulary and comprehension, which requires students to choose pictures to illustrate passages. *Group administration:* 55 min.

Levels 3–10/12
Grades 3.0–12.9
Subtests include vocabulary and comprehension. Vocabulary consists of four choices to define a target word. Comprehension consists of short passages followed by multiple choice questions. *Group administration:* 55 min.

Gates–McKillop–Horowitz Reading Diagnostic Tests
Grades 1–6
Teachers College Press
Tests oral reading, sight knowledge, phonics, spelling, and writing. Subtests include: Sets of graded short oral reading paragraphs; four reading sentences with regular words; flashwords presented with tachistoscope; untimed word list for sight recognition and analysis; word attack test, using nonsense words to test syllabication, recognizing and blending word parts, reading words, letter sounds, and naming capital and lowercase letters; identifying spoken vowel sounds; auditory blending and discrimination; spelling test; informal writing sample. Provides grade equivalent scores and informal ratings. Also provides analysis of oral reading errors and phonics skills. *Individual administration:* 60–90 min.

Gray Oral Reading Test, Third Edition (GORT–3)
Ages 7–17
Riverside
Two equivalent forms containing thirteen sequenced passages. Each passage is followed by five comprehension questions. Provides standard scores and percentile ranks. Provides a system to analyze miscues by meaning similarity, function similarity, graphic/phonemic similarity, and self-correction. Norm referenced. *Individual administration:* 45 min.

Gray Oral Reading Test–Diagnostic (GORT–D)
Grades K–6
Pro-Ed

Used as a supplement to the GORT–3. Two equivalent forms to use with beginning readers. Subtest on paragraph reading administered first. Other subtests, administered to students who perform poorly on paragraph reading, include decoding, word identification, word attack, morphemic analysis, contextual analysis, and word ordering. Provides grade equivalents, standard scores for subtests and composites, and percentile ranks. *Individual administration:* 45 min.

Stanford Diagnostic Reading Test, Third Edition
Grades 1.5–12
Psychological Corporation

Includes auditory discrimination, phonetic analysis, and structural analysis. Four levels, with two equivalent forms at each level. Norm and criterion referenced. Provides raw scores for each subtest, percentile ranks, stanines, grade equivalents, and scaled scores.

Red Level
Grades 1.5–3.5

Subtests include auditory vocabulary, auditory discrimination, phonetic analysis with consonants and vowels, word reading, and reading comprehension in sentences and paragraphs. *Group administration:* 105 min.

Green Level
Grades 3.0–5.5

Subtests include auditory vocabulary, auditory discrimination, phonetic analysis, structural analysis, and reading comprehension. *Group administration:* 114 min.

Brown Level
Grades 5.0–9.5

Subtests include auditory vocabulary, reading comprehension, phonetic analysis, structural analysis, and reading rate. *Group administration:* 108 min.

Blue Level
Grades 8.5–12.8

Subtests include reading comprehension, vocabulary, word parts, phonetic analysis, structural analysis, scanning and skimming, and fast reading. *Group administration:* 116 min.

Test of Reading Comprehension, Third Edition (TORC–3)
Ages 7–17
Psychological Corporation

Measures silent reading. Four subtests include general vocabulary, syntactic similarities, paragraph reading, and sentence sequencing. Supplementary subtests include reading vocabulary in math, science, social studies, and directions. Provides standard scores. *Group administration:* 30 min.

Woodcock Reading Mastery Tests–Revised (WRMT–R)
Ages 5–75+
American Guidance Service, Inc.
Consists of two forms. Form G includes two readiness tests and four achievement tests: visual–auditory learning, letter identification, word identification, word attack, word comprehension, and passage comprehension. Form H includes four achievement tests: word identification, word attack, word comprehension (measures reading vocabulary in reading, science/mathematics, social studies, and humanities), and passage comprehension. Provides percentile ranks, standard scores, normal curve equivalents, and age and grade equivalents. *Individual administration:* 10–30 min.

Observational Survey

An Observation Survey of Early Literacy Achievement
Beginning Literacy
Marie M. Clay
Heinemann
Systematic observational procedures for teachers to be used with *Sand* and *Stones* and *Reading Recovery: A Guidebook for Teachers in Training,* also by Marie M. Clay. *Introduction* provides techniques for observing progress in oral language and emergent literacy, detecting difficulties, and early intervention. *The Observation Survey: Part One* includes directions for taking running records, procedures for observing text reading, a sample running record sheet, and directions for analyzing reading behaviors. *The Observation Survey: Part Two* includes letter identification; the "Concepts about Print" test, a sample score sheet; Word Tests and score sheets; Writing Samples, a sample writing vocabulary observation sheet, and a Weekly Record Sheet; a Dictation Task, and an observation sheet. Directions for administration and scoring and guidelines for interpretation of results included for each task. Also includes suggestions for summarizing results of the Observation Survey and a Survey Summary Sheet. *Individual administration:* 30–60 min.

Informal Reading Inventories

Analytical Reading Inventory, Fourth Edition
Levels: Primer–9
Mary Lynn Woods and Alden J. Moe
Macmillan Publishing Company
Includes three forms, with ten passages at each reading level and seven twenty-item word lists for each form, Primer–Sixth grade levels. Also includes science passages and social studies passages, written on Levels 1–9. Passages at Levels Primer–2 are followed by six comprehension questions. Passages at Levels 3–9 after followed by eight comprehension questions. Yields independent, instructional, and frustration reading levels. Also provides suggestions for analyzing miscues. Includes some guidelines for retellings. *Individual administration:* 30–60 min.

Basic Reading Inventory, Sixth Edition
Levels: Pre-Primer–10
Jerry L. Johns
Kendall/Hunt Publishing Company

Includes five forms. Equivalent forms A, B, and C each consist of word lists for Levels Pre-primer through Grade 10 and graded passages at the Pre-primer level through Grade 8. Form A is used for oral reading, Form B for silent reading, and Form C to determine a listening level. Form LN includes longer narrative passages at Levels 3 through 10. Form LE includes expository passages written on Levels 3 through 10. Yields independent, instructional, frustration, and listening comprehension levels. Analysis of miscues and retellings also included. *Individual administration:* 30–90 min.

Flynt–Cooter Reading Inventory for the Classroom
Grades 1–9
Gorsuch Scarisbrick, Publishers

Includes three forms. Forms A and B are narrative passages Levels 1 through 9. Form C has expository passages Levels 1 through 9. Sets of three sentences written at each level determine initial passage selection. Each passage is introduced with a background statement. Next, students read the passage silently and retell it. Then the examiner asks comprehension questions. Next, the examiner asks students to read the passage orally in order to access miscues. Yields reading levels. *Individual administration:* 30–60 min.

Qualitative Reading Inventory–II
Levels: Pre-primer–Jr. High
Lauren Leslie and JoAnne Caldwell
HarperCollins, Publishers, Inc.

Includes twenty-item word lists at Preprimer through Junior High reading levels. Provides four passages written on each level for Preprimer through Level 2, six passages at each of Levels 3 through Junior High. Includes both fiction and nonfiction passages at all levels. Features questions to tap students' prior knowledge of concepts crucial to comprehension of passages. Includes both retellings and questions about each selection. Includes explicit and implicit comprehension questions. Yields independent, instructional, and frustration levels. Includes a miscue analysis worksheet and excellent retelling scoring guides for examiners for each passage. Some passages at Preprimer through Level 2 include pictures to determine students' dependence on context clues.

Includes a miscue analysis worksheet. Authors have also provided retelling scoring guides for each passage.

Classroom Reading Inventory, Seventh Edition
Grades 1–Adult
Nicholas J. Silvaroli
Brown and Benchmark, Publishers

Contains four forms, each consisting of graded word lists and graded passages, with five comprehension questions for each passage. Also includes an optional spelling survey, levels 1 through 6. Forms A and B contain word lists and passages for levels pre-primer through grade 6. Form A is a more traditional, skills-based format, and Form B is a more literature-based format. Forms C and D contain graded word lists and passages from levels 1 through 8, written for more mature students. Yields independent, instructional, and frustrational reading levels, as well as listening capacity. Provides guidelines to analyze oral reading errors and comprehension errors. *Individual administration*: Approximately 12 minutes

Informal Reading Inventory, Second Edition
Grades 1–12
Paul C. Burns & Betty D. Roe
Houghton Mifflin

Contains four equivalent forms, each consisting of graded word lists and passages, levels pre-primer through grade 12, with comprehension quetions for each passage. Passages for upper grades include articles about science and social sciences. Yields independent, instructional, and frustrational levels. Provides guidelines to analyze oral reading errors and comprehension errors. *Individual administration:* 20-40 minutes

Appendix: Instructional Materials for Students with Reading Problems

HIGH INTEREST BOOKS
PREDICTABLE BOOKS
MATERIALS FOR FOCUSED INSTRUCTION
    MULTI-AREA DEVELOPMENT
    WORD RECOGNITION
    VOCABULARY DEVELOPMENT
    COMPREHENSION
    STUDY STRATEGIES/CONTENT AREAS
    RATE
REAL-LIFE MATERIALS/FUNCTIONAL READING

Abbreviations Used in This Appendix
    RL denotes Reading Level

    IL denotes Interest Level

Both interest and reading levels are given in grades throughout this table. Interest Levels are only listed when they differ from Reading Levels.

High-Interest Books
    A Matter for Judgment (Globe Fearon) **RL** 4–5 **IL** 6–12, adult

        A collection of stories involving moral conflict that invites reader judgment of character.

    Achievers (The Learner Group) **RL** 4+ **IL** reluctant reader, adult

        Composed of 9 biographies.

Adventures in Reading (Dominie Press) **RL** K–1

Recommended for reluctant readers, early literacy intervention programs, and Chapter I programs.

All Aboard Reading Books. (Putnam & Grosset Group) **RL** K–3

Books designed to be appealing to children.

Adventures of Ranger Rick (Soundprints) **RL** K–5

Nature/environmental themes with audiocassette tapes available.

Amazing Adventures (Globe Fearon) **RL** 3 **IL** 6–adult

Eight short novels.

Animals Question and Answer Series (Phoenix Learning Resources) **RL** 2–3 **IL** K–4

Books about animals with striking illustrations.

Beginning Reading (Children's Press/Franklin Watts) **RL** 1–2

Six classroom sets. Some big books available.

Best Sellers (Globe Fearon) **RL** 1–4 **IL** 6–12, adult

Four sets of easy to read novels on topics of mystery, science fiction, suspense, and adventure.

Beyond Victory Anthologies (Perfection Learning Corporation) **RL** 2–6 **IL** 6–9

A series of high-interest, low-vocabulary anthologies containing nonfiction and sports stories.

Big Books: Collections for Emergent Readers (Scholastic) **RL** K–1

Three levels of books moving from simple, predictable books to more challenging literature selections.

Bookline (Scholastic) **RL** K–6

Two Bookline libraries at each level: science and social studies. Includes activity cards, student notebooks and teacher resource booklets.

Book Center (Scholastic) **RL** 1–8

Units for grades 2 through 6. Each unit is composed of single copies of 52 titles and 7 copies each of 4 core titles. The selections in each unit represent varied levels of difficulty.

Bookshelf (Scholastic) **RL** K–2

Offers a wide variety of genres. Each level contains 6 copies of 18 titles, an audio package, and a teacher's resource book.

Bridges (Scholastic) **RL** 1–6

Each level includes 35 copies of 1 title, small group books (10 copies each of 3 titles) and buddy books (2 copies each of 10 titles).

Carousel Readers (Dominie Press) **RL** K–1

Recommended for reluctant readers, early literacy intervention programs, and Chapter I programs.

Celebrity Biography Paperbacks (Curriculum Support Materials) **RL** 4

Twelve titles with accompanying workbooks.

Content Area Reading (Children's Press/Franklin Watts) **RL** 2–6 **IL** varies

A wide variety of nonfiction books with reading levels well below interest levels.

Creative Minds Biographies (The Learner Group) **RL** 3+ **IL** reluctant readers and adults

Thirty stories of courageous individuals with text suitable for "older reluctant readers."

Discovery Readers (Phoenix Learning Resources) **RL** 1–2 **IL** K–4

A series of nonfiction early readers.

Dolch First Reading Books (SRA) **RL** 1
Dolch Basic Vocabulary RL 2
Dolch Classic Folklore of the World Books RL 3
Dolch Classic Pleasure Books RL 3–6

Stories with vocabulary based upon the Dolch Basic Sight Words, the Dolch list of Storyteller's Vocabulary words, and the Dolch list of First Thousand Words.

Double Fastbook Books, Fastback Books (Globe Fearon) **RL** 4–5 **IL** 6–12

Six series (mystery, romance, horror, spy, strange occurrences, sports) in Double Fastback Books. Seven sets (spy, crime, science fiction, mystery, romance, horror, sports) in Fastbook Books.

Early Science (Troll Associates) **RL** K–4

Nonfiction. Big books available for some of the primary books. Word for word cassettes available.

Easy Reading (Troll Associates) **RL** K–2

Books with simple sentences and easy vocabulary intended for beginning or remedial readers. Word for word cassettes available.

Emergent Readers (Children's Press/Franklin Watts) **RL** 1 **IL** K–2

Five classroom sets. Big books available.

Entertainment World (The Learner Group) **RL** 4+ **IL** reluctant reader, adult

Six brief biographies.

Freedom Fighters (Globe Fearon) **RL** 3–4 **IL** 6–adult

Five short biographies.

Great Series (Steck-Vaughn) **RL** 2–4 **IL** 6–12

Short selections on past and present events. Exercises follow each selection.

Great Unsolved Mysteries (Steck-Vaughn) **RL** 4–6 **IL** 4–adult

Motivating and intriguing selections.

Fantastic Mystery Stories (Curriculum Support Materials) **RL** 3.5–6

Tales of UFO's, ghosts, monsters, etc.

Flights of Fantasy (Globe Fearon) **RL** 3 **IL** 6–adult

Eight short novels.

Hello USA (The Learner Group) **RL** 3+ **IL** reluctant reader, adult

Thirty-five books addressing the richness and diversity of our country.

Heroic Acts (Perfection Learning Corporation) **RL** 3–5 **IL** 6–9

Nonfiction anthologies of famous and everyday heroes.

High-Action Series (Globe Fearon) **RL** 1–4 **IL** 6–12, adult

A variety of series books: Laura Brewster Books, South City Cops, Jim Hunter Books, Crisis Series, Dilemmas and Decisions.

High-Interest Low-Vocabulary for Reluctant Readers (Crestwood House) **RL** 3–7

A wide variety of titles and topics.

Holidays and Heroes (Phoenix Learning Resources) **RL** 2 **IL** K–4, ESL

Selections based upon a variety of holidays and well known heroes.

Hopes and Dreams (Globe Fearon) **RL** 1–2 **IL** 6–12, adult, ESL

Selections on immigrants.

In America Books (The Learner Group) **RL** 5+ **IL** Reluctant reader, adult.

Fifteen titles about ethnic groups in America.

In Fact Series (Vanwell Publishing) **RL** K–6

A series of nonfiction book on topics that are "interesting and relevant" to children.

Jamestown Classics (Jamestown) **RL** 4–5 **IL** 4–12

Short stories adapted from Poe, Stevenson, London, Harte, O.Henry, Sir Arthur Conan Doyle. Questions and activities accompany each story.

Laugh Aloud Puffins (Puffin Books) **RL** 1–5

Designed to entice reluctant readers

Little Indestructible Books (Aro) **RL** K–4

Three sets of books that progress from wordless picture books to books containing multisyllabic words.

Multicultural Biographies Collection (Globe Fearon) **RL** 6 **IL** 6–12

Six sets: Asian American, Native American, African American, Hispanic, World, and American biographies.

Nature Watch (The Learner Group) **RL** 2+ **IL** reluctant reader, adult

Thirty-five books about animals.

Nature Science Books (The Learner Group) **RL** 4+ **IL** reluctant reader, adult

Thirty-five books on a variety of nature topics: ants, apple trees, bats, beetles, etc.

One Small Square (W. H. Freeman) **RL** 3–6

Selections that promote environmental awareness with "engaging text, instructions for activities, and vibrant full color illustrations."

On My Own Books (The Learner Group) **RL** K+ **IL** reluctant reader and adult

Nine nonfiction books.

Open-Ended Plays; Open-Ended Stories (Globe Fearon) **RL** 3–5 **IL** 6–12, adult

Twenty books of short, open-ended plays and stories let students work out real life problems. Topics include lifestyles, values, drugs, cheating, prejudice and loneliness.

Our Century Magazine (Globe Fearon) **RL** 3–4 **IL** 6–12, adult

Nine 64 page magazines each focusing on events of a single decade.

Pacemaker Classics (Globe Fearon) **RL** 3 **IL** 5–12

Cassette tapes and study guides accompany 32 classics.

Perform Theater Workshop Playbook (Scholastic) **RL** 2–5

Series of short plays suitable for expressive oral reading.

Phoenix Everyreader (Phoenix Learning Resources) **RL** 4 **IL** 4–adult, ESL

Easy paperback adaptations of famous adventures.

Points of View (Globe Fearon) **RL** 4–5 **IL** 6–12, adult

Short stories that encourage readers to examine multiple viewpoints.

Puffin Speedsters (Puffin Books) **RL** 3–9

Suitable for "reluctant readers and children who have just learned to enjoy independent reading."

Read More Books (Dominie Press) **RL** K–1

A collection of nonfiction books based on real life situations for the emergent reader.

Reading About Science (Phoenix Learning Resources) **RL** 2–6 **IL** 2–Adult, ESL

High-interest science articles.

Reading Corners (Dominie Press) **RL** K–1

Recommended for reluctant readers, early literacy intervention programs, and Title I programs.

Reading for Today (Steck-Vaughn) **RL** K–6 **IL** adult

Six books in magazine format stress contemporary adult themes. Controlled vocabulary.

Reluctant Readers Collections (Scholastic) **RL** 5–8

"Exciting books to motivate the hard-to reach student."

Reluctant Readers Roundup (Troll Associates) **RL** 2–4; 3–5

A collection of books for students "not yet completely at home with books." The selections cover a wide range of interests.

Science and Social Studies. (Troll Associates) **RL** 1–6

Nonfiction. Big books available for some of the primary books. Word for word cassettes available.

Short Classics (Steck-Vaughn) **RL** 4–6 **IL** 4–adult

Shortened versions of classical literature with controlled vocabulary. Teacher guides available.

Something True, Something Else (Globe Fearon) **RL** 4–5 **IL** 6–12, adult

Lively anthology of short stories.

Silver Press Easy Reader Program (Silver Burdett Press) **RL** K–2.

Books by well-known authors and illustrators.

Silver Screen (The Learner Group) **RL** 5+ **IL** Reluctant reader, adult

Seven books for readers interested in movies.

Smithsonian Wild Heritage Collection (Soundprints) **RL** K–5

Nature/environmental themes with audio cassettes available.

Spellbinders (Globe Fearon) **RL** 3–5 **IL** 6–12, adult

Eight theme-based anthologies on sports, adventure, mystery, and science fiction.

Sports Achievers (The Learner Group) **RL** 4+ **IL** Reluctant reader, adult

Highly readable biographies of popular sports figures.

Spotlight on Literature (SRA) **RL** 3–6

Eight anthologies feature more than 60 authors. A teacher's guide is available.

Spotlight on Readers Theatre (Phoenix Learning Resources) **RL** 2–4 **IL** 1–5

Content-based plays with a social studies emphasis.

Stars (Curriculum Support Materials, Inc.) **RL** 3–4

Stories about famous celebrities.

Super Sports (Troll Associates) **RL** 4–9

Nonfiction. Word for word cassettes available.

Talk About Books (Dominie Press) **RL** K–1

Recommended for reluctant readers, early literacy intervention programs, and Title I programs.

Top Shelf Literature (SRA) **RL** 1–5 **IL** 1–9

Fiction and nonfiction with full color illustrations to encourage all reading levels. Comes with a correlated workbook, *Clues to Cloze.*

Troll First-Start Easy Readers (Dale Seymour Publications) **RL** K–3

Ten stories featuring simple sentences and carefully controlled vocabulary. A word list in each book identifies the basic words used.

Winners (Steck-Vaughn) **RL** 2–4 **IL** 6–12

Short selections on real people in a magazine style format.

10 Word Books (Aro) **RL** K–1

Books with a 10-word controlled vocabulary, repetition and excellent word-picture relationships.

20 Word Books (Aro) **RL** K–1

Books with a 20-word controlled vocabulary taken from early basal reading lists.

Zero Word Books (Aro) **RL** K **IL** K–6

Wordless picture books

Zoobooks. (Wildlife Education) **RL** 4–8

Expository selections with many titles available in Spanish as well as English.

Predictable Books

Big Book Predictable Library (Scholastic) **RL** K–1

One hundred and twenty-four books, each featuring rhyme, rhythm and repetition. Standard sized books in sets of 8 with one accompanying big book.

Big Books: Rhyme, Big Books: Repetition, Big Books: Rhyme and Repetition (Scholastic) **RL** K–3

Three different collections with standard sized books, big books, audiocassette tapes, and a teaching guide.

City Kids (Cypress, Rigby) **RL** 2–3 **IL** 3–6

Short comic paperbacks about irreverent kids who get into trouble. Good for older students at beginning levels.

Infomazing (Rigby) **RL** 1–2

Beginning books of expository information on several levels.

Literacy 2000 (Rigby) **RL** Emergent–3

Hundreds of titles include **Traditional Tales** and **Planet Earth**, as well as many other series by this company. Eight levels.

Look Together Books. (Around the World Books) **RL** K–3

Six stories that have rhyming and/or predictable repetitive language, detailed illustrations and lively text.

Planet Earth (Rigby) **RL** 1–2

Beginning series of short texts. Topics include dinosaurs, space, technology, and wild animals, with several booklets for each topic.

Traditional Tales (Rigby) **RL** 1–2

A variety of excellent and colorful books, including a three-dimensional-like version of Goldilocks.

Predictable Books (Scholastic) **RL** 1–3

A variety of predictable book collections, some with audiocassette tapes. All include a resource book.

Primary Fiction Series. (Vanwell Publishing) **RL** K–1

Based on themes relevant for young readers. Contains rhyme, rhythm and predictable text.

Ready to Read Packages (Richard C. Owen) **RL** K–2

Eight packages containing a variety of books from New Zealand.

Sunshine Books (Wright Group) **RL** K–1 **IL** K–2

Short predictable books. Contains eleven levels. Plays are also included.

The Story Box (Wright Group) **RL** K–3 **RL** K–4

Short enchanting predictable books including 111 titles. Big books and cassettes available.

Tiger Cub Books (Peguis Publishing) **RL** K–3

Thirty-two titles with highly predictable text using rhyme, rhythm and repetition.

Unicorn (Phoenix Learning Resources) **RL** 1–3 **IL** K–6, ESL

A collection of classic children's stories, fables, songs, and poems.

Willie MacGurkie and Friends; Finnigan and Friends (Curriculum Associates) **RL** K–7 **IL** K–7

Books with rhyme, rhythm and humorous characters. Audiocassette tapes and big books available.

Materials for Focused Instruction

Multi-area Development

Biographies from American History (Globe Fearon) **RL** 2 **IL** 6–12

Thirty short biographies with pre- and post-reading exercises included.

Conquests in Reading (Phoenix Learning Resources) **RL** 1–8 **IL** 4–adult, ESL

Text and workbooks that focus on basic word attack and comprehension.

Final Chapter (SRA) **RL** 3–6

Stories about real people from diverse cultures. Each story has a surprise ending and is accompanied by vocabulary, comprehension, and writing activities.

Focus on Reading (SRA) **RL** 1–3, 2–6

High interest reading experiences. Plentiful vocabulary exercises and a focus on literal and inferential comprehension.

Globe Reader Collection (Globe Fearon) **RL** 3–8 **IL** 6–12

Eight texts containing short high interest selections followed by reading improvement exercises.

Headlines of the Century (Steck-Vaughn) **RL** 2–4 **IL** 5–8

Major events of the 20th century written at low reading levels. Exercises to develop vocabulary and critical thinking follow each story.

Insights: Reading as Thinking (Charlesbridge Publishing) **RL** K–8

Features three related strands: comprehension, study skills and word attack.

Interactive Reading Program (SRA) **RL** 1–4

Contemporary stories each accompanied by audiocassette tapes. Workbook exercises develop problem solving, predicting, and critical thinking skills.

Language Arts Resources: Reading Strategies (Charlesbridge Publishing) **RL** 3–adult

Materials "target specific skills for improvement" and are "ideal for successful inclusion of special needs, Chapter I students."

Merrill Reading Skilltext Series (SRA) **RL** 1–6

Appealing story content and easy-to-understand directions. Diagnostic tests determine problem areas and progress tests monitor growth.

Passages Reading Program (Perfection Learning Corporation) **RL** 3–6 **IL** 7–12

Novels with reading levels at least two grade levels below interest levels. Matching workbook for each novel.

Reading Booster (Phoenix Learning Resources) **RL** 1–4 **IL** 1–6

A program designed to bring "poorer readers up to grade level and beyond quickly and effectively."

Reading Scene. (Continental Press) **RL** 1–5 **IL** 6–12

Four sets of books accompanied by a teacher's guide containing vocabulary and comprehension activities. Reproducible pre- and post-tests available.

Skill by Skill Workbook (Modern Curriculum Press) **RL** 2–6

Separate workbook series for comprehension, vocabulary, study skills. Each book covers 4 to 6 skills.

SRA Reading Laboratory Series (SRA) **RL** K–14

Selections grouped according to colors. Reading selections with accompanying skill exercises boxed according to levels.

Sprint Reading Skills Program (Scholastic) **RL** 2–5

Three levels. Each includes 3 skills books, a short story and a play book, and a teaching guide.

Turning Point (Phoenix Learning Resources) **RL** 1–4 **IL** 7–adult, ESL

"A high interest program for older students with marginal reading skills."

Word Recognition

Basic Reading Series (SRA) **RL** K–2

"Systematic organization of vocabulary ensures that students are never asked to read any phonetic element that has not been specifically taught and practiced."

Brigance Prescriptive Word Analysis: Strategies and Practices (Bomar/Noble) **RL** 1–3 **IL** 1–adult

Two volumes of activities, strategies and reference materials for teaching word analysis skills.

Get Ready, Get Set, Read! (CSM) **RL** K–2

Twelve books emphasizing the word families approach to word recognition instruction.

Merrill Phonics Skilltext (SRA) **RL** K–6

Builds skills in four areas: phonics, structural analysis, vocabulary and dictionary.

MCP Phonics Program (Modern Curriculum Press) **RL** 1–6

Series of workbooks presenting phonics skills.

Merrill Linguistics (SRA) **RL** K–3

Organized around the basic spelling patterns of the English language. Includes readers, skills books, and tests.

Phonics: A Sound Approach (Curriculum Associates) **RL** 1–4 **IL** 4–adult, ESL

Series of workbooks on phonics skills.

Phonics for Reading (Curriculum Associates, Inc.) **RL** 1–4 **IL** 1–adult, ESL

A five-level series to develop word attack skills.

Phonics Practice Readers (Modern Curriculum Press) **RL** 1–2 **IL** 1–4.

Each book tells a short story, using words focusing on one phonics element.

Reading Step by Step (Continental Press) **RL** 1–3

Slow paced phonics for primary and special needs students.

SRA Phonics (SRA) **RL** K–1

Readers accompanied by skills activities. Big books available for some selections.

Vocabulary Development

Lessons in Vocabulary Development (Curriculum Associates) **RL** 4–6

Words in student skillbook are introduced thematically. Pre- and post-tests and writing activities are included.

Lessons for Vocabulary Power (Curriculum Associates) **RL** 6–10

Twenty thematic lessons promoting the transfer of vocabulary to speaking and writing.

Stanford Vocabulary (Phoenix Learning Resources) **RL** 4–10 **IL** 7–Adult, ESL

A self instructional program for building vocabulary for secondary students.

Survival Vocabulary (Globe Fearon) **RL** 1–3 **IL** 6–12, adult, ESL

Ten texts each teaching 80 words or phrases associated with common settings such as banking. clothing, medicine, etc.

Vocabulary Booster (Phoenix Learning Resources) **RL** 4–5 **IL** 4–6

A vocabulary development program in 60 story lessons.

Vocabulary Drills (Jamestown) **RL** 6–8, 9–12

Twenty selections present words that students encounter regularly. A variety of activities follow each selection: composing definitions, using context; completing analogies, and connecting words to synonyms and antonyms.

Vocabulary for the Twenty-First Century (Curriculum Associates) **RL** 3–6 **IL** 2–adult

Four books, each containing 12 regular and 3 review lessons. Writing activities are part of the program.

Vocabulary: Meaning and Message (Globe Fearon) **RL** 2–4 **IL** 5–12

Four texts each present essential vocabulary in history, math, science, life skills, survival skills, jobs, sports, and entertainment.

World of Vocabulary (Globe Fearon) **RL** 2–3 **IL** 6–12, adult

An eight volume series of contemporary short nonfiction articles. Short skill exercises follow the articles.

Comprehension

Building Basic Reading Skills (Continental Press) **RL** 1–6

Three workbooks on main ideas, inferencing and sequencing using high interest real-world reading selections.

Caught Reading Program (Globe Fearon) **RL** 1–4 **IL** 6–12

Novels incorporating a planned cycle of instruction: pre-reading, review, reading, and comprehension.

Clues for Better Reading (Curriculum Associates) RL K–5

"High-interest reading and integrated skills are the CLUES that solve the mystery of reading comprehension"

Comprehension Skills Series (Jamestown) **RL** 3–5, 4–8, 8–12

Provides concentrated help in 10 reading comprehension categories: recognizing main idea, making judgments, understanding characters, drawing conclusions, making inferences, understanding literary forms, understanding organization, understanding significant details, and understanding vocabulary.

Critical Reading Skills Series (Jamestown) **RL** 6–8

High-interest nonfiction to motivate "tentative readers." Each selection is followed by 4 exercises: finding the main idea, recalling facts, making inferences, and using words precisely.

Developing Reading Strategies. (Steck-Vaughn) **RL** 2–6 **IL** 6–12

Skill and strategy instruction interspersed between thematically grouped reading selections

Essential Skills Series (Jamestown) **RL** 3–12

Develops comprehension in six key areas: subject matter, supporting details, conclusions, clarifying devices, vocabulary in context and main idea.

Instructional Fair Workbooks (Scholar's Choice) **RL** 1–8

Booklets "perfect for students who need extra practice."

Matchbook Five Minute Thrillers (Globe Fearon) **RL** 3 **IL** 6–12, adult

Twenty short tales with comprehension exercises.

Multiple Skills Series (SRA) **RL** K–9

Develops 4 key comprehension skills: getting the main idea, making inferences and drawing conclusions, interpreting context clues, and grasping significant facts.

New Practice Readers (Phoenix Learning Resources) **RL** 2–6 **IL** 2–Adult, ESL

A developmental and remedial program containing articles from across the curriculum to teach comprehension.

New Reading Thinking Skills (Continental Press) **RL** 3–5 **IL** 6–12, adult

Six leveled workbooks for comprehension and critical thinking.

Reading Comprehension Series (Steck-Vaughn) **RL** 1–6 **IL** 1–9

Eight workbooks of stories containing controlled vocabulary followed by varied exercises. Review lessons.

Reading for Comprehension (Continental Press) **RL** 1–8

Readability below target level to insure success. Nonfiction selections with teacher's guide and audiocassette tapes available.

Reading for Concepts (Phoenix Learning Resources) **RL** 1–6 **IL** 2–Adult, ESL

A developmental and remedial program with articles from a variety of disciplines to teach comprehension and critical thinking.

Reading for Information, Critical Reading, Read and Think (Scholastic) **RL** 3–6

Each workbook offers lively and imaginative reading material to develop a wide range of comprehension skills.

Reading for Today (Steck-Vaughn) **RL** K–6 **IL** adult

Five books in magazine format stress contemporary adult themes.

Reading Reinforcement Skilltext Series (SRA) **RL** 1–8

Theme based stories followed by exercise that develop comprehension and vocabulary skills. Controlled vocabulary.

Single Skills Series (Jamestown) **RL** 3–12

Ten levels for each skill: subject matter, main idea, supporting details, conclusions, clarifying devices and vocabulary in context. A placement test places the student in the appropriate skill. Factual and high-interest selections.

Six-Way Paragraphs (Jamestown) **RL** 4–8, **IL** 8–12

High interest passages and questions focus on six essential comprehension skills: main idea, subject matter, supporting details, conclusions, clarifying devices, and vocabulary in context. Each book begins with a lesson followed by 100 passages, each with its own set of comprehension questions.

Spotlight (Steck-Vaughn) **RL** 2–4 **IL** 4–8

Selections on famous celebrities. Reading and critical thinking exercises follow each selection.

Spotlight on Reading (SRA) **RL** 2–8

Skills workbooks provide practice in eight comprehension skills at each level: main idea, sequence, critical reading, details, inference, story elements, charts, graphs and maps, and vocabulary.

Tales for Thinking (Curriculum Associates) **RL** 1–3 **IL** 2–8

Multicultural fairy tales. The program employs the Directed Reading Thinking Activity.

Talewinds Books (Continental Pres) **RL** 3–5 **IL** 6–12

Three collections of novelettes accompanied by a teacher's guide for developing vocabulary and comprehension.

Thinking about Reading (Modern Curriculum Press) **RL** 2–6 **IL** 2–10

Each worktext contains ten stories divided into segments. Students read using the Directed Reading-Thinking Activity. Story mapping and vocabulary self selection included.

Study Strategies/Content Areas

Brigance Prescriptive Study Skills (Curriculum Associates) **RL** 1–7 **IL** 3–adult

Provides objectives, rationale, skill sequence, etc. for each skill area. Teaches reference and map skills.

Cloze in the Content Areas: Science and Social Studies (Continental Press) **RL** 2–6

High-interest nonfiction articles correlated to the science and social studies curricula. Teacher guides available.

Connections (Steck-Vaughn) **RL** 6–8 **IL** 9–12

Practice in content area reading skills: writing, literature, mathematics, science and social studies.

Learning to Study (Jamestown) **RL** 2–8

A step by step approach in seven categories: location. organization, interpretation, retention, test-taking, skimming/scanning, and study strategies.

Spotlight on Content Area Reading (SRA) **RL** 4–6

Eighteen books aimed at improving making inferences, analyzing data, organizing and synthesizing information, drawing conclusions and making judgments, and using information for different purposes.

Reading in the Content Areas (Modern Curriculum Press) **RL** 2–6

Five graded worktexts for teaching graphic aids, textbook aids, outlining, summarizing, etc.

Rate

Reading Drills (Jamestown) **RL** 4–6, 6–8, 7–12

Each volume contains 30 timed passages taken from fiction and nonfiction selections. Comprehension activities after each selection include questions, cloze test and vocabulary questions.

Timed Readings and Timed Readings in Literature (Jamestown) **RL** 4–college

Fifty 400-word passages for lasting rate improvement. Ten questions following each passage maintain a focus on comprehension.

Real-life Materials/Functional Reading

Career Awareness (Troll Associates) **RL** 2–8

Nonfiction. Word for word cassettes available.

Like Times (Globe Fearon) **RL** 1–2 **IL** 9–12, adult

Two seven book sets about realistic situations such as returning to school, dealing with alcoholism and choosing between family and career.

Pacemaker Career Readers (Globe Fearon) **RL** 2 **IL** 7–12

Career exploration books including nurse's aid, machinist, retail sales, beauty operator, security guard.

Pacemaker Vocational Readers (Globe Fearon) **RL** 2 **IL** 7–12

Career-oriented stories on entry level jobs (gardener, waitress, cook) and information on the work world.

The Lifeschool Program (Globe Fearon) **RL** 1–4 **IL** 9–12

Six binders containing 60 learning modules in a variety of areas: consumer economics, occupations, health, community resources, government and law, interpersonal relations

Working for Myself (Lake Education) **RL** 3–4 **IL** 6–12

Stories about people who successfully build their own businesses.

Worktales (Globe Fearon) **RL** 1–2 **IL** 9–12, ESL

Dramatizes workplace issues such as job stress, sexism, safety, substance abuse, etc.

Appendix: An Informal Reading Inventory

This informal reading inventory was developed by Dr. Joyce Jennings. It was field-tested in the Reading Center of Northeastern Illinois University and several schools in the Chicago metropolitan area, with the help of graduate students in the Departments of Reading and Special Education at Northeastern Illinois University.

The word lists consist of twenty-five words each. They were developed using *Basic Reading Vocabularies* (Harris & Jacobson, 1982). Each word presented in the word lists is included in the passages read by the students. For those words appearing in the oral reading passages, you can compare students' ability to recognize words in isolation and in context.

The reading passages consist of two passages per level, Preprimer through Grade 8. One set of these graded passages can be used to assess students' oral reading, and the other can be used to assess silent reading. You may also wish to use the silent reading passages to assess students' listening comprehension.

Abbreviations used in this instrument include:

Lit. = Literal   Ind. = Independent Level
Inf. = Inferential   Inst. = Instructional Level
Comp. = Comprehension   Frust. = Frustration Level

When you have completed the IRI, use the Summary Record Sheet to record your results. Then determine the oral, silent, and estimated overall reading levels as described in Chapter 3.

INFORMAL READING INVENTORY

SUMMARY SHEET

Level	Oral Passages			Silent Passages	Total Reading	Listening
	Word Rec Level	Comp Level	Passage Level	Comp & Passage Level	Passage Level	Passage Level
PRE-P						
PRIMER						
1						
2						
3						
4						
5						
6						
7						
8						

Informal Reading Assessment
Word List

Preprimer Level	Preprimer Level	Level 1
and	bed	again
day	box	bake
dog	dad	bark
good	duck	best
he	fast	brother
home	frog	cake
in	fun	chairs
is	got	children
it	green	clean
jump	had	coming
like	his	doctor
make	house	family
no	lake	heard
pet	made	hurt
play	mother	leg
ride	next	noise
run	over	other
said	rock	soon
she	sat	sound
the	still	stay
they	swim	stuck
this	then	tiger
to	tree	watch
with	went	while
yes	why	zoo

Word List, Continued

Level 2	Level 3	Level 4
brush	accident	approval
camp	arrive	article
card	bandage	athlete
classroom	camera	brilliant
clothes	capture	challenger
dress	chosen	champion
egg	dangerous	compete
forever	discover	confidence
hundred	dusk	convince
kitchen	excitement	countless
knew	film	daybreak
packed	harbor	disappointment
playground	information	gear
seemed	maple	icicles
shirt	miserable	instruction
short	parent	international
spend	passenger	junior
teacher	police	ladybug
teeth	reporter	mountainside
tent	rescue	performance
toast	screech	permit
week	seaweed	represent
whole	study	skater
world	underwater	slope
year	unusual	sunrise

Word List, Continued

Level 5	Level 6	Level 7	Level 8
adventurous	acknowledge	acrobatic	administrtor
belongings	alternate	algebra	agonizing
civilization	biology	alternative	ambassadors
continuous	declined	ample	biological
cramped	downpour	appreciative	contemplation
destruction	drainage	bifocals	correspondent
firelight	effective	bolstered	corrugated
frontier	embarrassment	cartoonist	devastated
injured	enterprising	cartwheel	dishearened
machinery	equipped	comical	dismantled
mechanic	frustration	computation	dissect
mountaintop	inspection	confront	envision
placid	midafternoon	contempt	eroded
rainfall	observation	coodination	excelled
rampaging	orangutan	desperation	extensive
ranger	parallel	elegance	hysteria
reassured	✳ perspeiration	enthusiastically	inclination
refreshing	placement	expectation	innermost
restore	✳ rainwqater	gymnastics	journalist
roused	recommended	kindergarten	overpowering
spectacular	specialize	mistrust	phenomenal
stallion	sunup	perceived	preserved
surroundings	surgery	quizzical	presitgious
tension	veterinarian	tolerated	seacoasts
thrashed	zookeeper	unison	southeastern

Preprimer Level, Oral Passage   **62 Words**
Background: *What is a pet? Read this story to find out what happened when Bill wanted a pet.*

Bill wanted a **pet**. **He** asked his mom for a **pet**. **She said he** had **to** wait.

One **day**, Bill saw a little **dog**. **The dog** was crying.

Bill **said**, "**This dog is** lost." Bill took **the dog home**.

Bill's mom saw **the dog**. Bill asked, "May **I** keep **it**?"

Bill's mom **said he** could keep **the dog**.

Bill had **a pet**!

Comprehension Questions

Lit - 1. What did Bill want in this story?
          Accept either: *a pet/a dog*
Lit - 2. In the beginning of the story, what did Bill's mother say when he asked for a pet?
          Accept either: *he had to wait/no*
Inf - 3. Why did Bill think the dog was lost?
          It was crying
Lit - 4. Where did Bill and the dog go?
          home
Inf - 5. Why did Bill take the dog home?
          Accept any: *he wanted to keep it/It was crying/ it was lost*
Inf - 6. How did Bill finally get a pet?
          Accept either: *he took a lost dog home to show his mother/she let him keep it*

Primer Level, Oral Passage   **100 Words**
Background: *What kinds of things can you make with your friends? Read this story to find out what Meg and Jane made one day.*

Jane and Meg are friends. One day, Meg **went** to Jane's house to play.

They **went** outside. Jane showed Meg a big **tree**. Jane said, "I want to make a **house next** to this **tree**."

Meg said, "I know! Come to my house! My **mother** just **got** a new **bed**! It came in a very big **box**. Maybe we can have the **box** for our house!"

Meg and Jane **went** to Meg's house. They asked Meg's **mother** if they could have the **box**. Meg's **mother** said yes.

Jane and Meg took the **box** to make a house. They **had fun**.

Comprehension Questions

Lit - 1. Where were Meg and Jane playing?
        Accept either: *At Jane's house/in the yard*
Lit - 2. What did Jane want to make?
        a house
Lit - 3. Where did Jane want to make the house?
        Next to the tree
Inf - 4. How did Meg's mother help the girls?
        she said they could use the box from her mom's new bed
Inf - 5. Why did Meg's mother have a box?
        her new bed came in it
Inf - 6. Why did Meg think the box will be good for a house?
        it is big

Level 1, Oral Passage   **98 Words**
Background: What kinds of books do you like to read? *Read this story*
about Jan and her favorite kind of book.

Jan loves to read books!

Most of all, Jan loves books about animals. She likes books about dogs that help put out fires. She likes books about cats that get **stuck** in trees.

The **best** book is about a **doctor**. This **doctor** takes care of animals. Jan loves to read about him.

In the book, a **tiger** at the **zoo** was **hurt**. The **doctor** came to the **zoo**. He put something on the **tiger's leg**. **Soon** the **tiger** was well **again**. When Jan grows up, she wants to be a **doctor**. She will take care of animals, too.

Comprehension Questions

Lit - 1. What does Jan like to do?
          read books

Lit - 2   What does Jan like to read about?
          Accept either: *animals/animal doctor*

Inf - 3   Why do you think Jan likes to read about animals so much?
          Accept any of these: *She wants to take care of them/she likes to read about them/she wants to be a vet*

Lit - 4   What are two animals that Jan likes to read about?
          Any two: *dogs, cats, tiger*

Lit - 5   What is Jan's favorite book about?
          Accept either: *A doctor that takes care of animals/animals*

Inf - 6   Why did the doctor in the book have to go to the zoo?
          to take care of the tiger

Inf - 7   What kind of doctor does Jan want to be?
>   *one that takes care of animals*

Inf - 8   How do you know Jan likes animals?
>   *she likes to read about them and she wants to be a doctor who*
>   *takes care of animals*

Level 2, Oral Passage   **140 Words**
Background: *What is it like to be so excited about something that you can't sleep? Read this story to find out why Danny is so excited.*

Danny is very happy this morning! This is the first day of **camp**! Last **year**, Danny went to day **camp**. This **year**, he can **spend** nights at camp. He is going to stay a **whole week**, just like his brother!

Last night, Danny **packed** his **clothes**. This morning, he **dressed** and **brushed** his **teeth**. Then he went to the **kitchen**. Danny's dad gave him some **eggs** and **toast**. But Danny was too happy to eat!

Danny's dad drove him to **camp**. The trip **seemed** like it would take **forever**! Finally, they came to the **camp**. There were **hundreds** of boys and girls all **dressed** in blue **shorts** and yellow **shirts**.

As soon as the car stopped, Danny saw his friend Joe. Joe told him they would be sleeping in the same **tent**. Danny **knew** this would be a great **week**!

Comprehension Questions

Lit - 1. Where was Danny going?
          To camp
Inf - 2. What is different between this camp and last year's?
          Last year Danny couldn't stay overnight, but this year he can
Lit - 3. How long will Danny be at camp?
          A week
Lit - 4. Why couldn't Danny eat?
          He was too excited
Lit - 5. How did Danny get to camp?
          His dad drove him

Inf - 6. How do you know this was a big camp?
> *There were hundreds of boys and girls*

Inf - 7. How did Danny feel about sleeping in the tent with Joe?
> *He was happy that he would be with Joe*

Inf - 8 Why does Danny think this will be a great week?
> *He wanted to go to camp and now he will be with his friend*

Level 3, Oral Passage   **187 Words**
Background: *What is an island? Can you imagine what it would be like to live on an island? Read this story to find out what it is like for Kim.*

Kim lives on an island far out in the ocean. You may think that it would be fun to live on an island. But Kim is **miserable**. Kim hasn't seen her friends in a year. There is no one to play with or talk to. There isn't even a school!

Why has Kim's family **chosen** such a lonely life? Kim's **parents study** animals that only live in the **harbor** of this island. But Kim's dad knows how unhappy Kim is. He wants to do something to make her happy.

Kim's dad **discovered** a new kind of fish. It has bright orange fins and a blue tail. Dad named this **unusual** fish after Kim. He calls it the Kimfish. It hides in the **seaweed**. It only comes out in the morning and at **dusk**.

Kim's dad takes his **underwater camera** to the harbor every day. He hopes to **capture** the Kimfish on **film**. Maybe someday her dad will learn enough about the Kimfish. Then Kim can go back to her old school. Then she can see all her old friends again. Kim hopes that day will come soon.

Comprehension Questions

Lit - 1. Where does Kim live?
          On an island
Lit. - 2. Why is Kim unhappy?
          Accept either: *she doesn't have any friends/she is lonely*
Inf. - 3. How long has Kim's family lived on the island?
          A year
Lit. - 4. Why do Kim's parents want to live on the island?
          They are studying the animals

Inf. - 5. Why do you think Kim's father plans to name his discovery after her?

He knows she is unhappy and wants to make her feel better

Lit. - 6. What colors is the fish that Kim's father discovered?

Accept either: *orange/blue*

Inf. - 7. Why is it so hard for Kim's father to take a picture of the Kimfish?

Accept either: *It only comes out in the morning and just before night/it hides in the seaweed*

Inf. - 8. Why does Kim want to go back to her old home?

Accept either: *To go to her old school / to see her friends*

Level 4, Oral Passage   **179 Words**
Background: *What is ice skating? In this story, Jessie is an ice skater.*

More than anything, Jessie wants to be a **champion skater**! She can't remember a time she didn't want to skate or a time she didn't want to be the best.

Jessie began skating **instruction** when she was three years old. In her first ice show, she played the part of a **ladybug**. She still remembers her red and black spotted costume. Most of all, Jessie remembers the audience clapping their **approval**.

Jessie doesn't have much time for ice shows anymore. Now she must practice jumps and turns. When Jessie was six, she started skating in contests for ages six to twelve. By the time she was eight, Jessie was the **junior** state champion. Now that she is thirteen, Jessie **competes** with adults. She is the state **champion** in ice skating.

Last week, a sports writer wrote an **article** about Jessie's **performance**. It said she was a "**brilliant** young **athlete**." It said her skating showed "**confidence** and grace. Jessie thought about the **countless** falls she had taken to make each jump look perfect. She didn't feel very graceful or confident!

Next week, Jessie will **represent** her state in a **national** meet. This will be the first time she has skated at this level. She hopes all her practice and hard work will pay off. Jessie hopes that her **confidence** and grace will help her win.

Comprehension Questions

Lit - 1. What does Jessie want to be?
a champion ice skater

Inf - 2. Why doesn't Jessie have time to be in ice shows any more?
Accept either: *she's too busy competing/she has to practice*

Lit - 3. When did Jessie start taking skating lessons?
when she was three

Inf - 4. How did Jessie know the audience liked her first performance?
they applauded

Lit - 5. How old is Jessie now?
thirteen

Inf - 6. Why doesn't Jessie feel graceful?
she falls so many times in practice

Inf - 7. Why did the sports writer describe Jessie as brilliant?
Accept either: *she is competing with adults although she is so young/she can skate better than other people*

Lit - 8. What kind of competition will Jessie be in next week?
national

Level 5, Oral Passage   **246 Words**
Background: *What do you think it would be like to live on a farm? In this story, Beth wishes she could live in the country.*

Sometimes Beth hated towns and cities! They were taking over and the farms and open land were disappearing. Beth wished she could live on a farm, but her dad was a **mechanic**. He repaired **machinery** for a mill in town.

Beth's favorite times were spent with Grandpa on his farm. Beth spent almost all her weekends with Grandpa. On cool evenings, Grandpa would light a fire. Beth loved to read by the **firelight**, just like girls did when this was the **frontier**.

On Saturday mornings, Grandpa was always up early, ready for his long day of chores. First, the pigs had to be fed, and the chicken coop had to be cleaned. Then the **stallion** had to be brushed. When Beth was little, Grandpa let her help milk the cows, but now he used milking machines.

In the afternoon, Beth and Grandpa walked the horses. This was Beth's favorite chore. Grandpa's favorite place to walk the horses was Bear Mountain. It took most of the afternoon to ride all the way out to the mountain and back. Grandpa and Beth always packed a lunch to eat on the **mountaintop**. As they shared their fruit and milk, they talked. Grandpa told her how much he liked to look out over the farms and towns for miles. These trips to the mountain **reassured** Beth. They made her know that there was still enough land and open spaces. They helped her to not feel so closed in by **civilization**.

Comprehension Questions

Inf - 1. Why didn't Beth like where she lived?
          Accept any of these: *She had to live in town/It was too crowded for her/no open land or farms*

Lit - 2. Where did Beth like to spend her weekends?
          on Gramps' farm

Lit - 3. Why did Beth's family live in town?
          because her dad was a mechanic

Inf - 4. Why did Beth like going to her grandfather's farm?
          Accept any of these: *Liked to do chores/liked to read by firelight/liked to go to the mountain/It had lots of space*

Lit - 5. What were some of the chores that Beth and her grandfather did?
          Name two: *feed the pigs, clean the chicken coop, brush the stallion, walk the horses*

Inf - 6. Why do you think Beth's favorite core was walking the horses?
Accept either: *because she like to go to the mountain/she likes horses*

Lit - 7. What did Beth and Gramps take with them to the mountain?
lunch

Inf - 8. Why did Beth like to go to the mountain?
It made her feel there was enough space for people like her

Level 6, Oral Passage   **300 Words**
Background: *What is a veterinarian? In this passage, Pam wants to be a veterinarian.*

More than anything, Pam wanted to be a **veterinarian**. She was great with animals. For the last two years, Pam had volunteered at the zoo. But this summer, she was going to be paid. Pam's **biology** teacher had **recommended** that she work in a special science program.

Pam was disappointed when she found out she was assigned to the petting zoo. She had hoped for something more exciting, like reptiles. Pam decided to talk to the zoo's vet, Dr. Mack. Maybe she would understand how Pam felt, and Pam could ask her to convince the **zookeeper** to change her **placement**.

When Pam arrived at the zoo, Dr. Mack was in the nursery. There had been an emergency, and Dr. Mack had been called to help. The nurse asked Pam to wait for Dr. Mack in the **observation** room. She was surprised to find that the **observation** room overlooked a small operating room. There she saw Dr. Mack, working frantically to save a baby **orangutan**. After several minutes, the tiny ape started to breathe on its own, and Dr. Mack came out to greet Pam, "I thought we were going to lose her! Since we rescued her from a fire, we've been trying to bottle-feed her, but suddenly she stopped breathing. The nurse called me because I **specialize** in great apes. Now that I'm sure she'll be all right, how can I help you?"

"I'm glad she's going to be okay," replied Pam, "I didn't know you were **equipped** for **surgery**."

"That's why we need someone like you. We need someone who can handle frightened animals and comfort them while they wait for **surgery** and while they recover. Now, what was it you wanted to discuss?"

Pam replied, "I think you've answered all my questions. When can I start?"

Comprehension Questions
Inf - 1. Who helped Pam get the job at the zoo?
      her biology teacher
Lit - 2. Where did the zookeeper want Pam to work?
      in the children's zoo
Inf - 3. Why didn't Pam want to work in the baby animal zoo?
      she didn't think it was an important job

Inf - 4. What did Pam think would happen if she talked to the zoo's veterinarian?
she thought the veterinarian would convince the zookeeper to let her work with other animals

Lit - 5. Why wasn't Dr. Mack in her office when Pam arrived at the zoo?
she had been called to help with an emergency

Lit - 6. Where did the nurse ask Pam to wait for Dr. Mack?
In an observation room

Lit - 7. What was wrong with the baby orangutan?
Accept either: *She had stopped breathing/She had been in a fire*

Lit - 8. How did the zoo get the baby orangutan?
they rescued her from a fire

Lit - 9. What was the job that Dr. Mack wanted Pam to do?
handle the frightened animals and take care of them while they recovered from surgery

Inf - 10. Why didn't Pam ever ask Dr. Mack to talk to the zookeeper?
after she learned about the job Dr. Mack wanted her to do, she realized it was important

Level 7, Oral Passage   **352 Words**
Background: *What happens when someone gets in trouble in class? In this passage, Peter gets in trouble with Mr. Galvin. Read it to find out what happens.*

I knew I shouldn't be drawing in **algebra** class, but I just couldn't resist. Mr. Galvin had such a **comical** look as he peered over his **bifocals** at Jamie's futile attempt to solve the problem on the board. Maybe I could call this brilliant work of art "Galvin-eyes" or something equally insulting!

I suddenly realized Mr. Galvin was calling my name, "Peter, what is your solution to this problem?" Oh no, Mr. Galvin was walking in my direction! If I got in trouble again, I could be suspended. In **desperation**, I tried to adjust my book to cover the drawing, but it was too late. "Peter, have you completed the **computation** for problem number seven?" Even though I hadn't even started the problem, I replied in my most respectful tone, "Not quite, sir." When he stopped at the front of the row, it **bolstered** my confidence. "I'll have it done in just a couple of minutes." Why did I always have to open my big mouth, instead of leaving well-enough alone? Now he was coming directly toward my desk.

Mr. Galvin, in a tone of total **mistrust**, suggested, "Why don't you come to the board and show us how far you've gotten, and perhaps your classmates can help you complete the problem?"

As I fumbled for an answer, Mr. Galvin reached my desk. He lifted my book with the **expectation** of finding a partially solved algebra problem. Instead, he found a drawing of himself, **bifocals** and all, glaring at Jamie with a **quizzical** look on his face. At least I hadn't had time to write the caption!

"Peter!" boomed Mr. Galvin, "just what do you expect to make of yourself with this kind of behavior?"

Without thinking how it might be taken, I replied, "A **cartoonist**."

Wrong answer! The class gave an **appreciative** round of applause. But Mr. Galvin **perceived** this as yet another attempt on my part to **confront** him. Once again, I had tried to undermine his authority with the class.

I had **ample** opportunity to think of **alternative** replies while I waited in the assistant principal's office.

Comprehension Questions

Lit - 1. What was Peter doing instead of his algebra problem?

He was drawing a cartoon of Mr. Galvin

Inf - 2. Why was Peter drawing a picture of Mr. Galvin?

Accept any of these: *Because he thought he looked so funny/he didn't like him/he wanted to be a cartoonist*

Inf - 3. Why did Peter lie when Mr. Galvin asked him if he had finished the problem?

He knew if he got in trouble any more his dad would ground him

Lit - 4. Who did Mr. Galvin say would help Peter finish the problem?

His classmates

Lit - 5. What did Mr. Galvin expect to find under Peter's algebra book?

His algebra problem

Lit - 6. What did Mr. Galvin really find under the algebra book?

Peter's drawing

Inf - 7. Why do you think Peter was glad he hadn't written a caption?

It was even more insulting to his teacher than the drawing

Lit - 8. What does Peter want to be when he grows up?

A cartoonist

Inf - 9. Why did Peter's answer make Mr. Galvin so angry?

He thought Peter was making fun of him

Inf - 10. How do you know this isn't the first time Peter has gotten in trouble in algebra class?

When Mr. Galvin gets angry, he thinks this was another attempt by Peter to disrupt the class, and when Peter lies to Mr. Galvin, he thinks if he gets in trouble again, he will be suspended

Level 8, Oral Passage   **336 Words**
Background: *What is biology? What does dissecting mean? In this passage, James is about to take biology.*

James had always **excelled** in science, winning every science fair and making straight A's. But this year, he would be taking **Biological** Studies, and he knew that meant **dissecting** animals. He was **agonizing** over the thought of cutting up a creature that had been alive. He couldn't even **envision** cutting into a cockroach—and he hated those! James started the summer with an **overpowering** fear of embarrassing himself. By July, he had worked himself into a state of near **hysteria**.

To solve his problem, James bought a dissecting kit to practice. Inside the kit, he found an address to order **preserved** animals. After some **contemplation**, James chose an earthworm, a crawfish, a frog, and a snake.

When the animals arrived, James carefully **dismantled** the **corrugated** box so he wouldn't damage the contents. When he reached the **innermost** container, he was shocked beyond words! There must have been a mistake! Not only were these animals not **preserved**, they weren't even dead! James looked at the order form and discovered his mistake. He had marked the wrong code!

Suddenly, James was the proud owner of four creatures who were very much alive. He had no idea what to feed any of these animals, nor any desire to find out. Deciding to dispose of them as quickly as possible, he biked to the nearest pet shop to sell the animals. The manager told him they only bought from licensed dealers. He tried the **administrator** of the zoo, but she didn't have room for any more animals just now. James was **disheartened**. He realized he would have to accept responsibility for the animals himself.

First, James went to the library. There he learned that the animals would have to be housed in separate containers. He went back to the pet store and bought four small aquariums. By the end of the summer, James had learned an **extensive** amount of information about his new pets. What had started as a dissection project had turned into a valuable study of live animals.

Comprehension Questions

Lit - 1. What was school subject was James best at?
Science

Inf - 2. Why was James worried about taking biology?
Accept either: *He was afraid he would embarrass himself/he didn't want to cut up animals*

Lit - 3. How did James decide to solve his problem?
He bought a dissecting kit to practice

Lit - 4. What is one kind of animal that James thought he would need?
Accept any: *Earthworm, crawfish, snake, frog*

Inf - 5. Why was James surprised when he opened the boxes?
He expected dead animals, but these were alive

Lit - 6. Why wouldn't the pet shop take the animals?
They were only allowed to buy from licensed dealers

Lit - 7. Why wouldn't the children's zoo take the animals?
They didn't have room

Inf - 8. How do we know that James cared about animals?
Accept any of these: *He tried to find a home for them/fed them/took care of them/didn't want to dissect them*

Inf - 9. What did James finally do with the animals?
He kept them and took care of them

Inf - 10. How did James' mistake become a positive experience?
Accept either: *He learned a lot about the animals/he got four new pets*

Preprimer Level, Silent Passage   **86 Words**
Background: *Do you have a special friend? In this story, Jill and Pat are friends. Read this story to find out what they like to do together.*

Jill likes to **play with** Pat. **They like to run and jump. They like to ride** bikes, too.

One **day, they** wanted **to make a** cake. Jill asked her mom if they could **make a** cake **in** her house. Jill's mom **said no.** She did not have time to help.

Jill **and** Pat went **to** Pat's house. Pat asked her mom if **they** could **make a** cake **in** her house. Pat's mom **said yes.**

Jill **and** Pat made a cake. Pat's mom helped. **It** was **good.**

Comprehension Questions

Inf - 1. Who is Jill's friend?
          Pat
Lit - 2. What are two things they like to do together?
          Name two: *play, run, jump, play games, ride bikes*
Lit - 3. What did they ask Jill's mother?
          If they could bake a cake
Inf - 4. Why couldn't they make the cake at Jill's house?
          Jill's mom didn't have time to help them
Lit - 5. What did Pat's mother say when they asked to make the cake at Pat's house?
          Yes
Inf - 6. How do you know that Jill and Sue liked the cake?
          It was good

Primer Level, Silent Passage　　　　　　　　　　　**96 Words**
Background: *What kinds of animals could you find near water? Read this story about Nick and his dad watching animals.*

Nick and **his dad** like **animals**. One day, Nick and **his dad went** to the **lake**. They went to see the **animals**. They **sat next** to the **lake**. They were very **still**.

Then Nick **saw** a big **duck**. He **saw** the **duck swim** to a big **rock** in the **lake**. Something **made** the duck fly away **fast**.

Nick asked **his dad**, "**Why** did the **duck** fly away?"

Nick's **dad** said, "Look **over** there." He showed Nick something in the **lake**. Nick thought he would see something big.

What a surprise to see a little **green frog**!

Comprehension Questions
Lit - 1.　Where did Nick and his dad go?
　　　　　To the lake
Inf - 2.　Why do you think Nick and his dad were trying to be still?
　　　　　So the animals would come close to them
Lit - 3.　What animals did Nick and his dad see?
　　　　　Duck, frog

Lit - 4. What did the duck do?

      Accept either: *Swam to the rock/Flew away*

Inf - 5. What made the duck fly away?

      The frog

Inf - 6. Why was Nick surprised to see the frog?

      Accept either: *He thought he would see something big, and the frog was little; Duck was big and frog is little, but it scared the duck*

Level 1, Silent Passage   **109 Words**
Background: *How do you feel when you want to do something fun and*
your mom or dad want you to work? Read this story about
how Ben helped his mom.

Ben was sad. He wanted to go to the park with the **other children**. But his mom said he had to **stay** home.

Ben's **grandma** was **coming** to see his **family**. He had to help **clean** the house.

Ben had to put away his toys. He had to make his bed. He had to move the **chairs**. Then Mom **cleaned** the floor.

Then he had to **watch** his baby **brother** while Mom **baked** a **cake**.

At last, **Grandma's** car was **coming** down the road! Sh e got out of the car. She had a big box. Ben **heard** a **noise**. It came from the box. It **sounded** like a **bark!**

Comprehension Questions
Lit - 1. What did Ben want to do?
            He wanted to go to the park
Lit - 2. What did Ben's mom want him to do?
            Help her clean the house
Inf - 3. Why did Ben s mom want him to move the chairs?
            So she could clean the floor
Inf - 4. Why did Ben's mom want the house to be clean?

Ben's grandma was coming to visit

Lit - 5. What were two jobs that Ben's mom wanted him to do?

Put away his toys, moved chairs, or watched brother/make his bed

Inf - 6. What do you think was in the box that Ben's grandma had?

A dog

Level 2, Silent Passage   **173 Words**
Background: *Have you ever been so worried about having a new teacher that you didn't want to go to school? Read this story to find out how Sarah felt about having a new teacher.*

Today is the first day of school. But Sarah doesn't want to go. This **year**, Sarah should have Mrs. Black for her **teacher**. But last June, Mrs. Black told the class she would not be back this **year**. She told them their new **teacher** would be very nice.

Mrs. Black is the best **teacher** in the **world**! Sometimes the big girls on the **playground** don't let Sarah and her friends jump rope. Then Mrs. Black comes out to turn the rope just for them. Sarah doesn't think a new **teacher** will do that.

Sarah was surprised when she got to her **classroom**. The new **teacher's** name was Mr. Black. He said, "Good morning, boys and girls. My name is Mr. Black. I will be your new **teacher**. Mrs. Black asked me to tell you that she had a baby on Friday. I brought a picture of Mrs. Black and the baby." Sarah and her friends made a **card** for Mrs. Black and the baby. Maybe the new **teacher** won't be so bad after all!

Comprehension Questions
Inf - 1. Why didn't Sarah want to go to school?
          Accept either: *Mrs. Black wouldn't be there/she was going to have a new teacher*

Lit - 2.   What did Mrs. Black tell the class about the new teacher?
           She said the new teacher would be nice

Inf - 3   Why did Sarah think Mrs. Black was so nice?
           She turned the jump rope for Sarah and her friends

Inf - 4.   Why wasn t Mrs. Black coming back this year?
           She was going to have a baby

Inf - 5.   What did Sarah find out when she got to her classroom?
           Accept either: *The new teacher was Mr. Black/ Mrs. Black had had a baby*

Lit - 6.   Who is the new teacher?
           Accept either: *Mr. Black/Mrs. Black s husband*

Lit - 7.   What did Sarah and her friends do for Mrs. Black?
           Made cards for her and the baby

Lit - 8.   What does Sarah think of the new teacher at the end of the story?
           Accept either: *She thinks he won't be so bad/she thinks he is nice*

Level 3, Silent Passage   **219 Words**
Background: *What does a person have to do to be a hero? Read this story to find out how Bill's dad became a hero.*

      Yesterday, Bill's dad ran into the kitchen, shouting, "There has been an **accident**!" He told Bill to call the **police**. He said to tell them a bus had hit a car at the corner of Oak and **Maple** Streets.

      Bill wanted to go back to the corner with his dad. He wanted to join the **excitement**. But his dad said it was too **dangerous**. Bill watched out the window as his dad ran back out to the street. He hoped his dad wouldn't go on the bus. It was leaning against a wall. Only two wheels were on the ground.

      But his dad did go back on the bus. Bill watched as his dad carried people from the bus to the grass. Bill saw his dad carry a little girl from the bus. She was clinging to a teddy bear. He said, "Thank goodness, that's the last one!" Just then, a truck **screeched** to a stop as the **rescue** workers **arrived**. The **rescue** workers rushed to care for the people who were hurt. They even put a **bandage** on the little girl's bear! Then the news **reporters** arrived. They wanted **information** about Bill's dad. This morning there was a picture of Bill's dad in the paper. Under the picture, in big print, it said, "LOCAL HERO SAVES **PASSENGERS**".

Comprehension Questions
Inf - 1. How did Bill find out about the accident?
                Accept either: *His dad told him/ his dad ran into the kitchen shouting about it*
Lit - 2. What did Bill's dad tell him to do?
                Accept either: *To call the police/tell them there had been an accident*
Lit - 3. Why didn't Bill's dad let him go to the corner with him?

> *He said it was too dangerous*

Inf - 4. Why didn't Bill want his dad to go on the bus?

> Accept either: *He was afraid it would fall over/he thought it was too dangerous*

Lit - 5. How did Bill's dad help the people on the bus?

> *He carried them off the bus*

Lit - 6. What did the rescue workers do?

> Accept either: *Cared for the people who were hurt/put a bandage on the little girl's bear*

Inf - 7. Why did the news reporters come to the accident?

> Accept either: *They wanted to find out about Bill's dad/they wanted to put the accident on the news*

Inf - 8. Why did the news reporters want information about Bill's dad?

> *He was a hero, and they wanted to write an article about him*

Level 4, Silent Passage   **237 Words**
Background: *What is skiing? What do you have to have to ski? What do*
you think it would be like to ski down a mountain? Read this
story about Josh's ski trip.

At **daybreak**, Josh looked out the window of the cabin. He looked through the **icicles**, to the snow-covered **mountainside**. He couldn't wait to get out on the **slopes**! This year he would get to go on the **Challenger Slope**. He wanted to feel the wind rushing past his face as he raced down the hill.

When Josh's family came to Bear Mountain last year, Josh was the best skier in his class. But he was too short, and the ski patrol wouldn't **permit** him on the more difficult **slopes**. He tried to **convince** the captains of the ski patrol. He knew he was good enough to go on the tougher **slopes**, but they wouldn't bend the rules for anyone.

But during the long summer months, Josh had grown to five feet, seven inches, and nobody could stop him! The mountain was just outside the window, but everyone else was still sleeping peacefully. Josh couldn't stand it any longer! In silence, he picked up his boots and goggles and crept downstairs. He quietly lifted his **gear** down from the rack and slipped out the door.

The morning was perfect! The air was crisp, and the snow sparkled in the **sunrise** like silver as Josh made his way to the ski lift. He was anxious to feel the wind in his face. What a **disappointment** when he saw the new sign: "No children under fifteen without an adult"!

Comprehension Questions

Lit - 1. Where is Josh?
> Accept any of these: *On a ski trip/at Bear Mountain/in a cabin*

Lit - 2. What does Josh want to do?
> Accept any of these: *Go out on the mountain/ski/go on the Challenger slope*

Lit - 3. Why couldn't Josh ski on the Challenger slopes last year?
> *He was too short*

Inf - 4. How do you know Josh is a good skier?
> Accept any of these: *He was the best in his class, he could handle more difficult slopes/he liked skiing*

Inf - 5. Why did Josh decide to sneak out of the house?
> *Everyone else was sleeping and he didn t want to wait*

Inf - 6. How far away Is the ski slope?
> *On the mountain, just outside the window*

Inf - 7. Why did Josh creep downstairs?
> *He was trying to sneak out of the house*

Inf - 8. Why can't Josh go on the "Challenger" slope now?
> *He is too young*

Level 5, Silent Passage   **289 Words**
Background: *What is it like to go camping? Read this story to find out what happened when Ted and his family went camping.*

Ted's family was taking one last camping trip before school started. They found the perfect campsite! It was just where a clear stream trickled into **placid** Green Lake. The **surroundings** were ideal! Ted and his brothers could swim to their hearts' content. They could row into hidden coves along the shore. It was a perfect place to fish or relax.

The first two days were great, with **spectacular** sunrises and **adventurous** days. The nights were cool and **refreshing**. Just before **nightfall** on the third day, a **rainfall** began. Everyone joked and laughed as they packed their **belongings**. But, by the second day of **continuous** rain, **tensions** rose. The four boys grew tired of sharing their **cramped** tent. Late that night, Ted was awakened by a loud crash. He realized he was floating! Their quiet stream had become a **rampaging** river and their tent had been washed into it! Ted **roused** his brothers and they **thrashed** about in the darkness as they struggled to pull themselves onto the riverbank. Streaks of lightning flashed across the sky. **Thunderbolts** shook the earth. The storm raged through the night.

Near daybreak, the lightning and thunder ceased. The brothers could see the path of **destruction** left by the storm. The huge oak across the stream had been struck down. Now it was no more than a jumbled **woodpile**. Their canoes had been tossed about the shore like toys. They worked hard all morning to **restore** their campsite. During lunch, a park **ranger** came by to see if they were okay. He told them a **camper** had been **injured** when a tree was hit by lightning and fell on his tent. Ted and his brothers were lucky to have escaped with only scratches and bruises.

Comprehension Questions
Inf - 1. Why did Ted and his family think the campsite was perfect?

Accept either: *They could do all the things they liked to do/it was quiet, near a lake*

Lit - 2. What were some of the things that Ted and his brothers liked to do?
Swim, fish, row

Inf - 3. What was the loud crash that Ted heard?
Accept either: *Lightning and thunder/The oak tree falling*

Lit - 4. What awoke Ted?
A loud noise

Inf - 5. How did the stream become a dangerous river?
All the rain made it bigger and faster

Lit - 6. What did the brothers see when the storm was over?
How much of the area had been destroyed

Lit - 7. Why did the park ranger come to the campsite?
To see if they were okay

Inf - 8. Why did Ted and his brothers have to work so hard to restore the campsite?
Because the storm had done so much damage

Level 6, Silent Passage   **332 Words**
Background: *What do you have to do if you don't have enough money to buy something special? Read this story to find out how Mike worked to earn money for something he wanted very badly.*

Mike squinted at the midday sky. He had been working since **sunup** and needed a break. Wiping the **perspiration** from his face, he continued his exhausting work.

Mike had been working all summer to earn enough money for a new bike. His ancient, beaten up bike was a total **embarrassment.** But his mom said they couldn't afford a new one. Even though Mike knew she was right, in his **frustration**, he shouted back at her, "You never give me anything!"

He only needed fifty more dollars. Mr. Painter had offered him forty dollars to dig a new **drainage** ditch. He wanted to stop the flooding in his rose garden. Mr. Painter wanted the new ditch to run **parallel** to the old one. Mike didn't think that would be **effective** in a **downpour**. So he suggested an **alternate** plan to direct the **rainwater** away from the house.

Mike noticed Mr. Painter watching him from behind a curtain. Knowing the old grouch, he'd deduct that little brow-wiping break from his pay! As he returned to his work, Mike waved. Mr. Painter **acknowledged** the wave and disappeared.

Mike worked steadily until **midafternoon**. Then Mr. Painter came out for an **inspection**. "Why don't you lay off for today, and get a fresh start tomorrow?"

"I'd rather finish up," replied Mike. It's supposed to rain tonight, and I'd like to have this operational before the next storm."

About six-thirty, Mike laid the last pipe in place. As he was returning the tools to the shed, Mr. Painter walked up, "Mike, you're an **enterprising** young man! You don't see many young people these days who care about their work." He handed Mike an envelope and went to inspect his roses.

When Mike opened the envelope, he counted three twenty-dollar bills. He ran to catch Mr. Painter and started to hand one back to him. Mr. Painter **declined** the offer, "Take it as thanks for keeping an old man from making the same mistake twice."

Comprehension Questions
Lit - 1. Why was Mike trying to earn money?
           To buy a bike

Lit - 2. What was Mike doing to earn money?
> *Digging a ditch*

Inf - 3. What was wrong with Mike's old bike?
> Accept either: *It was an embarrassment/it was old and beaten up*

Inf - 4. Why did Mike yell at his mom?
> Accept either: *He was frustrated or angry that she said she couldn't buy him a bike*

Inf - 5. Why didn't Mike think Mr. Painter's plan for the drainage ditch would work?
> *It was going to be in the same direction as the old ditch*

Inf - 6. How do you think Mike felt about Mr. Painter as he was working?
> *He didn't like him*

Lit - 7. How much more money did Mike need to buy the bike he wanted?
> *Fifty dollars*

Lit - 8. Why didn't Mike want to stop when Mr. Painter suggested he quit for the day?
> *He wanted to finish before it rained*

Lit - 9. How much did Mr. Painter promise to pay Mike for digging the ditch?
> *Forty dollars*

Inf - 10. Why do you think Mr. Painter paid Mike more than her had promised?
> Accept any of these: *suggested how to dig the ditch, wanted to stay and finish, cleaned tools*

Level 7, Silent Passage   **360 Words**
Background: *What do people do in gymnastics? In this passage, Debbie has to do gymnastics in gym class.*

Sometimes, Debbie wondered how she and Kim even **tolerated** each other, much less remained best friends. While Debbie was outgoing, Kim was quiet and shy. While Debbie was famous for her total lack of **coordination**, Kim was the most **acrobatic** person in the entire school. Yet the girls were **inseparable**, best friends since **kindergarten**. They were thrilled to find out they would be gym class together. But as usual, the had opposite opinions about actually taking gym. Kim greeted the class **enthusiastically**, and Debbie had nothing but **contempt** for it.

Today, they began the **gymnastics** unit, and Debbie wished she could crawl into a deep hole and disappear. Down the hall came the new **gymnastics** teacher, Ms. Bain. She announced that today they would be tumbling. Then Ms. Bain described some of the moves the girls would be doing, the forward roll, the backward roll, and the **cartwheel**.

Ms. Bain asked if anyone could demonstrate any of the moves for the class. The whole class sang out in **unison**, "Kim!" Then Ms. Bain asked Kim if she had taken lessons, and she nodded shyly. When Ms. Bain asked if Kim had gotten far enough along to demonstrate any of these moves, the class giggled. Debbie realized that Kim was too modest to tell Ms. Bain the truth, so she spoke up proudly, "Ms. Bain, Kim is the state champion in **gymnastics**. She's a competitor at the national level."

Ms. Bain smiled at Kim and said, "Maybe you could give us a demonstration of the routine you performed at the state meet." With some encouragement from her classmates, Kim agreed to show the class part of her tumbling routine.

As Debbie watched in admiration, Kim stepped onto the floor mat. As soon as she started to perform, her whole personality changed. Usually, Kim was awkward in front of people, but when she stepped onto the gym floor her body became **elegance** in motion. Kim's normal shyness disappeared and she seemed to be an actress playing the part of a gymnast. Even Ms. Bain was taken aback! She applauded approvingly and said she hoped Kim would invite her to her next meet.

Comprehension Questions

Inf - 1. Why didn't Debbie like gym class?
> *She is clumsy*

Inf - 2. Why did Kim like gym class?
> Accept either: *She is acrobatic/likes gymnastics*

Lit - 3. When did Debbie and Kim become friends?
> *In kindergarten*

Lit - 4. What tumbling moves did the teacher want the girls to do?
> Accept any: *forward roll, backward roll, or cartwheel*

Inf - 5. Why did the girls in the gym class suggest that Kim demonstrate the tumbling moves?
> Accept either: *They knew she was good at gymnastics/she was state champion*

Inf - 6. Why did the girls giggle when Ms. Bain asked if Kim had enough experience to demonstrate for the class?
> Accept either: *They all knew that Kim was state champion/had been taking gymnastics a long time*

Lit - 7. Why didn't Kim tell the teacher about her experience in gymnastics?
> Accept either: *She was too modest/she was too shy*

Inf - 8. Why did Kim need encouragement from her classmates before she would perform?
> Accept either: *She was shy/she felt awkward in front of people/she was modest*

Inf - 9. Why did Debbie admire Kim?
> Accept any: *She was coordinated/she was state champion/she was good at gymnastics*

Lit - 10. What did Ms. Bain do when Kim finished her performance?
> Accept either: *She applauded/said she would like to go to Kim's next meet*

Level 8, Silent Passage   **337 Words**
Background: *What is a journalist? In this passage, Kate has decided she wants to be a kind of journalist.*

Kate's greatest ambition is to be a **journalist**. Throughout her high school years, she has been a photographer on the school newspaper. Now she is the senior editor of her high school newspaper, but her goal is to be a foreign **correspondent**. Kate is taking a class in photography and learning how to use pictures to tell a story. Kate would like to find a way to combine writing about international relations and photography, perhaps writing for a news magazine or for a TV news show, but using her own photographs.

Two years ago, Kate's history class took a trip to the southeastern states. She took her camera and photographed the **eroded seacoasts**. When Kate's pictures were published in the local newspaper, there were many letters to the editor, praising her work.

Last year, when Kate was a junior, her class went to Mexico. Kate took pictures of how the recent earthquake had **devastated** the entire region. When Kate showed her pictures to the editor of the town newspaper, he asked her to write an article to go with her pictures. He told Kate that she had a unique talent for capturing people's attention with a profound photograph. He said if she wrote an article go with the pictures, people would understand the message in the photographs better. This time, public reaction was **phenomenal**! Kate could finally see a way to combine her ability to write with her interest in photography!

Now in her senior year, Kate is deciding where to go to college. Kate's **inclination** is to go to a **prestigious** college in Washington, D.C. or New York. She wants to be near the **ambassadors** and diplomats. Kate has never abandoned her goal to be a foreign **correspondent**. She keeps that in mind through all her decisions.

Comprehension Questions

Lit - 1. What does Kate want to be?
        Accept either: *A journalist/A foreign correspondent*
Lit - 2. How did Kate get started in journalism?
        She is on the staff of the high school newspaper
Inf - 3. How will Kate's experiences in high school help her accomplish her goals?

Accept any of these: *She is the editor of the high school news-paper/She is a photographer for the high school paper/She is taking a class to learn about photography*

Inf - 4. Why did Kate take her camera with her to Mexico?
So she could take pictures of the damage caused by the earth-quake

Lit - 5. How did Kate get her pictures published the first time?
The local newspaper published them ✓

Inf - 6. How did the newspaper readers feel about Kate's pictures from the southeast?
They liked her work

Lit - 7   Who helped Kate get her photographs and writing published?
The local newspaper editor

Inf - 8. How did the local editor help Kate see a way to accomplish her goal?
He asked her to write about her pictures

Lit - 9. Why did the newspaper editor suggest that Kate write an article to go with her pictures about the earthquake?
To help people understand the message of the photographs bet-ter

Inf - 10. How will Kate make her decision about which college to attend?
She will choose one where she can be near people who make political decisions ✓

References

Aaron, P. G. (1993). Is there a visual dyslexia? *Annals of Dyslexia, 43,* 110–124.

Abramson, L. Y., Garber, J., & Seligman, M. E. (1980). Learned helplessness in humans: An attributional analysis. In J. Garber & M. E. Seligman, *Human helplessness: Theory and applications* (pp. 3–34). New York: Academic Press.

Ada, A. F. (1988). The Pajaro Valley experience: Working with Spanish-speaking parents to develop children's reading and writing skills in the home through the use of children's literature. In T. Skutnabb-Kangas & J. Cunnins (Eds.), *Minority education: From shame to struggle* (pp. 223–238). Clevedon, UK: Multilingual Matters.

Adams, A. (1991). The oral reading of learning-disabled readers: variations produced within the instructional and frustration ranges. *Remedial and Special Education, 12,* 48–52, 62.

Adams, M. J. (1990). *Beginning to read: Thinking and learning about print.* Boston: MIT Press.

Afflerbach, P. P. (1987). How are main idea statements constructed? Watch the experts. *Journal of Reading Behavior, 30,* 512–518.

Allen, V. G. (1994). English books that foster concepts in limited-English students. In K. Spangenberg-Urschat & R. Pritchard, *Kids come in all languages* (pp. 108–131). Newark, DE: International Reading Association.

Allington, R. L. (1977). If they don't read much, how they ever gonna get good? *Journal of Reading, 21,* 57–61.

Allington, R. L. (1980). Teacher interruption behaviors during primary grade oral reading. *Journal of Educational Psychology, 72,* 371–377.

Allington, R. L. (1982). The persistence of teacher beliefs in the perceptual deficit hypothesis. *Elementary School Journal, 82,* 351–359.

Allington, R. L. (1983). The reading instruction provided readers of differing abilities. *The Elementary School Journal, 83,* 548–559.

Allington, R. L. (1984). Content coverage and contextual reading in reading groups. *Journal of Reading Behavior, 16,* 85–97.

Allington, R. L. (1986). Policy constraints and effective compensatory reading instruction: A review. In J. B. Hoffman (Ed.), *Effective teaching of reading: Research and practice* (pp. 261–289). Newark, DE: International Reading Association.

Allington, R. L., & Broikou, K. A. (1988). Development of shared knowledge: A new role for classroom and specialist teachers. *The Reading Teacher, 41,* 806–812.

Allington, R. L., & Johnston, P. H. (1989). Coordination, collaboration, and consistency: The redesign of compensatory and special education interventions. In R. E. Slavin, N. L. Karweit, & N. A. Madden (Eds.), *Effective programs for students at risk* (pp. 195–219). Needham Heights, MA: Allyn and Bacon.

Allington, R. L., & McGill-Frazen, A. (1989). School response to reading failure: Instruction for Chapter I and special education students in grades 2, 4, and 8. *Elementary School Journal, 89,* 529–543.

Allington, R. L., & Walmsley, S. A. (1995). Redefining and reforming instructional support programs for at-risk students. In R. L. Allington & S. A. Walmsley, *No quick fix: Rethinking literacy in America's elementary schools* (pp. 19–41). New York: Teachers College Press, and Newark DE: International Reading Association.

American Academy of Pediatrics (1992). Learning disabilities, dyslexia, and vision. *American Academy of Pediatrics,* volume 90, 124–126.

American Psychiatric Association (1994). *Diagnostic and statistical manual of mental disorders (DSM IV)* (4th ed.). Washington, DC: American Psychiatric Association.

Anderson, B. (1981). The missing ingredient: Fluent oral reading. *Elementary School Journal, 81,* 173–177.

Anderson, R. C., & Freebody, P. (1981). Vocabulary knowledge. In J. Guthrie (Ed.), *Comprehension and teaching: Research views* (pp. 77–117). Newark, DE: International Reading Association.

Anderson, R. C. (1984). Role of the reader's schema in comprehension, learning, and memory. In R. C. Anderson, J. Osborn, & R. J. Tierney (Eds.), *Learning to read in American schools* (pp. 243–258). Hillsdale, NJ: Earlbaum.

Anderson, R. C., & Pearson P. D. (1984). A schema-theoretic view of basic processes in reading comprehension. In P. D. Pearson, R. Barr, M. L. Kamil, & P. Mosenthal (Eds.), *Handbook of reading research* (Vol. I, pp. 255–291). White Plains, NY: Longman.

Anderson, R. C., Hiebert, E. H., Scott, J. A., & Wilkinson, I. A. G. (1985). *Becoming a nation of readers.* Washington, DC: National Institute of Education.

Anderson, R. C., & Nagy, W. E. (1991). Word meanings. In R. Barr, M. L. Kamil, P. Mosenthal, & P. D. Pearson (Eds.), *Handbook of reading research* (Vol. II, pp. 690–724). White Plains, NY: Longman.

Anderson, R. C., Wilson, P., & Fielding, L. (1988). Growth in reading and how children spend their time outside of school. *Reading Research Quarterly, 23,* 285–303.

Anderson, R. C., Wilkinson, I. A. G., & Mason, J. M. (1991). A micro-analysis of the small-group guided lesson: Effects of an emphasis on global story meaning. *Reading Research Quarterly, 26,* 417–441.

Anderson, S. (1984). *A whole-language approach to reading.* Landham, MD: University Press of America.

Anderson, T. H., & Armbruster, B. B. (1984). Content area textbooks. In R. C. Anderson, J. Osborn, & R. J. Tierney (Eds.), *Learning to read in American schools: Basal readers and content texts* (pp. 193–226). Hillsdale, NJ: Erlbaum.

Appleby, A. N. (1978). *The child's concept of story: Ages 2–17.* Chicago: University of Chicago.

Armbruster, B. B. (1986). Using frames to organize expository text. Paper presented at National Reading Conference, Austin, TX.

Armbruster, B. B., & Anderson, T. H. (1982). *Idea-mapping: The technique and its use in the classroom* (Reading Education Report No. 36). Champaign, IL: Center for the Study of Reading, University of Illinois.

Asher, J., & Price, B. (1969). The learning strategy of total physical response: Some age differences. *Child Development, 38,* 1219–1227.

Aulls, M. (1986). Actively teaching main idea skills. In J. F. Baumann (Ed.), *Teaching main idea comprehension* (pp. 96–132). Newark, DE: International Reading Association.

Badian, N. A., Duffy, F. H., Als, H., & McNaulty, G. B. (1991). Linguistic profiles of dyslexic and good readers. *Annals of Dyslexia, 41,* 221–245.

Baker, K. (1993, December). At-risk students and literature-based instruction, low-achieving students and self-selected reading. Presentation at the National Reading Conference, Charleston, SC.

Ball, E. W., & Blachman, B. A. (1991). Does phoneme awareness training in kindergarten make a difference in early word recognition and spelling? *Reading Research Quarterly, 26(1),* 49–66.

Bannatyne, A. D. (1974). Diagnosis: A note on recategorization of the WISC scaled scores. *Journal of Learning Disabilities, 7,* 272–273.

Baumann, J., & Murray, B. (1994). Current practices in reading assessment. In K. Wood & B. Algozzine (Eds.), *Teaching reading to high risk learners: A unified perspective* (pp. 149–196). Needham Heights, MA: Allyn and Bacon.

Baumann, J. F. (1986). The direct instruction of main idea comprehension ability. In J. F. Baumann (Ed.), *Teaching main idea comprehension* (pp. 133–178). Newark, DE: International Reading Association.

Baumann, J. F., & Serra, K. K. (1984). The frequency and placement of main ideas in children's social studies textbooks: A modified replication of Braddock's research on topic sentences. *Journal of Reading Behavior, 16,* 27–40.

Beach, R., & Hynds, S. (1991). Research on response to literature. In R. Barr, M. L. Kamil, P. Mosenthal, & P. D. Pearson (Eds.), *Handbook of reading research* (Vol. 2, pp. 453–489). White Plains, NY: Longman.

Bear, D. (1994). Word sort: An alternative to phonics, spelling, and vocabulary. Paper presented at the National Reading Conference, San Diego, CA.

Beattie, J. (1994). Characteristic of students with disabilities and how teachers can help. In K. Wood & B. Algozzine (Eds.), *Teaching reading to high-risk learners: A unified perspective* (pp. 99–122). Needham Heights, MA: Allyn and Bacon.

Beck, I. L., Omanson, R. C., & McKeown, M. G. (1982). An instructional redesign of reading lessons: effects on comprehension. *Reading Research Quarterly, 17,* 462–481.

Beck, I. L., Perfetti, C. A., & McKeown, M. G. (1982). The effects of long-term vocabulary instruction on lexical access and reading comprehension. *Journal of Educational Psychology, 74,* 506–521.

Becker, N., & Carnine, D. (1980). Direct instruction: an effective approach to educational intervention with disadvataged and low performers. In B. Lahey & A. Cazden (Eds.), *Advances in clinical psychology* (Vol. 3). New York: Plenum.

Berliner, D. C. (1981). Academic learning time and reading achievement. In J. T. Guthrie (Ed.), *Comprehension and teaching: Research views* (pp. 203–226). Newark, DE: International Reading Association.

Berninger, V. W., Lester, K., Sohlberg-McKay, M., & Mateer, C. (1991). Interventions based on the multiple connections model of reading for developmental dyslexia and acquired deep dyslexia. *Archives for Clinical Neuropsychology, 6(4),* 375–391.

Berrueta-Clement, J. R., Schweinhart, L. J., Barnett, W. S., Epstein, A. S., & Weikart, D. P. (1985). *Changed lives. The effects of the Perry pre-school program on youths through age 19.* Ypsalanti, MI:

Monographs of the High/Scope Educational Research Foundation, 8.

Biemiller, A. (1994). Some observations on acquiring and using reading skills in elementary schools. In C. K. Kinzer & D. J. Leu (Eds.), *Multidimensional aspects of literacy research, theory, and practice: Forty-third yearbook of the National Reading Conference* (pp. 209–216). Chicago, IL: National Reading Conference.

Birman, B. F., Orland, M. E., Jung, R. K., Anson, R. J., Garcia, G. N., Moore, M. T., Funkhouser, J. E., Morrison, D. R., Turnbull, B. J., & Reisner, E. R. (1987). *The current operation of the Chapter I program: Final report from the National Assessment of Chapter I.* Washington, DC: U.S. Government Printing Office.

Blachman, B. A. (1994). What we have learned from longitudinal studies of phonological processing and reading, *and* some unanswered questions: A response to Torgesen, Wagner, and Rashotte. *Journal of Learning Disabilities 27,* 287–291.

Blachowicz, C. L. Z. (1986). Making connections: Alternatives to the vocabulary notebook. *Journal of Reading, 29,* 643–649.

Bowlby, J. (1969). *Attachment.* New York: Basic Books.

Breen, M. J. (1986). Cognitive patterns of learning disability subtypes as measured by the *Woodcock–Johnson Psycho-Educational Battery. Journal of Learning Disabilities, 19,* 86–90.

Bridge, C. A., & Tierney, R. J. (1981). The inferential operations of children across text with narrative and expository tendencies. *Journal of Reading Behavior, 31,* 210–214.

Brophy, J. (1988). Research linking teacher behavior to student achievement: Potential implications for instruction of Chapter I students. *Educational Psychologist, 23,* 235–86.

Brown, A., & Campione, J. (1986). Psychological theory and the study of learning disabilities. *American Psychologist, 41,* 1059–1068.

Brown, A. L., Armbruster, B. B., & Baker, L. (1986). The role of meta-cognition in reading and studying. In J. Orasanu (Ed.), *Reading Comprehension: From research to practice* (pp. 49–75). Hillsdale, NJ: Erlbaum.

Brown, A. L., & Day, J. D. (1983). Macrorules for summarizing text: The development of expertise. *Technical Report No. 270.* Champaign, IL: Center for the Study of Reading, University of Illinois.

Brown, A. L., & Palincsar, A. S. (1982). Inducing strategic learning from texts by means of informed, self-control training. *Technical Report No. 262*. Champaign, IL: Center for the Study of Reading, University of Illinois.

Bryan, T. (1991). Social problems and learning disabilities. In B. Wong (Ed.), *Learning about learning disabilities* (pp. 195–231). San Diego: Academic Press.

Burke, C. (1976). The Burke reading interview. Bloomington, IN: Indiana University, School of Education, Reading Department.

Byrne, B., & Fielding-Barnsley, R. (1991). Evaluation of a program to teach phonemic awareness to young children. *Journal of Educational Psychology, 83(4)*, 451–455.

Caldwell, J. (1985). A new look at the old informal reading inventory. *The reading teacher, 39*, 168–173.

Caldwell, J. (1990). Using think cards to develop independent and strategic readers. *Academic Therapy, 25*, 561–566.

Caldwell, J. (1991, April). Subtypes of reading/learning disabilities: Do they have instructional relevance? Paper presented at the Learning Disabilities Association of America.

Caldwell, J. (1993a). Developing a metacognitive strategy for comprehension monitoring for narrative text. Milwaukee, WI: Cardinal Stritch College. Unpublished strategy.

Caldwell, J. (1993b). Developing an expectation grid for understanding expository text. Milwaukee, WI: Cardinal Stritch College. Unpublished strategy.

Caldwell, J. (1993c). Developing an text coding strategy for understanding expository text. Milwaukee, WI: Cardinal Stritch College. Unpublished strategy.

Carbo, M., Dunn, R., & Dunn, K. (1986). *Teaching students to read through their individual learning styles*. Reston, VA: Reston Publishing Co.

Cardon, L., Smith, S., Fulker, D., Kimberling, W., Pennington, B., & DeFries, J. (1994, October 14). Quantitative trait locus for reading disabilty on chromosome VI. *Science 26*, 276–279.

Carnegie Corporation (1994). *Starting points: Meeting the needs of our youngest children*. New York: Carnegie Corportation.

Carrasquillo, A. L., & Baecher, R. E. (Eds.) (1990). *Teaching the bilingual special education student*. Norwood, NJ: Ablex Publishing Co.

Carver, R. B. (1990). *Reading rate: A review of research and theory*. San Diego, CA: Academic.

Cazden, C. B. (1986). Classroom discourse. In M. C. Wittrock (Ed.), *Handbook of research on teaching* (3rd ed., pp. 432–462). New York: Macmillan.

Cazden, C. B. (1988a). *Classroom discourse: The language of teaching and learning*. Portsmouth, NH: Heinemann.

Cazden, C. B. (1988b). *Interactions between Maori children and Pakeha teachers*. Aukland NZ: Aukland Reading Association. Quoted in Johnston, P., & Allington R. L. (1991). Remediation. In R. Barr, M. L. Kamil, P. Mosenthal, & P. D. Pearson, *Handbook of reading research* (Vol. 2, pp. 984–1012). White Plains, NY: Longman.

Chall, J. S. (1967). *Learning to read: The great debate*. New York: McGraw-Hill.

Chall, J. S. (1979). The great debate: Ten years later with a modest proposal for reading stages. In L. B. Resnick & P. A. Weaver (Eds.), *Theory and practice of early reading* (Vol. 1, pp. 29–55). Hillsdale, NJ: Erlbaum.

Chall, J. S. (1983a). *Learning to read: The great debate* (updated version). New York: McGraw-Hill.

Chall, J. S. (1983b). *Stages of reading development*. New York: McGraw-Hill.

Chall, J. S. (1987). Reading development in adults. *Annals of Dyslexia, 37*, 252–263.

Chall, J. S. (1994). Patterns of adult reading. *Learning Disabilities: A Multidisciplinary Journal, 5(1)*, 1–33.

Chall, J. S., Jacobs, V., & Baldwin, L. (1990). *The reading crisis: Why poor children fall behind*. Cambridge, MA: Harvard University Press.

Chamot, A. U., & O'Malley, J. M. (1994). Instructional approaches and teaching procedures. In K. Spangenberg-Urbschat & R. Pritchard (Eds.), *Kids come in all languages* (pp. 82–107). Newark DE, International Reading Association.

Chicago Tribune (1994, April 6). Rising risks for our nation's children, Section 1, p. 1.

Chira, S. (1994, April 12). Study confirms worst fears on U.S. children. *New York Times*, p. A1, A11. Carnegie Corporation of New York: Carbo and Hodges.

Chomsky, C. (1978). When you still can't read in third grade. After decoding, what? In S. J. Samuels (Ed.), *What research has to say about reading instuction*. Newark, DE: International Reading Association.

Clay, M. M. (1993a). *An observation survey of early literacy achievement.* Portsmouth, NH: Heinemann Educational Books.

Clay, M. M. (1993b). *Reading recovery: A guidebook for teachers in training.* Portsmouth, NH: Heinemann Educational Books.

Clymer, T. (1963). The utility of phonic generalizations in the primary grades. *The Reading Teacher, 16,* 252–258.

Cohen, J. (1986). Learning disabilities and psychological development in childhood and adolescence. *Annals of Dyslexia, 36,* 287–300.

Cooper, H. (1979). Pygmalion grows up: A model for teacher expectation, communication, and performance influence. *Review of Educational Research, 49,* 389–410.

Cosden, M., Gerber, M., Semmel, D., Goldman, S., & Semmel, M. (1987). Microcomputer uses within micro-education environments. *Exceptional Children, 53,* 399–409.

Cox, A. (1986). Alphabetic phonics : An organization and expansion of the Orton–Gillingham. *Annals of Dyslexia, 35,* 187–189.

Crawford, J. (1989). Instructional activities related to achievement gains in Chapter I classes. In R. E. Slavin, N. L. Karweit, & N. A. Madden (Eds.), *Effective programs for students at risk* (pp. 264–290). Needham Heights, MA: Allyn and Bacon/Simon and Schuster.

Critchley M. (1970). *The dyslexic child.* Springfield, IL: Charles C. Thomas.

Crook, W. (1977). *Can your child read? Is he hyperactive?* Jacobson, TN: Professional Books.

Cummins, R. (1989). A theortical framework for bilingual special education. *Exceptional Children, 56,* 111–120.

Cunningham, A. E., & Stanovich, K. E. (1993). Children's literacy (environments and early recognition subskills. *Reading and Writing: An Interdisciplinary Journal, 5,* 193–204.

Cunningham, P. M. (1995). *Phonics they use: Words for reading and writing* (2nd ed.). New York: Harper Collins.

Cunningham, P. M., & Cunningham, J. W. (1992). Making words: Enhancing the invented spelling–decoding connection. *The Reading Teacher, 46,* 106–115.

Cunningham, P. M., & Hall, D. P. (1994a). *Making words.* Carthage, IL: Good Apple.

Cunningham, P. M., & Hall, D. P. (1994b). *Making big words.* Carthage IL: Good Apple.

Dale, E. (1965). Vocabulary measurement: Techniques and major findings. *Elementary English, 42,* 895–901, 948.

Daneman, M. (1991). Individual differences in reading skills. In R. Barr, M. L. Kamil, P. Mosenthal, & P. D. Pearson (Eds.), *Handbook of reading research* (Vol. II, pp. 512–538). White Plains, NY: Longman.

Davey, B. (1983). Think aloud: Modeling the cognitive processes of reading comprehension. *Journal of Reading, 27,* 44–47.

Davis, F. B. (1968). Research in comprehension in reading. *Reading Research Quarterly, 3,* 499–545.

DeFries, J. C., & Decker, S. N. (1982). Genetic aspects of reading disability: A family study. In R. Malatesha & P. Aaron (Eds.), *Reading disorders: Varieties and treatments* (pp. 255–279). New York: Academic Press.

DeFries, J. C., Olson, R. K., Pennington, B. F., & Smith, S. D. (1991). Colorado reading project: An update. In D. D. Duane & D. B Gray (Eds.), *The reading brain: The biological basis of dyslexia.* Parkton, MD: York Press.

Delain, M. T., Pearson, P. D., & Anderson, R. C. (1985). Reading comprehension and creativity in black language use: You stand to gain by playing the sounding game. *American Educational Research Journal, 22,* 155–173.

Delpit, L. D. (1988). The silenced dialogue: Power and pedagogy in educating other people's children. *Harvard Educational Review, 58,* 280–298.

Diener, C. I., & Dweck, C. (1978). An analysis of learned helplessness: II. The processing of success. *Journal of Personality and Social Psychology, 39,* 940–952.

Doctorow, M., Wittrock, M. C., & Marks, C. (1978). Generative processes in reading comprehension. *Journal of Educational Psychology, 70,* 109–118.

Dowhower, S. L. (1987). Effects of repreated readings on second-grade transitional readers' fluency and comprehension. *Reading Research Quarterly, 22,* 389–406.

Dreher, M. J., & Zenge, S. D. (1990). Using metalinguistic awareness in first grade to predict reading achievement in third and fifth grades. *Journal of Educational Research, 84,* 13–21.

Duane, D. (1989). Neurobiological correlates of learning disorders. *Journal of the American Academy of Child and Adolescent Psychiatry, 28,* 314–318.

Duffy, F. (1988). Neurophysiological studies in dyslexia. In D. Plum (Ed.), *Language, communication, and the brain.* New York: Raven Press.

Duffy, G., & Roehler, L. (1987). Improving classroom reading instruction through the use of responsive elaboration. *The Reading Teacher, 40,* 514–521.

Durkin, D. (1978–9). What classroom observations reveal about reading comprehension instruction. *Reading Research Quarterly. 14 (4),* 481–533.

Dymock, S. (1993). Reading but not understanding. *Journal of Reading, 37,* 86–91.

Elley, W., & Mangubhai, F. (1983). The impact of reading on second language learning. *Reading Research Quarterly, 19,* 53–67.

Ellis, E., Deshler, D., Lenz, K. Schumkaer, J., & Clark, F. (1991). An instructional model for teaching learning strategies. *Focus on Exceptional Children, 23(6),* 1–23.

Enfield, M. (1988). The quest for literacy. *Annals of Dyslexia, 38,* 8–21.

Engelmann, S., & Bruner, H. (1974). *DISTAR READING.* Chicago: Science Research Associates.

Englert, C. S., & Hiebert, E. (1984). Children's developing awareness of text structure in expository material. *Journal of Educational Psychology, 26,* 65–74.

Evans, B. J. W. (1993). Dyslexia: The Dunlop test and tinted lenses. *Optometry Today, 33,* 26–30.

Farr, R., Lewis, M., Fasholz, J., Pinsky, E., Towle, S., Lipschutz, J., & Faulds, B. P. (1990). Writing in response to reading. *Educational Leadership, 47(6),* 66–69.

Feingold, B. (1975). *Why your child is hyperactive.* New York: Random House.

Fernald, G. (1943/1988). *Remedial techniques in basic school subjects.* Austin, TX: Pro-Ed. (Original work published in 1943.)

Feuerstein, R. (1980). Instrumental Enrichment: An intervention program for cognitive modifiability. Baltimore: University Press.

Fisher, C. W., Filby, N. W., Marliave, R., Cahen, L. S., Dishaw, M. M., & Moore, J. E. (1978a). *Teaching and learning in the elementary school: A summary of the beginning teacher evaluation study* (Beginning Teacher Evaluation Study [BTES] Report VII–I). San Francisco: Far West Laboratory for Educational Research and Development.

Fisher, C. W., Filby, N. W., Marliave, R., Cahen, L. S., Dishaw, M. M., Moore, J. E., & Berliner, D. C. (1978b). *Teaching behaviors, academic learning*

time and student achievement (Final report of Phase III–B BTES). San Francisco: Far West Laboratory for Educational Research and Development.

Flesch, R. (1979, November). Why Johnny still can't read. *Family Circle, 92,* 26–46.

Fletcher, J., & Martínez, G. (1994). An eye-movement analysis of the effects of scotopic sensitivity correction on parsing and comprehension. *Journal of Learning Disabilities, 27,* 67–70.

Flowers, D. L. (1993). Brain basis for dyslexia: A summary of work in progress. *Journal of Learning Disabilities, 26,* 575–582.

Foorman, B. R., Francis, D. J., Novy, D. M., & Liberman, D. (1991). How letter–sound instruction mediates progress in first-grade reading and spelling. *Journal of Educational Psychology, 83(4),* 456–469.

Fractor, J. S., Woodruff, M. C., Martinez, M. G., & Teale, W. H. (1993). Let's not miss opportunities to promote voluntary reading: Classroom libraries in the elementary school. *The Reading Teacher, 46,* 476–484.

Galaburda, A. (1989). Ordinary and extraordinary brain development: Anatomical variations in developmental dyslexia. *Annals of Dyslexia, 39,* 67–80.

Galda, L., Cullinan, B. E., Strickland, D. S. (1993). *Language, literacy and the child.* New York: Harcourt Brace Jovanovich.

Gambrell, L. B. (1986, December 3). Functions of children's oral language during reading instruction. Paper presented at the 36th annual meeting of the National Reading Conference, Autsin, TX.

Gambrell, L. B., & Bales, R. J. (1986). Mental imagery and the comprehension-monitoring performance of fourth- and fifth-grade poor readers. *Reading Research Quarterly, 21,* 454–464.

Gambrell, L. B., Pfeiffer, W., & Wilson, R. (1985). The effects of retelling upon reading comprehension and recall of text information. *Journal of Educational Research, 78,* 216–220.

Garcia, G. E., Pearson, R. D., & Jiménez, R. T. (1994). *The at-risk dilemma: A synthesis of reading research.* Champaign IL: Center for the Study of Reading, University of Illinois.

Garcia, S. B., & Malkin, D. H. (1993). Toward defining programs and services for culturally and linguistically diverse learners in special education. *Teaching Exceptional Children, 26(1),* 52–58.

Gardner, H. (1985). *Frames of mind: The theory of multiple intelligences.* New York: Basic Books.

Gaskins, I. W., & Downer, M. (1986). *Benchmark word identification/vocabulary development program: Beginning level.* Media, PA: Benchmark Press.

Gaskins, R. W. (1988). The missing ingredients: Time on task, direct instruction, and writing. *The Reading Teacher, 41,* 750–756.

Gaskins, R. W., Soja, S., Indrisano, A., Lawrence, H., Elliot, T., Rouch, S., O'Donnell. D., Young, J., Audley, S., Bruinsma, S., MacDonald, E., Barus, B., Gutman, A., & Theilacker, S. (1989). *Benchmark word identification/vocabulary development program: Intermediate level.* Media, PA: Benchmark Press.

Genesee, F. (1985). Second-language learning through immersion: A review of U.S. programs. *Review of Educational Research, 55(4),* 541–561.

Gentry, J. R., & Gillet, J. W. (1993). *Teaching kids to spell.* Portsmouth, NH: Heinemann.

Gersten, R., Brengleman, S., & Jiménez, R. (1994). Effective instruction for culturally and linguistically diverse students: A reconceptualization. *Focus on Exceptional Children, 27(1),* 1–16.

Giacobbe, M. E. (1986). Learning to write and writing to learn in the elementary school. In A. R. Petrosky & D. Bartholomae (Eds.), *The teaching of writing: Eighty-fifth yearbook of the National Society for the Study of Education* (pp. 131–147). Chicago, IL: University of Chicago.

Gillingham, A., & Stillman, B. (1970). *Remedial training for children with specific disability in reading, spelling and penmanship.* Cambridge, MA: Educators Publishing Service.

Gipe, J. P. (1980). Use of relevant context helps kids learn new word meanings. *The Reading Teacher, 33,* 398–402.

Golden, J., & Guthrie, J. (1986). Convergence and divergence in reader response to literature. *Reading Research Quarterly, 21,* 408–421.

Goldman, S. R., & Pellegrino, J. W. (1987). Information processing and educational microcomputer technology: Where do we go from here? *Journal of Learning Disabilities, 20,* 144–154.

Goldstein, R. (1969). *The poetry of rock.* New York: Bantam.

Gollnick, D. M., & Chinn, P. C. (1990). *Multicultural education in a pluristic society.* Columbus, OH: Charles Merrill.

Good, T. (1983). Research on classroom teaching. In L. S. Schulman & G. Sykes (Eds.), *Handbook on teaching and policy.* White Plains, NY: Longman.

Goodman, K. S. (1965). A linguistic study of cues and miscues in reading. *Elementary English, 42,* 639–643.

Goodman, K. S. (1969). Analysis of oral reading miscues. *Reading Research Quarterly, 5,* 9–30.

Goodman, K. S. (1979). Reading: A psycholinguistic guessing game. In H. Singer & R. Ruddell (Eds.), *Theoretical models and processes of reading* (pp. 497–508). Newark, DE: International Reading Association.

Goodman, K. S. (1992). Why whole language is today's agenda in today's education. *Language Arts, 69,* 353–363.

Goodman, K. S., & Gollasch, F. V. (1980–1). Word omissions: Deliberate and non-deliberate. *Reading Research Quarterly, 14,* 6–31.

Goodman, K. S., & Goodman, Y. (1983). Reading and writing relationships: Pragmatic functions. *Language Arts, 60,* 590–599.

Goodman, K. S., & Goodman, Y. M. (1979). Learning to read is natural. In L. B. Resnick & P. A. Weaver (Eds.), *Theory and practice of early reading* (Vol. 1, pp. 137–154). Hillsdale, NJ: Earlbaum.

Goodman, Y. M. (1976). Miscues, errors and reading comprehension. In J. Merritt (Ed.), *New horizons in reading.* Newark, DE: International Reading Association.

Gottesman, R. (1994). The adult with learning disabilities: An overview. *Learning Disabilities: A Multidisciplinary Journal, 5(1),* 1–13.

Gough, P. B., & Hillinger, M. L. (1980). Learning to read: An unnatural act. *Bulletin of the Orton Society, 30,* 171–176.

Graesser, A., Golding, J. M., & Long, D. L. (1991). Narrative representation and comprehension. In R. Barr, M. L. Kamil, P. Mosenthal, & P. D. Pearson (Eds.), *Handbook of reading research* (Vol. 2, pp. 171–205). White Plains, NY: Longman.

Graves, D. H. (1994). *A fresh look at writing.* Portsmouth, NH: Heinemann.

Gross, A. (1978). The relationship between six differences and reading ability in an Israeli kibbutz system. In D. Feitleson (Ed.), *Crosscultural perspectives on reading and reading research* (pp. 72–88). Newark, DE: International Reading Association.

Guthrie, J. T., & Greaney, V. (1991). Literacy acts. In R. Barr, M. L. Kamil, P. Mosenthal, & P. D. Pearson

(Eds.), *Handbook of reading research* (Vol. 2, pp. 68–96). White Plains, NY: Longman.

Hagerman, R. J., Jackson, C., Amiri, K., Silverman, A. C., O'Connor, R., & Sobsesky, W. (1992). Girls with fragile X syndrome: Physical and neurocognitive status and outcome. *Pediatrics, 89, 395–400.*

Hakuta, K. (1990). Language and cognition in bilingual children. In A. M. Padilla, H. H. Fairchild, & C. Valadez (Eds.), *Bilingual education: Issues and strategies* (pp. 47–59). Newbury Park, CA: Sage.

Hakuta, K., & Garcia, E. (1989). Bilingualism and education. *American Psychologist 44, 234–239.*

Hammechek, D. (1990). *Psychology in teaching, learning, and growth.* Boston, MA: Allyn and Bacon.

Hansen, J. (1981). The effects of inference training and practice on young children's reading comprehension. *Reading Research Quarterly, 16, 391–417.*

Harp, B. (1989). What do you do when the principal asks: "Why aren't you using phonics workbooks?" *The Reading Teacher, 42, 326–327.*

Harris, A., & Sipay, E. R. (1985). *How to increase reading ability* (8th ed.). White Plains, NY: Longman.

Hayes, D. P., & Ahrens, M. (1988). Vocabulary simplification for children: A special case of 'motherese'? *Journal of Child Language, 15, 395–410.*

Heath, S. B. (1981). Questioning at home and at school: A comparative study. In G. Spindler (Ed.), *Doing ethnography: Educational anthropology in action* (pp. 102–131). New York: Holt, Rinehart, and Winston.

Heath, S. B. (1983). *Ways with words: Language, life, and work in communities and classrooms.* Cambridge, MA: Harvard University Press.

Heckelman, R. G. (1969). The neurological impress method of remedial reading instruction. *Academic Therapy, 4, 277–282.*

Henderson, E. H. (1981). *Learning to read and spell: The child's knowledge of words.* DeKalb, IL: Northern Illinois University.

Henderson, E. H. (1985). *Teaching spelling.* Geneva, IL: Houghton Mifflin.

Hensley, M. (1994). From untapped potential to creative realization: Empowering parents of multicultural backgrounds. Paper presented at the meeting of the Society of Applied Anthropology, Cancun, Mexico. Cited in L. C. Moll & N. González, (1994). Lessons from research with language-minority children. *Journal of Reading Behavior, 26, 439–456.*

Herman, P. A. (1985). The effect of repeated readings on reading rate, speech pauses, and word recognition accuracy. *Reading Research Quarterly, 20, 553–564.*

Hinshelwood, J. (1917). *Congenital word-blindness.* London: H. K. Lewis.

Hirsch, E. D., Jr. (1987). *Cultural literacy.* Boston: Houghton Mifflin.

Hodgkinson, H. (1991). Reform versus reality. *Phi Delta Kappan, 73, 9–16.*

Hoffman, J. V. (1987). Rethinking the role of oral reading in basal instruction. *The Elementary School Journal, 87, 367–373.*

Hoffman, J. V., McCarthey, S. J., Abbott, J., Christain, C., Corman, L., Curry, C., Dressman, M., Elliot, B., Matherne, D., Stahle, D. (1994). So what's new in the basals? A focus on first grade. *Journal of Reading Behavior, 26, 47–73.*

Hoffman J. V., O'Neal, S. V., Kastler, L. A., Clements, R. D., Segel, K. W., & Nash, M. F. (1984). Guided oral reading and miscue focused verbal feedback in second grade classrooms. *Reading Research Quarterly, 14, 367–384.*

Holdaway, D. (1979). *The foundations of literacy.* Portsmouth, NH: Heinemann.

Holt-Ochsner, L. K. (1992). Automaticity training for dyslexics: An experimental study. *Annals of Dyslexia, 42, 222–241.*

Hornsby, D. Sukarna, D. W., & Parry, J. A. (1986). *Read on: A conference approach to reading.* Portsmouth NH: Heinemann.

Horowitz, R. (1985). Text patterns: Part I. *Journal of Reading Research, 28, 448–454.*

Hynd, G. (1992). Neurological aspects of dyslexia: Comments on the balance model. *Journal of Learning Disabilities, 25, 110–113.*

Idol, L. (1987). Group story mapping: A comprehension strategy for both skilled and unskilled readers. *Journal of Learning Disabilities, 20, 196–205.*

Improving America's Schools Act (1993). *Education Week, 20,* 31.

Individuals with Disabilities Education Act (1990). PL 101–476. U.S. Congress.

Ingham, J. (1982). *Books and reading development: The Bradford book flood experiment* (2nd ed.). Exeter, NH: Heinemann.

Iversen, S., & Tunmer, W. E. (1993). Phonological processing skills and the reading recovery program. *Journal of Educational Psychology, 85, 112–126.*

Jenkins, J. R., Heliotis, J., Haynes, M., & Bweck, K. (1986). Does passive learning account for readers' comprehension deficits in ordinary reading situations? *Learning Disability Quarterly, 9, 60–76.*

Jenkins, J. R., Pious, C., & Peterson D. (1988). Categorical programs for remedial and handicapped students: Issues of validity. *Exceptional Children, 55,* 147–158.

Jennings, J. H. (1991). A comparison of summary and journal writing as components of an interactive comprehension model in social studies. In *The fortieth yearbook of the National Reading Conference* (pp. 67–82). Chicago, IL: National Reading Conference.

Jennings, J. H., Richek, M. A., Chenault, L. R., & Ali, S. L. (1993, December). A parental literacy support program: Helping parents to help at-risk children. Paper presented at the National Reading Conference, Charleston, SC.

Johns, J. L. (1993). *Informal reading inventories: An annotated reference guide.* DeKalb, IL: Communitech.

Johnson, D. D. (1971). The Dolch list reexamined. *The Reading Teacher, 24,* 449–457.

Johnson, D. D., & Baumann, J. F. (1984). Word identification. In P. D. Pearson (Ed.), *Handbook of reading research* (pp. 583–608). White Plains, NY: Longman.

Johnson, D., & Johnson R. (1975). *Learning together and alone.* Englewood Cliffs, NJ: Prentice Hall.

Johnson, D., & Myklebust, H. (1967). *Learning disabilities.* New York: Grune and Stratton.

Johnson, M. J., Kress, R. A., & Pikulski, J. L. (1987). *Informal reading inventories* (2nd ed.). Newark, DE: International Reading Association.

Johnston, P. H. (1984). Instruction and student independence. *Elementary School Journal, 84,* 338–344.

Johnston, P. H., & Allington, R. (1991). Remediation. In R. Barr, M. L. Kamil, P. Mosenthal, & P. D. Pearson (Eds.), *Handbook of reading research* (Vol. 2, pp. 984–1012). White Plains, NY: Longman.

Johnston, P. H., Allington, R. L., & Afflerbach, P. (1985). Congruence of classroom and remedial reading instruction. *Elementary School Journal, 85,* 465–478.

Josel, C. A. (1986). A silent DRTA for remedial eighth graders. *Journal of Reading, 29,* 434–439.

Josel, C. A. (1988). In a different context. *Journal of Reading, 31,* 374–377.

Jouzaitis, C. (1994, July 13). Unwed mother a common target in welfare debates. *Chicago Tribune,* Section 1, p. 3.

Juel, C. (1983). The development and use of mediated word identification. *Reading Research Quarterly, 18,* 306–327.

Juel, C. (1994). *Learning to read and write in one elementary school.* New York: Springer-Verlag.

Kameenui, E. J. (1993). Diverse learners and the tyranny of time: Don't fix blame; fix the leaky roof. *The Reading Teacher, 46,* 376–393.

Kamhi, A. G. (1992). Response to historical perspective: A developmental language perspective. *Journal of Learning Disabilities, 25,* 48–52.

Kaufman, A. S. (1981). The WISC and learning disabilities assessment: State of the art. *Journal of Learning Disabilities, 14,* 520–526.

Kauffman, J. M. (1993). How we might achieve the radical reform of special education. *Exceptional Children, 60,* 6–16.

Kavale, K. A., & Forness, S. R. (1987). The far side of heterogeniety: A critical analysis of empirical subtyping research in learning disabilities. *Journal of Learning Disabilities, 6,* 374–382.

Keogh, B., Tchir, C., & Windeguth-Behn, A. (1974). Teachers' perceptions of educationally high-risk children. *Journal of Learning Disabilities, 7,* 367–374.

Kerr, M., Nelson, C., & Lambert, D. (1987). *Helping adolescents with learning and behavior problems.* Columbus, OH: Merrill.

Kirk, S., Kirk, W., & Minskoff, E. (1985). *Phonic remedial reading lessons.* Novato, CA: Academic Therapy.

Koskinen, P. S., Gambrell, L. B., Kapinus, B. A., & Heathington, B. S. (1988). Retelling: A strategy for enhancing students' reading comprehension. *The Reading Teacher, 41,* 892–896.

Kramer, J. J., & Conoley, J. C. (1992). *Eleventh mental measurements yearbook.* Lincoln, NE: Borow Institute of Mental Measurements.

Kutiper, K., & Wilson, P. (1993). Updating poetry preferences: A look at the poetry children really like. *The Reading Teacher, 47,* 28–34.

LaBerge, D., & Samuels, S. M. (1974). Toward a theory of automatic information processing in reading. *Cognitive Psychology, 6,* 293–323.

Labov, W. (1967). Some sources of reading problems for Negro speakers of nonstandard English. In A. Frasier (Ed.), *New directions in elementary English* (pp. 293–323). Champaign, IL: National Council of Teachers of English.

Labov, W., Cohen, P., Robins, C., & Lewis, J. (1968). *A study of the nonstandard English of Negro and*

Puerto Rican speakers in New York City: Final report (Cooperative Research Project, 3288). Washington, DC: Office of Education.

Langdon, W. (1989). Language disorder or difference? Assessing the language skills of Hispanic students. *Exceptional Children, 56,* 160–167.

Lansdown, S. (1991). Increasing vocabulary knowledge using direct instruction, cooperative grouping, and reading in junior high school. *Illinois Reading Council Journal, 19,* 15–21.

Larry P. v. *Riles,* 495. Supp. 96 (N. D. Cal, 1979). *affd,* 1988–84. E.H.I R.D.E.C. 555;304 (9th Cir. 1984).

Lee, N. G., & Neal, J. C. (1993). Reading rescue: Intervention for a student "at promise." *Journal of Reading, 36,* 276–282.

Lerner, J. W. (1993). *Learning disabilities: Theories, diagnosis, and teaching strategies* (6th ed.). Boston: Houghton Mifflin.

Lerner, J. W., Lowenthal, B., & Lerner, S. (1995). *Attention deficit disorders: Assessment and teaching.* Pacific Grove, CA: Brooks/Cole.

Leslie, L. (1993). A developmental–interactive approach to reading assessment. *Reading and Writing Quarterly, 9,* 5–30.

Leslie, L., & Caldwell, J. (1995). *The qualitative reading inventory* (2nd ed.). New York: HarperCollins.

Levine, D. U., & Havighurst, A. J. (1992). *Society and education.* Boston: Allyn and Bacon.

Levinson, H. N. (1984). *Smart but feeling dumb.* New York: Warner Books.

Lewis, R. B. (1993). *Special education technology: Classroom applications.* Pacific Grove, CA: Brooks/Cole.

Liebert, R. E. (1970–1). Ten minutes as a retarded reader. *Journal of Reading Behavior, 3,* 74–76.

Lipson, M. Y., Cox, C. H., Iwankowski, S., & Simon, M. (1984). Exploration of the interactive nature of reading: Using commercial IRI's to gain insights. *Reading Psychology: An International Quarterly, 5,* 209–218.

Lubs, H. S., Rabin, M., Feldman, E., Gross-Glen, K., Ruara, R., & Elston, R. C. (1993). Familial dyslexia: Genetic and medical findings in eleven three-generation families. *Annals of Dyslexia, 43,* 44–60.

Lyons, C. A., & Beaver, J. (1995). Reducing retention and learning disability placement through Reading Recovery: An educationally sound cost-effective choice. In R. L. Allington & S. A. Walmsley, *No quick fix: Rethinking literacy in America's ele-*

mentary schools (pp. 116–136). New York: Teachers College Press, and Newark DE: International Reading Association.

Lyons, G. R., Newby, R., Recht, D., & Caldwell, J. (1991). Neurpsychology and learning disabilities. In B. Wong (Ed.), *Learning about learning disabilities: Research and practice* (pp. 376–406). San Diego: Academic Press.

MacArthur, C., Schwartz, S., & Graham, S. (1991). Effects of a receptor peer revision strategy in special education classrooms. *Learning Disabilities: Research and Practice, 6,* 201–210.

Male, M. (1994). *Technology for inclusion: Meeting the special needs of all students.* Boston: Allyn and Bacon.

Martin, H. (1980). Nutrition, injury, illness, and minimal brain dysfunction. In H. Rie & E. Rie (Eds.), *Handbook of minimal brain dysfunction: A critical view.* New York: Wiley.

Mayher, J. S., Lester, N. B., & Pradl, G. M. (1983). *Learning to write/writing to learn.* Upper Montclair, NJ: Boynton/Cook.

McCormick, S. (1995). *Instructing students who have literacy problems* (2nd ed.). Englewood Cliffs, NJ: Merrill/Prentice Hall.

McCormick. S. (1994). A nonreader becomes a reader: A case study of literacy acquisition by a severely disabled reader. *Reading Research Quarterly, 29,* 156–177.

McDermott, R. P. (1978). Pirandello in the classroom: On the possibility of equal educational opportunity in American culture. In M. C. Reynolds (Ed.), *Futures of exceptional children: Emerging structures* (pp. 41–64). Reston, VA: Council for Exceptional Chidren.

McGinley, W. J., & Denner, P. R. (1987). Story impressions: A prereading/writing activity. *Journal of Reading, 31,* 248–253.

McKenna, M. C. (1983). Informal reading inventories: A review of the issues. *The Reading Teacher, 36,* 670–679.

McKeown, M. G. (1993). Creating effective definitions for young word learners. *Reading Research Quarterly, 28,* 16–31.

Mead, M. (1995). Enriching the reading process with software. *Closing the Gap, 13(5),* 1, 11.

Meyer, B. S. F., & Freedle, R. O. (1984). Effectiveness of discourse type on recall. *American Educational Research Journal, 21,* 121–143.

Miller, G. A., & Gildea, P. (1987). How children learn words. *Scientific American, 257,* 94–99.

Miller, S. D., & Yochum, N. (1991). Asking students about the nature of their reading difficulties. *Journal of Reading Behavior, 23,* 465–485.

Moffett, J. M., & Wagner, B. J. (1983). *Student-centered language arts and reading, K–13: A handbook for teachers* (3rd ed.). Boston: Houghton Mifflin.

Moll, L. C., & González, N. (1994). Lessons from research with language-minority children. *Journal of Reading Behavior, 26,* 439–456.

Moore, D., & Arthur, S. V. (1981). Possible sentences. In E. D. Dishner, T. W. Bean, & J. E. Readence (Eds.), *Reading in the content areas: Improving classroom instruction* (pp. 138–142). Dubuque IA: Kendall/Hunt.

Moore, D., & Wieland, O. (1981). WISC–R indexes of children referred for reading diagnosis. *Journal of Learning Disabilities, 14,* 511–514.

Morrow. L. M., Gambrell, L., Kapinus, B., Koskinen, P., Marshall, N., & Mitchell, J. N. (1986). Retelling: A strategy for reading instruction and assessment. In J. A. Niles & R. Lalik (Eds.), *Solving problems in literacy: Learners, teachers, and researchers: Thirty-fifth yearbook of the National Reading Conference* (pp. 73–80). Rochester, NY: National Reading Conference.

Morrow, L. M., & Weinstein, C. S. (1986). Encouraging voluntary reading. The impact of a literature program on children's use of library corners. *Reading Research Quarterly, 21,* 330–346.

Mossburg, J. (1989). A new approach to an old problem: Remediation not just another pull-out. *The Reading Teacher, 42,* 342–343.

Moustafa, M. (1993). Recoding in whole language reading instruction. *Language Arts, 70,* 483–487.

Nagy, W., Anderson R., & Herman, P. (1987). Learning word meanings from context during normal reading. *American Educational Research Journal, 24,* 237–270.

Nass, R. D. (1993). Sex differences in learning abilities and disabilities. *Annals of Dyslexia, 43,* 61–77.

National Center for Education and Statistics (1994). *Language characteristics and schooling in the United States: A changing picture: 1979–1989.* U.S.A. Department of Eudcation, Office of Educational Research and Improvement.

New Directions in Reading Comprehension (flip chart) (1987). Tallahasee, FL: Department of Education, in connection with Florida Reading Association; now available from Newark, DE: International Reading Association.

Newman, A. P. (1994). Adult literacy programs: An overview. *Learning Disabilities: A Multidisciplinary Journal, 5(1),* 51–61.

Norton, A., & Glick, P. (1986). One parent families: A social and economic profile. *Family Relations, 35,* 9–17.

Office of Bilingual Education and Minority Languages Affairs (1994, November 1). *NABE News,* pp 5–6.

Ogle, D. (1986). KWL: A teaching model that develops active reading of expository text. *The Reading Teacher, 39,* 564–570.

Olson, G. H. (1989, March). Date of birth and its effect upon performance in school over subsequent years. Paper presented at the annual meeting of the American Educational Research Association, San Francisco, CA.

Ortiz, A. (1988). *Effective practices in assessment in instruction for language minority students: An intervention model.* Arlington, VA: Innovative Approaches Research Project, Office of Bilingual Education and Minority Languges Affairs. U.S. Department of Education.

Orton, S. (1937). *Reading, writing, and speech problems of children.* New York: Norton.

Orton Dyslexia Society (1986). Some facts about illiteracy in America. *Perspectives on Dyslexia, 13,* 1.

Pace, A. J., Marshall, N., Horowitz, R., Lipson, M. Y., & Lucido, P. (1989). When prior knowledge doesn't facilitate some text comprehension: An examination of some of the issues. In S. McCormick & J. Autell (Eds.), *Cognitive and social perspectives for literacy research and instruction: Thirty-eighth yearbook of the National Reading Conference* (pp. 213–224). Chicago, IL: National Reading Conference.

Paris, S. G. (1986). Teaching children to guide their reading and learning. In T. Raphael (Ed.), *Contexts of school-based literacy* (pp. 115–130). New York: Random House.

Paris, S. G., Wasik, B. A., & Turner, J. C. (1991). The development of strategic readers. In R. Barr, M. L. Kamil, P. Mosenthal, & P. D. Pearson (Eds.), *Handbook of reading research* (Vol. 2, pp. 609–640). White Plains, NY: Longman.

Parker, H. C. (1992). *The ADD hyperactivity handbook for schools.* Plantation, FL: Impact Publications.

PASE v. Hannon, 506 F. Supp 832 (N. D. Ill, 1980).

Pearl, R., Donahue, M., & Bryan, T. (1986). Social relationships of learning disabled children. In J. Toregeson & B. Wong (Eds.), *Psychological and educational perspectives on learning disabilities* (pp. 257–296). Orlando, FL: Academic Press.

Pearson P. D., & Fielding L. (1991). Comprehension instruction. In R. Barr, M. L. Kamil, P. Mosenthal, & P. D. Pearson, *Handbook of reading research* (Vol. 2, pp. 815–860). White Plains, NY: Longman.

Perfetti, C. A. (1985). *Reading ability.* New York: Oxford University Press.

Pflaum, S. W., Walberg, H. J., Karegianes, M. L., & Rasher, S. W. (1980). Reading instruction: A quantitative analysis. *Educational Researcher, 9,* 12–18.

Phillips, M. (1990, December 2). Ephemeral ixia plant kept off federal endangered list *Miami Herald,* p. 6B.

Pikulski, J. J., & Shanahan, T. (1982). Informal reading inventories: A critical analysis. In J. J. Pikulski & T. Shanahan (Eds.), *Approaches to the informal evaluation of reading* (pp. 94–116). Newark, DE: International Reading Association.

Pinnell, G. S. (1989). Reading recovery: Helping at-risk children learn to read. *The Elementary School Journal, 90,* 161–183.

Pinnell, G. S., Fried, M. D., & Estice, R. M. (1990). Reading recovery: Learning to make a difference. *The Reading Teacher, 43,* 282–295.

Pinnell, G. S., Lyons, C. A., Deford, D. E., Bryk, A. S., & Seltzer, M. (1994). Comparing instructional models for the literacy educaton of high-risk first graders. *Reading Research Quarterly, 29,* 9–39.

Pressley, M. (1977). Imagery and children's learning: Putting the picture in developmental perspective. *Review of Educational Research, 47,* 585–622.

Pressley, M., & Harris, K. R. (1990). What we really know about strategy instruction. *Educational Leadership, 48,* 31–34.

Preston, R. (1979). Reading achievement of German boys and girls related to sex of teacher. *The Reading Teacher, 32,* 521–526.

Public Law 93–112 (1973). Section 504 of the Rehabilitation Act.

Purcell-Gates, V. (1986). Lexical and syntactic knowledge of written narrative held by well-read-to kindergarteners and second graders. *Research in the Teaching of English, 22,* 128–157.

Purves, A. C., Rogers, T., & Soter, A. O. (1990). *How porcupines make love II: Teaching a response-centered literature curriculum.* White Plains, NY: Longman.

Quirk, T. J., Tristman, D. A., Nailn, K., & Weinberg, S. (1975). Classroom behavior of teachers during compensatory reading instruction. *Journal of Educational Research, 68,* 185–192.

Rabinovitch, R. (1989). Dyslexia: Psychiatric considerations. In J. Money (Ed.), *Reading disability: Progress and research needs in dyslexia.* Baltimore, MD: Johns Hopkins University Press.

Rapp, D. (1979). Food allergy treatment for hyperkinesis. *Journal of Learning Disabilities, 12,* 608–616.

Rashotte, C. A., & Torgesen, J. K. (1985). Repeated reading and reading fluency. *Reading Research Quarterly, 20,* 180–188.

Read, C. (1971). Preschool children's knowledge of English phonology. *Harvard Educational Review, 41,* 1–34.

Read, C. (1975). *Children's categorization of speech sounds in English* (NCTE Research Reports, No. 17). Urbana, IL: National Council of Teachers of English.

Reyes, M. D. (1992). Challenging venerable assumptions: Literacy instruction for linguistically different students. *Harvard Education Review, 62,* 427–446.

Richek, M. A. (1969). A study of the affix structure of English: Affix frequency and teaching methods. Unpublished paper, University of Chicago.

Richek, M. A. (1987). DRTA: 5 variations that facilitate independence in reading narratives. *Journal of Reading, 30,* 632–636.

Richek, M. A. (1989). *Increasing the achievement of your remedial reading students.* Paso Robles, CA: Bureau of Education and Research.

Richek, M. A. (1994). Field project at the Piccolo Elementary School. Chicago, IL.

Richek, M. A. (1995). *Reading success for at-risk children: Ideas that work.* Bellevue, WA: Bureau of Education and Research.

Richek, M. A., & Glick, L. C. (1991). Coordinating a literacy-support program with classroom instruction. *The Reading Teacher, 45,* 474–479.

Richek, M. A., & McTague, B. (1988). The "Curious George" strategy for students with reading problems. *The Reading Teacher, 42,* 220–225.

Richek, M. A., McTague, B. K., Anderson, C. A., Baker, K. S., Luchitz, M. M., Hendler, L. W., Hatchett, M. B., McGuier, D., & Nevel, M. (1989). The "Curious George" strategy: Experiences of nine teachers. *Reading: Issues and Practices, Maryland Reading Journal of the International Reading Association, 6,* 36–44.

Robinson, H. M. (1946). *Why pupils fail in reading.* Chicago: University of Chicago.

Robinson, H. M. (1972). Visual and auditory modalities related to methods for beginning reading. *Reading Research Quarterly, 8,* 7–41.

Rosenberger, P., & Hier, D. (1980). Cerebral assymetry and verbal intellectual deficits. *Annals of Neurology, 8,* 300–304.

Rosenblatt, L. (1983). *Literature as exploration* (4th ed.). New York: Modern Language Association.

Rosenshine, B., & Stevens, R. (1986). Teaching functions. In M. Wittock (Ed.), *Handbook of resarch on teaching* (pp. 376–391). New York: Macmillan.

Rosenthal, R., & Jacobson, L. (1968). *Pygmalion in the classroom.* New York: Holt, Reinhart, and Winston.

Roswell, F., & Chall, J. (1994). *Diagnostic assessments of reading with trial teaching strategies (DARTTS).* Chicago: Riverside.

Roswell, F., & Chall, J. (1994). *Creating successful readers: A practical guide to testing and teaching at all levels.* Chicago: Riverside.

Roswell, F., & Natchez, G. (1989). *Reading disability: A human approach to evaluation and treatment of reading and writing difficulties.* New York: Basic Books.

Rowan, B., & Guthrie, L. T. (1989). The quality of Chapter I instruction: Results from a study of twenty-four schools. In R. E. Slavin, N. L. Karweit, & N. A. Madden (Eds.), *Effective programs for students at risk* (pp. 195–219). Needham Heights, MA: Allyn and Bacon.

Rumelhart, D. E. (1985). Toward an interactive model of reading. In H. Singer & R. B. Ruddell (Eds.), *Theoretical models and processes of reading* (3rd ed.). Newark, DE: International Reading Association.

Runion, H. J. (1980). Hypoglycemia—fact or fiction? In W. Cruckshank (Ed.), *Approaches to learning disabilities: Vol. 1. The best of ACLD.* Syracuse, NY: Syracuse University Press.

Sadowski, M. (1985). The natural use of imagery in story comprehension and recall. *Reading Research Quarterly, 20,* 658–667.

Salvia, J., & Ysseldyke, J. E. (1995). *Assessment* (6th ed.). Boston, MA: Houghton Mifflin.

Samuels, S. J. (1979). The method of repeated readings. *The Reading Teacher, 32,* 403–408.

Samuels, S. J. (1988). Decoding and automaticity: Helping poor readers become automatic at word recognition. *The Reading Teacher, 41,* 756–761.

Santa, C., Havens, L., & Harrison, S. (1989). Teaching secondary science through reading, writing, studying, and problem solving. In D. Lapp, J. Flood, & N. Farnan (Eds.), *Content area reading and learning: Instructional strategies.* Englewood Cliffs, NJ: Prentice Hall.

Schiller, E., & Hauser J. (1992). OSERS' initiative for meeting the needs for children with attention deficit disorders. *OSERS News in Print, 4,* 30–31.

Schlagal, R. C. (1989). Constancy and change in spelling development. *Reading Psychology: An International Quarterly, 10,* 207–232.

Sebesta, S. (1993). Creative drama and language arts. In B. E. Cullinan (Ed.), *Children's voices: Talk in the classroom* (pp. 33–46). Newark, DE: International Reading Association.

Shapiro, S. (1994). From reading poetry to poetry reading in the classroom. *Illinois Reading Council Journal, 21,* 67–71.

Shapiro, S., & Welch, M. (1991). Using poetry with adolescents in a remedial reading program: A case study. *Reading Horizons, 31,* 318–331.

Sheenan, L. D., Feldman, R. S., & Allen, V. L. (1976). Research on children tutoring children: A critical review. *Review of Educational Research, 16,* 355–385.

Shelfelbine, J. (1991). *A syllabic-unit approach to teaching syllabication strategies.* New York: Teachers College, Columbia University.

Siegel, L. S. (1992). An evaluation of the discrepancy definition of dyslexia. *Journal of Learning Disabilities, 25,* 618–629.

Silver, A., & Hagin, R. (1990). *Disorders of learning in childhood.* New York: Wiley.

Silver, L. (1992). *The misunderstood child.* Blue Ridge Summit, PA: Tab Books.

Silver, L. B. (1986). Controversial approaches to treading learning disabilities and attention deficit disorders. *American Journal of Diseases of Children, 140,* 1045–1052.

Simpson J. (1987, October 28). A shallow labor pool spurs business to act to bolster education. *Wall Street Journal,* p. A1.

Singer, H., & Donlan, D. (1982). Active comprehension: Problem-solving schema with question generation for compehension of complex short stories. *Reading Research Quarterly, 17,* 166–186.

Slavin, R. (1991). *Educational psychology.* Englewood Cliffs, NJ: Prentice Hall.

Slavin, R. E. (1984). Students motivating students to excel: Cooperative incentives, cooperative tasks, and student achievement. *Elementary School Journal, 85,* 53–64.

Slavin, R. E., Madden, N. A., Karweit, N. L., Dolan, L., & Wasik, B. A. (1992). *Success for all: A relentless approach to prevention and early intervention in elementary schools.* Arlington, VA: Educational Research Service.

Slingerland, G. (1981). *A multisensory approach to language arts for specific language disability children.* Cambridge, MA: Educators Publishing Service.

Smith, S. (1992). Familial patterns of learning disabilities. *Annals of Dyslexia, 42,* 143–158.

Snider, V. E., & Tarver, S. G. (1987). The effect of early reading failure on acquisition of knowledge among students with reading disabilities. *Journal of Learning Disabilities, 20,* 351–356.

Something about the author (1986). Detroit: Gale Research Company.

Spache, G. D. (1981). *Diagnosing and correcting reading disabilities.* Boston: Allyn and Bacon, 1981.

Spiro, R. J., Bruce, B. C., & Brewer, W. F. (Eds.). (1980). *Theoretical issues in reading comprehension.* Hillsdale, NJ: Erlbaum.

Stahl, S. A. (1988). Is there evidence to support matching reading styles and initial reading methods? A reply to Carbo. *Phi Delta Kappan, 70,* 317–322.

Stahl, S. A. (1992). Saying the "p" word: Nine guidelines for exemplary phonics instruction. *The Reading Teacher, 45,* 618–625.

Stahl, S. A., & Fairbanks, M. (1986). The effects of vocabulary instruction: A model-based meta-analysis. *Review of Educational Research, 56,* 72–110.

Stahl, S. A., & Heubach, K. (1993). *Changing reading instruction in second grade: A fluency-oriented program.* University of Georgia: National Reading Research Center.

Stahl, S. A., & Murray, B. A. (1994). Defining phonological awareness and its relationship to early reading. *Journal of Educational Psychology, 86,* 221–234.

Stahl, S. A., Richek, M. A., & Vandiver, R. J. (1991). Learning meaning through listening: A sixth-grade replication. In J. Zutell & S. McCormick (Eds.), *Learner factors/teacher factors: Issues in literacy reserach and instruction* (pp. 185–192). Chicago, IL: National Reading Conference.

Stanovich, K. E. (1982a). Individual differences in the cognitive processes of reading: I. Word decoding *Journal of Learning Disabilities, 15,* 485–493.

Stanovich, K. E. (1982b). Individual differences in the cognitive processes of reading: II. Text level processes. *Journal of Learning Disabilities, 15,* 549–554.

Stanovich, K. E. (1986). Matthew effects in reading: Some consequences of individual differences in the acquisition of literacy. *Reading Research Quarterly, 21,* 360–407.

Stanovich, K. E. (1988a). *Children's reading and the development of phonological awareness.* Detroit: Wayne State UniversityPress.

Stanovich, K. E. (1988b). The right and wrong places to look for the cognitive locus of reading disability. *Annals of Dyslexia, 38,* 154–177.

Stanovich, K. E. (1993–4). Romance and reality. Distinguished educator series. *The Reading Teacher, 47,* 280–290.

Stanovich, K. E., & Cunningham, A. E. (1993). Where does knowledge come from? Specific associations between print exposure and information acquisition. *Journal of Educational Psychology, 85,* 211–229.

Stauffer, R. G. (1975). *Directing the reading–thinking process.* New York: Harper and Row.

Stauffer, R. G. (1980). *The language experience approach to the teaching of reading* (2nd ed.). New York: Haper and Row.

Stein, M. K., Leinhardt, G., & Bickel, W. (1989). Instructional programs for teaching students at risk. In R. E. Slavin, N. L. Karweit, & N. A. Madden, *Effective programs for students at risk* (pp. 145–194). Needham Heights, MA: Allyn and Bacon.

Sternberg, R. J. (1985). *Beyond IQ: A triarchic theory of human intelligence.* New York: Cambridge University Press.

Sternberg, R. J. (1987). Most vocabulary is learned from context. In M. G. McKeown & M. E. Curtis (Eds.), *The nature of vocabulary acquisition* (pp. 89–105). Hillsdale, NJ: Erlbaum.

Stotsky, S. (1983). Research on reading/writing relationships: A synthesis and suggested directions. *Language Arts, 60,* 627–642.

Sulzby, E., & Teale, W. (1991). Emergent literacy. In R. Barr, M. L. Kamil, P. Mosenthal, & P. D. Pearson (Eds.), *Handbook of reading research* (Vol. 2, pp. 727–758). White Plains, NY: Longman.

Sundbye, N. (1987). Text explicitness and inferential questioning: Effects on story understanding and recall. *Reading Reserach Quarterly, 22,* 82–98.

Taylor, B., Harris, L. A., Pearson, P. D., & Garcia G. (1995). *Reading difficulties: Instruction and assessment* (2nd ed.). New York: McGraw-Hill.

Taylor, B. M. (1992). Text structure, comprehension, and recall. In S. J. Samuels & A. E. Farstrup (Eds.), *What research has to say about reading comprehension* (pp. 220–235). Newark, DE: International Reading Association.

Taylor, R. L., Partenio, I., & Ziegler, E. (1983). Diagnostic use of WISC–R subtest scatter: A note of caution. *Diagnostique, 9,* 26–31.

Teale, W. H. (1988). Developmentally appropriate assessment of reading and writing in the early childhood classroom. *Elementary School Journal, 89(2),* 173–183.

Thomas, A., & Chess, S. (1977). *Temperament and development.* New York: Bruner/Mazel.

Thomson, N. (1987). *Understanding teenagers' reading.* New York: Nichols.

Thorndike, R. L. (1973). *Reading comprehension education in fifteen countries.* New York: Wiley.

Tierney, R. J. (1990). Redefining reading comprehension. *Educational Leadership, 47,* 37–42.

Torgesen, J. D., Wagner, R. K., & Rashotte, C. A. (1994). Longitudinal studies of phonological processing and reading. *Journal of Learning Disabilities, 27,* 276–286.

Trachtenburg, P. (1990). Using children's literature to enhance phonics instruction. *The Reading Teacher, 43,* 648–654.

Traub, N., & Bloom, F. (1978). *Recipe for reading.* Cambridge, MA: Educators Publishing Service.

U.S. Census Bureau (1994). *Marital status and living arrangements.* Washington, DC: U.S. Census Bureau.

U.S. Department of Education (1991, September 16). Clarification of policy to address the needs of children with attention deficit disorders within the general and/or special education. Memorandum.

U.S. Department of Education (1994). *To assure the free appropriate public education of all children with disabilities: Sixteenth annual report to Congress on the implementation of the Individuals with Disabilities Act.* Washington, DC: U.S. Government Printing Office.

U.S. Office of Secretary of Education. (1994). *The Goals 2000: Educate America Act.* Washington, DC: U.S. Department of Education.

van den Bosch, K., van Bon, W. H. J., & Schreuder, R. (1995). Poor readers' decoding skills: Effects of training with limited exposure duration. *Reading Research Quarterly, 30,* 110–125.

van Dijk, T. A., & Kintsch, W. (1983). *Strategies of discourse comprehension.* San Diego, CA: Academic.

van Ijzendoorn, M. H., & Bus, A. G. (1994). Meta-analytic confirmation of the nonword reading deficit in developmental dyslexia. *Reading Research Quarterly, 29(3),* 250–264.

Vaughn, S. (1991). Social skills enhancement in students with learning disabilities. In B. Wong (Ed.), *Learning about learning disabilities* (pp. 408–440). San Diego, CA: Academic Press.

Vellutino, F. R. (1987). Dyslexia. *Scientific American, 256,* 34–41.

Vellutino, F. R., & Denckla, M. B. (1991). Cognitive and neuropsychological foundations of word identification in poor and normally developing readers. In R. Barr, M. L. Kamil, P. B. Mosenthal, & P. D. Pearson (Eds.), *Handbook of reading research: Vol. II.* (pp. 571–608). White Plains, NY: Longman.

Venezsky, R. L., Kaestle, C. F., & Sum, A. M. (1987). *The subtle danger: Reflections on the literacy abilities of American's young adults.* Princeton, NJ: Educational Testing Service.

Vogel, S. A. (1974). Syntactic abilities in normal and dyslexic children. *Journal of Learning Disabilities, 7,* 103–109.

Wallace, G., & Larsen, S. C. (1978). *Educational assessment of learning problems: Testing for teaching.* Boston: Allyn and Bacon.

Walsh, D. J., Price, G. G., & Gillingham, M. G. (1988). The critical but transitory importance of letter naming. *Reading Research Quarterly, 23(2),* 108–122.

Ward, B. J. (1992). [Letter to the editor]. *Journal of Learning Disabilities, 25,* 274–275.

Warner, S. A. (1963). *Teacher.* New York: Simon and Schuster.

Wasik, B. A., & Slavin, R. E. (1993). Preventing early reading failure with one-to-one tutoring: A review of five programs. *Reading Research Quarterly, 28,* 179–200.

Wechsler, D. (1975). *The measurement and appraisal of adult intelligence.* Baltimore, MD: Williams and Wilkins.

Weinberg, W., & Rehmet, A. (1983). Childhood affective disorders and school problems. In D. Cantwell & G. Carlson (Eds.), *Affective disorders in childhood and adolescence—an update.* Jamaica, NY: Spectrum Publications.

Wesson, M. D. (1993). Diagnosis and management of reading dysfunction for the primary care optometrist (symposium). *Optometry and Vision Science, 70,* 357–368.

West, R. F., Stanovich, K. E., & Mitchell, H. R. (1993). Reading in the real world and its correlates. *Reading Research Quarterly, 28,* 35–50.

Wiig, E., & Semel, E. (1984). *Language assessment and intervention for the learning disabled.* Columbus, OH: Charles E. Merrill.

Will, M. (1986). Educating children with learning problems: A shared responsibility. *Exceptional Children, 52,* 411–416.

Williams, J. P. (1993). Comprehension of students with and without learning disabilities: Identification of narrative themes and idiosyncratic text representations. *Journal of Educational Psychology, 93,* 631–641.

Wilson, P. T. (1988). *Let's think about reading and reading instruction: A primer for tutors and teachers.* Dubuque, IA: Kendall/Hunt.

Wittrock, M. C. (1984). Writing and the teaching of reading. In J. M. Jensen (Ed.), *Composing and comprehending* (pp. 77–83). Urbana, IL: ERIC Clearinghouse on Reading and Communication Skills.

Wixson, K. (1983). Questions about a text: What you ask about is what children learn. *The Reading Teacher, 37,* 287–293.

Wixson, K., Peters, C., Wever, E., & Roeber, E. (1987). New directions in statewide reading assessment. *The Reading Teacher, 40,* 749–755.

Wolf, M. (1991). Naming speed and reading: The contribution of the cognitive neurosciences. *Reading Research Quarterly, 26,* 123–141.

Wolf, S. A., & Enciso, P. E. (1994). Multiple selves in literacy interpretation: Engagement and the language of drama. In C. K. Kinzer, & D. J. Leu, J. A., *Multidimensional aspects of literacy research, theory, and practice* (pp. 351–369). Chicago, IL: National Reading Conference.

Wolfram, W. (1969). *A sociolinguistic description of Detroit Negro speech.* Washington, DC: Center for Applied Linguistics.

Wong, B. Y. (1986). A cognitive approach to teaching spelling. *Exceptional Children, 53,* 169–172.

Wong, B., & Wong, W. (1980). Role-taking skills in normal-achieving and learning-disabled children. *Learning Disabilities Quarterly, 3,* 11–18.

Wood, K. D., & Algozzine, B. (1994). Reading and special education in the twenty-first century: Time to unify perspectives. In K. Wood & B. Algozzine (Eds.), *Teaching reading to high-risk learners: A unified perspective* (pp. 1–8). Needham Heights, MA: Allyn and Bacon.

Yopp, H. K. (1992). Developing phonemic awareness in young children. *The Reading Teacher, 45,* 696–703.

Zametkin, A. J., Nordahl, T. E., Gross, M., King, A. C., Semple, W. E., Rumsey, J., Hamburger, S., & Cohen, R. M. (1990). Cerebral glucose metabolism in adults with hyperactivity with childhood onset. *New England Journal of Medicine, 323,* 1361–1364.

Zigmond, N. (1990). Rethinking secondary programs for students with learning disabilities. *Focus on Exceptional Children, 23,* 1–23.

Zigmond, N., Vallecorsa, A., & Leinhardt, G. (1980). Reading instruction for students with learning disabilities. *Topics in Language Disorders, 1,* 89–98.

Name Index

Subject Index

Test Index